Check Point™
Next Generation

with Application Intelligence
Security Administration

Chris Tobkin
Daniel Kligerman   **Technical Editor**

KEY	SERIAL NUMBER
001	GH74K9LLNB
002	9MVXZ35G7J
003	2NFRRSI87N
004	GC29MLKC89
005	8HXXDRPMQ8
006	36HYIUXBTS
007	TYHK9MN9NH
008	326KMNYGTS
009	HKMN567B2N
010	IYBASCLITH

PUBLISHED BY
Syngress Publishing, Inc.
800 Hingham Street
Rockland, MA 02370

Check Point™ Next Generation with Application Intelligence Security Administration

Printed in the United States of America
1 2 3 4 5 6 7 8 9 0
ISBN: 1-932266-89-5

Acquisitions Editor: Catherine B. Nolan
Page Layout and Art: Patricia Lupien
Indexer: Rich Carlson

Cover Designer: Michael Kavish
Copy Editor: Darlene Bordwell,
    Judy Eby, Amy Thomson

Distributed by O'Reilly & Associates in the United States and Jaguar Book Group in Canada.

Acknowledgments

We would like to acknowledge the following people for their kindness and support in making this book possible.

Syngress books are now distributed in the United States by O'Reilly & Associates, Inc. The enthusiasm and work ethic at ORA is incredible and we would like to thank everyone there for their time and efforts to bring Syngress books to market: Tim O'Reilly, Laura Baldwin, Mark Brokering, Mike Leonard, Donna Selenko, Bonnie Sheehan, Cindy Davis, Grant Kikkert, Opol Matsutaro, Lynn Schwartz, Steve Hazelwood, Mark Wilson, Rick Brown, Leslie Becker, Jill Lothrop, Tim Hinton, Kyle Hart, Sara Winge, C. J. Rayhill, Peter Pardo, Leslie Crandell, Valerie Dow, Regina Aggio, Pascal Honscher, Preston Paull, Susan Thompson, Bruce Stewart, Laura Schmier, Sue Willing, Mark Jacobsen and to all the others who work with us, but whose names we do not know (yet)!

The incredibly hard working team at Elsevier Science, including Jonathan Bunkell, Ian Seager, Duncan Enright, David Burton, Rosanna Ramacciotti, Robert Fairbrother, Miguel Sanchez, Klaus Beran, and Rosie Moss for making certain that our vision remains worldwide in scope.

David Buckland, Wendi Wong, Daniel Loh, Marie Chieng, Lucy Chong, Leslie Lim, Audrey Gan, and Joseph Chan of STP Distributors for the enthusiasm with which they receive our books.

Kwon Sung June at Acorn Publishing for his support.

Jackie Gross, Gayle Voycey, Alexia Penny, Anik Robitaille, Craig Siddall, Darlene Morrow, Iolanda Miller, Jane Mackay, and Marie Skelly at Jackie Gross & Associates for all their help and enthusiasm representing our product in Canada.

Lois Fraser, Connie McMenemy, Shannon Russell, and the rest of the great folks at Jaguar Book Group for their help with distribution of Syngress books in Canada.

David Scott, Tricia Wilden, Marilla Burgess, Annette Scott, Geoff Ebbs, Hedley Partis, Bec Lowe, and Mark Langley of Woodslane for distributing our books throughout Australia, New Zealand, Papua New Guinea, Fiji Tonga, Solomon Islands, and the Cook Islands.

Winston Lim of Global Publishing for his help and support with distribution of Syngress books in the Philippines.

A special thanks to all the folks at Malloy who have made things easy for us and especially to Beth Drake and Joe Upton.

Author

Chris Tobkin (CCSI, CCSE+ CCSE, CCSA, MCP) is a security engineer for Check Point Software Technologies, Ltd. and a member of the Minnesota chapter of the ISSA. Chris began his career over a decade ago programming C, C++, and Perl at the University of Minnesota. While there obtaining his bachelors of business administration with emphasis on management information systems degree, his job expanded to include project management, as well as database, network, and systems administration. His talents in security were recognized and leveraged as a part of the computer security group for the university. Chris later moved on to a security services and integration company where he was able to hone his skills in penetration testing, social engineering, firewalling, policy development, intrusion detection and prevention, and teaching courses in security, including the Check Point curriculum. In 2001, Chris moved to a position inside Check Point designing and architecting solutions for customers. Chris has also done many presentations and other writing including contributing to *Check Point NG VPN-1/FireWall-1: Advanced Configuration and Troubleshooting* (Syngress Publishing, ISBN: 1-931836-97-3) and the *CCSA Next Generation Check Point Certified Security Administrator Study Guide* (McGraw-Hill, ISBN: 0-072194-20-0).

Technical Editor and Contributor

Daniel Kligerman (CCSA, CCSE), author of *Building DMZs for Enterprise Networks* (Syngress Publishing, ISBN: 1-931836-88-4), *Check Point NG VPN-1/Firewall-1: Advanced Configuration and Troubleshooting* (Syngress Publishing, ISBN: 1-931836-97-3), *Nokia Network Security Solutions Handbook* (Syngress, ISBN: 1-931836-70-1), and *Check Point Next Generation Security Administration* (Syngress, ISBN: 1-928994-74-1), is a senior network specialist with TELUS, Canada's second-largest telecommunications company. Leading the eastern Canadian network team, he is responsible for the architecture, deployment, and support of enterprise customer networks, including LAN and WAN routing and switching, and all aspects of network security.

Daniel holds a bachelor of science degree from the University of Toronto in computer science, statistics, and English, and resides in Toronto, Canada with his wife Merita.

Contributors

Drew Simonis (CISSP, CCNA, SCSA, SCNA, CCSA, CCSE, IBM CS) is a senior security engineer with the RL Phillips Group, LLC, where he provides senior level security consulting to the United States Navy, working on large enterprise networks. Drew is a security generalist, with a strong background in system administration, Internet application development, intrusion detection and prevention, and penetration testing. He is a co-author of *Hack Proofing Your Web Applications* (Syngress Publishing, ISBN: 1-928994-31-8) and *Hack Proofing Sun Solaris 8* (Syngress, ISBN: 1-928994-44-X). Drew's background includes various consulting positions with Fiderus, serving as a security architect with AT&T and as a technical team lead with IBM. Drew has a bachelor's degree from the University of South Florida and is also a member of American MENSA. He lives in Suffolk, Virginia with his wife, Kym and daughters, Cailyn and Delany. He would like to pay special thanks to Travis Corson and Ron Ostrenga for helping him break into the industry.

Corey S. Pincock (CISSP, MCSE, GSEC, MCDBA, CCSA, CCNA) is the senior information security architect for CastleGarde in Tampa, Florida. As an expert in the information security aspects of Graham-Leach-Bliley and HIPAA, Corey consults with financial and healthcare organizations on a national level to implement information security programs that include policy development, risk assessments, security infrastructure design, implementation, training, and monitoring. His other specialties include firewall assessments and audits, Windows 2000, and cryptography. Corey's background includes positions as a network administrator for CommerceQuest, systems engineer for MicroAge, and senior instructor for Certified Tech Trainers. Corey holds a bachelor's degree from the University of Washington and is a member of ISSA. Corey lives in Tampa, Florida with his wife and two daughters. He would like to thank his wife, Shelly, for encouraging him to be his best, and Allen Keele of Certified Tech Trainers.

Jeff Vince (CCSA, CCSE) is a security consultant in Waterloo, Ontario where he specializes in secure network architecture and firewall configuration for medium- to large-scale network installations. His specialties focus on security products ranging from antivirus software to intrusion detection and enterprise security management software running on the Microsoft Windows and Linux platforms. In addition to normal client consulting work, Jeff has—as part of a team of security professionals—performed successful attack and penetration tests on networks owned by companies ranging from major financial institutions and broadband service providers to smaller software development companies. Working as both an outsider trying to break in and as a security manager responsible for securing corporate assets has given Jeff a unique perspective on network security. Applying this dual vision of security has allowed him to help clients build network infrastructure that provides the high availability and security required in today's Internet environment.

Doug Maxwell (CCSI) is a senior network engineer with Activis, Ltd. in East Hartford, Connecticut. He currently works as a third-tier engineer in the technical support division, and is a certified Check Point instructor. His specialties include Unix network security and firewall network integration. Doug holds a bachelor of science degree in computer science from the University of Massachusetts at Amherst, and is a member of the Association for Computing Machinery (ACM), USENIX, and SAGE, the System Administrator's Guild. He happily resides in Ellington, Connecticut with his wife and 1-year-old son.

Simon Desmeules (CCSE, ISS, MCSE+I, CNA) is an independent security perimeter specialist. He currently provides architectural design, technical consulting, and tactical emergency support for perimeter security technologies for several Fortune 1000 companies in Canada and the United States. Simon's background includes positions as a firewall / intrusion security specialist for a pioneer of Canadian Security, Maxon Services, and their Managed Security clients. He is an active member of the FW-1, ISS, and Snort mailing lists where he discovers new problems and consults with fellow security specialists.

Cherie Amon (CCSA, CCSE, CCSI) is a senior network security engineer and security instructor for Integralis. She is a Check Point Certified Security instructor and has been installing, configuring, and supporting Check Point products since 1997. Cherie teaches the Check Point courses at the Integralis Authorized Training Center (ATC) in East Hartford, Connecticut, which is the only Check Point ATC in the state. Prior to working at Integralis, she held a position at IBM supporting the IBM Global Dialer, which is now the ATT Global Dialer. Cherie lives in Tampa, Florida and attended college at the University of South Florida in Tampa, where she is now pursuing a math degree. She would like to thank her husband, Kyle Amon, and father, Jerry Earnest, for leading her in the direction of computers and technology.

Contents

Foreword

Security is seldom simple. Over the years, companies have done an excellent job of mandating that security and privacy be transparent to users in the name of productivity. Some of us long for a simpler time when security response wasn't measured in minutes and availability wasn't measured in milliseconds.

With the rise in the number and complexity of vulnerabilities and attacks, security professionals must defend their systems against more threats, more quickly than ever before. Check Point has produced a solution, which makes it possible for these goals to be achieved in organizations both small and large. Check Point's Simple Management Architecture (which has been mimicked, but never replicated) has been heralded for its ease-of-use and flexibility since its inception a decade ago.

Effective management alone, however, was not enough to make Check Point the industry standard. Security must be of foremost concern when deciding on a firewall platform and Check Point has best balanced security with the ever-changing business needs of companies over time. Providing the highest level of security without sacrificing performance has been a corner-stone of Check Point's success.

Check Point also created the Open Platform for Security (OPSEC) consortium. This allows the capabilities of the firewall to be extended to hundreds of other solutions to meet the unique needs of each organization in a fully supported and certified manner. This also provides choice to companies who do not want to be locked into a certain vendor or product. Covering the 350+ partners who integrate with Check Point is well beyond the scope of any book; however, we will cover the methods that are used to extend the Check Point solution so you can better understand the interoperability.

Within this book we will cover the basic concepts of security and how to configure a simple firewall all the way to some very advanced VPN scenarios.

This book is written by experts in the field as well as certified instructors to give the depth desired by the most advanced users, but also to allow even the most basic administrator to learn the do's and don'ts of security. The ultimate goal of this book is to instruct you on the capabilities and configurations of Check Point's product line. As each chapter builds on the previous ones, it covers not only the basics of Check Point VPN-1/FireWall-1, but also the new features introduced in Check Point Next Generation with Application Intelligence R54, which provides proactive attack protection with SmartDefense. For the most complex and advanced configuration scenarios outside the scope of this book, many of the authors have also contributed to the already best-selling *Check Point NG VPN-1/FireWall-1 Advanced Configuration and Troubleshooting* (Syngress Publishing, ISBN: 1-931836-97-3).

We all hope you will find this book useful as both a learning tool and reference guide as you use the software 93% of the Global Fortune 100 use to secure their networks.

—*Chris Tobkin*, Technical Editor and Contributor
Check Point Certified Security Professional: CCSA, CCSE, CCSE+, CCSI
Security Engineer, Check Point Software Technologies, Ltd.

## Chapter 1

Introduction to Check Point Next Generation with Application Intelligence

Solutions in this Chapter:

- Introducing the Check Point Next Generation with Application Intelligence Suite of Products
- Understanding VPN-1/FireWall-1 SVN Components
- Looking at Firewall Technology
- Complete Secure Virtual Network Concept

☑ Summary

☑ Solutions Fast Track

☑ Frequently Asked Questions

Introduction

The Check Point Next Generation (NG) with Application Intelligence (AI) suite of products provides the tools necessary for easy development and deployment of enterprise security solutions. Check Point VPN-1/FireWall-1 has been beating out its competitors for years in every category, and the NG AI software continues to improve the look, feel, and ease of use of this software. Most notably, there is a new security dashboard that gives security administrators a more detailed view of the Security Policy and management objects in one window. The user interface is easy to comprehend and provides optimal functionality, all in one place.

With the NG AI software, you can manage multiple firewalls from a central management server, and can centrally manage licenses and software upgrades with the SmartUpdate application. Other useful tools in the NG AI suite include Lightweight Directory Access Protocol (LDAP) account management, Large Scale Manager (SmartLSM), SecuRemote virtual private networks (VPNs), bandwidth usage services, Domain Name System (DNS)/dynamic host control protocol (DHCP) services, reporting, logging, and high availability configurations.

This chapter introduces you to each of these tools, and discusses the various components of VPN-1/FireWall-1 in more detail. You will learn the difference between proxy firewalls, packet filtering firewalls, and the technology that Check Point NG AI uses, called Stateful Inspection. You will become familiar with the inspection engine, which is the nuts and bolts of the software, and learn how it analyzes traffic going through the firewall.

Introducing the Check Point Next Generation with Application Intelligence Suite of Products

It seems that the Internet moves a little further into the network everyday, and along with it comes new network security and management challenges. A few years ago, it was easy to define and visualize a network into simple security zones: "trusted" for anything behind the firewall and "un-trusted" for anything in front of it. Security at that time seemed easy: stick a firewall where the internal network met the Internet, and maybe add a Demilitarized Zone (DMZ) for the Web and e-mail servers. Now, however, with new Internet applications, extranets, and VPNs becoming common, the un-trusted network is creeping into the DMZ and even right into the trusted network. To address the security needs of this new network, we not only need secure scaleable firewall technology but also the tools to provide Quality of Service (QoS) and network management, and to log and report on the usage and health of the network infrastructure.

The Check Point NG AI suite is composed of several different products bundled to create a complete enterprise security solution. The combination of these specialized tools allows the NG AI suite to address the major security and network management challenges facing today's security managers. Rather than look at network security solely from the firewall or VPN solution, Check Point set out with its Secure Virtual Network (SVN) architecture to encompass all areas of enterprise security into a single, easy-to-use product. Until recently, many enterprise security managers believed that simply firewalling their network at the Internet connection provided all the security they needed. In today's network world there are Intranet and extranet connections and remote dial and VPN access to secure. The SVN architecture looks at the entire enterprise network, encompassing not only Local Area Network (LAN) and Wide Area Network (WAN) connections, but extending right down to the individual VPN-connected user. This new enterprise level view of security defines a complete, scalable, and secure architecture that requires the integration of several products to achieve.

The NG with AI suite is designed to fill the security and management needs of the SVN architecture. Using VPN-1/FireWall-1 to firewall between networks and provide a robust endpoint for VPN traffic addressed most companies' primary security needs. Having secured the front door, SecuRemote was added to the NG AI suite as a desktop application to enable easy VPN setup. SecureClient was designed to build on to the functionality of SecuRemote by enabling security managers to set and enforce a desktop Security Policy for desktop machines connecting to the VPN service. Having addressed the firewall and user VPN capabilities most companies are looking for, NG AI turned to address the user management problems identified by the SVN. Two products were added to the suite to enable security managers to easily manage users and accounts. The Account Management component was added to manage user accounts stored on LDAP servers, and UserAuthority (UA) was introduced to make authentication information acquired by VPN-1/FireWall-1 available to other applications to provide Single Sign-On (SSO) capabilities. To help manage the Internet Protocol (IP) network, two more tools where added to the NG AI suite. Meta IP allows easy management of DNS and DHCP servers, while FloodGate-1 provides the QoS and bandwidth management needed for VPN and Internet networks. To provide the scalability necessary for deploying hundreds or thousands of firewalls,

Check Point added a SmartLSM to provide profile (or template) based management. Finally, to provide detailed security and usage reports from not only the NG AI suite of products, but also from supported third-party applications, Check Point added the SmartView Reporter tool. By combining all of these tools into a comprehensive suite, NG AI provides network and security managers with the security and management tools needed in today's enterprise networks in one integrated, scaleable package.

To tie all of these products together into an easy-to-manage solution, NG AI includes a new Security Dashboard that incorporates the best features of the Policy Editor with additional object display windows and the optional Smart Map. The Security Dashboard, as shown in Figure 1.1, not only provides a single point of access for managing the entire NG AI suite, but also shows how the different products integrate together allowing configuration information to be moved and shared between applications quickly and easily.

Figure 1.1 NG AI Security Dashboard

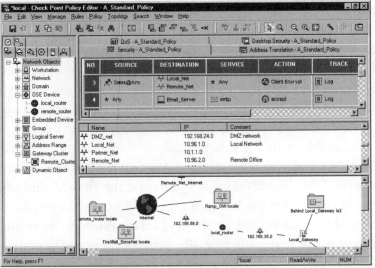

VPN-1/FireWall-1

At the cornerstone of the NG AI suite is VPN-1/FireWall-1. The VPN-1 and FireWall-1 (FW-1)products are designed to prevent unauthorized access to or from the networks connected to the firewall, based on the rules defined by the security manager. VPN-1/FW-1 uses a set of rules to create a Security Policy. This policy is compiled and loaded into the inspection engine component of the firewall and is applied to all traffic that traverses the firewall's network interfaces. VPN-1/FW-1 enforces part of the overall security policy from a technical aspect. Of course, you should have a written security policy that is enforced via procedures, audits, and other technical implementations.

Although it is common to think of VPN-1 and FW-1 as a single product, and although many people use the term FW-1 to refer to both products, they have very different functions. FW-1 provides the data filtering, logging, and access control as expected of any firewall gateway. VPN-1 integrates tightly into FW-1 to add VPN tools alongside the firewall. Combining VPN-1 with FW1 has allowed Check Point to provide firewall and VPN products that not only leverage each other's strengths, but that also function together seamlessly and are managed through a single management application. Tying VPN-1 and FW1 together enables you to build VPN gateways into your firewall rather than having to maintain two separate machines to provide firewall and VPN services. This can simplify the network complexity and Security Policy required, allowing for easier management and reducing the possibility of configuration errors.

Although VPN-1 provides all the tools you need to support site-to-site VPNs, and has even improved support for easy setup with third-party firewall products, there is still the issue of individual user-to-site VPN connections. To ensure that VPN-1 could provide the level of encryption, security, and control required when used with user-to-site VPNs, Check Point has updated the SecuRemote and SecureClient software packages. By integrating SecuRemote and SecureClient tightly with VPN-1, Check Point has not only provided you with the tools you need to secure your user-to-site VPN, but has also ensured their continued dominance in the VPN market space.

In the NG AI suite, Check Point provides the tools required to manage VPN-1/FW-1 in a distributed environment, allowing security managers to define and enforce a single Security Policy across the entire enterprise. By building FW-1 on a distributed model, Check Point has designed a product that functions equally well as a stand-alone single gateway product, as it does in large multiple firewall gateway networks. This distributed nature allows multiple VPN-1 and FW-1 gateways to be managed from a single management station, simplifying not only Security Policy definition, but also logging functions since the logs from all gateways are available from a centralized server.

Managing NG AI products has been simplified by the creation of the Security Dashboard. This new application took the best features of the Policy Editor from FW-1 4.1 (CP2000) and added new tools to simplify firewall and other product management. New drag-and-drop lists and the SmartMap not only speed up the rule creation process, but also provide an easy-to-understand visual look at your Security Policy, hopefully reducing security holes caused by errors in the policy. To further enhance the manageability of VPN-1/FW-1 in a distributed environment, several new tools were added to the NG AI suite. SmartUpdate enables security managers to maintain the newest product code levels not only on FW-1 products but also on Open Platform for Security (OPSEC) certified products from a centralized location. To ensure that communication between firewall enforcement points, the management station, and the management client is reliable, Check Point uses the Secure Internal Communication (SIC) function to encrypt and validate traffic between modules.

Designing & Planning…

What is Provider-1?

Standard installations, which are covered in this book, work wonderfully for most customers, but the security infrastructure of a large enterprise or a Managed Service Provider (MSP) requires a much more robust solution with separate policies, objects, and logs for each customer, business unit, or other logical grouping of firewalls. With the standard enterprise management solution (SmartCenter or SmartCenter Pro), the only way to separate logs, polices, and objects was to run multiple management stations, which led to a much higher hardware cost as well as more management overhead. Provider-1 was developed from customer requests by large enterprises and MSPs whose scale and requirements went beyond the capabilities of an individual management station.

By design, Provider-1 allows role-based administration of multiple virtual management stations to run on a single physical system. Based on the same three-tier management infrastructure, each virtual management station contains its own logs, policies, and objects. However, enabling virtual management stations did not solve all the management scalability concerns faced by large implementations. Provider-1 Superusers can also leverage the Multi-Domain GUI (a graphical user interface [GUI] that oversees all the virtual management stations; also referred to as the MDG) to administer global policies, administrators, objects, and VPNs that span multiple virtual management stations. This enables an administrator to make a single change, which is applied across the entire enterprise (or multiple virtual management stations) to quickly react to new threats.

Designing & Planning…

What is OPSEC?

Although the NG AI suite contains many products to help you secure your network, no one vendor can account for every security challenge you may face and do it well. Whether it is load balancing network hardware or two-factor authentication software, there will almost always be a requirement to use additional, third-party applications to achieve the level of security and robustness you need. Using OPSEC-certified solutions will guarantee central management, interoperability, and ease of use by ensuring the security products you implement will work together.

Check Point's OPSEC Partner Alliance program allows Check Point to extend their security suite well beyond what any one company can offer, by certifying hardware and software solutions from third-party vendors in the security enforcement, network management and reporting, performance, and high availability, as well as eBusiness markets. To ensure the broadest number of solutions available to customers, Check Point even allows its competitors to join the alliance if they meet the standards. For example, even though Check Point develops a reporting solution, there are other vendors in the same category including WebTrends.

To become OPSEC-certified, applications are tested to ensure compliance with the defined OPSEC standards as well as the SVN architecture. This ensures that solutions you invest in today will operate and integrate with legacy OPSEC applications as well as new applications as they come to market. With the support of over 350 vendors, finding OPSEC security solutions for even your most unique issues while ensuring compatibility in your environment, is fast and easy. For more information, including a list of certified partners, go to www.opsec.com

On the surface, VPN–1/FW–1 NG AI looks like an update to version 4.1, but when you dig deeper you find that, although the core FW–1 technology of Stateful Inspection is still the heart of the system, new tools and updated applications work together to provide an updated and complete security solution. VPN–1/FW–1 NG AI provides the security tools that enterprises are looking for with the ease of manageability that security managers need. The following sections examine the additional products that enable FW–1 NG AI to be a complete security solution, and then discuss FW-1, pointing out the technology and features that have made Check Point the market leader in Internet and VPN gateway solutions.

Smart Directory (LDAP)

One of the many features that distinguish VPN-1 and FW-1 from the competition is the ability to easily authenticate users at the gateway. Whether it is as simple as verifying a user's access to surf the Internet or as sensitive as authenticating VPN connections, managing user accounts quickly becomes a big part of managing your enterprise Security Policy. To help make user management easier, Check Point provides the Smart Directory (formerly called the account management module) component integrated into SmartDashboard. Smart Directory allows one or more OPSEC-compliant LDAP servers, including Microsoft's Active Directory and Novell's Novell Directory Services (NDS), to provide user identification and security information to FW-1. Once enabled, FW-1 can use information stored on the defined servers to enforce rules within the Security Policy.

The Smart Directory module also integrates a specialized GUI that can be used to manage user accounts and define user level access. Users and privileges defined with the Account Manager are then available not only to FW-1 but also to any other application that is able to query the LDAP database. The Smart Directory tool is available as a tab on the Objects List, allowing you to manage user accounts stored in LDAP directories as easily as users defined in the local FireWall-1 user database.

To ensure that sensitive user information is not collected or tampered with in transit, Secure Sockets Layer (SSL) communications can be enabled between the Smart Directory machine and the LDAP server. SSL can also be enabled between the LDAP server and the firewall module, ensuring that sensitive information such as user encryption schemes or account passwords are always protected.

SecuRemote/SecureClient

As part of the VPN-1 solution, Check Point developed the SecuRemote application to provide the VPN endpoint on client machines. Designed for the Microsoft 32-bit Windows, Apple Macintosh, and Linux operating systems (OSs), SecuRemote provides the authentication and encryption services required to support simple desktop-to-firewall VPNs. SecuRemote can not only be used to encrypt traffic from Internet-based clients, but also for LAN and WAN and intra-LAN users who deal with sensitive information. By encrypting all data between the user's desktop and the VPN-1 gateway, you can be sure that information transferred has not been read or modified in transit.

The explosion in affordable home broadband cable modem and Digital Subscriber Line (DSL) access revealed the need to secure these "always on" VPN-connected users, which lead to the SecureClient product. SecureClient is an extension to the SecuRemote software; along with the standard encryption and authentication services, it also provides powerful client-side security and additional management functions. The SecureClient application contains "personal firewall" software that is centrally managed by the VPN-1 security manager and uses the same proven Stateful Inspection technology found in VPN-1/FW-1. To ensure that the client machine cannot be configured in a way that would circumvent the Security Policy set by the security manager, VPN-1 uses a set of Secure Configuration Verification (SCV) checks to ensure that the desired security level is in place. The SCV checks can be as simple as setting the Security Policy enforced at the client, right down to ensuring that the newest version of your chosen virus-scanning software is installed. Coupled with the encryption and authentication services found in SecuRemote, SecureClient provides the security tools needed to build a secure VPN tunnel between individual desktop hosts and the VPN-1 gateway. This enables you to extend the enterprise network to include the client PC, whether that machine is LAN-connected in the next office, or a mobile user working via an Internet connection.

To make user setup easier, VPN-1 SecureClient enables you to build custom install packages with all the connection options pre-defined. This reduces the set up complexity for the end user, which ultimately results in fewer support calls to your helpdesk. SecureClient also includes centrally managed Security Policy update and VPN client software update capabilities to ensure that VPN clients are always up-to-date with the newest software version and policy settings.

SecureClient and SecuRemote support the industry standard encryption algorithms, including 256-bit Rijndael Advanced Encryption Standard (AES) and 168-bit Triple Data Encryption Standard (3DES) all the way down to 40-bit single Data Encryption Standard (DES), to ensure compatibility with whatever application you have in mind. Add flexible user authentication including everything from token-based two-factor mechanisms through X.509 Digital Certificates and biometrics, down to OS- or FW-1-stored passwords, and you have a VPN solution that can be easily integrated and scaled into almost any environment.

To keep your users connected and working, both SecuRemote and SecureClient support Multiple Entry Point (MEP) VPN-1 gateway configurations. This allows the SecuRemote or SecureClient software to be aware of more than one gateway that is available to provide VPN access to a protected network or system. Should one path or gateway become unavailable for any reason, the connection will be attempted through another VPN-1 gateway, if defined. This provides not only for redundancy to maintain high availability statistics on your VPN solution, but can also allow you to spread the network and firewall load out to reduce latency.

SmartView Reporter

Although the built-in log viewer (SmartView Tracker) is perfect for most day-to-day log file examinations, the FW-1 suite has, until NG, lacked a good tool to produce "state of the network" and diagnostic graphs. The SmartView Reporter fills this need to produce summary and detailed reports from the log data. To provide the best view possible of your network, you can create reports with the detail level you specify not only from log data generated from traffic intercepted by Check Point products, but also from the logs of other OPSEC applications.

Using the SmartView Reporter to create reports from your logs enables you to check the security and performance of your network, firewalls, and Security Policy at a glance. Generating network traffic reports can help ensure that you dedicate your bandwidth budget dollars where needed and reduce spending on services that are underutilized. The network traffic reports also enable you to see trends in network usage, which, with a little luck, will allow you to increase capacity proactively rather than have to scramble when network users start to complain of slow access.

Generating reports of dropped or rejected session attempts can turn up suspicious traffic you may not otherwise notice. This may enable you to see "low and slow" port scans that take days or weeks to complete, in an effort to be stealthy or to see that one of your servers is acting funny. I once worked with a company whose Web server had been "rooted," or taken over by an unauthorized user. The server administrator had not noticed the server malfunctioning or failing in any way, but the firewall logs showed dropped packets from attempted connections to hosts on the Internet and to the firewall's own interface (presumably from a host scan to identify other machines in the DMZ) from the Web servers' network address. Seeing this dropped traffic alerted the administrator to a problem, since anyone authorized to work on the Web server would have known that they did not have any network access from its console and would normally not attempt these connections. Situations like this are difficult to distinguish from the filtered log data with the SmartView Tracker [Log Viewer]) since, instead of filtering for something specific, what you want to see is everything from a high level to be able to spot odd behavior that is easy to achieve by generating overview reports.

One of the best reasons to use this tool, aside from trending usage of your network and security resources, is what has been referred to as the "pretty picture effect." Especially when trying to increase bandwidth budgets or lobbying to double some of your infrastructure and enable load balancing, a picture is worth more than a thousand words. You can try to explain to the budget managers that your Internet connection is running at capacity and will soon become a bottle-neck with no results, but pull out six months' worth of bandwidth graphs that show a steady increase in bandwidth usage that is now approaching the limit, and things may start moving. To help automate this, trending and history creation of your Security Policy enforcement and network health reports can be scheduled to automatically generate. This allows you to have the most current reports waiting in your e-mail inbox every Monday at 8:00 A.M. if you like, or have the reports saved in HTML format that is easy to share via an internal Web site. SmartView Reporter is also ideal for providing regular reports to end-users, auditors, or customers who are also intrigued by the "pretty picture effect".

The SmartView Reporter is made up of two components:

- The Consolidation Policy Editor
- The Reporting Tool

The Consolidation Policy Editor is integrated into the Security Dashboard and can be viewed from the **View | Products | Log Consolidator** menu. The Consolidation Policy Editor enables you to set the level of detail recorded into the log database as well as to summarize log entries into meaningful con-nection data. For example, rather than log every session that is established with the Web server, you can consolidate this information and log it every 10 minutes. You can create consolidation rules for an individual Web server or for the entire farm, enabling you to trend and report the data in whatever format is most useful in your environment. Since the report module logs are stored onto a separate log server (or at least in a separate application database on the same server, if you choose) the original raw log data is still stored in the source device's logs. Using FW1 as an example, you could see the individual sessions allowed through to your Web server in the FW-1 logs, and see the summarized data in the Report

Server database. Another advantage of this architecture is the ability to consolidate and correlate the logs from all your supported OPSEC applications; this enables you to create reports that show the interaction of devices and give a more complete picture of your environment.

The second half of the SmartView Reporter is the Report Tool, which is used to actually mine data from the report database and create the final output. Built on the same model as FW-1, the Report Tool can be run as a separate client to the report server from another PC. The Report Tool contains many default reports that can be used out of the box or customized as needed. As well, you can create your own reports from scratch, enabling you to see as much or as little data from only the devices and servers that you need to see.

ClusterXL

With VPN connections being used for more critical day-to-day network operations, and with more businesses selling online though e-commerce sites 24 hours a day, 7 days a week, keeping firewall and VPN services always up and online is becoming increasingly important. Aside from the lost productivity from a service outage, businesses also have to consider customer confidence. Even the shortest outage may be all it takes to lose a potential customer to a competitor. The Check Point ClusterXL module enables you to create highly available VPN-1 and FW-1 services to help keep your infrastructure online and running 24 hours a day, 7 days a week.

The ClusterXL module enables you to create clusters of VPN-1/FW-1 machines, providing seamless failover for critical services and network connections. By tightly integrating into VPN-1/FW-1, the ClusterXL module allows one or more of the cluster machines to fail without impacting the users' ability to connect and maintain established sessions with your servers. By keeping state information synchronized between the individual machines in the cluster, when a failure occurs, another machine is able to seamlessly take over the sessions that had been using the now-failed gateway. Since users never see the failover, any file transfers or VPN sessions continue as normal, without the need to restart or re-authenticate.

In addition to having a highly available cluster of firewalls, systems can participate in load sharing to aggregate the total throughput capabilities of each individual firewall together to scale linearly. This combination of the processing power of multiple systems ensures that connections are handled quickly even for CPU-intensive applications such as authentication, encryption, and the use of

Security Servers. Aside from protecting against hardware or OS failures, creating high availability clusters can also be useful for performing routine maintenance such as backups, disk checks, or upgrades that may require a machine to be taken offline or rebooted. In the always-on, always-connected world of the Internet, there no longer exists a good time to take services offline for maintenance, and many companies are turning to clusters and redundancy to keep their availability statistics as close to 100 percent uptime as possible. In addition to creating highly available VPN and Internet gateways, you can also create highly available management stations, so that logging and Security Policy creation and maintenance can continue as normal in the event that the primary management station is unavailable. This enables you to geographically separate additional gateways and management stations, if needed, to provide for disaster recovery and offsite maintenance of your security infrastructure.

Once a previously down server is back online, either from being repaired or from finishing its maintenance programs, the cluster will automatically return the machine to active duty without administrator intervention. This means that if your servers are configured to automatically reboot after a failure, and the reboot successfully repairs the problem so that the server returns to the cluster, the only evidence of the failure may be in the logs.

UA

The UA module provides authentication services to VPN-1/FW-1 and other third-party applications. By extending the user account and group information from multiple sources such as VPN-1/FW1, Windows NT, or LDAP servers to the firewall and other eBusiness applications, the UA module reduces the need to maintain multiple user information databases for application authentication services. This provides not only reduced complexity for the users by being able to use the same account information for multiple applications, but also simplifies development of new applications by providing the necessary authentication procedures.

The UA module can be used to enable a SSO solution for multiple applications. Many companies have seen increased support calls and user dissatisfaction from the need for users to authenticate themselves to multiple systems and applications, often with different credentials each time. Companies have also seen development costs for new applications drop by leveraging a pre-built authentication mechanism—especially when using less known means of authentication, such as biometrics, two-factor authentication, and digital certificates. The UA module allows authentication services and information to be shared between applications so that users only need to provide authentication credentials once, per session, to be able to use multiple applications. To enable this, the authorization information is captured by the UA module and is made available to all trusted UA-enabled applications.

FloodGate-1

FloodGate-1 enables you to improve performance of your IP networks by assigning and controlling QoS priority to traffic passing through the VPN-1/FW-1 gateway. Like FW-1, FloodGate-1 is policy-based and managed from the Policy Editor. The integration with VPN-1/FW-1 is what allows FloodGate-1 to outperform other QoS solutions. For example, by working with VPN-1, FloodGate-1 can manage VPN traffic with finer control than other QoS products because it can manage data before it is encrypted and assign weighting to different types of VPN data, whereas other applications can only see and manage the entire encrypted data stream as one. Being built into VPN-1/FW-1 also allows the same objects and user definitions to be used in the QoS policy as in the Security Policy.

To control QoS, FloodGate-1 enables you to set a weighting on individual types of traffic. The weighting for each rule is relative to that of the other active rules in the database. For example, if data is applied to a rule that has a weight of 10 and, when combined, all the rules with open connections have a total weight of 90, then the data gets 10 percent of the available bandwidth dedicated to it. However, if the rule has a weight of 10 and the rules with open connections have a total weight of only 10, then the data receives 50 percent of the available bandwidth. This allows QoS to be applied dynamically, maximizing use of the available bandwidth and ensuring that no class of traffic is starved completely, even under heavy load. Figure 1.2 shows a FloodGate-1 policy loaded into the Policy Editor in the same fashion as the Security or Network Address Translation (NAT) policy.

Figure 1.2 FloodGate-1 Policy

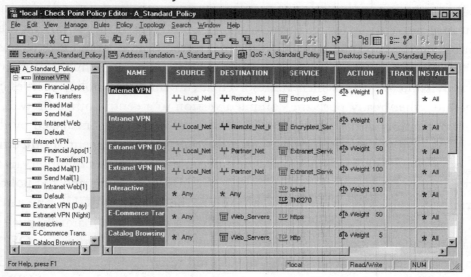

QoS performance can be monitored from the SmartView Monitor application, and can be selected to show all rules and networks or can be customized to only show VPN or specific application traffic. Since FloodGate-1 integrates with VPN-1/FW-1, general QoS overview statistics are available from the System Status viewer. This enables you to check the health and effectiveness of your QoS policy by looking at the current number of connections as well as pending byte and packet information. Since FloodGate-1 integrates so tightly into FW-1, data logged by your QoS policy (if enabled) is stored in the normal VPN-1/FW-1 logs, enabling you to correlate your policy actions with QoS information with the standard log viewing tools.

Another added benefit of this integration with VPN-1/FireWall-1 is the ability to prioritize and mark packets for QoS even inside the VPN tunnel. This allows an administrator to, for example, limit remote VPN clients' Simple Mail Transfer Protocol (SMTP) sessions to a specific bandwidth, and for uploading quarterly sales data, allow unlimited bandwidth and mark the encrypted packets with Differential Services (DiffServ). This type of complexity is impossible without an integrated VPN and QoS solution.

SmartLSM

In extremely large deployments where configurations are going to be similar, profile- or template-based management may be more suited for the task. For example, when deploying small devices to 1,500 stores across the country or 5,000 devices to regional offices for an insurance company, the standard management may prove to be less efficient than one would like. Even routine tasks like pushing a policy become unmanageable due to the time it would take to push 1,500 policies. SmartLSM simplifies this task by allowing an administrator to create dynamic objects (which are resolved at run-time) and policy profiles centrally and, when ready, push the compiled version to a central office firewall, which becomes a distribution point to all the remote firewalls managed by the SmartLSM. All the remote firewalls fetch the policy from the central office firewall on a given interval (if necessary) and because they all start the intervals at random times based on when they startup, the load of sending updated policies is distributed over a longer period of time. From the SmartLSM GUI, one can quickly see the status of hundreds of firewalls at a glance and manually push the dynamic objects or policy immediately, update the software, update the OS, manage licenses, get extended status details, and restart/reboot the gateway. Even more useful is that SmartLSM can manage both normal installations of VPN-1/FW-1 as well as low-end devices running Sofaware's Safe@ software.

SmartLSM can be used with a normal SmartCenter Pro or inside a Provider-1 virtual management station to provide similar policies to many systems whose logs will all come to the same system. Contrasted to SmartLSM, Provider-1 virtual management stations are most useful when managing systems that have very different functions and differing policies. SmartLSM is used primarily for managing systems with very similar configurations.

Meta IP

As your network grows larger and more complex, IP addressing and name resolution services can become time consuming and often difficult to manage. Not only are DHCP and DNS services important to keep your network running smoothly, but they may also be a large part of your overall network security architecture. We often write security rules by creating groups of IP addresses or defining entire networks as objects, and grant access to services based on a client machine's membership in one of these IP address ranges. For example, it is common to allow all user workstation machines to be used to browse the Internet, but restrict operators from browsing when logged onto a server. This is a good practice if you are concerned that someone may inadvertently download and execute a virus or another malicious code on a server where it could do more damage than it would if just run on a workstation. This raises the issue of keeping the workstations out of the server IP network space and ensuring that the servers are not configured with "workstation" addresses. To help mitigate network addressing problems and the security issues that can arise as a result of poor address management, Check Point designed Meta IP to provide you with the ability to securely manage DHCP and DNS services on your network.

The centrally managed DHCP and DNS servers provided by Meta IP can interoperate with any existing standards-based service, making integration into your network easy as well as providing the framework necessary to scale up as your network expands. These features not only help you manage the IP address and namespace on your network, but also can help you reduce support costs by managing related services from a central location. The built-in analysis tools help you manage the often complex server configuration files and enable you to periodically check all files for errors and corruption, either interactively or as an automated, scheduled task.

High availability has been built into the Meta IP DNS and DHCP servers to help ensure that the IP address management services stay up and service clients 24 hours a day. The DNS servers support the primary and secondary configuration that we are all used to, but DHCP Check Point has something unique. The Meta IP DHCP service supports a one-to-one failover module as well as a many-to-one model that will enable you to have a single centrally located server provide backup for any number of severs in a distributed network, reducing the hardware and support costs of maintaining service availability.

To protect the IP address and name service database and configuration from being tampered with or corrupted, Meta IP servers can use Transactional Signatures (TSIGs) to digitally sign and verify the configuration update and replication information they send and receive. This ensures that only services with the appropriate TSIG keys can modify the DHCP scope or DNS zone information.

Arguably the most exciting feature of Meta IP is the ability to provide the SecureDHCP service. By integrating with VPN-1/FW-1 and the UA, Meta IP's DHCP service enables you to authenticate users to a Windows domain or to the FW-1 user database before being issued a useable IP address. To accomplish this, the client machine is first given a non-routable IP address that provides them with sufficient connectivity to authenticate. Once authenticated, the user's workstation is issued a new address that allows the user to work normally. This not only increases the security of your network by allowing only authenticated users access to network services, but also improves user accountability, by showing users that all network access can be logged, if needed, back to their username. This can be particularly useful if your company needs to enforce an "acceptable use" policy for accessing LAN or Internet resources. The access users are provided before and after authenticating is all controlled via the same SmartDashboard security policy discussed throughout this book.

Understanding VPN-1/FireWall-1 SVN Components

Now that you have seen the major components of the NG AI suite of products, you have likely noticed an underlying theme develop. Everything in the NG AI suite seems to integrate into, requires, or works best in combination with VPN-1/FW1. Although some of the NG AI suite products can operate alone, parts of Meta IP, for example, the product's true power and full feature set is only available when used in conjunction with VPN-1/FW-1. The next few pages look at the individual components of FW-1 itself, and examine how these individual components combine to provide the network security and management tools required to satisfy the SVN specifications.

The GUI, management, and VPN/firewall modules make up the core of VPN-1/FireWall-1. These three modules can reside on a single computer or be built on separate, distributed machines depending on the size and specific needs of your network. The management module provides a centralized point to manage and log data from a single or multiple network security enforcement point. The GUI provides an easy-to-use interface for the management module, simplifying configuration and maintenance. Since the GUI and management modules are what you interact with most when working with VPN-1/FireWall-1, we will explore them before looking at the VPN/Firewall module that does the actual traffic inspection.

VPN-1/FireWall-1 Management Module

At the center of Check Point's three-tier architecture is the management module (SmartCenter server). The management module is most commonly configured using the GUI client and resides on the management server (SmartCenter). The management module not only stores the Security Policy but is also responsible for maintaining the logs, user databases, and the various network objects used in the Security Policy. The management module moves the logging and policy maintenance functions away from the core inspection module. This allows a single SmartCenter to service multiple enforcement points, and allows VPN/firewall modules to perform better by not having to maintain and sort the log files. The management module also checks that the Security Policy is defined correctly and compiled into the format that the inspection module needs. The management module also expands the Security Policy beyond just Check Point VPN-1/FW-1 devices by enabling you to define and push out an access control list (ACL) to any number of supported third-party devices.

Although the management module can be deployed on the same physical machine as the GUI clients and even on the VPN/firewall module, the true benefit of separating the management aspect from the GUI configuration and enforcement point really shows in a larger, distributed environment.

Central Management of VPN-1/FireWall-1 Modules

The management module leverages the Client/Server architecture to enable you to manage an entire enterprise from a single SmartCenter. This configuration provides performance, scalability, and centralized control of your security environment from a single supported platform that could, if needed, be duplicated and made into a highly available service. Figure 1.3 shows a typical distributed configuration of a single management server maintaining multiple FireWall-1 and VPN-1 enforcement points.

Figure 1.3 Distributed Client/Server Architecture

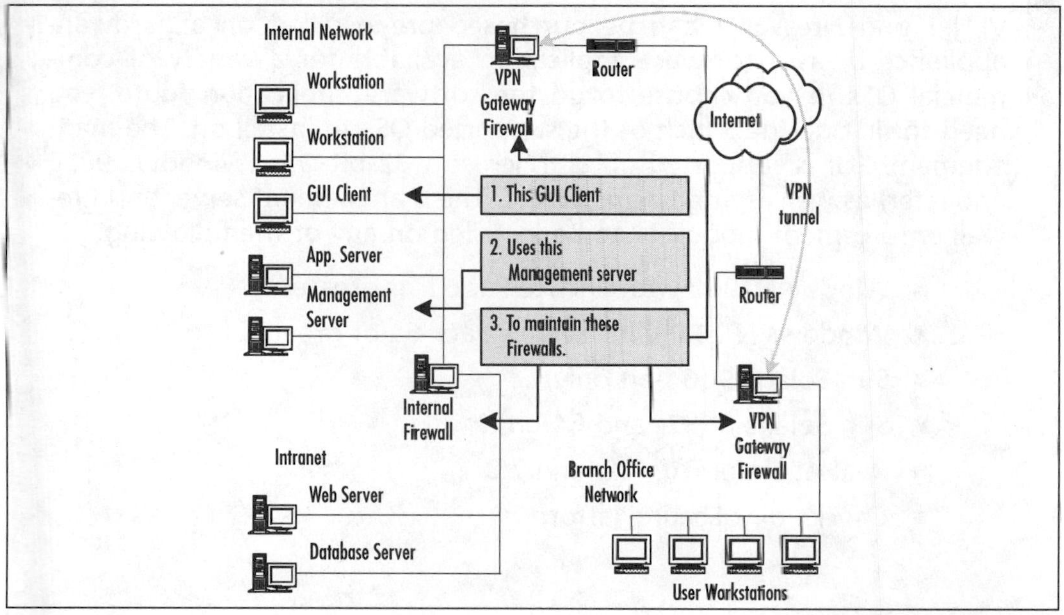

The key point to notice in the above example is that the management server can be accessed from a workstation that is running the management GUI, and that a single server can manage multiple firewalls. If desired, the management server could be used to manage the ACLs on the routers and other supported network equipment. This enables you, from a GUI client running on your desktop workstation, to securely create and maintain a single Security Policy, stored on a centralized management server and enforced on any number of enforcement points. The enforcement points can be Check Point firewall or VPN modules running on any supported OS or purchased pre-installed onto network appliances, as well as a number of routers, switches, and other network devices from different vendors. This allows a single centrally managed Security Policy to define and enforce the basic security needs of your entire enterprise. Without the management server layer, an administrator would have to connect to each firewall to make a change. This introduces the possibility for policies to become disjointed and security vulnerabilities to be introduced without an administrator realizing it.

Designing & Planning…

Choosing Your OS

VPN-1 and FireWall-1 can be purchased pre-installed on a hardware appliance or as a software application available for a variety of commercial OSs. If you choose to go the software application route, you need to first decide which of the supported OSs to install on. The management GUI is supported on all Microsoft 32-bit OSs (Windows 98SE and later) as well as Sun Solaris SPARC. The management server and firewall enforcement modules can be installed on any of the following:

- Windows 2000 with Service Pack 1 or greater
- Windows NT 4.0 with Service Pack 6a or greater
- Sun Solaris 9 (64-bit only)
- Sun Solaris 8 (32- and 64-bit)
- RedHat Linux 7.0, 7.2, and 7.3
- Check Point SecurePlatform

Continued

Choosing the platform that is right for your company has more to do with your ability to support the OS than with actual security. When you choose your OS, you need to consider what your company is best able to maintain and troubleshoot if problems arise. We have all heard that one OS is more secure than another is, but when it comes to the firewall configuration, mistakes can lead to security problems faster than OS vulnerabilities. By working with the OS you are most comfortable with, you reduce the chances of making configuration mistakes, which generally outweigh any perceived benefit from running on a "more secure" platform. A skilled administrator can make any supported OS just as secure as any other, and after VPN-1/FWI-1 is installed, it will take care of securing the machine via the firewall security policy.

Furthermore, many companies "harden" the OS before installing the firewall by uninstalling or locking down unneeded services and restricting user and application access to the firewall just to be extra cautious. This type of configuration requires an in-depth knowledge of the OS that is hard to get if the firewall is running on a "one of" OS in your enterprise.

Optionally, Secured by Check Point Appliances and Check Point's SecurePlatform OS come with web-based interfaces for OS management and configuration. This reduces the need for you to be an expert at securing and navigating the OS and simplifies administration.

SIC

We all know that any time data is in transit over our networks it is vulnerable. Sensitive network data could be recorded in order to reconstruct the session later, or it could even be modified or corrupted while in transit using standard man-in-the-middle (MITM) tactics. For most network data, this is not much of a concern since the risk of loss or corruption is low, or the data is simply not worth the effort involved to secure it (such as users browsing the Internet). However, when working with firewall configuration and logs, the risk is much higher, and trusting the configuration and logs from your firewall is paramount to securing your network. To address this issue, Check Point developed the SIC module.

SIC is used to encrypt the data passed between modules and applications, such as information passed between the GUI client, management server and firewall module for policy downloads and sending log data, as well as for a variety of other communication between devices that work with VPN-1/FW-1. For example, SIC can be used between the firewall module and a Content Vectoring Protocol (CVP) server or a Log Export API (LEA) application, in addition to various other OPSEC products and components.

SIC provides three basic functions that enable you to trust communication between supported devices, most notably between your management server and enforcement points. Along with the encryption that you would expect between devices or modules, SIC also ensures that communication is proceeding only with the host intended by authenticating that host using an internal Public Key Infrastructure (PKI) infrastructure. When running on the server side of the client/server model, SIC checks that the client has been granted access to the function or procedure that it is trying to execute even after the peer has successfully authenticated. By authenticating its peers, applying access control, and encrypting traffic, the SIC module ensures that communication between components is accurate and private. By using SIC's internal PKI solution to authenticate systems to each other and encrypt data over any link, trusted or un-trusted, this enables a much more scalable and manageable infrastructure.

NG SIC is certificate-based and makes use of the management server as a party that all hosts trust. The management server hosts the internal Certificate Authority (CA) that is used to issue new certificates, as well as maintains the certificate revocation list (CRL). The internal CA is also used to service certificate pull requests generally issued by third-party OPSEC applications. This again shows off the central nature of the management server and makes another argument for running the management server on a separate machine, even though it can be hosted with the firewall module, so as to remove this extra functionality and overhead from your Security Policy enforcement point.

SmartUpdate

SmartUpdate is an application, included with the management module, which enables you to maintain and upgrade software and licenses for Check Point, OPSEC applications, and some OSs from a central server. For example, SmartUpdate can be used to install a new feature pack or OS update onto your VPN-1/FW-1 NG AI installation as well as push out updated license information when you need to renew expired licenses or if you license additional features.

SmartUpdate enables you to track OS and application versions from all of your Check Point modules as well as supported OPSEC applications. Figure 1.4 shows a typical SmartUpdate window displaying OS, service pack and IP address information for all the modules currently defined to the management server.

Figure 1.4 SecureUpdate Products Tab

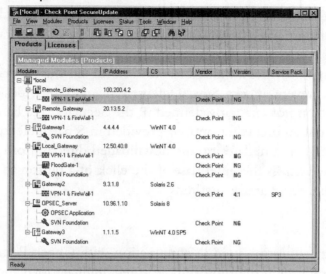

The Licenses tab of SmartUpdate allows you to see the installed license details for all your firewalls and supported OPSEC applications in one convenient location. Aside from showing you the features currently licensed on all your gateways, SmartUpdate can also be used to upgrade those licenses remotely. This feature is extremely useful if you need to change the external IP address and, therefore, to update the license for a remote gateway since, with SmartUpdate, you can change the license properties without the need to reinstall the license, which might otherwise require you to be at the gateway's console. Most commonly, the License tab is used to install new licenses for modules whose existing license is about to expire or when upgrading licensed features, such as adding encryption or adding SecureClient licenses to an existing gateway.

New integration with Check Point's UserCenter has also streamlined the process of downloading new packages and importing them into the SmartUpdate Product Repository. By using this feature, SmartUpdate will go to Check Point's Web site and, after signing in with your UserCenter username and password, download all the new versions of software you require to update your systems.

SmartDefense

In Check Point NG AI, there is a new tab in the SmartDashboard GUI called SmartDefense. SmartDefense brings global security mechanisms that were configured in text files and obscure areas of the GUI (and sometimes not well known, such as Check Point Malicious Activity Detection) into its own tab to provide a single, straightforward interface for configuring these advanced security options. The purpose of SmartDefense is to provide the configuration of active defense against attacks.

SmartDefense provides a unified framework for various security components to identify and prevent attacks. SmartDefense efficiently provides proactive protection, even when not explicitly defined in the Security rule base. In addition to the strict protocol enforcement options provided in SmartDefense, real time attack information and updates can be downloaded directly from Check Point and implemented across the enterprise at the click of a button to protect from new vulnerabilities and attack methods.

SecureXL

SecureXL is a specification used in conjunction with Check Point's hardware partners to help develop the most fully featured, high-performance firewall devices at varying price points. In general terms, SecureXL is helping Check Point service partners develop the hardware and software required to embed VPN-1 and FW-1 into devices that meet the requirements of as many applications as possible.

SecureXL aims to provide smaller companies with affordable firewall appliances as well as develop high-end machines with multi-gigabyte throughput for larger networks. To accomplish this, the SecureXL framework is employing the newest technology developments from the microprocessor field as well as Network Processors (NPs), Application-Specific Integrated Circuits (ASICs), and board-level encryption to develop high performance VPN-1 gateways. A direct benefit from the SecureXL work is the ability to use low-cost encrypting network interface cards (NICs), built to SecureXL specification, to boost VPN-1 encryption throughput.

In addition to encrypting NIC cards, the SecureXL standard allows vendors to increase device performance by moving firewall functions, such as NAT and anti-spoofing, to specialized hardware for processing. Even core firewall processes like access control and the connection tables can be replicated or moved to dedicated devices for improved performance and scalability. For more information, see the Check Point VPN-1/FW-1 performance brief at www.checkpoint.com/products/security/vpn-1_firewall-1_perfdetails.html

The ultimate goal of SecureXL is to develop the security products that enterprise network managers are looking for, at a variety of price points, by using the newest hardware and software technology and customizing the features included. This creates a variety of firewall and VPN solutions that enable you to not only pick the feature set, but in some cases also pick from multiple vendors to ensure that you get the products you need to secure your network, at a price that will fit your budget.

GUI

The GUI is the component of the management module that you will interact with the most. The GUI is made up of several tools and modules, designed to help you create and enforce a Security Policy and monitor the current and historical state of your security infrastructure. As a FW-1 security manager, you will spend most of your time in the two main GUI tools: the SmartDashboard and SmartView Tracker (Log Viewer). These two tools enable you to create the rules that make up your Security Policy and to check the effectiveness of those rules in action. The SmartDashboard contains the Policy Editor that will help you to build your Security Policy from objects that you define, as well as to build in definitions. SmartView Tracker enables you to sort and process data generated by your Security Policy in action on your network, and is explored in detail in Chapter 3.

The SmartDashboard GUI is designed to help you create the most accurate policy possible. Many companies expose themselves to risk, not from a lack of security understanding, but from poorly written firewall rules or policy. The graphical rule base of the Policy Editor, combined with the optional components such as the SmartMap, aim to help you quickly visualize and better understand your network topology and firewall rule base, enabling you to write an effective, enforceable Security Policy.

SmartDashboard

The combination of the Policy Editor, Object Tree, Object List, and Visual Policy Editor make up the majority of what Check Point calls the SmartDashboard. The Smart Dashboard provides you with the tools you need to analyze and manage your company's network security through the creation and maintenance of a Security Policy. The main advantage of the macro-level view provided by the SmartDashboard, is the elimination of having to hunt through menus and other dialogs to find the objects and resources required to efficiently build your Security Policy rules.

The Policy Editor has been designed to help show the relationships between objects better with the use of the SmartMap, as well as generally making the job of building security policies easier by enabling you to drag and drop objects from the Objects Tree, and making detailed object information readily available from the Objects List. Figure 1.5 shows the integration of all these components to create the SmartDashboard.

Figure 1.5 SmartDashboard

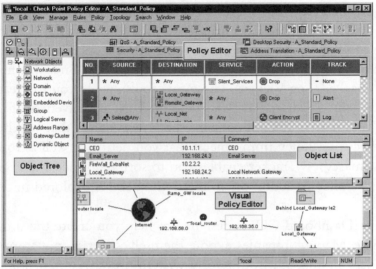

Policy Editor

The easiest and quickest way to manage your Security Policy is to use the Policy Editor, although a command-line interface is available. The Policy Editor has seen major improvements from previous versions to provide a user-friendly, GUI-based approach to security rule base creation and management. The Policy Editor has been designed to give a more detailed, visual representation of your Security Policy providing fast, easy, and more accurate rule creation.

Depending on the products licensed, all six VPN-1/FW-1 policies are available from the main Policy Editor window. Along with the standard Security and NAT policy tabs, the QoS, SmartDefense, UA WebAccess, and Desktop Security policies are also available. This all-in-one approach to maintaining all the major policies from a single GUI is a direct result of Check Point's SVN architecture that attempts to treat network security as an easy-to-manage, end-to-end solution rather than separate, isolated components. The added advantage of managing all four policies together is the reduction in duplicating objects into multiple applications, since the same set of network and user definitions are used in all four policies. The SVN-inspired SmartDashboard enables you to maintain the entire network, from the Internet-based, VPN-connected user desktop through NAT and QoS rules, right up to your Internet gateway Security Policy using a single, easy-to-use tool.

Expanding on the distributed nature of FireWall-1, Check Point has developed the SmartDashboard to work as a separate product that can be installed on the average workstation as part of the normal GUI tools. This enables you to use the SmartDashboard to work with the Security Policy stored on the management station from another computer known as a GUI client. Using this distributed design enables you to manage your firewall security rules, whether you are sitting at the console of the management server or working from a GUI client on the other side of the country.

Object Tree

The Object Tree provides the security administrator with quick access to all the objects that make up the Security Policy. Normally found running down the left side of the Policy Editor window, the Object Tree displays and sorts all the objects defined for use in the Security Policy. To make what you need easier to find, the Object Tree groups available objects into eight tabs: Network Objects, Services, Resources, OPSEC Applications, Servers, Users, Time Objects, and Virtual Links. For more information on how to use each of these objects, see Chapter 3.

Besides categorizing the policy objects to make it easier to find what you are looking for, the Object Tree also speeds up policy building by enabling you to drag and drop objects directly into policy rules, rather than requiring an administrator to open dialog boxes from the Manage menu.

Object List

The Object List is normally used simultaneously with the Object Tree to show the details of all objects available under the currently selected heading on the Object Tree. The main advantage of the Object List is the ability to see all the objects' important properties in a convenient table format rather than having to open each object's properties panel. Using the Object List enables you to quickly ensure that you are working with the object you intend (for example, when selecting workstation objects, you will be able to compare IP addresses and comments for each object, rather than just relying on the object names). This is especially handy when your object-naming convention is not completely clear, in that you can quickly verify that you are using the proper objects to build a new rule.

Another efficiency the Objects List provides is the ability to sort on any of the columns shown. This allows an administrator to show all network objects in the Objects List, but sort them by IP address, comment, version, or net mask. The same functionality for services allows one to sort by port. As with the Object Tree, you can drag and drop objects from the list directly into new or existing rules.

SmartMap

Check Point designed the SmartMap to help security managers better visualize the network topology contained within the Security Policy. Prior to FW-1 NG (and the VPE beta for FW-1 4.x), I often found myself used a white board or scrap of paper to draw network device connections and services to help build and verify the rule base. With the SmartMap, the whiteboard network diagram is automatically created and updated in SmartMap, providing not only a visual display of the network built from defined objects, but also allowing you to define new groups and other objects easily right in the visualization.

Along with making it easier to visualize the security rules, the ability to build and keep the network diagram with the Security Policy solves a couple of administration issues. First off, white board or even printed network diagrams, although often necessary for visualizing the network layout, are very difficult to keep secure. When network diagrams contain sensitive information, such as Intrusion Detection System (IDS) locations or other sensitive security device IP address information, it is important to keep that information secured. Keeping the diagram with the policy ensures only users allowed to view the Security Policy have access to the diagram. Secondly, if you have multiple security managers, using the SmartMap ensures that everyone is working from the same diagram. This can be very important when the primary security manager is unavailable and a secondary operator must finish or troubleshoot a new service installation. As well, this is extremely useful when one or more of your security administrators work offsite or in another office where SmartMap diagrams may be the most convenient way to share network diagrams.

Because of the tight integration with the Policy Editor and the objects, SmartMap automatically updates the diagram as your addressing changes, removing the need to continually update a shared document, which contains the current network topology. The always up-to-date SmartMap can also be exported to an image file (bitmap or JPEG) as well as directly to Microsoft Visio.

One of the most useful features of the Visual Policy Editor's integration with the Policy Editor is the ability to highlight individual rules from the Policy Editor on the network diagram. This feature is perfect for displaying complex rules to ensure that you have actually created what you expected, as shown in Figure 1.6. To make the visualization easy to read, different colors are used for different actions (accept, drop, encrypt, and so forth), which can be customized to suit your needs.

Figure 1.6 Visual Policy Editor Showing Rule

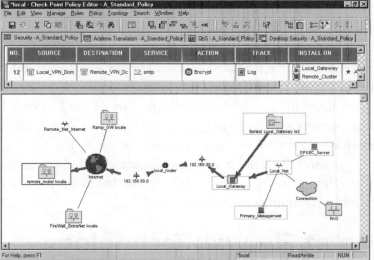

Policy Server

The Policy Server integrates into VPN-1, enabling you to manage the SecureClient software installed on a VPN user's machine from a central location. The Policy Server is responsible for sending SecureClient policy information for the specific desktop security settings to load, pushing down new versions of the client to the desktop, and enforcing SCV to ensure that the SecureClient machine's configuration meets your policy requirements.

In addition to verifying the clients' configuration and sending the desktop Security policy, the Policy Server is also responsible for handling logs from the SecureClient machines. As a final step of logging into the Policy Server, the software will package its local alert logs and send them to the Policy Server. The

Policy Server then opens these files and sends each alert log entry to the management server to be incorporated into the log database, where it is viewable through the VPN-1/FW-1 Log Viewer. This enables you to view alert data from not only VPN-1/FW-1 and local OPSEC applications, but also from remote VPN desktops with SecureClient installed.

Desktop Security

The Desktop Security policy is created with the Policy Editor on the Desktop Security tab. In addition to the actual policy, which is similar to the main Security Policy, operational settings can be modified from the Desktop Security section of the global policy properties. Once defined, the Desktop Security policy is downloaded to your policy server, making it available to your SecureClient v 4.1 and NG AI users when they next log on.

Desktop Security enables you to control the tiny or "personal" firewall built into the SecureClient software package. This enables you to extend the security of your network down to encompass the Internet-connected VPN client machines, as specified in the SVN architecture. Part of the Desktop Security policy can also incorporate checking to ensure that a minimum configuration level is maintained on the VPN client machine, by using the SCV module. This enables you to expand the default Desktop Security options to include custom checks that you define, grant, or deny VPN access based on the configuration state of the computer attempting to connect.

Looking at Firewall Technology

The final component of VPN-1/FW-1 is the actual firewall module. The firewall module enforces NAT, access control, logging, content security, and user, client, and session authentication services. The firewall module contains, among other functions, the inspection module that actually makes control decisions, based on the Security Policy, on how to handle traffic attempting to traverse the firewall's network interfaces. VPN-1/FW-1 uses a Check Point-patented technology called Stateful Inspection to examine IP data packets, and after applying knowledge of previous communication and the Security Policy, decide what action to perform on that data.

To understand the benefits of Stateful Inspection to control network traffic, it is necessary to look at the other types of firewall technology available today. The next few sections examine proxy or application gateway and packet filtering device technology and compare the advantages and disadvantages with those of Check Point's Stateful Inspection firewall technology.

Proxy Server versus Packet Filter

When comparing firewall technology, it is necessary to consider the layer of the Open System Interconnection (OSI) reference model where the firewall inspects traffic. Table 1.1 lists the seven layers of the OSI reference model and explains the type of data at each layer. In general terms, firewalls that inspect close to the top of the model have very detailed control over application-specific data, whereas firewalls inspecting farther down the model have less control over many types of traffic. As well, the position of the firewall's control module in the IP stack has an effect on how much of the underlying OS can be exposed to unfiltered traffic.

Table 1.1 OSI Reference Model

OSI Layer	Function
7 - Application Layer	Provides a set of interfaces allowing applications' network access
6 - Presentation Layer	Converts application data into a generic format for transmission
5 - Session Layer	Allows two network devices to hold ongoing communication (session)
4 - Transport Layer	Manages the transmission of the data on the network (packet sizes, and so forth)
3 - Network Layer	Addresses packets by resolving physical addresses from logical names
2 – Data Link Layer	Translates physical frame data into network layer format (NIC drivers)
1 - Physical Layer	Converts bits into signals (NIC and network medium at this layer)

Packet filtering examines data at the Network layer of the OSI model. This allows the packet filter device to apply a user-defined rule base on the source and destination service port and IP address only. Although this is relatively effective and can be made completely transparent to users, it is also often difficult to configure and maintain as your rule set grows. Packet filtering is inexpensive and can be found in many network devices from entry-level routers to enterprise firewall solutions. Packet filtering can offer complete application transparency and greater data throughput performance than application or proxy gateways.

The limitations of the packet filtering method of controlling data stem from the inability to apply rules to data above the network layer. This ignores a large part of the data packet when making a control (allow or deny) decision. In addition to often being difficult to configure and monitor due to their command-line only interface, packet filtering does not provide detailed logging of network data, again because of the lack of knowledge of the packets' contents above layer three and the simplicity of the devices often used. Since the packet filter device cannot keep or use application or session state to make decisions on what to do with specific data packets and subsequent connections, and only having a limited ability to manipulate traffic (such as address substitution), it is often considered to have a lower security level than a proxy or Stateful Inspection solution.

Application gateway (often called proxy) firewalls inspect network data at the very top of the OSI model, the Application layer. By using the underlying OSs IP stack, this typically gives the proxy firewall more detailed control over the applications' data since packets are fully decoded before a decision to pass or drop the traffic is made. This provides good security, but only for applications that the proxy is aware of; as new applications are introduced new proxy components must be developed, which is a long and programming-intensive process.

The main disadvantages of the proxy firewall technology are that the gateway cannot always be made transparent to the users and that the firewall is more vulnerable to OS or application security problems and bugs than other technologies, because the firewall sits so high on the IP stack. Proxies also have problems supporting User Datagram Protocol (UDP), Remote-Procedure Call (RPC), and other common connectionless services and protocols, such as Internet Control Message Protocol (ICMP).

Furthermore, even though application gateways inspect at the Application layer, they typically only enforce basic protocol rules and have no dedicated attack protection and prevention. Many attacks today (Nimda, Code Red, and so forth) are designed to conform to protocol specifications and exploit weaknesses in the design of the application running. By designing worms and exploits in this manner, these attacks often pass right through an application gateway or proxy server to the destination server, exploiting it.

Performance and Scalability

The need to continuously increase the Internet bandwidth available to your network to support new applications and services, as well as the need to segregate other high-speed networks, makes performance and scalability a high priority for any firewall solution. The ability of a solution to fit your current needs and grow as your network grows needs to be considered alongside the overall feasibility of the solution to fill your security requirement.

Although a proxy firewall can provide good security, scaling up to new applications is not always easy. Each application or protocol (such as HTTP or FTP) needs to have its own application gateway; this makes controlling new applications difficult and sometimes impossible—especially for proprietary applications and protocols. The performance or data throughput of a proxy solution is often lower, and the latency higher, than other options, since data must be decoded all the way up to the Application layer before a control decision can be made. In addition, the maintenance of terminating a connection, decoding of the packets, and creating a new connection outbound require more processing and because they are a function of the OS and not the application, connection information is difficult, if not impossible, to synchronize across multiple gateways to provide transparent failover.

Packet filters, on the other hand, often scale up to large installations easily. This is partially due to the fact that the packet-filtering firewall is often built into network routers and switches and, as such, can operate at or near network line speed. This makes packet filtering scale up with growth very easily since most networks already use routers; it is just a matter or purchasing devices capable of filtering and installing them where needed, and creating some rules. Even when built as an application running on a server, from the performance side, the packet filtering firewall is inspecting at a lower layer of the OSI model, meaning less processing overhead is introduced and greater throughput can be achieved. It is for these reasons that packet filtering is often used at the edges, or borders, of the network to reduce the volume of traffic before passing it to a firewall that can provide better security. It is easiest to think of this implementation as a kind of basic filter applied to the data stream; once you have reduced the volume of noise, you can use a more secure firewall, which may or may not perform at a lower rate to provide fine control over the network data.

FireWall-1's Inspection Engine

FW-1's Inspection Engine inspects all data inbound and outbound on all of the firewall's network interfaces. By inserting it into the Transmission Control Protocol (TCP)/IP stack between the Data Link and Network layer, the Inspection Engine is running at the lowest level of the OSI model accessible by software, since the Data Link layer is actually the NIC driver and the Network layer is the first layer of the IP protocol stack.

With FW-1 inspecting data at the lowest point possible, it is possible to keep state and context information from the top five layers of the OSI model that can be used when making control decisions. To obtain this state information, the Inspection Engine examines the source and destination service port and IP address fields from the data packets as well as other application information. This data is then used to determine what action to take based on the Security Policy. Figure 1.7 shows an overview of the firewall's position during a typical session between a client and server, as well as an overview of how data flows through the inspection module.

Figure 1.7 FireWall-1 Data Flow and Inspection Engine Detail

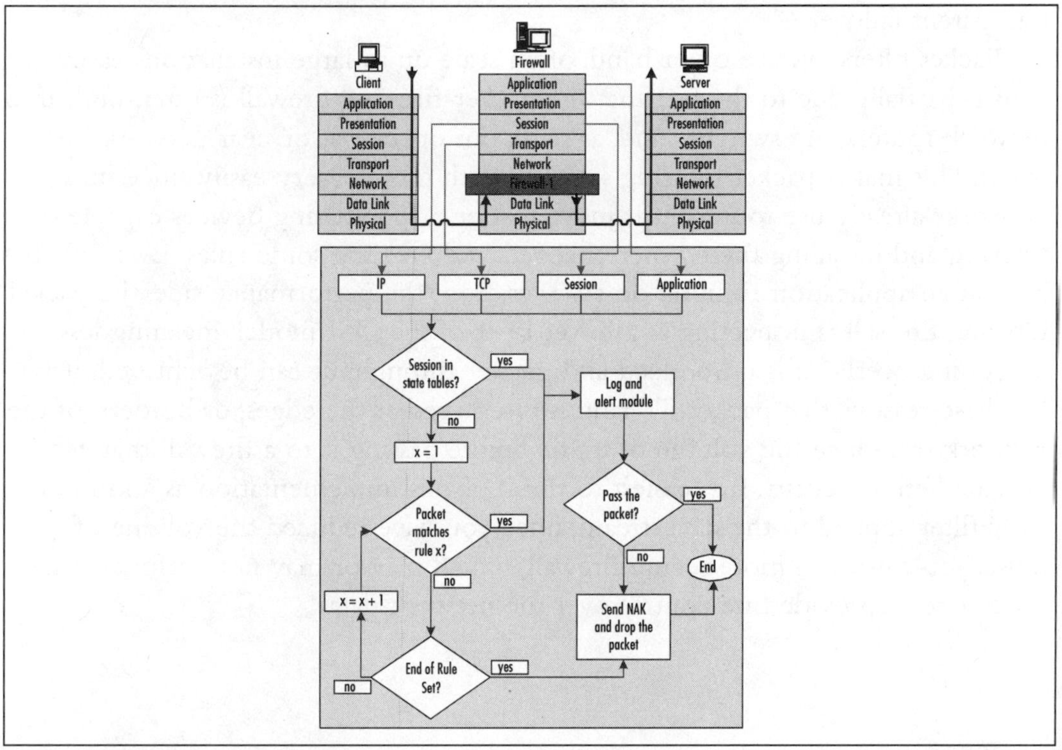

The Stateful Inspection technology maintains two types of state information. The communication-derived state is information that is gained from previous communication. For example, the Inspection Engine will note an outgoing FTP PORT command and will allow the incoming FTP data session to pass through to the client even though the data session on TCP port 20 is completely separate from the control session between a client and server on TCP port 21. The application-derived state is information saved by FW-1 from other applications, such as a user authenticating to the firewall to be allowed HTTP access, and can also be allowed HTTPS access if both rules in the Security Policy require the same type of authentication.

Collecting state and context information allows FW-1 to not only track TCP sessions, but also connectionless protocols such as UDP or RPC. Consider a standard DNS query; if the query were done with TCP, tracking the response would be easy, since it would be part of the established connection between the client and the server. However, DNS queries are always done with UDP, usually on port 53 (TCP port 53 being used for DNS zone transfers); this complicates allowing the DNS response to pass through the firewall since it is not part of an existing connection. A packet-filtering device would have to allow defined (or all) hosts to send UDP port 53 data to the client at any time, regardless of whether or not a request was made, since no application tracking can be done. In contrast, by keeping state information, FW-1 will be expecting a DNS response from a specific server after recording that the client had made a request, which was permitted by the Security Policy, into the state tables. To make this work, FW-1 allows data on UDP port 53 from the server back to the client that made the request, but this "open port" is only held open until a user-configurable timeout has expired, and then it will be closed again. This ensures that a request must go out from the client before any data from the server will be accepted, and that if no response is received, the port will not be held in an open state.

Developing & Deploying…

Caveat Emptor

Be aware when comparing differing firewall technologies, that even though Check Point developed Stateful Inspection in 1993 and is the undisputed market leader in the firewall marketplace, there are many products out there riding on Check Point's coattails, which claim to use "Stateful Firewalling," "Stateful Packet Filtering," "Deep Packet Inspection," or even "Stateful Inspection" itself. However, unless the product itself has been certified by Check Point and runs Check Point's software (i.e., Secured by Check Point Appliances), its capabilities are not as flexible, robust, and secure. Today, even free software can enforce the three-way handshake of TCP and dynamically open ports for FTP, but being able to enforce very stringent security for uncommon or complex protocols like SQL*Net, SIP and H.323, and being able to differentiate encrypted protocols from each other (without terminating the secure connection) like SSH v1 from v2 or SSL v2 from v3, is where you see the real difference between Check Point and its competitors.

Check Point's solution, built ground-up on the Inspection Engine, three-tiered management infrastructure, and a GUI-based management, is the only solution available today that can provide the security, flexibility, manageability, integration, and scalability in a single solution to meet the needs of small, medium, and large organizations alike. In addition to the unique technology Check Point provides, the OPSEC Alliance of best-of-breed third-party companies ensures that your investment can also meet your needs in the future without locking you into a single vendor's chosen solution.

Performance and Scalability

Controlling traffic using Stateful Inspection is very efficient and introduces minimal load to the firewall and very little latency to the network data stream. This is partly because the Inspection Engine is inserted into the OS kernel, allowing it to control data quickly and efficiently, but also because of the use of state tables to help make control decisions. As Figure 1.6 shows, incoming data packets are compared to information in the state tables before evaluating the rules in the

Security Policy. Since the state tables are kept in kernel memory, access to them is considerably faster than checking the rule base rule by rule, which allows traffic to be handled faster. To help increase performance of the Security Policy, try to keep frequently used rules near the top of the rule base; this will help to ensure that the minimum number of rules will need to be evaluated before making a control decision.

Adding encryption or logging with the account option will add a noticeable amount of overhead to your firewall. Performance is always traded for additional functionality, but purchasing or upgrading to a faster hardware platform will help to relieve most performance problems if your network grows beyond what your existing firewall was built to serve. For firewalls doing a lot of encryption, consider using a multiple CPU machine or adding a hardware encryption accelerator to handle some of the load.

Taking advantage of the VPN-1/FW-1 distributed design helps not only with scalability, but also with performance issues. As your network grows, you can add additional firewalls, either in a clustered load-balancing configuration or as stand-alone enforcement points, to spread different functions to separate gateways. Transparent high availability and load sharing can be achieved because the state information stored in the kernel memory is synchronized with all other cluster members, thus allowing them to immediately take over for a down system without effecting the connection. For example, some medium-sized organizations use one firewall for outbound user traffic (such as HTTP and FTP access) and for protecting an Intranet segment, a second firewall to provide inbound services such as access to the corporate Web servers, for internal and external (Internet) users, and a third machine to serve as a VPN gateway for employees and business partners. Since a single management server can manage multiple firewalls, scaling up to new growth and application demands by adding another firewall, when a simple hardware upgrade will not meet the performance requirement, can be done quickly and easily without significantly increasing your management overhead.

Complete SVN Concept

The real power of Check Point's solution comes to fruition when multiple components are used together. With the tight integration of the different technologies, very complex designs become not only possible but also manageable, ensuring complete end-to-end security throughout the enterprise and all related systems. You can mix and match technologies together to see how they can compliment each other.

For example, a virus or worm that propagates through Windows File Sharing (CIFS or Network Basic Input/Output System [NetBIOS]) can be blocked from infecting laptop users at home on broadband connections using the desktop firewalling and SCV capabilities of SecureClient. It can also be blocked from infecting your organization through a VPN with a business partner using the SmartDefense features on your gateway firewall. If you have laptop users on your LAN without SecureClient or visiting users, you can further contain infections by deploying firewalls to protect between network segments (i.e., Finance, Accounting, Internal Servers, and Wireless). With OPSEC solutions, you can extend this protection to protect against viruses propagating via HTTP and SMTP at the gateways, by leveraging the resources objects and the OPSEC CVP API (CVP), enforcing anti-virus updates, and ensuring that the virus is not present (i.e., checking to see if the *MSBlast.exe* file is running) on SecureClient users through SCV API. An administrator can enforce all these protections very quickly, view violations in a single log, and cover all entry points to the network to provide true end-to-end security.

Summary

The Check Point NG AI suite of products provides a combination of market-leading tools and applications aimed to meet the basic security needs of the entire enterprise. By using the SVN architecture to view security, not only from the firewall or stand-alone VPN-connected user, but also from an end-to-end solution perspective, has allowed Check Point to bring together the tools you need to secure your data assets.

VPN-1/FW-1 is the cornerstone of the NG AI suite, providing network security and VPN capabilities, as well as serving as the foundation for many of the other NG AI products. To complete the VPN capabilities of VPN-1, SecuRemote and SecureClient were included in the NG AI suite. SecuRemote provides a mechanism to authenticate users and encrypt data between the user's desktop and the VPN-1 gateway, while SecureClient adds a personal firewall to the user's computer that can be managed from the Policy Server integrated into VPN-1. This effectively enables you to expand the perimeter of your network to encompass and secure all entry points into your network including Internet-connected VPN users.

Although VPN-1/FW-1 meets the basic security need of providing gateway protection and a secure VPN endpoint, additional products have been added to the NG AI suite to address other security challenges identified in the SVN architecture. Since efficient network management so often becomes a big part of network security, Check Point developed Meta IP to provide and manage DNS and DHCP services and introduce new features to these crucial services such as Secure DHCP. To help you make efficient use of your limited bandwidth, FloodGate-1 enables you to prioritize network traffic and provide QoS on data passing through your gateways, ensuring timely delivery of high priority data, such as traffic to your Web site, or of time-sensitive application data like streaming video.

Managing and sharing user account and authorization information is critical to ensuring that legitimate users get access to the resources they need while blocking access to unauthorized parties. Proper authentication mechanisms can also increase user satisfaction by not forcing multiple, often redundant, logons. Two tools were added to the NG AI suite to help manage user credentials and authorization information. The account management module allows LDAP-stored user accounts and associated information to be easily created and maintained alongside the Security Policy that uses them. To help share user authorization information between OPSEC applications, the UA module was developed, allowing other applications access to the user privilege information already gathered by VPN-1/FW-1.

Finally, the SmartView Reporter and tools for real-time status monitoring were added to help you keep track of how your security infrastructure is performing. By monitoring and trending your network usage, the monitoring and reporting tools aim to help you not only spot security problems or attempted violations and suspicious activity, but also can enable you to proactively monitor network traffic levels, allowing you to plan for growth or reduction of provided services.

After looking at the entire NG AI suite, this chapter focused on the VPN-1/FW-1 module, looking at how the three major components of FW-1 work together in a distributed or stand-alone environment. The GUI client enables you to remotely manage the Security Policy and provides the main interface for most NG AI products. The GUI is comprised of several modules and tools including the SmartMap and Object Lists that help you maintain your network policies. These tools help you easily create and visualize your network security rules, reducing the chances for configuration errors caused by oversight or confusion when creating and updating the rule base.

The GUI client is the tool you use to create the Security Policy that is stored on the SmartCenter (management) server. The SmartCenter's management module not only stores the Security Policy used by FW-1-based devices, but can also create and distribute ACLs for OPSEC-certified network devices such as routers and switches. The management module is also responsible for keeping the logs from all VPN-1/FW-1 enforcement modules and from SecureClient machines. Network traffic between the GUI, management server, and firewall module is encrypted using SIC to ensure that an unauthorized third party cannot read or modify sensitive data while in transit.

After being compiled into the appropriate format, the Security Policy is pushed from the management server to the firewall inspection module to be enforced. To understand how the inspection module makes control decisions for data attempting to pass through the firewall, it is necessary to understand the technology Check Point calls Stateful Inspection. By comparing the pros and cons of proxy firewalls (that provide good application control with limited scalability) and packet filters (that scale well but cannot provide in-depth application control) to Check Point's Stateful Inspection, you should have a basic understanding of how the FW-1 Inspection Engine works, and why Stateful Inspection simplifies security management while increasing overall security with application awareness.

Although network security application vendors would like to produce a single product or suite that could storm the market by providing all the security tools any organization will need, the fact is, it is not possible. Although Check Point VPN-1/FW-1 and the NG AI suite cover the basic security needs of most enterprises, there will always be small gaps where third-party applications are needed. To help ensure that you can leverage your existing investment and provide easy integration with your Check Point security infrastructure, OPSEC was created to certify that the third-party products you require will work well with VPN-1/FW-1 and other OPSEC applications.

Combining the proven, market-leading NG AI versions of VPN-1 and FW-1 with the NG AI suite of products and with Check Point OPSEC partner applications enables you to build and manage the highly available and secure network infrastructure needed to support today's eBusiness models and to scale up to future growth in enterprise network security.

Solutions Fast Track

Introducing the Check Point Next Generation Suite of Products

- ☑ FireWall-1 is the cornerstone of the NG AI suite, providing data filtering, logging, and authentication in stand-alone, distributed, and high-availability clustered gateway models.

- ☑ VPN-1 builds onto the features of FireWall-1, adding encryption and VPN support.

- ☑ The LDAP account management now runs integrated into the Security Dashboard, enabling you to manage LDAP database-stored user accounts more easily.

- ☑ SecuRemote is used with VPN-1 and creates the client or user end of the VPN tunnel, providing the authentication and encryption needed to establish and maintain the VPN connection.

- ☑ SecureClient adds a personal firewall to the SecuRemote feature set. This firewall, running the same robust Stateful Inspection engine, installed onto the user's computer enables you to centrally control the security settings of VPN-connected desktops. In addition to the firewall capabilities, SecureClient can send its logs to the central management server, once connected.

☑ The SmartView Reporter helps you trend and analyze your network by using predefined or customized report criteria to generate data traffic statistics and reports.

☑ The Check Point ClusterXL module helps you create clusters of firewalls to reduce service downtime by providing seamless failover from one gateway to another using either high availability or load sharing. Load sharing allows for the aggregation of available resources across all systems in the cluster.

☑ FloodGate-1 has been integrated into VPN-1/FireWall-1 to provide QoS prioritization of network traffic as it passes through the gateway. This allows for providing QoS and traffic prioritization inside the VPN tunnel, a task difficult for separate solutions.

☑ Meta IP provides you with secure, scalable solutions for DNS and DHCP server management. As well as providing standards-based servers, Meta IP provides additional tools such as Secure DHCP that you use to authenticate your users before giving their machine a fully functional IP address.

☑ The UA module extends the user-authorization information acquired by VPN-1/FireWall-1 to trusted third-party applications. This can help reduce multiple logons and reduce development time for new applications.

Understanding VPN-1/FireWall-1 SVN Components

☑ The VPN-1/FireWall-1 management module resides on the SmartCenter (management) server, and not only stores and pushes out the Security Policy to the enforcement points, but is also responsible for storing all the objects and definitions used in the policy. Logs from Check Point enforcement modules, including SecureClient, are stored in the log database hosted by the management server.

☑ The management module is at the heart of the distributed model for firewall deployment, allowing for centralized logging and easy security management even for environments with several firewalls.

☑ The GUI client is used to manage and configure the options and policies stored on the management server. The GUI is made up of a number of tools and components combined into the SmartDashboard that allows for easy, visual configuration of the Security, NAT, QoS, and Desktop Security polices.

☑ The firewall module contains the inspection engine that uses a compiled version of the Security Policy to control traffic attempting to pass between the firewall's interfaces.

☑ The SIC module ensures that communication between GUI clients, management servers, and the inspection engine is secure to prevent modification or copying of data in transit.

Looking at Firewall Technology

☑ Proxy or application gateway firewalls provide in-depth control of a single application, allowing for very detailed filtering. However, this makes scaling to new applications difficult and can reduce performance of the firewall.

☑ Packet filters offer great performance and affordability because this type of firewall is often built-in routers or similar network devices. Since packet filtering firewalls are unaware of the application layer, granular control is not possible.

☑ VPN-1/FireWall-1 uses a Check Point-patented technology called Stateful Inspection to control IP network data.

☑ Stateful Inspection is able to make control decisions based on information from the top five layers of the OSI model, providing granular control and application awareness.

☑ The firewall tracks communications data, and as a result, throughput performance is increased by leveraging the ability to determine continuations of previously accepted sessions versus new connection attempts that need to be applied to the rule set.

Complete SVN Concept

☑ The real power of Check Point's solution comes to fruition when multiple components are used together. With the tight integration of the different technologies, very complex designs become not only possible but also manageable, ensuring complete end-to-end security throughout the enterprise and all related systems.

Frequently Asked Questions

The following Frequently Asked Questions, answered by the authors of this book, are designed to both measure your understanding of the concepts presented in this chapter and to assist you with real-life implementation of these concepts. To have your questions about this chapter answered by the author, browse to **www.syngress.com/solutions** and click on the **"Ask the Author"** form. You will also gain access to thousands of other FAQs at ITFAQnet.com.

Q: What is this "fingerprint" I see when first connecting to the management server?

A: In order to verify that you are connecting to the intended management station (rather than an imposter), FW-1 uses a fingerprint phrase. To ensure that secure communication between the GUI client and management server is set up properly, be sure that you have the server's fingerprint to verify before initiating the first connection to a new server. If you choose to cancel and not accept the fingerprint, your authentication credentials will not be sent.

Q: What happened to the "Apply gateway rules to interface direction" property?

A: In previous versions of FW-1 you could specify, in the policy properties, the data direction (inbound, outbound, or eitherbound) in which the security policy would be applied on the firewall's interfaces. In VPN-1/FW-1 NG, Check Point has removed this option and the security policy rules are now applied both inbound and outbound (also known as eitherbound) on all interfaces. Aside from not being needed in the new version of the Inspection Engine, removing this option is likely for the best, since few people actually understood how it worked or why it was needed.

Q: How are the rules in the Security Policy applied to incoming data?

A: The Security Policy rules are applied from top to bottom. Data for which no rule applies will be dropped after falling to the bottom of the Security Policy. Data dropped in this fashion is not logged, which is why a "drop all" rule is used with source: any, destination: any, service: any and track set to log is normally written at the bottom of the rule base.

Q: VPN-1/FW-1 just looks like an application running on my server; how does it protect the underlying OS from attack?

A: The FW-1 Inspection Engine is inserted into the OSs kernel just above layer two of the OSI model. Since Layer two is actually the firewall's NIC driver, this means that data must pass through the firewall Security Policy before being allowed to move onto the OSs' IP stack. Therefore, the underlying OS is never exposed to raw, unfiltered network data.

Q: How does the Inspection Engine handle fragmented packets?

A: When you look at fragmented packets individually, most of the information needed to make a control decision is in the first packet. However, FW-1 needs the entire assembled packet for a couple of reasons. First, the data section of the packet is most likely to be fragmented since it is at the end of the packet and is the largest section. Depending on the rules in your policy, this data may need to be inspected in its entirety to make a control decision. Second, the second and subsequent fragments only contain the remainder of the original packet (usually the data portion), not another copy of the full packet headers, which may also be needed to make the control decision. Without reassembling the packet, it may not be possible to apply it to the security policy, since information about source and destination ports would be missing. To get around this, FW-1 will completely reassemble a packet before applying it to the Security Policy. To prevent a Denial of Service (DoS) attack caused by a high volume of incomplete packet fragments, a timer is used when the first fragment arrives. If the timer expires before the complete packet is reassembled, the fragments are discarded. Once a packet is reassembled and a control decision is made to pass the packet on, the original fragments are released in the same fragmented condition and order as they arrived in, to the destination. The behavior of whether to allow fragmented packets and the timer are both configurable now in SmartDefense.

Q: Can I get a copy of VPN-1/FW-1 for evaluation?

A: To request an evaluation package with the software, documentation, and licenses required to fully test VPN-1/FW-1 in your network, head to www.checkpoint.com/getsecure.html.

## Chapter 2

Installing and Configuring VPN-1/FireWall-1 Next Generation with Application Intelligence

Solutions in this Chapter:

- **Before You Begin**

- **Installing Check Point VPN-1/FireWall-1 NG AI on Windows**

- **Uninstalling Check Point VPN-1/FireWall-1 NG AI on Windows**

- **Installing Check Point VPN-1/FireWall-1 NG AI on Solaris**

- **Uninstalling Check Point VPN-1/FireWall-1 NG AI on Solaris**

- **Installing Check Point VPN-1/FireWall-1 NG AI on Nokia**

- **Installing Check Point VPN-1/FireWall-1 NG AI on SecurePlatform**

Introduction

This chapter is written to familiarize you with the installation and configuration options available in the Check Point Next Generation (NG) with Application Intelligence (AI) Enterprise Suite of Products. Specifically, we will be installing and configuring VPN-1/FireWall-1 NG on the Windows, Solaris, Nokia, and SecurePlatform platforms. The installation process is pretty straightforward. We will focus on installing a Management Module and enforcement module on each platform, and will point out the subtle differences you will encounter if you choose to install these components in a distributed environment instead. After installing and configuring each platform, we will walk you through the uninstall process so you will know what you need to do in case you have to remove the software from your system.

Prior to starting the installation procedure of VPN-1/FireWall-1 NG, there are several steps that you should take to prepare the system and get ready for the installation screens you will be presented with. Most systems are not secure out-of-the-box, and we will help you to secure the host computer before you turn it into a firewall. We will also advise you on some good techniques you can use when preparing for your firewall installation. The information in this chapter is built on five years of experience installing, configuring, and supporting the Check Point VPN-1/FireWall-1 product.

Before You Begin

This section will prepare you to install the Next Generation product. There are several things that you need to consider prior to installing a firewall. We will discuss each step so that you understand its importance, and guide you in your endeavor to secure your network. The list of minimum system requirements as defined by Check Point is outlined in Table 2.1. You will need to ensure that your hardware meets these requirements at the very least. You can find these online at www.checkpoint.com/products/security/firewall-1_sysreq.html.

Table 2.1 Minimum System Requirements

System Requirement	Primary Management & Enforcement Module	SmartConsole Clients
Operating Systems	Microsoft Win2k Server (SP1, SP2, SP3) Microsoft Win2k Advanced Server (SP1 and SP2) Windows NT 4.0 SP6a Sun Solaris 8 (32- or 64-bit mode)* Sun Solaris 9 (64-bit only)** RedHat Linux 7.0, 7.2*** and 7.3**** Nokia IPSO 3.7***** Check Point SecurePlatform IBM AIX 5.2	Microsoft Win2k Professional(SP1, SP2, SP3) Microsoft Win2k Server (SP1, SP2) MicrosoftWindows 98SE/ME Mcrosoft Windows XP Home/Professional Windows NT 4.0 SP6a Sun Solaris 8*******
Disk Space	40 MB	55 MB (100 MB for Solaris)
CPU	300+ MHz Pentium II (UltraSparc II for Solaris)	300+ MHz Pentium II
Memory	128 MB (130 MB for Windows and Linux)	128 MB
Network Interfaces	ATM, Ethernet, Fast Ethernet, Gigabit Ethernet, FDDI, Token Ring	Any supported by the operating system.
Media	CD-ROM	CD-ROM

* You must have patches 108528-17, 113652-01, 109147-18, 109326-07, 108434-01 (32-bit) and 108435-01 (64-bit) or newer on Solaris 8

** You must have patch 112902-07 or newer applied to Solaris 9

*** Requires Kernel version 2.4.9-31

**** Requires Kernel version 2.4.18-5

****** See Nokia website for latest release for each specific IPSO platform

******* The following SmartConsole clients are not supported on Solaris 8 UltraSPARC: SmartView Reporter, SmartView Monitor, SmartLSM, and SecureClient Packaging Tool

Tools & Traps…

Solaris 32-bit vs. 64-bit

To check whether your Solaris machine is in 32- or 64-bit mode, use the following commands:

```
isainfo -b
isainfo -vk
```

To change from 64- to 32-bit mode in Solaris 8 or 9, perform the following actions:

1. Enter EEPROM mode using the STOP-A keyboard combo.
2. Type *setenv boot-file kernel/unix* and press **Return**.
3. Reboot.
4. If the machine has difficulty booting, use the *set-defaults* command to return to 64-bit mode.

To change from 32- to 64-bit mode, do the following:

1. Enter EEPROM mode using the **STOP-A** keyboard combo.
2. Type *setenv boot-file /platform/sun4u/kernel/sparcv9/unix*.
3. Reboot.

Performance of your firewall will rely on the hardware you choose. It is highly recommended that you increase your hardware requirements above the minimum listed in Table 2.1 in real-world environments. Keep in mind that your management station will be handling logs from each module it controls, so you will want to ensure that you have adequate disk space, memory, and CPU to handle these connections. Check Point provides a Platform Selection Guide on its website to assist in sizing your solution. The Platform Selection Guide is based on the system being dedicated to only running the Check Point software on the operating system (OS). If you are running other software, you may degrade performance or require more resources. It is highly recommended, though, that your systems be dedicated to their tasks as management stations and firewalls.

Before you start your installation, make sure that you complete the items listed below:

- Get your licenses.
- Secure the Host.
- Configure routing and test network interface cards.
- Enable IP forwarding.
- Configure DNS (domain name system).
- Prepare for Check Point Installation and Configuration Screens.

Obtaining Licenses

Check Point licenses have changed with the Next Generation release. In order to obtain a license, you can either get them through your Check Point Value Added Reseller (VAR) or use the Check Point User Center to license your products at http://usercenter.checkpoint.com (see Figure 2.1). You have two options when it comes to licensing your firewall modules. You can either have them tied to their individual IP addresses (external interface recommended by Check Point) as with previous versions, or you can tie them all to the management station's IP address. These licenses are called either *local* or *central*, respectively. All licenses are maintained on the management console, and administrators can add or remove licenses using the SecureUpdate management tool.

The management module itself must have a local license based on its own IP address. The nice thing about using central licenses for the enforcement modules is that you can change their IP addresses without needing to replace the license, and you can easily move a license from one module to another.

Starting with Check Point NG Feature Pack 3, the software comes with a built-in 15-day evaluation license. It is always best to obtain your permanent licenses before you install the firewall software. The program will ask you for your license details during the installation procedure. If you cannot obtain your permanent license prior to the installation, then you can use the built-in evaluation license. Check Point's evaluation licenses have full functionality for all features. If your evaluation lasts longer than 15 days, or if you need to test new features at any time, you can receive evaluation licenses from Check Point via your reseller or local Check Point office. These licenses show up in your UserCenter account at http://usercenter.checkpoint.com. Evaluation licenses downloaded from Check

Point's UserCenter are valid for one month, and the product is not compromised in any way while running on evaluation licenses.

Check Point changed its small to medium business licensing after the release of Application Intelligence, calling it Check Point Express. The new licenses integrate more functionality at a lower cost. If you purchased a Check Point Express license and you are installing NG with Application Intelligence (R54), you will need to download and install the Check Point Express Supplement Hotfix for the license to work correctly. Later versions will have the updated files included to recognize the new software keys.

Figure 2.1 Check Point's User Center

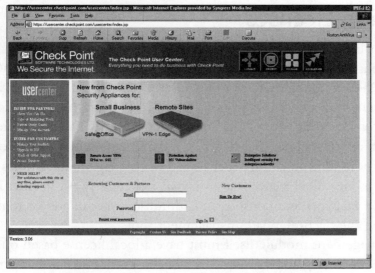

Securing the Host

With any firewall installation it is important to consider the security of the host computer on which you are installing the firewall software. There are some guidelines available on the Internet for securing the various operating systems. Below is a list of URLs to some good guides:

- **WinNT** http://support.checkpoint.com/kb/docs/public/os/winnt/ pdf/Securing_NT.pdf (SecureKnowledge Solution ID: 55.0.4232373.2607295)

- **WinNT** www.spitzner.net/nt.html

- **Solaris** http://support.checkpoint.com/kb/docs/public/os/ solaris/pdf/strip-sunserver.pdf (SecureKnowledge Solution ID: 55.0.4232382.2607295)

- **Solaris** www.spitzner.net/armoring2.html

- **Solaris** http://support.checkpoint.com/kb/docs/public/os/ solaris/pdf/solaris8_pkgs_fp3_rev2.pdf

- **Linux** www.spitzner.net/linux.html

- **Linux** http://support.checkpoint.com/kb/docs/public/os/linux/ pdf/linux_minimal_ng_fp2.pdf

You should start out by installing the base operating system without any bells or whistles, and then apply any necessary OS patches. You should not install any additional Internet servers on your firewall host. For example, you do not want to have an Internet Information Server (IIS) or an FTP (File Transfer Protocol) server running on your firewall, since these services could be vulnerable to attack.

Disabling Services

Probably the most important step in any of these guides is the process of disabling services on the firewall host. Almost any OS installation enables various services out-of-the-box, which are not needed for the operation of a firewall. Your firewall should have as few services running as possible. If you are installing on a Windows machine, you should disable NETBEUI and any other non-IP protocols. The kernel processes of the NG product do not inspect traffic on non-IP protocols, so your NETBEUI and IPX traffic would not be protected, therefore it should not be installed on the firewall.

NOTE

By default, the Nokia hardware platform comes with a hardened FreeBSD operating system out-of-the-box. There is nothing that needs to be done to secure a Nokia platform prior to installing the NG product when starting with a default installation. Because Nokia has done the work of hardening the OS, it is important to keep up to date with the version of IPSO installed. Security fixes are routinely distributed as new updates to the OS.

If you are installing the firewall on a Unix system, the most common method of disabling services is through the /etc/inetd.conf file. This file tells the system which services/protocols are enabled, and therefore which ports the system will be listening to. Illustration 2.1 shows the beginning of a typical inetd.conf file as installed in Solaris 2.7. As you can see, there are several services running that do not have to be enabled. Pretty much everything in the inetd.conf file can be disabled. If you want to leave FTP or telnet open temporarily, then that is your option. Also note that certain services are not spawned through the inetd process. These include secure shell (SSH), sendmail, and usually web servers.

Illustration 2.1 Example of inetd.conf File

```
# more inetd.conf
#
#ident   "@(#)inetd.conf 1.33    98/06/02 SMI"    /* SVr4.0 1.5    */
#
#
# Configuration file for inetd(1M).   See inetd.conf(4).
#
# To reconfigure the running inetd process, edit this file, then
# send the inetd process a SIGHUP.
#
# Syntax for socket-based Internet services:
#   <service_name> <socket_type> <proto> <flags> <user> <server_pathname>
<args>
#
# Syntax for TLI-based Internet services:
#
#   <service_name> tli <proto> <flags> <user> <server_pathname> <args>
#
# Ftp and telnet are standard Internet services.
#
ftp       stream  tcp     nowait  root    /usr/sbin/in.ftpd       in.ftpd
telnet    stream  tcp     nowait  root    /usr/sbin/in.telnetd    in.telnetd
#
# Tnamed serves the obsolete IEN-116 name server protocol.
#
#
```

Continued

Illustration 2.1 Example of inetd.conf File

```
name     dgram    udp      wait     root     /usr/sbin/in.tnamed        in.tnamed
#
# Shell, login, exec, comsat and talk are BSD protocols.
#
shell    stream   tcp      nowait   root     /usr/sbin/in.rshd          in.rshd
login    stream   tcp      nowait   root     /usr/sbin/in.rlogind       in.rlogind
exec     stream   tcp      nowait   root     /usr/sbin/in.rexecd        in.rexecd
comsat   dgram    udp      wait     root     /usr/sbin/in.comsat        in.comsat
talk     dgram    udp      wait     root     /usr/sbin/in.talkd         in.talkd
```

To disable services in this file, simply edit the file and insert a pound sign or hash mark in front of the line that you wish to disable. When completed, send a HUP signal to the inetd process running on the system as shown in Illustration 2.2.

Illustration 2.2 SIGHUP to inetd Process

```
# ps -ef | grep inet
    root    229     1   0    Nov 06 ?           0:00 /usr/sbin/inetd -s
# kill -HUP 229
```

You can verify that the processes are no longer listening on the system by running the *netstat –an* command. Because there are fewer services running on the firewall, there are fewer avenues of attack, and the system is more secure. You can think of each of those listening ports as holes into your operating system. Although the firewall software will protect the operating system from direct attack if you have the security policy defined properly, it is better to stay on the safe side and reduce the number of possible ingresses.

Routing and Network Interfaces

It is recommended that before you install the Check Point product, you first configure and test the networks that the firewall will be communicating on. When you install VPN-1/FireWall-1, the product binds to the interface adapters, and even begins configuring the firewall at this early stage. Regardless of the platform you are installing on, it is recommended that you configure the first interface on your firewall as the external interface, and that this IP address resolves to the name of the host computer in the hosts files. On Windows systems, that means the external

IP address of the enforcement firewall should go on the network interface that is displayed first in the interface pull-down list under the IP Address tab of the Microsoft TCP/IP Properties window. If this is not defined properly, then several problems may occur with SIC and virtual private network (VPN) configurations.

Prior to installation, configure your firewall interfaces with the correct IP addresses and subnet masks. See the Netmask Cheat Sheet available in Appendix A for a quick method of discerning subnet boundaries. Ideally, you can plug your system into a test network so that you are not putting your unprotected system on the live network before installing the firewall software. It is always best to install a firewall in an isolated environment so that it cannot be compromised before it has been protected. You will want to test routing and IP forwarding first. Check Point VPN-1/FireWall-1 NG will control IP forwarding once it is installed, but you must first enable it in the OS and test that your network adapters and routing are functioning properly. Just imagine if you didn't perform this test before installing the software, and then found that you had a faulty Network Interface Card (NIC). It would have saved you a lot of blood, sweat, and tears if you had determined this first. In addition, with Microsoft Windows 2000, if the network is down (link status), it can remove the interface altogether, which can cause many problems.

NOTE

When you are configuring your interfaces on a Windows system, be sure that you only configure one interface with a default gateway. This is a common mistake since each interface gives you the option of filling in a gateway, but you should never have more than one default gateway configured on your firewall.

Next, make sure you understand the wide area network (WAN) connections that will be coming into your firewall, and configure routing accordingly. You may decide to set up a dynamic routing protocol on your firewall to maintain its routing table, or you may decide that static routes are the way to go. If you add a route on a Windows system, then you should provide the –p switch so that the route will still be there after a reboot. This switch permanently adds the route into the system registry. For example, the following command will route the 172.17.2.0/24 network to the next hop router of 172.17.0.1 on a WinNT system:

Q89
Q84/80
Q19
Q53

```
route add -p 172.17.2.0 mask 255.255.255.0 172.17.0.1
```

In Solaris, you need to set up the route statements in a file that will be run at startup. A common location is the /etc/rc2.d directory. The file name has to begin with a capital S for the system to run it (e.g. S99local), and you should set the file modes to allow execution. The same route command above can be written in Solaris as follows:

```
route add 172.17.2.0 -netmask 255.255.255.0 172.17.0.1
```

If your firewall will be on the border of your network, connecting your local area networks (LANs) and WANs to the Internet, then you will need to ensure that default routes are configured throughout on all your workstations and routers so that they are routed to the next hop closest to the Internet. It may prove helpful if you create a network diagram that shows how your network looks prior to having a firewall, and another to show the network after the firewall is in place. This will help you to visualize which connections will be changing so that you can prepare accordingly. SmartMap can also help you visualize this as you define your objects in the SmartDashboard graphical user interface (GUI).

When using a firewall inside the network, you may be required to use dynamic routing protocols. Adding routing protocols to your firewall can add complexity to the configuration. To simplify your installation, leave the routing to the routers as much as possible.

Enabling IP Forwarding

To test your routing and interfaces you must enable IP forwarding in your OS. IP Forwarding allows traffic arriving at one interface to be routed to another and sent out that interface—essentially turning your server into a router. To do this on WinNT, access the **TCP/IP properties** window and select **Enable IP Forwarding** from the Routing tab as shown in Figure 2.2. To enable IP forwarding in Win2k, you must edit the registry as outlined in Microsoft's KB article Q230082 as follows:

1. Open the registry by running regedt32.exe.

2. Find the following registry key:
   HKEY_LOCAL_MACHINE\SYSTEM\CurrentControlSet\Services\Tcpip\Parameters

3. Add the following value to this key:

- Value Name: IPEnableRouter
- Value type: REG_DWORD
- Value Data: 1

Figure 2.2 Enable IP Forwarding in WinNT 4.0

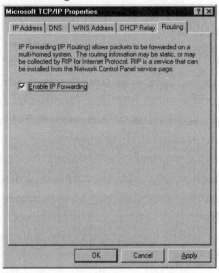

In Solaris, IP forwarding is usually enabled by default. You can switch it off and on with the following command: *ndd -set /dev/ip ip_forwarding 1*. The settings for this command are as follows:

- 0 disables IP forwarding
- 1 enables IP forwarding

You can also read the information from the operating system using the command: *ndd –get /dev/ip ip_forwarding*.

Configuring DNS

Since it is suggested that you install your firewall while it is not plugged into any untrusted networks, it will be best to start with DNS disabled on the firewall. If you have DNS enabled and the system cannot reach its name servers, then the system may become sluggish and system performance will be affected. It is important that once you do configure DNS that you configure it properly. The firewall should be able to resolve its own external IP address to the name of the host computer. This could be set up in advance by creating an A record in your domain for the firewall, and you should enter it into the firewall's hosts file. In Unix, this file is located in /etc/hosts, and in Windows it is located in c:\winnt\system32\drivers\etc\hosts. The Nokia platform also needs to have the host name associated with its external IP address, and this is done through the **Host Address Assignment** link found under the System Configuration heading in the Voyager GUI. You can use this interface to configure host entries instead of editing a host's file.

You should also include IP addresses in the host's file that your firewall may communicate with frequently, like a management server and/or enforcement module. Policy installation performance can be increased on a management server by having all network objects (which are defined in the next chapter) resolvable.

Another DNS record that you should create is a pointer (PTR) record for your firewall's external IP address or any other address(es) that you will be using for Network Address Translation (NAT). Some websites and FTP servers require that you have a reverse resolvable IP address before they will grant you or your users access to download their files. If you have obtained a block of IP addresses from your Internet service provider (ISP), then chances are that they control the PTR records for your addresses. Sometimes they will provide you with a Web site where you can administer these yourself. Other times, you will need to find the right person who can make the changes for you. If you have your own ASN, you can set up your own in-addr.arpa domain and create your own PTR records.

Preparing for VPN-1/FireWall-1 NG

During the installation process, you will be asked which components you want to install and then you will need to be prepared to fill in the configuration screens at the end of the installation procedure. The Check Point Next Generation with Application Intelligence CD gives you the following options for installation:

- **Demo Installation** Choose this option to only install the GUI clients in order to evaluate the user interface to the software. This option is also useful for installing only the software necessary for the administrator to work from his/her desktop system.

- **New Installation** Choose this option if you wish to install the Next Generation with Application Intelligence Suite.

- **Installation Using Imported Configuration** This option is for users who have used the installation CD to export their existing pre-NG AI configuration and wish to upgrade it during the installation process.

If you choose **New Installation**, you will be presented with a number of software packages to install. These should be reviewed carefully to ensure the correct packages are installed on your gateway and nonessential packages are not.

- **Gateway** These options are primarily used when the device you are installing will also be functioning as a security gateway.

  - **VPN-1 & FireWall-1** This includes FireWall-1 Management module and enforcement point software along with the VPN-1 encryption component.

- **VPN-1 Accelerator Cards** Install the appropriate drivers if you are utilizing hardware VPN acceleration devices.

  - **FloodGate-1** Provides an integrated Quality of Service (QoS) solution for VPN-1/FireWall-1.

  - **SecureClient Policy Server** Allows an enforcement module to install Granular Desktop Policies on mobile users' SecureClient personal firewalls.

  - **SmartView Monitor** Allows an organization to monitor their VPN connections, Internet connections, etc.

  - **UserAuthority** A user authentication tool that integrates with FireWall-1, FloodGate-1, and other e-business applications.

- **Management Server** In the event that this system will function as a management server (primary or secondary), you will utilize the following options.

  - **SmartCenter** Allows the software on this system to function as a management server for other enforcement points. It will also install the Internal Certificate Authority (ICA) which is necessary for Secure Internal Communications (SIC)

  - **Safe@ Connector** Provides management capabilities for SofaWare Safe@ Appliances such as the SofaWare S-Box and Nokia IP30.

- **Reporting Module** An integrated reporting tool that can generate reports, graphs and pie charts to display information obtained from the VPN-1/FireWall-1 logs.

- **Management Console** Management of the Check Point infrastructure requires Check Point's management clients. This will likely be installed anywhere one wishes to perform administrative functions related to the Check Point products.

  - **SmartConsole** The GUI for Check Point including the SmartDashboard, SmartView Tracker and SmartView Status GUI.

- **VPN Client** If you just want to install client software on your mobile users or desktops in the office as described below, then choose this option.

  - **VPN-1 SecuRemote/SecureClient** Client encryption software loaded on your mobile clients with or without the extended security features such as desktop firewalling and Secure Configuration Verification.

If you are installing from files, be sure that you download and install the Check Point SVN Foundation first. This package is the base of the entire Check Point Next Generation with Application Intelligence software suite as its name suggests. It's this program that allows the easy integration of all other NG components. The only VPN-1/FireWall-1 applications that don't rely on the SVN Foundation are the SmartConsole clients and VPN clients.

By far the simplest way to install the suite when using downloaded files is to download the installation wrapper (also known as the installation bundle) for your operating system. This package contains all the files and an installation program to guide you through setup of the software.

The next important question that the installation process will ask you (if you are installing a management server on your firewall) is whether you are installing a Primary or Secondary management server. The management servers can function in an active/standby relationship with each other for redundancy and disaster recovery. A secondary management station is only useful when paired with a primary. In earlier versions, the installation process would ask if you wish to configure backwards compatibility. In the NG AI installation wrapper, it automatically installs backwards compatibility for managing version 4.1 firewalls. The backward compatibility is also necessary for the Safe@ Connector, as it uses some of the same libraries.

The default folder installation in Windows is C:\WINNT\FW1\NG and Check Point installs files on Solaris in /opt and /var/opt. Make sure that you have partitioned your disk properly to accept the default installation folder, or be prepared to give a custom location for the installation (Windows only). If you don't accept the defaults, you should verify that the installation program configures the firewall's environment variables properly.

Configuring & Implementing…

FW-1 Environment Variables

You will see the use of the $FWDIR environment variable throughout this book. It is the nature of an environment variable to contain some value (similar to a variable used to represent a number in algebra). The $FWDIR variable contains the value of your firewall's installation directory, and it is configured upon installation. If you install on Windows, this variable is set to C:\WINNT\FW1\NG. In Solaris the $FWDIR environment variable is set to /opt/CPfw1-54.

There is also a $CPDIR variable, which contains the installation directory of the CPShared (SVN) components. In Windows, the $CPDIR variable is set to C:\Program Files\CheckPoint\CPShared\NG, and in Solaris it is set to /opt/CPshrd-54/.

So, whenever you see these terms used, $FWDIR or $CPDIR, then just substitute the appropriate directory for your firewall installation in their place. On a Unix system, you can type *echo $FWDIR* to see the value of the variable, or type *set* to see a list of all environment variables and their associated values. To be technically accurate, we should probably use %FWDIR% when talking about the Windows environment, but we are going to stick to the Unix method of describing variables in this book since it is the terminology that Check Point itself uses.

Next the installation program will install the SmartConsole software. The SmartConsole options are as follows:

- **SmartDashboard** Used to connect to your management server to configure your rulebase, NAT, VPN, FloodGate-1 QoS policy, WebAccess, and SecureClient Desktop Security Policies. There are a number of options below SmartDashboard, but they are all selected or not selected based on whether or not you are installing the SmartDashboard application. They are shown, but are integral to the operation of the SmartDashboard GUI, so they are always selected. For reference, these are SmartDefense, SmartMap, VPN Manager, Policy Manager, Users Manager, and Objects Manager.

- **SmartView Tracker** Used to view your VPN-1/FireWall-1 security logs, accounting logs, and audit logs on the management server.

- **SmartView Status** Used to view the status of your remote enforcement points connected to your management server.

- **SmartUpdate** Used for managing licenses and remotely upgrading software and Operating Systems of your remote enforcement points connected to your management server.

- **SecureClient Packaging Tool** Used to create custom packages for SecuRemote/SecureClient mobile users.

- **SmartView Monitor** Used to monitor an interface, QoS rule, or virtual link in real time. The display is in the form of a line or bar graph.

- **Reporting Tool** Used to generate historical reports with graphs and pie charts from the data in the VPN-1/FireWall-1 logs.

- **User Monitor** Used to monitor which users are logged into policy servers throughout the infrastructure.

- **SmartLSM** Used to manage hundreds or thousands of like-configured firewalls in a profile- or template-based method.

After the Check Point installation wizard copies files, it will run through a number of configuration screens. These will be identical if you are installing a management module with or without an enforcement module with the exception of the Simple Network Management Protocol (SNMP) option in Solaris, which is only configured if you are installing an enforcement module. The screens that you can prepare for in advance are the following:

- **Licenses** You should read the previous section on licenses above if you need help getting licenses. If you do not have your license(s), simply click **Next** and a 15-day evaluation license will be installed at the end of the installation. If you have your license(s), you will fill in the following fields:

- **Host/IP Address** The IP address associated with this license or "eval."

- **Expiration Date** The date that the license expires, which may be "never."

- **SKU/Features** These are the features that this license will enable (e.g. Management or 3DES).

- **String/Signature Key** The license string provided by Check Point to validate the license. This key will be unique for each license and IP Address.

- **Administrators** You will need to configure at least one administrator during installation. See below for more on adding Administrators. This administrator can be removed after you configure an alternate administrator through the SmartDashboard GUI.

  - **Administrator Name** Choose a login name for your administrator. This field is case-sensitive.

  - **Password** Choose a good alphanumeric password. It must be at least four characters long.

  - **Confirm Password** Repeat the same password entered above.

- **GUI Clients** These are the IP addresses of the management clients that your administrators will use when connecting to this management module. You may need to configure static IP addresses for your administrators. You may add as many GUI clients as you'd like or you may enter none (localhost is always allowed); it's up to you. See below for your GUI client options.

- **SNMP extension (UNIX only)** If you wish to utilize external network management tools such as HP OpenView, then you can install the Check Point FireWall-1 SNMP daemon. With the daemon installed and activated, you will be able to query the firewall status. You could use a network management tool to monitor the firewall's health and generate alerts based on certain criteria.

SECURITY ALERT

Around mid-February 2002 a CERT Advisory was posted warning about various vulnerabilities that have been found and exploited in many SNMP implementations. These vulnerabilities could lead to Denial of Service attacks or unauthorized access. Please ensure that you have applied any applicable security patches to your systems prior to accepting SNMP through your firewall. For more information, and links to patches visit the CERT Web site: www.cert.org/advisories/CA-2002-03.html. Nokia IPSO 3.4.2 and above already have the SNMP fix integrated.

Administrators

It is best to use individual administrator usernames instead of a generic username like *admin* or *fwadmin*. The problem with using a generic login ID is that you cannot properly audit the activities of the firewall administrators. It may be important for you to know who installed the last security policy when you are troubleshooting a problem. This becomes more and more important when there are several people administering a firewall system. But most important, it is a security risk to use a generic username as it is more easily guessed, especially by ex-employees. You will have to complete the following fields:

- **Administrator Name** Choose a login name for your administrator. This field is case-sensitive.
- **Password** Choose a good alphanumeric password. It must be at least four characters long.

NOTE

If you are installing just an enforcement module, then you will not have any administrators or GUI clients to configure.

There is a section labeled Permissions that enables you to define the access level you will require on an individual basis for each administrator. If you select **Read/Write All** or **Read Only All**, then your administrator will have access to all the available GUI client features with the ability to either make changes and updates or view the configuration and logs (perhaps for troubleshooting purposes) accordingly. You may also choose to customize their access so that they may be able to update some things and not others. To do this, select **Customized** and configure each of these options:

- **SmartUpdate** This GUI tool enables you to manage licenses and update remote modules.

- **Objects Database** This tool is used to create new objects to be used in the Security Policy rulebases. Objects will be covered in the next chapter.

- **Check Point Users Database** This tool is used to manage users for firewall authentication purposes.

- **LDAP Users Database** This tool is used to manage Lightweight Directory Access Protocol (LDAP) users.

- **Security Policy** This tool is used to create and manage rulebases using the SmartDashboard GUI.

- **QoS Policy** This tool is used to create and manage the bandwidth management rulebases.

- **Log Consolidator** This tool is used to create and manage rulebases regarding which logs will be consolidated from the log server into the SmartView Reporter database to run reports on.

- **Monitoring** This option enables access to the Log Viewer, System Status, and Traffic Monitoring GUI clients.

- **Web Policy** This tool allows administrators to create and manage the WebAccess rulebase in the SmartDashboard GUI.

- **ROBO Gateways Database** This allows an administrator to manage the Remote Office/Branch Office gateways defined in SmartLSM.

GUI Clients

When you enter GUI clients, you type their hostname or IP address into the **Remote hostname:** field, and then add them to the list of clients allowed to connect to your Management Module. You are allowed to use wildcards as follows:

- **Any** If you type in the word **Any**, this will allow anyone to connect without restriction (not recommended).

- **Asterisks** You may use asterisks in the hostname. For example, 10.10.20.* means any host in the 10.10.20.0/24 network, and *.domainname.com means any hostname within the domainname.com domain.

- **Ranges** You may use a dash (-) to represent a range of IP addresses. For example, 1.1.1.3-1.1.1.7 means the 5 hosts including 1.1.1.3 and 1.1.1.7 and every one in between.

- **DNS or WINS resolvable hostnames** It is recommend that you stay away from using hostnames or domain names, however, since it requires DNS to be configured and working on the firewall. Using IP addresses is the best method since it doesn't rely on resolving, and will continue to work even if you cannot reach your name servers from the firewall.

Upgrading from a Previous Version

Although this chapter will walk you through a fresh installation of NG in this chapter, some readers may be interested in upgrading from existing versions of FireWall-1. You can install or upgrade to NG from version 4.1, and it can manage v4.1 firewalls with the Backward Compatibility option. Although NG utilizes Secure Internal Communication (SIC) for other NG modules, it can also use the legacy *fw putkey* command to communicate with previous versions of the product. FireWall-1 NG with Application Intelligence is not compatible with versions earlier than 4.1.

It's very important that you upgrade your management console prior to upgrading any of your firewall enforcement modules to NG. A 4.1 management station cannot control an NG module. When you do upgrade your enforcement points, you will need to edit their workstation objects in the Policy Editor, and change their version to NG before you will be able to push or fetch a policy.

Read the release notes and utilize the upgrade tools (especially the pre-upgrade verifier) before you begin. This is very important since there is a list of limitations in the NG release notes that you will need to consider ahead of time. Some of these include, but are not limited to, your resources, VPNs, and external interface settings. NG does not support more than one resource in a rule. If you have rules configured with multiple resources, then NG will copy this rule into the new format with only one resource, and will not create new rules for the others. NG does not support Manual IPSec, FWZ, or SKIP VPNs any longer. If you have these types of VPNs in your rulebase before the upgrade, then they will be converted to IKE VPNs without notification during the upgrade to NG. If you have a limited license on your VPN-1/FireWall-1 v4.*x* firewall, your $FWDIR\conf\external.if settings will not be preserved during the upgrade. You will need to define your firewall's external interface in the workstation properties window under the **Topology** tab after the upgrade. You may also need to run the *confmerge* command to manually merge your objects.C file with the new objects in NG. These things and more are laid out for you in the product release notes.

It is also highly recommended that you have a back-out plan in place if your upgrade to NG does not go as smoothly as planned. Check Point recommends upgrading on a new piece of hardware; that way you will minimize downtime as well (even though the firewalls can run on their own without the management station). If you do it this way, remember that you may need to redo SIC or putkeys, and your Internet router or any routers directly connected to the firewall may need to have their ARP cache cleared after putting the new hardware in place.

Last but certainly not least, make sure that you have a backup of the entire system prior to an upgrade. It is especially important to save the $FWDIR/conf directory and any files that may have been edited from $FWDIR/state (like local.arp in Windows), $FWDIR/database, and $FWDIR/lib (for files like base.def and table.def that may have been modified). Also, always make sure to backup the registry on Windows systems as Check Point does utilize the registry to store numerous values and settings.

Installing Check Point VPN-1/FireWall-1 NG AI on Windows

Finally, all of your hard work at preparing for the firewall installation is about to pay off. This section is dedicated to installing the Check Point VPN-1/FireWall-1 NG on Windows. Hopefully you have read the previous section "Before you Begin" and are prepared to start with the Check Point software installation. If you did not read the "Before you Begin" section above, then you should go back and read it before you continue.

Although this section focuses on standalone installations, it will point out the different options you would make if you wanted to install the firewall on Windows in a distributed environment. In other words, you will be installing the management and enforcement modules as well as the GUI all on one machine; however, you could install each piece on separate machines (and use different operating systems) if that is what your network design calls for. You would typically use a distributed installation if you will be managing multiple firewalls, if you will be installing a cluster of firewalls, or if you are installing an appliance with limited disk space so the logging would go to a server with ample disk space. The distributed installation is not much different from the standalone installation, and the goal is for you to feel just as comfortable with the former as you do with the latter.

Installing from CD

This section will walk you through the Check Point VPN-1/FireWall-1 installation on Windows using the Check Point Next Generation CD. You can obtain a copy of this CD from Check Point by going to www.checkpoint.com/getsecure.html and requesting an evaluation of the software. If you have a login setup with Check Point, then you can download the software and updates from Check Point here: www.checkpoint.com/techsupport/downloadsng/ngfp1.html.

The following screenshots are taken from a new installation via CD to a Windows 2000 Server. If you are installing on Windows NT, the procedure is the same.

1. Insert the Check Point Next Generation CD into the CD-ROM drive on your firewall system. The Check Point NG Welcome Screen appears (Figure 2.3). If the Welcome screen does not appear after inserting the CD, then you may start it manually from the CD's wrappers\windows folder by running demo32.exe. From this screen you may choose to read the important information regarding evaluation licenses, purchased products, and the contents of the CD.

Figure 2.3 Welcome Screen

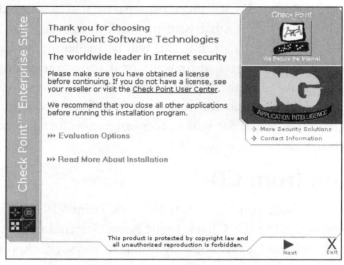

2. If you are ready to continue the installation, then select **Next** to start
    the Installation Wizard. You will be presented with the License
    Agreement as illustrated in Figure 2.4.

Figure 2.4 License Agreement

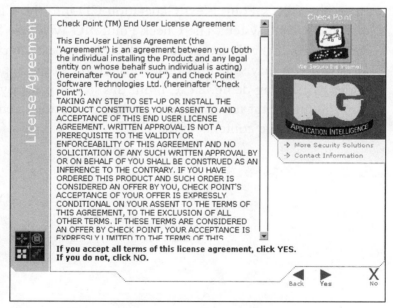

3. You must accept the license agreement in order to continue with installation. Select **Yes** when you are ready to continue. Otherwise, select **No** to exit the installation wizard.

4. The next screen, displayed in Figure 2.5, provides you with the Product Menu so that you can choose which Check Point products you want to install. You have three options:

   - **Demo Installation** Choose this option to only install the GUI clients to evaluate the user interface to the software. This option is also useful for installing only the software necessary for the administrator to work from his/her desktop system.

   - **New Installation** Choose this option if you wish to install the Next Generation with Application Intelligence Suite.

   - **Installation Using Imported Configuration** This option is for users who have used the installation CD to export their existing pre-NG AI configuration and wish to upgrade it during the installation process.

5. Make sure that **New Installation** is selected, and click **Next**.

Figure 2.5 Product Menu

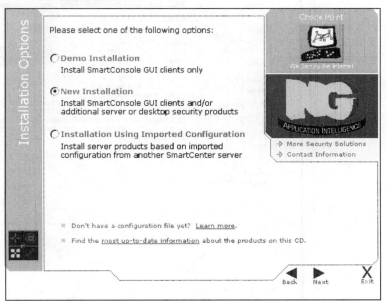

NOTE

During the installation process, use the **Back** button at any time to move to the previous screen, use the **Next** button to advance to the next screen, use the **Exit** option to exit at any time, and use the elevator buttons along the side of the page to scroll up and down.

6. The next screen is the Software Components (see Figure 2.6), which allows you to select the individual Check Point components to install. We will select **VPN-1 & FireWall-1**, **SmartCenter**, and **Management Clients** to install the management and enforcement modules as well as the Graphical User Interface. If you hold your mouse pointer over each item (without clicking), you will see a detailed description displayed on the right-hand side.

Figure 2.6 Server/Gateway Components

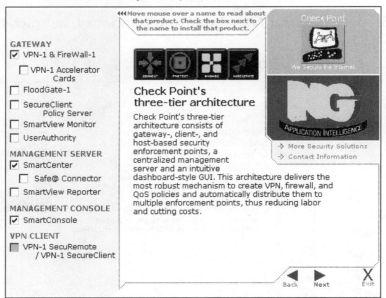

NOTE

If you wish to install the management module only, your selections here will not include VPN-1 & FireWall-1. If you wish to install the enforcement module only, then you will only select VPN-1 & FireWall-1.

7. Click **Next** when you are ready to begin the installation process.

8. The Check Point Installation Wizard will start the InstallShield Wizard program to begin the installation based on the options you've chosen thus far. Figure 2.7 illustrates the screen that you should see next. Click **Next** when you are ready to continue. A progress window will pop up as shown in Figure 2.8. You should see the window displayed in Figure 2.9 when the SVN installation begins. You should note that this is the first piece that is always installed on a Next Generation system. It will also be the last piece if you uninstall. The reason for this is that the SVN foundation contains the shared libraries which all Check Point applications use as well as it provides the secured communications layer for all communications between Check Point enabled systems.

Figure 2.7 Selected Products

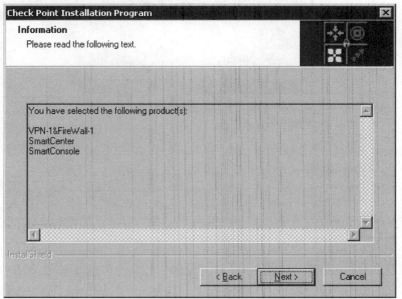

Figure 2.8 Progress Window

Figure 2.9 VPN-1 & FireWall-1 Installation

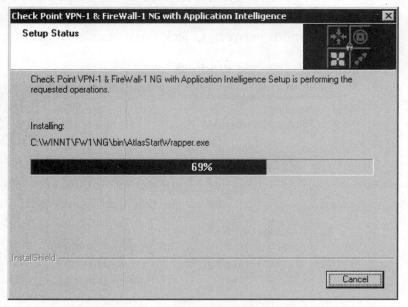

9. Following SVN installation, another window will pop up asking you for the specific components of VPN–1/FireWall-1 to install (see Figure 2.10). Of the following options, select **Primary SmartCenter** and click **Next**.

- **Primary SmartCenter** To install a management server only that will act in a primary capacity.

- **Secondary SmartCenter** To install a management server that will act in a backup capacity.

Figure 2.10 VPN-1 & FireWall-1 Product Specification

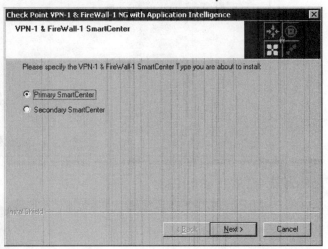

10. Next, Check Point will ask you where you want to install the product files. The default folder location in Windows is C:\WINNT\FW1\NG (actually %SystemRoot%\FW1\NG). If you wish to install to a different folder, click **Browse** and select the desired location; otherwise, click **Next** to accept the default location and continue. Whatever value you choose for the firewall's installation directory will be the value of the $FWDIR environment variable, which will be used throughout this book when referencing this directory. This is the last screen before VPN-1/FireWall-1 files are copied to your hard drive (Figure 2.11). Now the system copies files and installs the software. You should see a screen similar to the one in Figure 2.12 as the installation program shows you its progress. You may click the **Cancel** button on the bottom right-hand side of this screen if you wish to stop the installation at this point. However, remember that the installation program is modifying the operating system at a very low level (installing kernel modules and such) so it is preferred that you allow the installation to finish and uninstall it, rather than interrupting the installation and risk leaving the system in an uncertain state.

Figure 2.11 Choose Destination Location

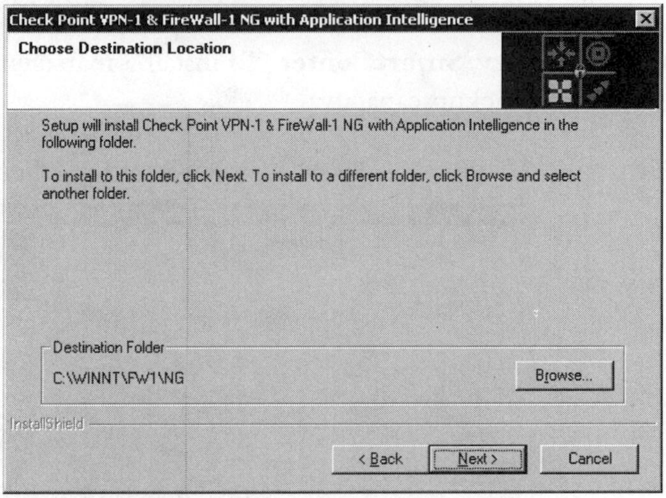

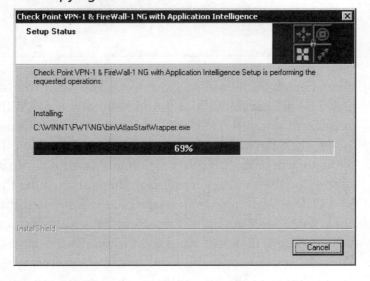

Figure 2.12 Copying Files

11. Once the system has finished copying files, you may see some messages
     pop up. This is normal to let the administrator that the installation pro-
     gram is hardening the Operating System as well as other operations as
     part of the installation process. The installation wizard will then display a
     final popup window from VPN-1/FireWall-1 explaining that the instal-
     lation was completed (as shown in Figure 2.13). Click **OK**.

Figure 2.13 Setup Information

12. The installation process will next install backward compatibility in case you require. It will then move to the next package to install, which is the SmartConsole (management clients). You will see a window like the one in Figure 2.14 asking if you wish to install the Check Point SmartConsole NG with Application Intelligence in the default folder C:\Program Files\CheckPoint\SmartConsole\NG_AI. You can either accept the default location or click **Browse** to choose a new target for the files. Accept the default folder location and click **Next** to continue.

Figure 2.14 Management Client Location

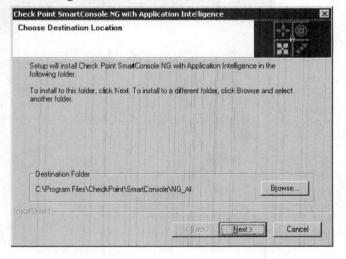

13. Now you will need to choose which of the SmartConsole components to install. Figure 2.15 displays the window you will see with the following options: Accept the default values to install all the clients and click **Next**. This is the last screen before the Check Point installation wizard begins copying files to your system (Figure 2.16).

Figure 2.15 Select Management Clients to Install

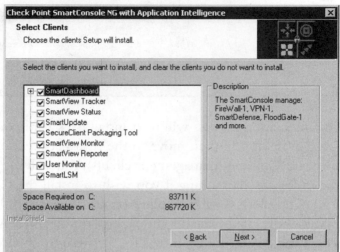

Figure 2.16 Management Clients Copying Files

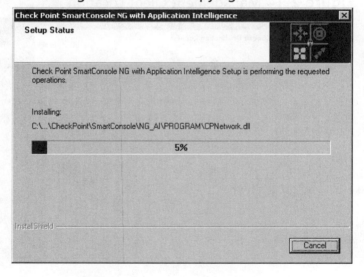

■ **SmartDashboard** Used to connect to your management server to configure the rulebase, Network Address Translation, VPN, FloodGate-1 QoS policy, WebAccess, and SecureClient Desktop Security Policies. There are a number of options below SmartDashboard, but they are all either selected or not selected based on whether or not you are installing the SmartDashboard application. They are shown, but are integral to the operation of the SmartDashboard GUI, so they are always selected. For reference, these are SmartDefense, SmartMap, VPN Manager, Policy Manager, Users Manager, and Objects Manager.

- **SmartView Tracker** Used to view the VPN-1/FireWall-1 security logs, accounting logs, and audit logs on the management server.

- **SmartView Status** Used to view the status of the remote enforcement points connected to the management server.

- **SmartUpdate** Used for managing licenses and remotely upgrading software and operating systems of the remote enforcement points connected to the management server.

- **SecureClient Packaging Tool** Used to create custom packages for SecuRemote/SecureClient mobile users.

- **SmartView Monitor** Used to monitor an interface, QoS rule, or virtual link in real time. The display is in the form of a line or bar graph.

- **Reporting Tool** Used to generate historical reports with graphs and pie charts from the data in the VPN-1/FireWall-1 logs.

- **User Monitor** Used to monitor which users are logged into policy servers throughout the infrastructure.

- **SmartLSM** Used to manage hundreds or thousands of like-configured firewalls in a profile- or template-based method.

14. When the system has finished copying files, the installation process is nearly complete. You can now click on any of the icons in the Check Point management clients folder. You can also open the management clients by selecting **Start | Programs | Check Point Management Clients**.

15. The installation procedure will next ask if you want shortcuts to the most commonly used clients placed on your desktop (Figure 2.17). Select **Yes** or **No**. Click **OK** to finish the installation (Figure 2.18) and begin the configuration process.

Figure 2.17 Desktop Shortcuts

Figure 2.18 Management Client Setup Finished

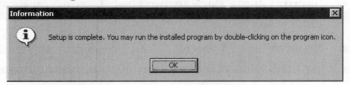

Configuring Check Point VPN-1/FireWall-1 NG AI on Windows

Once the system has finished copying files during the installation procedure, it will begin to go through the configuration screens. If you read the first section of this chapter, then you should be prepared to configure the firewall. After this initial configuration, you can always come back to any of these screens by opening the **Check Point Configuration** window via **Start | Programs | Check Point SmartConsole R54 | Check Point Configuration**.

The initial configuration will take you through the following screens:

- Licenses
- Administrators
- GUI Clients
- Certificate Authority Configuration

Licenses

You should have obtained all of your licenses before you get to this step. If you didn't, don't worry. There is a link to the Check Point User Center, where you can get your licenses, right in the Licenses window. If you need help with your license, read the first part of this chapter titled "Before you Begin." If you don't have any permanent licenses to install at this time, you can use the built-in 15-day evaluation license that will be created at the end of the configuration. And, of course, you can always request an evaluation license from either Check Point or your Check Point reseller.

Since you have installed a primary management module, you should be installing a local license that was registered with the local management station's IP address. Follow this step-by-step procedure for adding your license(s).

1. Click **Add** in the Licenses configuration window (Figure 2.19).

Figure 2.19 Licenses

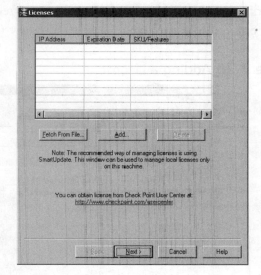

2. A window similar to the one in Figure 2.20 will be displayed. In this window you can either select **Paste License** or enter the license details into the appropriate fields. The figure below shows the following license installed: cplic putlic 192.168.0.1 never aoMJFd63k-pLdmKQMwZ-aELBqjeVX-pJxZJJCAy CPMP-EVAL-1-3DES-NG CK-CP. In addition, you will see the following fields:

- **IP Address** The IP address associated with this license or "eval" if you are utilizing an evaluation license.

- **Expiration Date** The date that the license expires, which is "never" for purchased products.

- **SKU/Features** These are the features that this license will enable (e.g. Management or 3DES).

- **Signature Key** The license string provided by Check Point to validate the license. This key will be unique for each license and IP Address.

    Enter your license details in the Add License window, and click **Calculate** to verify that the information you entered is correct. Match the Validation Code that you receive in this cell to the Validation Code on the license obtained from the Check Point User Center. You can also copy the entire *cplic putlic* command into your clipboard, and then click the **Paste License** button at the top of the screen to fill in all the fields. Click **OK** to continue, and if you entered everything correctly you should see the license entered into the main Licenses window (Figure 2.21).

Figure 2.20 Adding a License

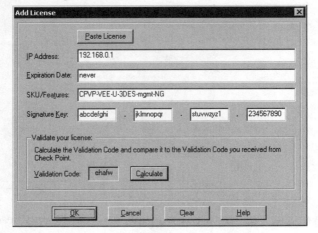

Figure 2.21 License Added Successfully

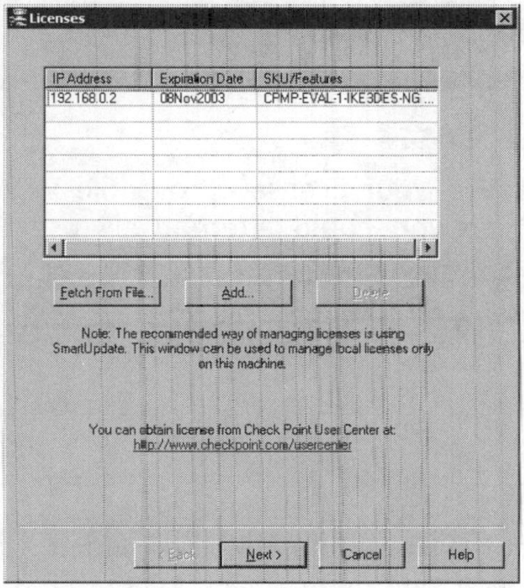

> **NOTE**
>
> The license configuration window will be displayed whether you are installing just the management or the enforcement module in a distributed installation. If you are utilizing centralized licensing for your remote enforcement modules, continue without a license and use SmartUpdate to license the module through the GUI.

3. Click **Next** to continue. The next screen deals with the Check Point configuration of the Management module.

Installing & Configuring…

Fetching Licenses

If you have saved your license(s) to a file with a .lic extension (e.g. licenses.lic), then you could alternatively use the **Fetch from File…** button, which would enable you to browse your file system for the license file. Once you've located the *.lic file, select **Open**, and the license details will be imported into the Licenses configuration window.

Administrators

After installing your licenses, you will be presented with another configuration window (see Figure 2.22) in which you need to configure your firewall administrators. You will need to define at least one administrator during this time. You can always come back to this window later to add, edit, or delete your administrative logins. If you utilize the management of administrative logins inside the SmartDashboard GUI, you should remove the administrative users defined here after they have been defined and applied.

Figure 2.22 Configuring Administrators

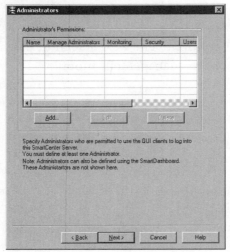

1. The first step to configuring your administrators is to click **Add**

2. You will be presented with a window similar to the one in Figure 2.23 where you can define the attributes for one administrator. It is best to use individual administrator usernames instead of a generic username like fwadmin. The problem with using a generic login ID is that you cannot properly audit the activities of the firewall administrators. It may be important for you to know who installed the last security policy when you are troubleshooting a problem. This becomes more and more important when there are several people administering a firewall system. The fields that you need to fill in are listed below. Enter the required fields in the Add Administrator Window and select **Read/Write All** for the permissions. Click **OK** to finish adding the administrator.

   - **Administrator Name** Choose a login name for your administrator. This field is case-sensitive.

   - **Password** Choose a good alphanumeric password. It must be at least four characters long and is also case-sensitive.

   - **Confirm Password** Repeat the same password entered above.
     The section labeled Permissions enables you to define the access level that you will require on an individual basis for each administrator. If you select **Read/Write All** or **Read Only All**, then your administrator will have access to all the available GUI client features with the ability to either make changes and updates or view the configuration and logs (perhaps for troubleshooting purposes), respectively. Notice that only Read/Write All administrators have the ability to manage administrative user accounts through the GUI. Any user with administrative privileges to the operating system of the management server can manage the Check Point administrators. You may also choose to customize their access so that they may be able to update some things and not others. To do this, select **Customized** and configure each of these options:

   - **SmartUpdate** This GUI tool enables you to manage licenses and update remote modules.

   - **Objects Database** This tool is used to create new objects to be used in the Security Policy rulebases. Objects will be covered in the next chapter.

www.syngress.com

- **Check Point Users Database** This tool is used to manage users for firewall authentication purposes.

- **LDAP Users Database** This tool is used to manage LDAP users.

- **Security Policy** This tool is used to create and manage rulebases using the SmartDashboard GUI.

- **QoS Policy** This tool is used to create and manage the bandwidth management rulebases.

- **Log Consolidator** This tool is used to create and manage rulebases regarding which logs will be consolidated from the log server into the SmartView Reporter database to run reports on.

- **SmartView Reporter** This tool is used to create reports based on information consolidated into its internal database from the logs stored on the management server.

- **Monitoring** This option enables access to the Log Viewer, System Status, and Traffic Monitoring GUI clients.

Figure 2.23 Adding an Administrator

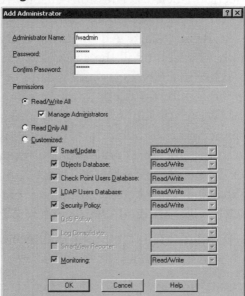

3. When you finish adding your administrator, you will be brought back to the main Administrators configuration window. Your administrator

should now be listed in the Administrator's Permissions window. From here you may choose to **Add**, **Edit**, or **Delete administrators** from this list (see Figure 2.24). When you are finished adding your administrators, click **Next** to continue with the configuration of the Check Point Management Module.

Figure 2.24 Administrators

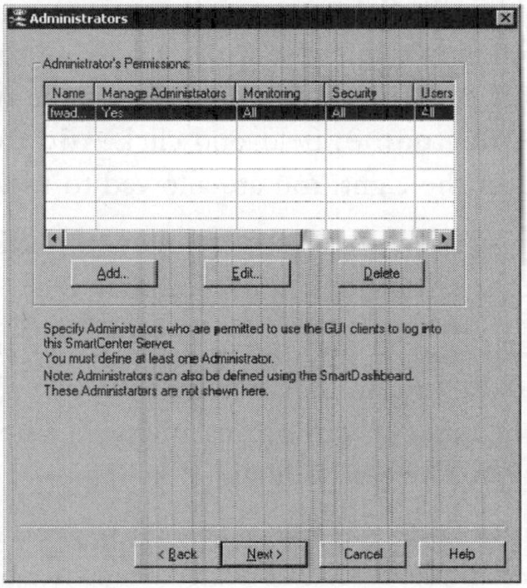

GUI Clients

The GUI clients are the SmartConsole programs we installed earlier. These clients could also be installed on as many desktops as you wish, but before they can connect to the management server, you need to enter their IP addresses into the GUI clients configuration window shown in Figure 2.25. You can use this feature, for example, if you install the GUI clients on your own workstation to enable you to control the management server from your PC. This will enable you to connect remotely to manage the Security Policy and view your logs and system status. You do not need to configure any clients at all during the installation (localhost is always allowed), but if you are already prepared for this step, you may enter as many clients into this window as necessary. This client information will be saved in a file on your firewall under $FWDIR/conf and will be named gui-clients. This file can be edited directly, or you can bring up this GUI Clients window at any time in the future. It is recommended, however, that you use the GUI to make all changes.

NOTE

If you have installed an enforcement module only, then you will not configure GUI clients or administrators.

---

1. For the example installation in this chapter, we are not going to enter any GUI clients. Select **Next** to continue on with the Check Point Management Module installation and read the next section. When you enter GUI clients, you type their hostname or IP address into the **Remote hostname:** field, and click **Add** to insert the clients to the window on the right. You are allowed to use wildcards as follows:

   ■ **Any** If you enter the word **Any**, this will allow anyone to connect without restriction (not recommended).

   ■ **Asterisks** You may use asterisks in the hostname. For example, 10.10.20.* means any host in the 10.10.20.0/24 network, or *.domainname.com means any hostname within the domainname.com domain.

   ■ **Ranges** You may use a dash (–) to represent a range of IP addresses. For example, 1.1.1.3–1.1.1.7 means the 5 hosts including 1.1.1.3 and 1.1.1.7 and every one in between.

   ■ **DNS** or **WINS resolvable hostnames**
   Figure 2.26 displays an example of the configured GUI cClients window with various options that you can use for your GUI client entries. It is recommended that you avoid using hostnames or domain names, however, since that requires DNS to be configured and working on the firewall. Using IP addresses are the best method since it doesn't rely on resolving, and will continue to work even if you cannot reach your name servers from the firewall. If, however, you have a very dynamic network with system names staying the same but addresses changing, or if you have many systems to add, hostnames may be the easiest solution.

Figure 2.25 Adding GUI Clients

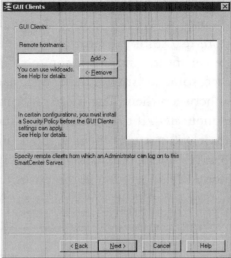

Figure 2.26 GUI Clients Added

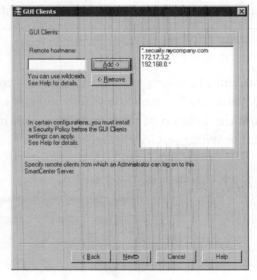

Certificate Authority Initialization

Check Point provides the highest level of security between its components using a PKI implementation. Your management server will be a Certificate Authority for your firewall enforcement modules, and will use certificates for Secure Internal Communication (SIC). This is the step in the installation process where the management server's certificate authority (CA) is configured, and a certificate is generated for the server itself.

You will be presented with a Key Hit Session window where you will be asked to input random text until you hear a beep. The data you enter will be used to generate the certificate, and it is recommended that you also enter the data at a random pace; some keystrokes may be close together and others could have a longer pause between them. The more random the data, the less likely that the input could be duplicated. If the system determines that the keystrokes are not random enough, it will not take them as input, and will display a bomb icon under Random Characters. If the input is good, the system will display a yellow light bulb. This is always a fun exercise in the classroom because of the sounds that are created when you frantically tap away at the keyboard.

NOTE

The Key Hit Session screen will also be presented to you if you have installed an enforcement module only so that you can generate a random number used to create an internal certificate for SIC.

1. Type random characters at random intervals into the Key Hit Session window until the progress bar is full, and the message "Thank you!" appears at the bottom of the window as seen in Figure 2.27. Click **Next** to continue with the CA configuration.

Figure 2.27 Key Hit Session

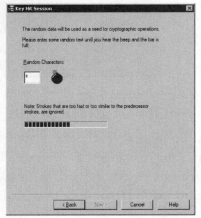

2. You will be presented with a window titled Certificate Authority
    (Figure 2.28). This window simply informs you that the CA is not yet
    configured and that it will be initialized when you select **Next**. Click
    Next to initialize the management module's Certificate Authority. The
    system will also prompt you for a name for the Internal Certificate
    Authority. This should be a Fully Qualified Domain Name (FQDN)
    due to the fact that it will be resolved by other devices to check the
    Certificate Revocation Lists (CRLs) for expired certificates, so this
    means it should be resolvable inside and outside your organization. If
    you did not install a license, you will be notified that your trial period
    will expire in 15 day. You should then receive a message that the initial-
    ization completed successfully, as shown in Figure 2.29.

Figure 2.28 Certificate Authority Initialization

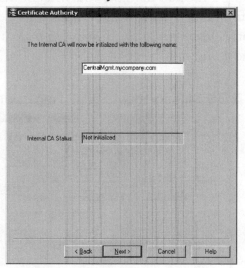

Figure 2.29 CA Initialized Successfully

3. Click **OK**.

4. Click **Finish** from the Fingerprint window (shown in Figure 2.30) to exit the configuration. This window will be the last one in the set of configuration screens during the installation process. This window displays the fingerprint of the management server's CA. You will be able to bring this window up again after the installation through the Check Point Configuration Tool, which is shown in the section titled "Getting Back to Configuration." When GUI clients first connect to the management server, they will be asked to verify the cryptographic fingerprint to ensure that they are connecting to the right machine. After that, the client software will compare the management server's fingerprints at each connect. If the fingerprints do not match, the client will be warned and asked if they wish to continue. The fingerprint could be exported to a file also, which the GUI clients would have access to.

5. If installing a firewall module, you will also receive a notice stating that a default firewalling policy will be installed when the Check Point services start. This will protect the system from attack until the first policy is applied to it.

Figure 2.30 Management Server Fingerprint

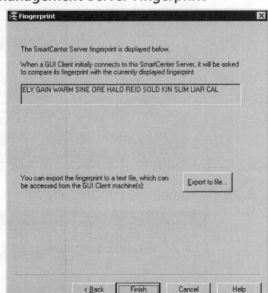

Installation Complete

Congratulations. You have now successfully installed and configured a Check Point VPN-1/FireWall-1 firewall on a Windows system. All you need to do now is navigate your way out of the Check Point Installation program and reboot your system. Check Point will thank you for installing Check Point Software (see Figure 2.31) and ask you if you wish to reboot now or reboot later (Figure 2.32).

1. To finish the installation process, click **OK**.

Figure 2.31 NG AI Configuration Complete

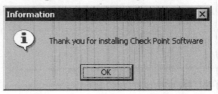

2. From the InstallShield Wizard dialog box illustrated in Figure 2.32, choose **Yes, I want to restart my computer now** and click **Finish**. Your computer will be shut down and restarted.

Figure 2.32 Reboot Computer

94   Chapter 2 • Installing and Configuring VPN-1/FW-1 NG with AI

Getting Back to Configuration

Now that installation is complete, you may need to get back into the
Configuration screens that you ran through at the end of the installation. You can
add, modify, or delete any of the previous configuration settings by running the
Check Point Configuration application.

1. Select **Start | Programs | Check Point SmartConsole R54 |
   Check Point Configuration**. This will bring up the Configuration
   Tool displayed in Figure 2.33. As you can see, all of the configuration
   options that we went through during the initial installation are available
   through the various tabs at the top of the Configuration Tool window.
   The tabs you can configure from this tool are listed below.

   - Licenses

   - Administrators

   - GUI Clients

   - PKCS#11 Token—Used to configure an add-on card, like a VPN
     accelerator card, for example.

   - Key Hit Session

   - Fingerprint
     Each of the options in Figure 2.33 is described previously in the
   chapter. If you are just starting to read the chapter at this point, jump to
   the top of this section "Configuring the Management Module" to get a
   walk-through of each of these screens and your options.

2. When satisfied with your firewall configuration, click on **OK** to exit the
   tool.

Figure 2.33 Check Point Configuration Tool

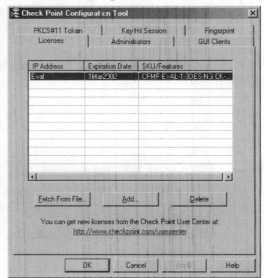

If you installed an enforcement module only, the Configuration Tool screens will be a little different (see Figure 2.34). The two new tabs are as follows:

- **Secure Internal Communication** Enables you to initialize an enforcement module for communication. You must enter the same password here as you enter in the SmartDashboard GUI (Figure 2.35).

- **High Availability** Enables this enforcement module to participate in a Check Point high availability (CPHA) or load sharing (CPLS) configuration with one or more other enforcement modules. This tab, illustrated in Figure 2.36, will not show up in your installation. The management module installed on an enforcement module participating in a cluster is not a supported configuration. State Synchronization is used to synchronize multiple firewalls together when using a 3rd party High Availability or Load Sharing solution.

Figure 2.34 Enforcement Module Configuration Tool

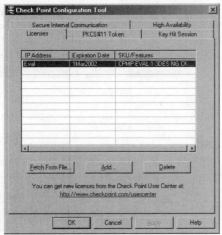

Figure 2.35 Secure Internal Communication

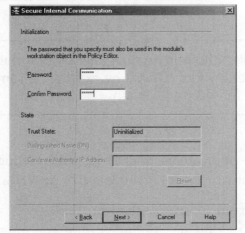

Figure 2.36 High Availability

Uninstalling Check Point VPN-1/FireWall-1 NG on Windows

When you uninstall VPN-1/FireWall-1, it is recommended that you make a full system backup before you begin. If you only need to back up the firewall configuration, then you should make a backup of the $FWDIR directory and all of its subdirectories. The default $FWDIR directory in Windows is C:\WINNT\FW1\NG. It is also advisable to back up the registry and the $CPDIR located by default at C:\Program Files\CheckPoint\CPShared\NG. Note that it is not necessary to uninstall the software to upgrade to a new version. The installation process will take care of upgrading the software.

> **WARNING**
>
> When you remove the Check Point VPN-1/FireWall-1 software from your system, you will lose all configuration data. The uninstall process deletes all the files, digital certificates, and directories associated with this package.

Uninstalling VPN-1 & FireWall-1

When you uninstall the firewall, you should remove the Check Point installed components using Add/Remove Programs in your system's Control Panel. The components should be removed in the reverse order in which they were installed. The following is a hypothetical order of removal:

1. Any Hotfixed versions of packages dependent on VPN-1/FireWall-1 NG AI such as Backward Compatibility, FloodGate-1, and Policy Server.

2. Any packages dependent on VPN-1/FireWall-1 NG AI such as Backward Compatibility, FloodGate-1, and Policy Server.

3. Check Point VPN-1 & FireWall-1 NG AI Hotfixes

4. Check Point VPN-1 & FireWall-1 NG AI

5. Check Point SVN Foundation NG AI Hotfixes

6. Check Point SVN Foundation NG AI

You can remove the management clients package at any time, but the order in which you remove these two packages is important.

Follow the steps below to completely uninstall all Check Point products from your Windows platform.

1. Exit all GUI Client windows that you may have open.

2. Open the Control Panel by selecting **Start | Settings | Control Panel**.

3. Click the **Add/Remove Programs** icon. If you are on Windows 2000, you should see a window similar to the window displayed in Figure 2.37. Next, select **Check Point VPN-1 & FireWall-1 4.1 Backward Compatibility** and click **Change/Remove** to uninstall this program.

Figure 2.37 Add/Remove Check Point VPN-1/FireWall-1 4.1 Backward Compatibility

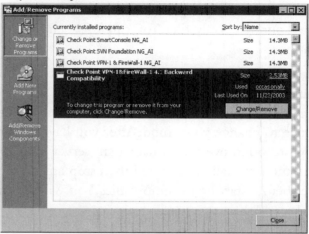

4. You will receive a message asking if you are sure that you want to remove this program. Click **OK** to continue and remove the VPN-1/FireWall-1 components. You may receive messages alerting you about shared and read only files. You can safely choose **Yes** to delete them and continue.

5. You will come back to the screen shown in Figure 2.38 in the Add/Remove Programs window. Select **Check Point VPN-1&FireWall-1 NG_AI** and click **Change/Remove** to uninstall this program.

Figure 2.38 Add/Remove Check Point VPN-1/FireWall-1 NG AI

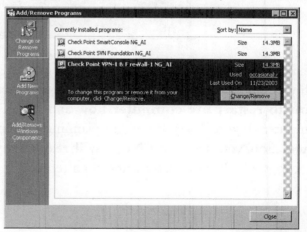

6. You will receive a message asking if you are sure that you want to remove this program. Click **OK** to continue and remove the VPN-1/FireWall-1 components. You may receive messages alerting you about shared and read only files. You can safely choose **Yes** to delete them and continue.

7. You will receive a Question/Warning message from Check Point (see Figure 2.39) asking if it is OK to continue with the uninstall of your primary management server. Click **Yes** to continue. This is your last chance to change your mind. After you have confirmed that you really do wish to remove the management server VPN-1/FireWall-1 component, the uninstall process will then stop any running Check Point services before starting to remove files. You will see the message displayed in Figure 2.40.

Figure 2.39 Check Point Warning

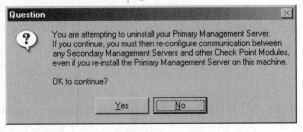

Figure 2.40 Stopping Services

8. Next, a window will be displayed to show you the progress of the uninstall process (Figure 2.41). Once the process has finished, select **Yes, I want to restart my computer now** and click **Finish** to reboot your computer (Figure 2.42). If you are planning on removing the SVN Foundation, you may select **No, I will restart my computer later**, remove the SVN Foundation, and then reboot.

Figure 2.41 Removing VPN-1/FireWall-1 Files

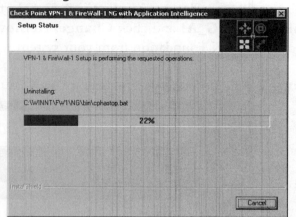

Figure 2.42 VPN-1/FireWall-1 Uninstall Complete

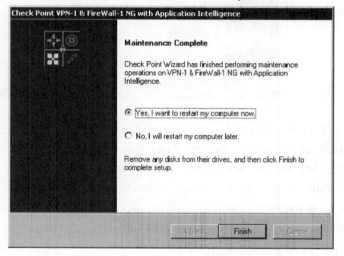

Uninstalling SVN Foundation

You have already uninstalled the VPN-1/FireWall-1 software, but now you must remove the SVN Foundation. This should always be removed after all other Check Point components, which are built on top of this foundation. If you had installed UserAuthority or the Policy Server, for example, these should be removed prior to removing the SVN program files.

1. Log into your computer
2. Choose **Start | Settings | Control Panel**.

3. Click the **Add/Remove Programs** Icon. You should see a window similar to the one illustrated in Figure 2.43. Select **Check Point SVN Foundation NG_AI** and click **Change/Remove** to completely remove the SVN Foundation from your system.

Figure 2.43 Add/Remove Check Point SVN Foundation NG AI

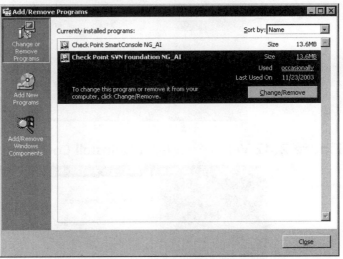

4. You will receive a notification stating that this is the only existing version of SVN foundation. After this package has been removed, the system will no longer be able to receive software updates through SmartUpdate. Click **Yes** to continue.

5. Click **OK** to confirm the removal of the selected application (see Figure 2.44). The InstallShield Wizard will then start up and begin uninstalling the SVN Foundation.

6. Click **Finish** when you receive the message **Maintenance Complete** as illustrated in Figure 2.44. You may be prompted to reboot instead. If so, select **Yes, I want to restart my computer now** and click **Finish** to reboot your computer. Once the machine reboots, log in again and open the Control Panel to remove the GUI clients.

Figure 2.44 SVN Foundation Maintenance Complete

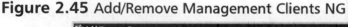

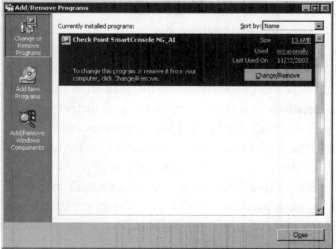

Uninstalling Management Clients

The management clients do not really depend on the SVN foundation installation; therefore, you could actually remove them at any time without any difficulty.

1. Access the **Add/Remove Programs** window after removing the SVN Foundation, and you should see a screen similar to that in Figure 2.45. Highlight **Check Point SmartConsole NG_AI** and click **Change/Remove** to uninstall all of the NG management clients (e.g. Policy Editor, Log Viewer, etc).

Figure 2.45 Add/Remove Management Clients NG

2. Choose to remove the GUI clients.

3. Click **OK** when you see the Maintenance Finished window displayed in Figure 2.46.

4. Click **Close** to exit the Control Panel, and you are done uninstalling all Check Point components.

Figure 2.46 Maintenance Finished

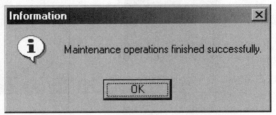

Installing Check Point VPN-1/FireWall-1 NG AI on Solaris

Finally all of your hard work at preparing for the firewall installation is about to pay off. This section is dedicated to installing the Check Point VPN-1/FireWall-1 NG on Solaris. Hopefully you have read the "Before you Begin" section at the beginning of the chapter and are prepared to start with the Check Point software installation. If you did not read the "Before you Begin" section above, then you should go back and read it before you continue. Although this section focuses on standalone installations, it will point out the different options you would make if you wanted to install the firewall on Solaris in a distributed environment. In other words, you will be installing the management and enforcement modules as well as the GUI all on one machine; however, you could install each piece on separate machines (and use different operating systems) if that is what your network design calls for. The distributed installation is not much different from the standalone installation, and the goal is for you to feel just as comfortable with the former as you do with the latter. This section assumes that you are already familiar with the Unix operating system, and know how to navigate the file system and list directories within Solaris.

If you are installing on Solaris 8, you can install in either 32- or 64-bit mode, and you must have patches 108434-01 (32-bit) or 108435-01 (64-bit), 108528-17, 113652-01 (only if 108528-17 is installed–anything later than 108528-17 is installed, 113625-01 is already included), 109147-18, and 109326-07 applied before you start installing VPN-1/FireWall-1 NG AI. In the event you are installing on Solaris 9 you will be required to install patch 112902-07. Solaris patches can be obtained from http://sunsolve.sun.com.

Installing from CD

In this section you'll see a Check Point VPN-1/FireWall-1 NG AI installation on Solaris using the Check Point Next Generation with Application Intelligence CD. You can obtain a copy of this CD from Check Point by going to www.checkpoint.com/getsecure.html and requesting an evaluation of the software. If you have a login setup with Check Point, then you can download the software and updates from Check Point at www.checkpoint.com/techsupport/downloads.jsp.

The following screenshots are taken from a new installation via CD to a Solaris 8 system. If you are installing on other versions of Solaris, the procedure is the same.

1. Insert the Check Point Next Generation with Application Intelligence CD into your computer's CD-ROM drive. If you have the automount daemon running on your Solaris system, then the drive will be mounted automatically. If not, mount the CD-ROM drive.

    The syntax for mounting the CD-ROM drive is below. You will need to determine which disk to mount before you type this command.

    ```
    mount -o ro -F hsfs <device> <mount point>
    ```

2. Move into the CD-ROM mount point directory by typing *cd /cdrom/cpsuite-r54* and press **Enter**. The directory name that you are using may vary depending on the version of the CD that you have. There is a file in this directory titled ReadmeUnix.txt, which explains the contents of the CD and how to begin the installation process.

Configuring & Implementing...

Installing Packages

If you have downloaded the packages to install on Solaris, you must first unzip and untar them to a temporary directory. Once the files are extracted, use *pkgadd –d <directory>* to install the Check Point VPN-1/FireWall-1 packages one at a time. Problems have been known to occur in previous versions if these temporary directories are several sub-directories away from the root of the file system. It would be best to extract these packages to /opt, /var/tmp, /tmp or directly to / instead of burying them too far down in the file system hierarchy. If you are in the same directory as the package, type *pkgadd –d*. to begin the installation.

You must install the SVN Foundation package prior to installing any other modules on your system. Make sure you download this package, too, if you want to install VPN-1/FireWall-1. You can install management clients without the SVN Foundation.

The simplest way to install the software, however, is to download the installation wrapper (also called the installation bundle), extract the files, and run the UnixInstallScript as shown below or install from the Check Point Next Generation with Application Intelligence CD.

3. When you are ready to start with the installation, type *./UnixInstallScript* and press **Enter** to initiate the Check Point installation wizard (see Figure 2.47). If you are in the Common Desktop Environment (CDE) then you can also use a file manager and double-click the **UnixInstallScript** file to begin.

    After you press **Enter**, you will be presented with Check Point's welcome screen.

NOTE

If you are installing Check Point NG on Linux, you use the same UnixInstallScript to begin the installation process. It will execute a separate executable behind the scenes (wrappers/unix/Install_Linux).

Figure 2.47 UnixInstallScript

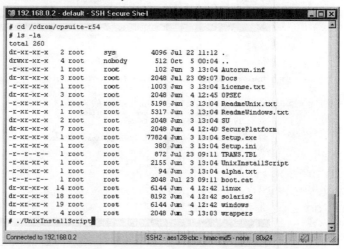

4. From the Welcome Screen (Figure 2.48) you have the options listed below. Type **n** to advance to the next screen.

- **V – Evaluation Options** Informational page on running this software on an evaluation license.

- **C – Contact Information** This option gives you telephone numbers on how to find and contact a local Check Point partner.

- **N – Next** Proceed to the next screen.

- **H – Help** To get help with navigating the installation screens.

- **E – Exit** To quit the installation and exit.
  It makes no difference in the installation process whether you are installing a purchased product or if you are installing for evaluation purposes. The software installation is exactly the same; the only thing that is different is the license you apply during configuration. You can always apply a permanent license to a system installed on evaluation at any time to turn it into a production firewall.

Figure 2.48 Welcome to Check Point NG

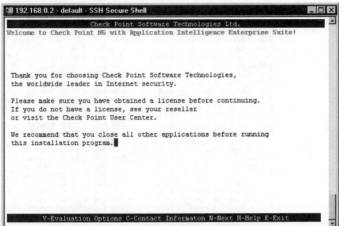

While running the UnixInstallScript, keep your eye at the bottom of the screen to see your navigation options. You will enter the letter associated with the menu item to perform the requested action. For example, to exit the system, you see E – exit at the bottom of the screen. Simply press e to exit and end the installation at any time.

5. You will receive the license agreement as shown in Figure 2.49. Press the **space bar** until you reach the end of the agreement. When you reach the end, the program will prompt you to indicate whether you accept the terms in the license agreement, "Do you accept all the terms of this license agreement (y/n) ?" Enter **y** and press **Enter**.

Figure 2.49 License Agreement

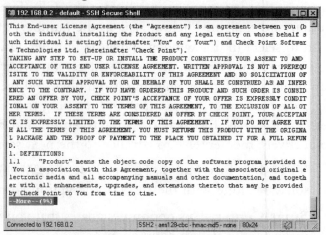

6. The next screen (Figure 2.50) will prompt you with two options to continue with the installation. They are somewhat self-explanatory; New Installation and Advanced Upgrade. The advanced upgrade can be used to export a configuration from a previous version into a single compressed file. It can also be used to import the aforementioned configuration file into a new installation to create a new NG AI system with the configuration of the old system. For the purposes of this installation, we will press **1** to choose New Installation and then **n** to continue.

Figure 2.50 Select Installation

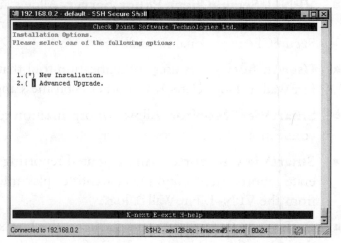

7. You will now be presented with a screen where you will select the
products that you want to install from this CD (Figure 2.51). Your
options are explained below. Type in the numbers of the packages you
wish to select in this window. Type the number again to unselect it. If
you enter **r** for Review, then you will get a new screen in which you
can select a product by entering its number, and then pressing **r** again to
get a description of the product. You're going to type **1, 2** and then **4** to
select **VPN-1 & FireWall-1, SmartCenter,** and **SmartConsole**
respectively, then enter *n* to advance to the next screen.

- **VPN-1 & FireWall-1** This includes FireWall-1 enforcement point
software along with the VPN-1 encryption component.

- **SmartCenter** This option designates that you wish to install the
management station component.

- **FloodGate-1** Provides an integrated Quality of Service (QoS)
solution for VPN-1/FireWall-1.

- **SmartConsole** The Graphical User Interface for Check Point
including the Policy Editor, Log Viewer, and System Status GUI.
Using the management clients on Solaris requires a Motif license
and you may need to tweak your environment to get them to run,
but you can connect with as many remote Windows GUI clients to
a Solaris management server as you wish without any additional
license.

- **VPN-1 SecureClient Policy Server** Allows an enforcement
module to install Granular Desktop Policies on mobile users'
SecureClient personal firewalls.

- **UserAuthority**   A user authentication tool that integrates with
FireWall-1, FloodGate-1, and other e-business applications.

- **SmartView Monitor** Allows an organization to monitor its VPN
connections, Internet connections, etc.

- **SmartView Reporter** An integrated reporting tool that can generate reports, graphs, and pie charts to display information obtained
from the VPN-1/FireWall-1 logs.

- **Performance Pack** Also available on the Linux platform
(including SecurePlatform), the Performance Pack replaces the Sun

Solaris kernel with a SunTone Certified kernel optimized for firewall and VPN functions. By removing excess functionalities in the kernel and enabling inspection closer to the hardware by removing unnecessary processing cycles, the throughput is increased significantly and latency through the firewall is reduced. This software acceleration requires a SecureXL (performance pack) license to be activated.

■ **SmartCenter Safe@ Connector** Provides the ability to manage Sofaware Safe@ Appliances (including the Sofaware S-Box and Nokia's IP30 and IP40) via the same management infrastructure (management station and clients) as enterprise firewalls.

Figure 2.51 Select Products to Install

NOTE

If you are installing the enforcement module only, then select **VPN-1 & FireWall-1**. For those who have been using Check Point for some time, the option for installing SmartCenter here will be new. The installation of management is actually just a configuration option, not an extra package. If you select VPN-1 & FireWall-1 and do not SmartCenter, you will be prompted with options analog to legacy version. The first option asks whether this system will be part of a Distributed or Stand Alone installation. When Distributed is chosen, you will be presented with the following options:

- **Enterprise Module** To install a firewall which will be managed by another system running the management software, choose this option.
- **Enterprise SmartCenter** Select this option if this system will only be a management server.
- **Enterprise SmartCenter and Enforcement Module** To install a firewall which will be managed by the management software which is also installed on this system, choose this option.
- **Enterprise Log Module** To send logs to a system which is only used for retaining logs..
- **Enterprise Module and Enterprise Log Server** To install an enterprise firea\s.

8. Next you will need to select the type of management installation you want on this system. You must select one of these options if you chose to install SmartCenter for management. Enter the desired option number. To select a different option number, simply enter that number. Select one of the options as shown in Figure 2.52. Enter *1* to select **Enterprise Primary SmartCenter**, and then press **n** to continue.

- **Enterprise Primary SmartCenter** To install a management server that will be acting primarily in a primary capacity.

- **Enterprise Secondary SmartCenter** To install a management server that will be acting primarily in a backup capacity. This option requires an Enterprise Primary SmartCenter to be already installed and licensed for Management High Availability in your infrastructure.

Figure 2.52 Choose the Type of Installation

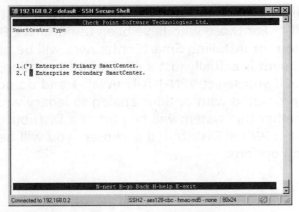

9. On the next screen (illustrated in Figure 2.53) press **n** to continue. This
    will be the last screen where you can exit the configuration before the
    installation script will start copying files. While the installation script is
    installing the package and copying files, you will see a screen similar to
    the one in Figure 2.54. The installation could take a few minutes. Next,
    the firewall will install the VPN-1/FireWall-1 kernel module and begin
    the configuration process.

Figure 2.53 Validation Screen

Figure 2.54 Installation Progress

Configuring Check Point VPN-1/FireWall-1 NG AI on Solaris

Once the system has finished copying files during the installation procedure, it will begin to go through the configuration screens shown in Figure 2.55. If you read the first section of this chapter, then you should be prepared to configure the firewall. After this initial configuration, you can always come back to any of these screens by running *cpconfig* from the root shell. It is recommended that you go through all of these screens during the installation without canceling; you can always go back in to change your initial configuration settings.

The initial configuration will take you through the following screens:

- SecureXL Acceleration
- Licenses
- Administrators
- GUI Clients
- SNMP Extension
- Certificate Authority Configuration

Figure 2.55 SecureXL Acceleration

SecureXL Acceleration

The first configuration option you are asked is in regard to SecureXL Acceleration. If you wish to offload the processing VPN encryption information onto a third-party hardware acceleration device, you can answer this question with **y** for yes to prepare the module for processing offload. For the installation within this chapter, enter **n** for no and press **Enter**.

Licenses

You should have obtained all of your licenses before you get to this step. If you need help getting your license, read the first part of this chapter titled "Before you Begin." If you don't have any permanent licenses to install at this time, you can either continue without a license and use the built-in 15-day evaluation license or at any time, request an evaluation license from either Check Point directly or your Check Point reseller.

> **NOTE**
>
> The license configuration option will be displayed regardless of which modules you have installed.

When installing a primary management module, one will be installing a local license that was registered with the local management station's IP address. Follow this step-by-step procedure for adding your license(s). You can see the license configuration input and output in Illustration 2.3.

1. When prompted to add licenses, enter **y** for yes and press **Enter**.

2. Enter **m** to add the license manually and press **Enter**. Now you will be prompted for each field of the license. The illustration below shows the following license installed: cplic putlic 192.168.0.1 never aoMJFd63k-pLdmKQMwZ-aELBqjeVX-pJxZJJCZy CPMP-VFE-U-NG CK-af80d80852ad

   - **Host** The IP address or hostid associated with this license.

   - **Date** The date that the license expires, which is "never" for any purchased license.

- **String** The license string provided by Check Point to validate the license. This key will be unique for each license and IP Address/Host.

- **Features** These are the features that this license will enable (e.g. management and/or 3DES).

   As you can see in Illustration 2.3, you also have the option of choosing **f** for Fetch from file. If you select this option, the configuration will prompt you to enter the file name of the file received from UserCenter.

3. Enter the values for **Host**, **Date**, **String**, and **Features**, pressing **Enter** after each entry.

Illustration 2.3 Configuring Licenses

```
Configuring Licenses...
=======================
The following licenses are installed on this host:


Host              Expiration Features



Do you want to add licenses (y/n) [n] ? y

Do you want to add licenses [M]anually or [F]etch from file?: M
Host:192.168.0.1
Date:never
String:aoMJFd63k-pLdmKQMwZ-aELBqjeVX-pJxZJJCZy
          Features:CPMP-VFE-U-NG CK- af80d80852ad
```

Administrators

If you have installed a management module, you will be prompted to add an administrator as soon as you enter a license into the configuration program. You must define at least one administrator at this time to allow you to log in using the SmartConsole GUI clients. You can always come back later to add, edit, or delete your administrators. Illustration 2.4 depicts the steps involved to add your administrator.

> **NOTE**
>
> If you have installed an enforcement module only, then you will not con-
> figure administrators.

It is best to use individual administrative usernames instead of a generic username like fwadmin. The problem with using a generic login ID is that you
cannot properly audit the activities of the firewall administrators. It may be
important for you to know who installed the last security policy when you are
troubleshooting a problem. This becomes more and more important when there
are several people administering a firewall system. You will have to complete the
following fields:

- **Administrator Name** Choose a login name for your administrator.
  This field is case-sensitive.

- **Password** Choose a good alphanumeric password. It must be at least
  four characters long and is also case-sensitive.

- **Verify Password** Repeat the same password entered above.

- **Permissions for all Management Clients** (Read/[W]rite All,
  [R]ead Only All, [C]ustomized)

Illustration 2.4 Adding an Administrator

```
Configuring Administrators...

==============================

No VPN-1 & FireWall-1 Administrators are currently

defined for this SmartCenter Server.

Administrator name: Joe

Password:

Verify Password:

Permissions for all Management Clients (Read/[W]rite All, [R]ead Only All,

[C]ustomized) w

        Permission to Manage Administrators([Y]es, [N]o) y
```

Continued

Illustration 2.4 Adding an Administrator

```
Administrator Joe was added successfully and has
Read/Write Permission for all products with Permission to Manage
Administrators

              Add another one (y/n) [n] ? n
```

Use the following steps to add an administrator:

1. Enter the login ID for your Administrator and press **Enter**. "Joe" is used in this example.

2. Enter the password for this username and press **Enter**.

3. Confirm the password entered in step 2 and press **Enter**.

4. Enter **w** for Read/Write All to give the administrator full permissions to access and make changes to all SmartConsole GUI clients.

Setting permissions enables you to define the access level that you will require on an individual basis for each administrator. If you select **Read/[W]rite All** or **[R]ead Only All,** then your administrator will have access to all the available GUI client features with the ability to either make changes and updates or to view the configuration and logs (perhaps for troubleshooting purposes) respectively. You may also choose to customize their access so that they may be able to update some things and not others. To do this, select **Customized** and configure each of these options (see Illustration 2.5):

■ **SmartUpdate** This GUI tool enables you to manage licenses and update remote modules.

■ **Monitoring** This option enables access to the Log Viewer, System Status, and Traffic Monitoring GUI clients.

Illustration 2.5 Setting Customized Permissions

```
Permissions for all products  (Read/[W]rite All, [R]ead Only All,
[C]ustomized) c
        Permission for SmartUpdate (Read/[W]rite, [R]ead Only, [N]one) w
        Permission for Monitoring (Read/[W]rite, [R]ead Only, [N]one) w


Administrator Doug was added successfully and has
Read/Write permission for SmartUpdate
Read/Write permission for Monitoring
```

GUI Clients

The Graphical User Interface clients are the management clients you installed. These clients can be installed on as many desktops as you wish, but before they can connect to the management server, you need to enter their IP addresses into the GUI clients configuration (Illustration 2.6). You can use this feature, for example, if you install the GUI clients on your own workstation to enable you to control the management server from your PC. This will allow you to connect remotely to manage the security policy and view your logs and system status. You do not need to configure any clients at all during the installation, but if you are already prepared for this step, you may enter as many clients into this window as necessary. This client information will be saved in a file on your firewall under $FWDIR/conf and will be named gui–clients. This file can be edited directly, but should be edited using the GUI clients window at any time in the future by running *cpconfig*. If you do not add any GUI clients, you will only be able to connect using the X-Motif GUI from this system.

> **NOTE**
>
> If you have installed an enforcement module only, then you will not configure GUI clients.

1. Press **y** to define the GUI clients.
2. Type in a GUI client IP address and press **Enter**.

3. Repeat step two for each GUI client you want to add to the list.

4. Press **Ctrl + D** to complete the list.

5. Verify that the list is correct, enter **y** for yes and press **Enter** to continue.

Illustration 2.6 Configuring GUI Clients

```
Configuring GUI clients...
===========================
GUI clients are trusted hosts from which
Administrators are allowed to log on to this SmartCenter Server using
Windows/X-Motif GUI.


No GUI Clients defined
Do you want to add a GUI Client (y/n) [y] ? y


You can add GUI Clients using any of the following formats:
1.  IP address.
2. Machine name.
3. "Any" - Any IP without restriction.
4. A range of addresses, for example 1.2.3.4-1.2.3.40
5. Wild cards - for example 1.2.3.* or *.checkpoint.com


Please enter the list of hosts that will be GUI Clients.
Enter GUI Client one per line, terminating with CTRL-D or your EOF
character.
192.168.0.10
172.17.3.2
^D
Is this correct (y/n) [y] ? y
```

As you enter GUI clients into this configuration, you type their hostname or IP address, one per line, pressing **Enter** at the end of each. When you are finished editing the client list, press **Ctrl + D** to send an end of file (EOF) control character to the program to continue. You are allowed to use wildcards as follows:

- **Any** If you enter the word **Any**, this will allow anyone to connect without restriction (not recommended).

- **Asterisks** You may use asterisks in the hostname. For example, 192.168.0.* means any host from 192.168.0.0 to 192.168.0.255, and *.domainname.com means any hostname within the domainname.com domain.

- **Ranges** You may use a dash (-) to represent a range of IP addresses. For example, 192.168.0.5-192.168.0.9 means the 5 hosts including 192.168.0.5 and 192.168.0.9 and each one in between.

- **DNS or WINS resolvable hostnames**

Illustration 2.7 displays an example of the configured GUI clients window with various options that you can use for your GUI client entries. It is recommended that you avoid using hostnames or domain names, however, since this requires DNS to be configured and working on the firewall. Using IP addresses is the best method since it doesn't rely on resolving, and will continue to work even if you cannot reach your name servers from the management station.

Illustration 2.7 GUI Client Wildcards

```
Please enter the list hosts that will be GUI clients.
Enter hostname or IP address, one per line, terminating with CTRL-D or your
EOF character.
*.mycompany.com
192.168.0.5-192.168.0.9
172.17.3.2
172.17.2.*
noc.mycompany.com
Is this correct (y/n) [y] ? y
```

Certificate Authority Initialization

Your management server will be a Certificate Authority for your firewall enforcement modules, and will use certificates for Secure Internal Communication (SIC). This is the step in the installation process where the management server's CA is configured, and a certificate is generated for the server and its components.

You will be presented with the Key Hit Session configuration option, where you will be asked to input random text until you hear a beep. The data you enter will be used to generate the certificate, and it is recommended that you enter the data at a random pace; some keystrokes may be close together and others could have a longer pause between them. The more random the data, the less likely that the input could be duplicated. If the system determines that the keystrokes are not random enough, it will not take them as input, and will display an asterisk to the right of the progression bar.

> **NOTE**
>
> The Key Hit Session screen will also be presented to you if you have installed an enforcement module, only so that you can generate an internal certificate for SIC.

1. Type random characters at random intervals into the Key Hit Session window until the progress bar is full, and the message "Thank you" appears at the bottom of the window as seen in Figure 2.56.

Figure 2.56 Random Pool

2. The next step is to initialize the internal Certificate Authority for SIC. It may take a minute for the CA to initialize. Figure 2.57 displays the

messages you will receive on the console while configuring the CA. Press **Enter** to initialize the Certificate Authority.

Figure 2.57 Configuring Certificate Authority

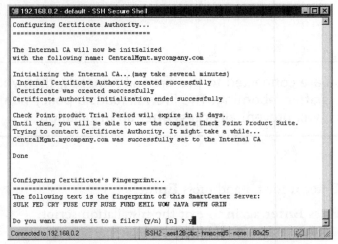

3. Once the CA is initialized successfully, you will be presented with the fingerprint of the management server's certificate. This fingerprint is unique to your CA and the certificate on your management server used for communication with the management server (another certificate would be generated for VPN). The first time your GUI clients connect to the management server, they will receive the fingerprint so that they can match it to the string listed here and verify that they are connecting to the correct manager. After the first connection, every time the clients connect to the management server, the fingerprint is verified. If the fingerprint presented by the management server doesn't match what's known on the workstation, a warning message will be displayed, and the administrator can decide whether or not to continue with the connection. Type **y** and press **Enter** to save the fingerprint to a file.

4. Enter the filename and press **Enter**. The file will be saved in $CPDIR/conf.

Installation Complete

When the configuration program ends, you may see a few messages on the screen, such as "generating GUI-clients INSPECT code," as the system finishes up the installation of the VPN-1/FireWall-1 package. Finally, you will receive the following question, "Would You like to reboot the machine [y/n]:" (shown in Figure 2.58). If you select not to reboot, then you will exit the installation and go back to a shell prompt. If you choose to reboot, then the system will be restarted.

WARNING

If you are connected to this firewall remotely, then you will not have access after rebooting. The firewall loads a policy named InitialPolicy, which will prevent all access after an installation.

1. Enter **n** for no and press **Enter**.
2. Press **Enter** again to exit the installation script.

Figure 2.58 Installation Complete

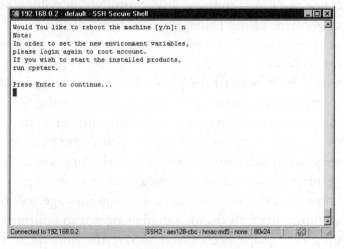

When you exit the installation script, you will see the shell. The last message you received on the console was concerning new environment variables. Let's address these environment variables for a moment. The firewall will create a .profile in root's home directory, which runs the Check Point environment script located at /opt/CPshrd-54/tmp/.CPprofile.sh (for bourne shell) or .CPprofile.csh (for c shell). This script sets your

Check Point variables such as $FWDIR and $CPDIR among others. See Figure 2.59 for a list of environment variables that are set after installation on a new system. Without setting these variables, various firewall commands will fail. For example, if you log in to the system as your standard user and then type *su* to root instead of *su –*, you will maintain the standard user's environment; then when executing *fw unload localhost* to unload the InitialPolicy, you will receive the following error message: "ld.so.1: /etc/fw/bin/fw: fatal: libkeydb.so: open failed: No such file or directory Killed."

3. When you are ready to restart the server, as a best practice, type *sync; sync; reboot* and press **Enter.**

Figure 2.59 Environment Variables

Continued

puter. You can log in to the console and verify that the filter is loaded with the *fw stat* command:

```
# fw stat
HOST        POLICY        DATE
localhost InitialPolicy  8Nov2003 16:51:48 :   [>hme1] [<hme1]
[>qfe0] [<qfe0] [>qfe1] [<qfe1] [>qfe2] [<qfe2]
```

If you have access to the console, then log in as root and unload the filter with the following command:

```
# fw unloadlocal
Uninstalling Security Policy from all.all@CentralMgmt
Done.
```

If you do not have access to the console, you can write a shell script to unload the filter and enable it in cron or place it in /etc/rc3.d/S99fwunload. Here's a sample /etc/rc3.d/S99fwunload script that one Check Point user used for his firewalls:

```
#!/bin/sh
. /.profile/opt/CPfw1-54/bin/fw unloadlocal
```

Unfortunately, just running the *unload* command is not enough. The various environment variables in the $CPDIR/tmp/.CPprofile.sh have to be defined. To do this, copy the contents of the .CPprofile.sh file into the middle of the script before the unload command or source them using the . /.profile command. Even before you reboot, you can test that the script works. To ensure the policy unload is run after reboot, first verify that you have enabled execute permissions on the file:

```
chmod +x /etc/rc3.d/S99fwunload
```

Now you can safely reboot the system and log back into it after it has booted. Don't forget to remove the file once you are back in the firewall. If you are using a version other than NG with Application Intelligence, the commands in the script may have to be changed because the package name will likely be different.

Getting Back to Configuration

Now that installation is complete, you may need to get back into the configuration screens that you ran through at the end of the installation. You can add, modify, or delete any of the previous configuration settings by running *cpconfig*.

If you did not log in as root or login and type *su −* to gain root access, then your Check Point environment variables may not be set, and you could receive the errors displayed in Illustration 2.8:

Illustration 2.8 Possible cpconfig Execution Errors

```
# /opt/CPshrd-54/bin/cpconfig
You must setenv CPDIR before running this program
# CPDIR=/opt/CPshrd-54/; export CPDIR
# /opt/CPshrd-54/bin/cpconfig
ld.so.1: /opt/CPshrd-54/bin/cpconfig_ex: fatal: libcpconfca.so: open failed:
No such file or directory
         Can not execute cpconfig
```

If this happens, simply login with *su −*. The dash is an optional argument to su, which provides you with the environment that you would have, had you logged in directly as root. You can also set your environment by sourcing root's .profile by executing . /.*profile* if using sh as your shell or *source /.cshrc* if you are using csh as your shell. See Figure 2.60 for the output of cpconfig on Solaris.

Figure 2.60 cpconfig

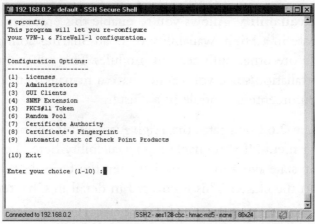

There are a few options listed here that did not come up during the initial installation process. Number 5 configures a PKCS#11 Token, which enables you to install an add-on card such as an accelerator card, and number 9 enables you to configure the automatic start of Check Point modules at boot time.

If you installed an enforcement module only, the cpconfig screens will also include the following:

- **Secure Internal Communication** Enables a one-time password that will be used for authentication between this enforcement module and its management server, as well as any other remote modules that it might communicate with (see Figure 2.61).

Figure 2.61 Secure Internal Communication Configuration

- **High Availability** Allows you to enable this enforcement module to participate in a High Availability or Load Sharing configuration with one or more other enforcement modules. This tab will not show up in your installation since you cannot have a management module installed on an enforcement module in a cluster.

Figure 2.62 illustrates the High Availability option available from the cpconfig menu. If you enable high availability here, then you will need to set up state synchronization between the firewalls that will be participating in the cluster. This is covered in detail in Chapter 12.

Figure 2.62 High Availability Configuration

```
192.168.0.2 - default - SSH Secure Shell
Configuration Options:
----------------------
(1)  Licenses
(2)  SNMP Extension
(3)  PKCS#11 Token
(4)  Random Pool
(5)  Secure Internal Communication
(6)  Enable Check Point ClusterXL and State Synchronization
(7)  Automatic start of Check Point Products

(8)  Exit

Enter your choice (1-8) :6


Enable Check Point ClusterXL and State Synchronization...
=========================================================

High Availability module is currently disabled.

Would you like to enable the High Availability module (y/n) [y] ?
Connected to 192.168.0.2          SSH2 - aes128-cbc - hmac-md5 - none   80x24
```

Uninstalling Check Point VPN-1/FireWall-1 NG AI on Solaris

When you uninstall Check Point VPN-1/FireWall-1 NG from Solaris, it is recommended that you make a full system backup before you begin. If you only need to back up the firewall configuration, then you should make a backup of /opt/CP★ and /var/opt/CP★ directories. If you are removing a primary management server, then the first time you run *pkgrm*, the removal will fail. Check Point does this on purpose to ensure that you do not unintentionally delete your management module without understanding that you will not be able to restore SIC to its current state after you remove it.

> **WARNING**
>
> When you remove the Check Point VPN-1/FireWall-1 software from your system, you will lose all configuration data. The uninstall process deletes all files and directories.

Uninstalling VPN-1 & FireWall-1

When you uninstall the firewall, you should remove the Check Point installed packages using the *pkgrm* program available on your Solaris system. The components should be removed in the following order:

1. Check Point VPN-1 & FireWall-1 NG
2. Check Point SVN Foundation NG

You can remove the management clients package at any time, but the order in which you remove the two packages listed above is important. Follow the steps below to completely uninstall all Check Point products from your Solaris platform. You may wish to run the command *pkginfo* to see which Check Point packages you have installed before you start. The packages you are going to uninstall are listed in Illustration 2.9.

Illustration 2.9 pkginfo Command

```
# pkginfo | grep "Check Point"
application CPclnt-54    Check Point SmartConsole NG with Application
                        Intelligence
application CPfw1-54     Check Point VPN-1/FireWall-1 NG with Application
                        Intelligence
application CPfwbc-41    Check Point VPN-1/FireWall-1 4.1 for Backward
                        Compatibility
application CPshrd-54    Check Point SVN Foundation NG with Application
                        Intelligence
```

1. Exit all GUI Client windows that you may have open.
2. Log in to the firewall and su to root: *su -*
3. Type *pkgrm* and press **Enter**. You will see a list of installed packages available for removal, as shown in Figure 2.63. In this example, you will choose the Check Point VPN-1/FireWall-1 4.1 for Backward Compatibility, which is number **3** in the list. We will uninstall this first because it extends the functionality of the VPN-1/FireWall-1 package which means the backward compatibility package is dependent on the firewall package. And the firewall package is dependent on the SVN Foundation. These dependencies determine the order in which the software should be removed.

Figure 2.63 Package Removal Choices

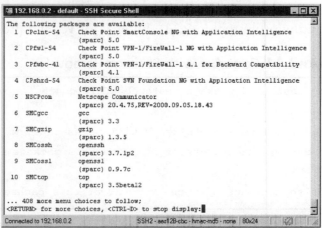

4. Press **Ctrl + D**, you will then be presented with the following message: Select package(s) you wish to process (or 'all' to process all packages). (default: all) [?,??,q]:

5. Enter **3** and press **Enter** to uninstall the CPfwbc-41 package.

6. Next, the system will ask you if you are sure you want to remove this package, as seen in Illustration 2.10. Enter **y** for yes and press **Enter**.

7. Repeat this process for the CPfw1-54 package and then for the CPshrd-54 package. The SmartConsole GUI clients can be removed at any time, as they are not dependent on any other Check Point packages.

Illustration 2.10 CPfwbc-41 Package Removal

```
Select package(s) you wish to process (or 'all' to process all packages).
(default: all) [?,??,q]: 3


The following package is currently installed:
   CPfwbc-41          Check Point VPN-1/FireWall-1 4.1 for
                      Backward Compatibility
                      (sparc) 4.1


Do you want to remove this package? y
```

8.   Next, the pkgrm program notifies you that the uninstall process will require the use of super-user privileges, and asks you if you want to continue (Illustration 2.11). Enter **y** for yes and press **Enter**.

Illustration 2.11 Continue with Package Removal

```
## Removing installed package instance <CPfwbc-41>


This package contains scripts which will be executed with super--user
permission during the process of removing this package.


Do you want to continue with the removal of this package [y,n,?,q] y
```

9.   When removing the CPfw1-54 package from a primary management station, the package removal will fail. Check Point has done this on purpose so that you can receive the WARNING notification that is displayed in Illustration 2.12. This message informs you that if you uninstall VPN-1/FireWall-1, then you will lose all configured SIC, and you will not be able to restore SIC to its current state by reinstalling the primary management server. The configuration can be recovered from a correctly performed backup. Run *pkgrm* again to uninstall the CPfw1-54 package.

Illustration 2.12 Removal Failed

```
## Verifying package dependencies.
## Processing package information.
## Executing preremove script.


There are no packages dependent on VPN-1/FireWall-1 NG with Application
Intelligence.
*********************************************************************


                    WARNING:
You are attempting to uninstall your Primary SmartCenter Server.

If you continue, you will be unable to communicate with any Secondary
SmartCenter Servers and other Check Point Modules, even if you later
reinstall the Primary SmartCenter Server on this machine.  The uninstall
program is now aborting.  If you still wish to uninstall your Primary
SmartCenter Server, then run it again.
```

Continued

Illustration 2.12 Removal Failed

```
******************************************************************

Please disregard the following error message:
pkgrm: ERROR: preremove script did not complete successfully.


Removal of <CPfw1-54> failed.
#
```

10. Press **Ctrl + D**.

11. Enter **2** and press **Enter** to select the CPfw1-54 package.

12. Enter **y** for yes and press **Enter**.

13. Enter **y** for yes and press **Enter**. This time the package removal will be
     successful. Figures 2.64 and 2.65 show you some of the messages you
     will see on your console as the package is removed from the system.

Figure 2.64 Uninstall of VPN-1/FireWall-1

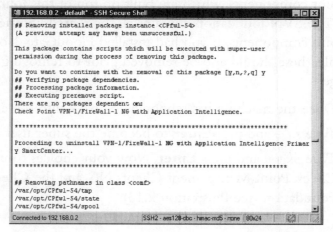

Figure 2.65 Uninstall of VPN-1/FireWall-1 Continued

```
192.168.0.2 - default* - SSH Secure Shell                        _ □ ×
/opt/CPfw1-54/bin/ChangeKeys
/opt/CPfw1-54/bin/AtlasStopWrapper
/opt/CPfw1-54/bin/AtlasStartWrapper
/opt/CPfw1-54/bin
/opt/CPfw1-54/SU/fw1/content.txt
/opt/CPfw1-54/SU/fw1/CPfwlPkgMod
/opt/CPfw1-54/SU/fw1
/opt/CPfw1-54/SU
/opt/CPfw1-54/LICENSE.TXT
## Executing postremove script.
***********************************************

IMPORTANT: You must REBOOT the machine !!!!

***********************************************

*****************************************************************
Check Point VPN-1/FireWall-1 NG with Application Intelligence uninstall complete
.
*****************************************************************
## Updating system information.

Removal of <CPfw1-54> was successful.
#
Connected to 192.168.0.2        SSH2 - aes128-cbc - hmac-md5 - none  80x24
```

14. Type *sync; sync; reboot* and press **Enter** to reboot the system.

Uninstalling SVN Foundation

You have already uninstalled the VPN-1/FireWall-1 software, but now you must remove the SVN foundation. This should always be removed after all other Check Point components, which are built on top of this foundation (as the name suggests). The SVN foundation contains all the shared libraries used by various Check Point components. If you had installed FloodGate-1 or the Policy Server, for example, these should also be removed prior to removing the SVN CPshrd-54 package.

1. Once the machine has rebooted, log back into the console.

2. Type *su –* and press**Enter** to become the super user (root).

3. Type *pkgrm* and press **Enter**. Now your choices to uninstall are the Check Point Management Clients NG and the Check Point SVN Foundation (see Illustration 2.13).

Illustration 2.13 Remove SVN Foundation

```
The following packages are available:
  1  CPclnt-50      Check Point Managment Clients NG
                    (sparc) 5.0
  2  CPshrd-50      Check Point SVN Foundation with Application
                    Intelligence
                    (sparc) 5.0
```

4. Press **Ctrl + D**.

5. Enter **2** and press **Enter** to select the SVN Foundation CPshrd–50 package.

6. When the pkgrm program asks you if you want to remove this program, enter **y** for yes and press **Enter.**

7. Again, pkgrm will print, "This package contains scripts that will be executed with super-user permission during the process of removing this package. Do you want to continue with the removal of this package [y,n,?,q]." Enter **y** for yes and press **Enter** to continue. See Illustration 2.14 for a complete view of the uninstall process of the Check Point SVN Foundation on Solaris. You do not need to reboot after uninstalling the SVN package.

Illustration 2.14 pkgrm SVN Foundation

```
$ su -
Password:
Sun Microsystems Inc.   SunOS 5.8      Generic February 2000# pkgrm

The following packages are available:
  1  CPclnt-54      Check Point SmartConsole NG with
                    Application Intelligence
                    (sparc) 5.0
  2  CPshrd-54      Check Point SVN Foundation with Apppication
                    Intelligence
                    (sparc) 5.0
```

Continued

Illustration 2.14 pkgrm SVN Foundation

```
... 148 more menu choices to follow;
<RETURN> for more choices, <CTRL-D> to stop display:^D

Select package(s) you wish to process (or 'all' to process
all packages). (default: all) [?,??,q]: 2

The following package is currently installed:
   CPshrd-54        Check Point SVN Foundation with Application
                    Ingelligence
                    (sparc) 5.0

Do you want to remove this package? y

## Removing installed package instance <CPshrd-54>

This package contains scripts that which will be executed with super-user
permission during the process of removing this package.

Do you want to continue with the removal of this package [y,n,?,q] y
## Verifying package dependencies.
## Processing package information.
## Executing preremove script.
There are no packages dependent on Check Point SVN Foundation NG installed.
## Removing pathnames in class <conf>
/var/opt/CPshrd-54/registry
/var/opt/CPshrd-54/conf/sic_policy.conf
/var/opt/CPshrd-54/conf/os.cps
/var/opt/CPshrd-54/conf/cp.macro
...
/opt/CPshrd-54/SU
/opt/CPshrd-54/LICENSE.TXT
## Executing postremove script.
****************************************************************
Rebooting the machine is recommended for successful removal of Check Point
NG with Application Intelligence products.
```

Continued

Illustration 2.14 pkgrm SVN Foundation

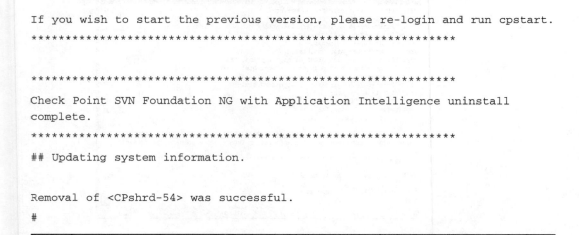

```
If you wish to start the previous version, please re-login and run cpstart.
*************************************************************


*************************************************************
Check Point SVN Foundation NG with Application Intelligence uninstall
complete.
*************************************************************
## Updating system information.


Removal of <CPshrd-54> was successful.
#
```

Uninstalling Management Clients

The management clients do not really depend on the SVN foundation installation; therefore, you could really remove them at any time without any difficulty.

1. Run **pkgrm** again to remove the SmartConsole package.

2. Press **Ctrl + D**.

3. At the prompt, "Select package(s) you wish to process (or 'all' to process all packages). (default: all) [?,??,q]:", enter **1** and press **Enter** to select the Check Point SmartConsole NG with Application Intelligence package (CPclnt-54).

4. Enter **y** for yes and press **Enter** when the pkgrm utility asks you, "Do you want to remove this package?"

5. Enter **y** for yes and press **Enter** when the pkgrm utility presents you with the following prompt, "This package contains scripts that will be executed with super-user permission during the process of removing this package. Do you want to continue with the removal of this package [y,n,?,q]."

   The package will be removed. Figure 2.66 illustrates the end of the uninstall process for the SmartConsole NG AI package.

Figure 2.66 Management Clients Package Removal

```
192.168.0.2 - default* - SSH Secure Shell                          _ □ ×
/opt/CPclnt-54/asm_help/ftp_bounce.html
/opt/CPclnt-54/asm_help/ftp.html
/opt/CPclnt-54/asm_help/fingerprint.html
/opt/CPclnt-54/asm_help/dynamic_ports.html
/opt/CPclnt-54/asm_help/dos.html
/opt/CPclnt-54/asm_help/dns.html
/opt/CPclnt-54/asm_help/cross_sites_scripting.html
/opt/CPclnt-54/asm_help/cifs_worm_catcher.html
/opt/CPclnt-54/asm_help/asm_help.css
/opt/CPclnt-54/asm_help/anti_spoof_hazard.html
/opt/CPclnt-54/asm_help
/opt/CPclnt-54/WindU
/opt/CPclnt-54/LICENSE.TXT
## Executing postremove script.

**********************************************************************
Check Point SmartConsole NG with Application Intelligence uninstalled successful
ly.
**********************************************************************

## Updating system information.

Removal of <CPclnt-54> was successful.
#

Connected to 192.168.0.2          SSH2 - aes128-cbc - hmac-md5 - none  80x24
```

Installing Check Point VPN-1/FireWall-1 NG AI on Nokia

Check Point's Next Generation with Application Intelligence Enterprise Suite on the Nokia IPSO appliance is a popular combination. Providing a combination of rack-mount appliance hardware, pre-hardened multi-purpose operating system, and the simple web and command-line interface, the IPSO platform currently claims nearly half of all Check Point installations. Nokia provides a web front-end called Voyager (see Figure 2.67) for easy package management and system configuration. Nokia also provides a fast failover mechanism utilizing VRRP and Check Point's state synchronization with an average failover time of just four seconds.

Check Point VPN-1/FireWall-1 NG with Application Intelligence requires Nokia IPSO 3.7 or later for installation (refer to Nokia's Support website for the latest compatible version of the operating system which runs Check Point NG AI). You can either order a Nokia box with Check Point preinstalled, or you can download the installation package from Check Point (with appropriate login ID) and install it yourself. If you need to upgrade your IPSO, you will need to obtain the IPSO image from Nokia's website. It may be necessary to upgrade your boot manager prior to upgrading your IPSO image. Please read all release notes prior to installing new packages or operating system (IPSO) images. It is not recommended to upgrade from 4.1 to NG AI if you have less than 128MB of memory; because this is the minimum memory required to run Check Point NG AI.

Figure 2.67 Nokia's Voyager GUI

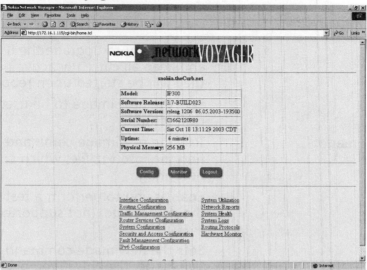

Installing the VPN-1/FireWall-1 NG AI Package

Since the Nokia appliance is already hardened, there is very little you need to do to prepare it for firewall installation. You must configure and test networking and DNS, set up the host address assignment through the Voyager GUI, and you may need to upgrade your IPSO and boot manager.

Upgrading IPSO Images

Nokia is actively developing the IPSO operating system and is continually adding new features. Before upgrading your system, you should always check Nokia's website for compatibility matrix of platforms, operating systems, and Check Point software (see Nokia Resolution 11253). The release notes for each IPSO version contain a list of versions of IPSO that are supported upgrade paths. The *newimage* command will automatically upgrade the boot manager on IP300, IP600, IP500, IP100, and IP700 series appliances. You can download the 3.7 image from https://support.nokia.com (login required). Once you have the image in /var/admin, you can run *newimage* to install it. The options for newimage are illustrated in Table 2.2.

Table 2.2 newimage Command Line Arguments

Switch for newimage	Description
-k	Enables you to upgrade the IPSO image and keep all currently active packages so they will be started upon reboot.
-R	Sets the new image to be used upon the next reboot.
-l <path to image>	Tells the newimage command where to find the ipso.tgz file, which contains the new image.
-T	Enables you to perform a test boot with the new image. (not supported on the IP440).
-I	Sets the newimage command in interactive mode. Use this if you need to ftp the file or use the CD-ROM drive (Platforms with CD-ROM only) to upgrade the IPSO image.
-b	Forces upgrade of bootmgr.

Assuming that you have the ipso.tgz file downloaded to /var/admin, and your system is on, the recommended command to upgrade your IPSO image is as follows:

```
newimage -k -R -l /var/admin
```

NOTE

The *-k* option should only be used if the software version you have installed and the one you are running are compatible with the current and new operating system versions.

After updating the image, reboot your system:

```
sync; sync; reboot
```

WARNING

If your IPSO hardware platform is an IP350 or IP380, you can run IPSO 3.5.1 or IPSO 3.7 (or later). Other IPSO versions previous to 3.7 were not compatible with the IP350 and IP380 hardware and when installed, required sending the system to Nokia for a newly formatted hard drive.

Installing VPN-1/FireWall-1 NG AI

To install the VPN-1/FireWall-1 NG AI package, you must first install the SVN foundation and then the VPN-1/FireWall-1 package. You will need to get the software from Check Point or from a Check Point reseller since Nokia does not provide VPN-1/FireWall-1 packages on their support Web site any longer. The simplest way to install the Check Point software on a Nokia appliance is to download the wrapper (also known as the NG with Application Intelligence bundle). Follow this step-by-step procedure to install the new packages. Of course, you should always read the release notes for the most recent information on installing the Check Point software and any applicable limitations. See Table 2.3 for available arguments to the newpkg command.

Table 2.3 newpkg Command Line Arguments

Switch for newpkg	Description
-i	Installs the package, but does not activate it. Prompts you for media type, new packages and old packages that you wish to install or upgrade.
-s <server>	Specifies the FTP server IP address.
-l <username>	Enter the FTP username (you don't need to enter a username if you will be using anonymous FTP).
-p <password>	Enter the FTP user's password.
-m <CDROM | AFTP | FTP | LOCAL>	Choose your media type; the options are CD-ROM, AFTP, FTP or LOCAL.
-d	Prints debug messages.
-v	Verbose mode for FTP.

Continued

Table 2.3 newpkg Command Line Arguments

Switch for newpkg	Description
-n <new package> package you are installing.	Enter the full pathname to the new
-o <old package>	Enter the full pathname of the package you are upgrading from.
-S	This sets the newpkg to install the package silently. If you enable silent mode, then you must specify the following arguments: -o, -m, -n and possibly –s and -l, –p if the media type is not LOCAL.
-h	Prints the usage for newpkg (help).

1. Put the installation wrapper package file in /var/admin. The NG with Application Intelligence wrapper file name at the time of release is IPSO_wrapper_R54.tgz.

> **NOTE**
>
> Do not unzip or untar the Nokia packages. When you run the *newpkg* command, it will do that for you.

2. From the /var/admin directory, type **newpkg –i** and press **Enter**. The newpkg installation program will begin, and will ask you where to install the new package as illustrated in Illustration 2.15.

Illustration 2.15 SVN Foundation Package Installation

```
ExternalFW[admin]# newpkg -i

Load new package from the following:
1. Install from CD-ROM.
2. Install from anonymous FTP server.
3. Install from FTP server with user and password.
4. Install from local filesystem.
```

Continued

Illustration 2.15 SVN Foundation Package Installation

```
5. Exit new package installation.

Choose an installation method (1-5):  4

Enter pathname to the packages [ or 'exit' to exit ]: .

Loading Package List

Processing package IPSO_wrapper_R54.tgz...
Package Description: Check Point SVN Foundation NG with Application
Intelligence

Would you like to  :

1. Install this as a new package
2. Upgrade from an old package
3. Skip this package
4. Exit new package installation

          Choose (1-4): 1
```

3. Choose the option for local filesystem number **4** and press **Return**.

4. When you are asked for the pathname to the package, type a period (.)
    for your current directory (which is /var/admin) and press **Enter**.

5. The newpkg program will locate any packages in this directory and
    begin processing them one by one. The Check Point SVN Foundation
    NG package will be presented to you. Choose **1** to install this as a new
    package and press **Enter**.

    Once the newpkg program has begun, it will process each package
    in the current directory until it has run through them all. If a package
    comes up that is already installed, or if you don't want to install it, then
    choose option **3** to skip the package and continue on with the others.
    You should reboot your Nokia appliance after each new Check Point
    package that you install; do not install them all simultaneously.

6. When the installation of SVN is finished, exit the newpkg installation and reboot with the command *sync; sync; reboot.*

7. When the system boots up, log in to Voyager and enable the SVN package.

   - Click **Manage Installed Packages.**

   - Turn on the new NG SVN package.

   - Click **Apply** | **Save.**

8. When done in Voyager, type *newpkg −i* once again and press **Enter** from the /var/admin directory.

9. Choose the option for localfile system number **4** and press **Enter**.

10. Type a period (.) for your current directory (/var/admin) and press **Enter**.

11. If you have an earlier version of VPN-1/FireWall-1 installed, then choose to number **1** to install this as a new package. If an earlier version of Check Point is currently enabled, select number **2** to upgrade this package from the existing, enabled version. If upgrading then:

    - Choose the package you are upgrading from the available choices.

    - Verify that you want to continue and that the correct packages are being processed by pressing **Enter**.

12. When the installation is complete, exit the newpkg installation and reboot by typing: **sync**; **sync**; **reboot**.

Configuring VPN-1/FireWall-1 NG AI on Nokia

If VPN-1/FireWall-1 NG is installed on your Nokia appliance, but it hasn't been configured, then you must run cpconfig before attempting to start the new package. If you just received your Nokia fresh from the factory NG AI is probably pre-installed installed, but you will still need to run cpconfig before the package will run properly. This is because you must accept the license agreement, choose which components you want to run (management and/or enforcement module), and configure licenses, administrators, GUI clients, etc. Your configuration options are the same as your options on the Solaris platform. See Figure 2.68 for the output of cpconfig on an NG FP1 Nokia appliance.

Figure 2.68 cpconfig on Nokia

After the NG package is installed on your system, you must run cpconfig to configure the package. Follow these steps to configure and activate your VPN-1/FireWall-1 NG package.

1. Run cpconfig and go through each screen. It is highly recommended that you do not enter CTRL-C at any time during the initial cpconfig configuration screens.

2. When finished with cpconfig, log in to Voyager and enable your NG package (see Figure 2.69).

   ■ Click **Manage Installed Packages**.

   ■ Turn off the old FireWall-1 package if enabled.

   ■ Turn on the new NG AI package.

   ■ Click **Apply | Save**.

   The Nokia package management makes it simple to back out of an upgrade. As you can see, it is easy to toggle back and forth between installed packages. You can also switch back and forth between IPSO images from Voyager's "Manage IPSO Images" page. After enabling or disabling a package or IPSO image, you must reboot your firewall. It is also very important to ensure that you do not leave two packages which would conflict (i.e. CPShared NG FP3 and CPShared NG AI) enabled at the same time.

Figure 2.69 Managing Installed Packages

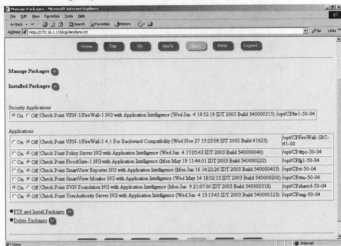

> **NOTE**
>
> Remember to always click **Apply** and then **Save** when making changes in the Voyager GUI. If you don't save your changes, then they will not be retained following a reboot.

3. After making changes to the FW-1 packages, then you must reboot the system again. You can either choose to restart the system from the Voyager GUI, or exit Voyager and type **sync**; **sync**; **reboot** from the command line to restart the box.

Installing Check Point VPN-1/FireWall-1 NG AI on SecurePlatform

Check Point's SecurePlatform operating system (Figure 2.70) is a pre-hardened, performance-tuned version of Linux that Check Point created and supports directly at no cost. Check Point provides SecurePlatform to its customers as another of the many platforms on which its software can be installed. SecurePlatform can turn a normal server into a network appliance in mere minutes.

Many "appliances" are often just x86 servers—sometimes with a specialized operating system or a few other basic features. Most times they are also more expensive than servers. SecurePlatform also takes advantage of the enormous and continued advancements in the open server market. Intel has continued to produce unprecedented performance in their processors. Hardware manufacturers like Dell, IBM, HP, and even Sun have been producing x86 servers that are inexpensive. Coupled with SecurePlatform, very high performance can be achieved at a very low cost. For example, a server that retails for around $5,000 at the time of this writing can process in excess of 3Gbps of traffic. Often, the question comes up, "How does SecurePlatform compare with Nokia's IPSO?" IPSO comes with web-based configuration of routing protocols, high availability (HA) and load sharing capabilities built-in, as well as the ability to have multiple versions of the operating system installed all at no extra cost. SecurePlatform does not currently have as many features in the web interface, but it runs on less expensive hardware, has routing protocols configured via the command line, and HA is now enabled in new licenses but load sharing is a separate license at extra cost. Check Point is placing much effort into developing the SecurePlatform operating system, but often the choice for SecurePlatform is based on the price and performance.

In addition, Check Point provides support for the operating system and all the updates (which can also be distributed via SmartUpdate) at no cost. Any hardware issues would be handled by your hardware manufacturer, but any software, driver, operating system, etc. issues are handled through you support contract with Check Point. This provides for a very cost-effective security solution for companies while providing a single source of support. This level of performance at such a low cost in combination with SmartDefense makes providing security to high-speed LANs a reality.

Figure 2.70 Check Point's SecurePlatform GUI

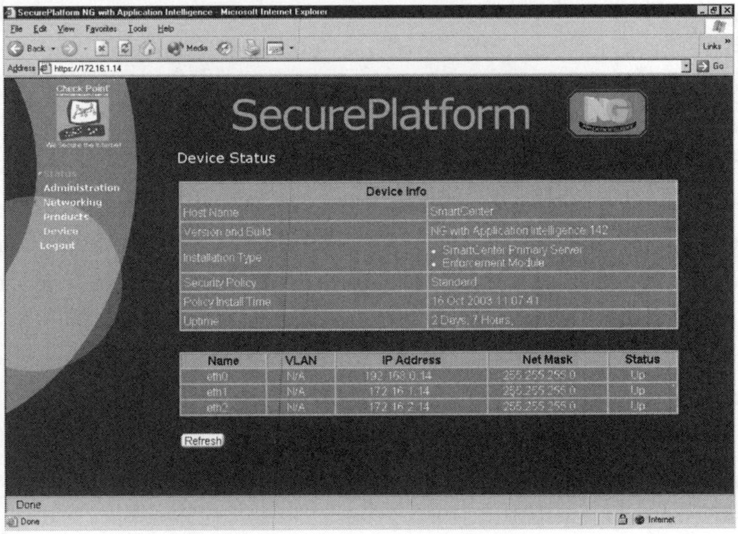

Installing and Configuring Check Point SecurePlatform AI

Check Point's SecurePlatform is streamlined to be installed easily and quickly. Simply place the CD in the server, set the BIOS to boot from CD, and boot the computer. The installation can be done via the serial port or the console. The only questions you will be asked during this part of the installation is what language you want the installation to be in and what IP address you wish to use to complete the second phase of the installation. At this point, the installation program will format the first drive it finds, partition it appropriately, install the software and prompt you for a reboot. After reboot, you will complete the installation by going to https://<IP Address you previously configured> to configure the rest of the interfaces, install the packages, and configure the management station or firewall.

Check Point's SecurePlatform is not simply an easy installation of Linux with web-based management. Check Point has gone through the work of hardening the operating system and even making the command-line access to the operating system similar to other appliances. For example, when you login to the system via the console, serial port, or SSH, you will be presented with a restricted shell that only allows a few select commands to be executed. The available commands depend on which packages are installed and the configuration of those packages.

Illustration 2.16 shows the commands available on a system with SmartCenter, VPN-1/FireWall-1, and the Policy Server installed. Simply executing *?* will give a list of the available commands.

Illustration 2.16 cpshell Usage

```
[patty.theCurb.net]# ?
Commands are:
?                  - Print list of available commands
LSMcli             - SmartLSM command line
LSMenabler         - Enable SmartLSM
SDSUtil            - Software Distribution Server utility
addarp             - Add permanent ARP table entries
adduser            - Add new user
arp                - Display/manipulate the arp table
audit              - Display/edit commands entered in shell
backup             - Backup configuration
checkuserlock      - Check if user is locked
cp_conf            - CheckPoint system configuration utility
cpconfig           - Check Point software configuration utility
cphaprob           - Defines critical process of High Availability
cphastart          - Enables the High Availability feature on the machine
cphastop           - Disables the High Availability feature on the machine
cpinfo             - Show Check Point diagnostics information
cplic              - Add/Remove Check Point licenses
cpshared_ver       - Show SVN Foundation version
cpstart            - Start Check Point products installed
cpstat             - Show Check Point statistics info
cpstop             - Stop Check Point products installed
date               - Set/show date
delarp             - Remove permanent ARP table entries
deluser            - Remove existing user
diag               - Send system diagnostics information
dns                - Add/remove/show domain name resolving servers
domainname         - Set/show domain name
exit               - Switch to standard mode/Logout
expert             - Switch to expert mode
```

Continued

www.syngress.com

Illustration 2.16 cpshell Usage

```
fips              - Turns on/off FIPS mode
fw                - VPN-1/FireWall-1 commands
fwaccel           - SecureXL commands
fwm               - FW-1/VPN-1 management utility
help              - Print list of available commands
hostname          - Set/show host name
hosts             - Add/remove/show local hosts/IP mappings
idle              - Set/show auto logout time in minutes
ifconfig          - Configure/store network interfaces
lockout           - Configure lockout parameters
log               - Log rotation control
netstat           - Show network statistics
ntp               - Configure ntp and start synchronization client
ntpstart          - Start NTP clock synchronization client
ntpstop           - Stop NTP clock synchronization client
passwd            - Change password
patch             - Install/Upgrade utility
ping              - Ping a host
reboot            - Reboot gateway
restore           - Restore configuration
route             - Configure/store routing tables
scroll            - Allow scrolling the output of various commands
showusers         - List SecurePlatform administrators
shutdown          - Shut down gateway
sim               - SecureXL Implementation Module commands
sysconfig         - Configure your SecurePlatform Gateway
time              - Set/show time
timezone          - Set/show the time zone
top               - Show the most active system processes
traceroute        - Trace the route to a host
unlockuser        - Unlock user
vconfig           - Configure Virtual LANs
ver               - Print the version
vpn               - Control VPN
webui             - Configure web UI
```

sysconfig is a menu–driven system for configuring the properties of the OS such as routing, date/time, and IP addresses. Expert requires another password (should be a different one) and presents the administrator a full Unix shell for advanced configurations. A detailed explanation of the commands as well as how to manage and appropriately size SecurePlatform is available in the sister book to this one: Check Point NG VPN-1/FireWall-1: Advanced Configuration and Troubleshooting (Syngress Publishing, ISBN: 1-931836-97-3).

Summary

The beginning of this chapter started out by preparing you to install the Check Point VPN-1/FireWall-1 NG with Application Intelligence product on a computer. There are several steps you can take to prepare your host computer prior to turning it into a firewall. First, make sure that your hardware meets and exceeds the minimum system requirements provided by Check Point. You will then need to install a base operating system, apply OS patches, configure and test your network interface cards and DNS, enable IP forwarding, disable any unnecessary services, and populate your hosts file with at least the external IP address of your firewall, which is configured on the first interface card in your computer.

Next, you will need to prepare for the various Check Point installation screens, you should know in advance which server/gateway components to choose and to be prepared for the initial configuration options by obtaining a license in advance, deciding on administrators' usernames, passwords, and privileges, and statically assigning IP addresses to your administrator's workstations so that you can add them as GUI clients.

If you are installing the VPN-1/FireWall-1 NG software on a Windows server, then you can start the installation wizard by inserting the CD or running windows\wrapper\demo32.exe. The SVN Foundation will be installed before any other Check Point components. After the installation wizard is done copying files, it will run through the initial configuration screens of Licenses, Administrators, GUI Clients, and then the CA initialization screens. Once the configuration is complete, you will need to reboot your firewall. To run the Configuration Tool again, select **Start | Programs | Check Point SmartConsole R54| Check Point Configuration NG.**

To uninstall the VPN-1/FireWall-1 NG software from a Windows System, you must uninstall the SVN foundation last. As the name suggests, this is the base of the VPN-1/FireWall-1 installation, and it cannot be removed prior to removing any components that depend on it. After uninstalling VPN-1/FireWall-1 you must reboot.

If you are installing the VPN-1/FireWall-1 NG software on Solaris 2.7 or 2.8, make sure you have the correct patches applied, and that you are in either 32- or 64-bit mode according to the system requirements in Table 2.1 in the beginning of the chapter. To install via CD-ROM, you will be running the ./UnixInstallScript. If you are installing from files, then you should unzip and untar the package, and then run *pkgadd −d* . from the directory where the package is located. The SVN Foundation package must be installed prior to installing VPN-1/FireWall-1; the UnixInstallScript will take care of this for you. After the installation program is done copying files, you will go through the initial configuration screens, which are Licenses, Administrators, GUI Clients, SNMP Extension, Group Permissions, and CA initialization. You can configure the firewall again at any time by running the *cpconfig* command. After installing VPN-1/FireWall-1, you must reboot.

After rebooting your firewall, an InitialPolicy will be installed that prohibits all connections to the firewall server. You can unload the InitialPolicy with the command *fw unloadlocal*. Keep in mind also that you must su to root with the dash (*su -*) in order to obtain the right environment variables to run the *fw unload* and most other FireWall-1 commands, including *cpconfig*.

To uninstall VPN-1/FireWall-1 on Solaris, use the *pkgrm* command. The first time you try to remove a Primary SmartCenter Server, the uninstall will fail. Simply run *pkgrm* a second time to successfully remove the package. Reboot your computer after uninstalling the VPN-1/FireWall-1 NG AI package.

If you are installing the VPN-1/FireWall-1 NG AI package on a Nokia appliance, make sure that you are on IPSO 3.7 before you begin. Like all the other platforms, you must install the SVN foundation prior to installing the VPN-1/FireWall-1 package. Also, you should reboot after each new package you install. You can toggle between installed packages in the Voyager GUI under the **Manage Installed Packages** link. Be sure to click **Apply** and **Save** after making any changes in Voyager. After the Check Point VPN-1/FireWall-1 package is installed, you must run *cpconfig* from the command line in order to finish the installation procedure.

Check Point's SecurePlatform provides a superb price/performance point while reducing administrative overhead and support complexity.

Solutions Fast Track

Before You Begin

- ☑ Your hardware must meet or exceed the minimum system requirements. Your hardware will determine the throughput performance of your firewall.

- ☑ Obtain your VPN-1/FireWall-1 licenses before you start installing the firewall software. The built-in evaluation license will only be valid for 15 days.

☑ You should configure the external IP address on the first interface that comes up on your firewall. This external IP should be configured in your hosts file to resolve to the hostname of the computer.

☑ IP forwarding must be enabled.

☑ Disable any unnecessary services on your operating system.

☑ Make sure DNS is configured properly, and get a PTR record setup for each NAT address you will be using on your firewall.

☑ Be prepared to answer questions during installation about your licenses, administrators, GUI clients, SNMP extension, and group permissions.

☑ Read the software release notes prior to installing or upgrading.

☑ Check Point Express requires a hotfix supplement for the licenses to work correctly on NG with Application Intelligence (R54).

Installing Check Point VPN-1/FireWall-1 NG on Windows

☑ Begin the installation by inserting the Check Point Next Generation CD.

☑ The SVN foundation must be installed first.

☑ The default folder installation location for VPN-1/FireWall-1 is c:\winnt\fw1\NG.

☑ A reboot after installing the VPN-1/FireWall-1 software should be performed.

☑ Configure your firewall licenses, administrators, GUI clients, and CA at any time by choosing **Start | Programs | Check Point Management Clients | Check Point Configuration NG**.

Uninstalling Check Point VPN-1/FireWall-1 NG on Windows

☑ The SVN foundation must be removed last.

☑ Remove packages by selecting **Control Panel | Add/Remove Programs**.

☑ Reboot after uninstalling VPN-1/FireWall-1.

Installing Check Point VPN-1/FireWall-1 NG on Solaris

- ☑ Begin the installation by inserting the Check Point Next Generation CD and running./UnixInstallScript.

- ☑ When installing from files, use the *pkgadd −d* command.

- ☑ The SVN foundation package CPshrd-54 must be installed first.

- ☑ Initial configuration screens include Licenses, Administrators, GUI Clients, SNMP Extension, Group Permissions, and CA initialization.

- ☑ A reboot after installing the VPN-1/FireWall-1 CPfw1-54 package should be performed.

- ☑ After reboot, the firewall will load the InitialPolicy, blocking any connection to the firewall. The policy can be unloaded by typing *fw unloadlocal*.

- ☑ You must *su −* to root to run *cpconfig*, which allows an administrator to reconfigure the firewall at any time.

Uninstalling Check Point VPN-1/FireWall-1 NG on Solaris

- ☑ Remove packages with the *pkgrm* command.

- ☑ The SVN foundation CPshrd-54 package must be uninstalled last.

- ☑ The first time you remove the Primary SmartCenter Server, the pkgrm will fail. Simply run it again to successfully remove the package.

- ☑ A reboot after uninstalling the VPN-1/FireWall-1 CPfw1-54 package should be performed.

Installing Check Point VPN-1/FireWall-1 NG on Nokia

- ☑ IPSO 3.7 is required before installing VPN-1/FireWall-1 NG FP1 on a Nokia appliance.

- ☑ The command *newimage* is used to install new IPSO images.

- ☑ The command *newpkg* is used to install new packages.
- ☑ The SVN foundation must be installed first.
- ☑ Reboot after installing the SVN foundation package.
- ☑ Reboot after installing the VPN-1/FireWall-1 package.
- ☑ After the package is installed, run *cpconfig* to finish the installation process.
- ☑ Use the Voyager GUI to activate installed packages via the **Manage Installed Packages** link. Always **Apply** and **Save** any change you make in the Voyager GUI.

Installing Check Point VPN-1/FireWall-1 NG AI on SecurePlatform

- ☑ SecurePlatform is a pre-hardened, performance-tuned version of Linux created and supported directly by Check Point at no charge.
- ☑ SecurePlatform turns a standard server into a security appliance in minutes.
- ☑ SecurePlatform has two levels of access to the command line: restricted and expert.

Frequently Asked Questions

The following Frequently Asked Questions, answered by the authors of this book, are designed to both measure your understanding of the concepts presented in this chapter and to assist you with real-life implementation of these concepts. To have your questions about this chapter answered by the author, browse to **www.syngress.com/solutions** and click on the **"Ask the Author"** form. You will also gain access to thousands of other FAQs at ITFAQnet.com.

Q: If I want to install FloodGate-1 or other add-ons to my firewall, in what order should I install the packages?

A: If installing from individual files, you should install the SVN foundation first, then VPN-1/FireWall-1 NG, and then FloodGate-1 NG or any other Check Point NG products. The wrapper handles this by presenting you with options in the correct order and installing them according to Check Point's recommendations.

Q: I installed NG AI Primary SmartCenter on a Nokia appliance, but I can't log in with the Check Point NG management clients. What am I doing wrong?

A: Your SmartConsole clients must be on the same build as your SmartCenter Server. Verify that your IP address is listed in the gui-clients file and upgrade your GUI clients to NG with Application Intelligence. If you have applied a hotfix, an updated version of the SmartConsole clients may be required.

Q: I just upgraded one of my 4.1 firewall modules to NG AI, and it's not able to fetch a policy. What can I do?

A: Verify that you have changed the module's version to NG in its workstation object, and that you have initialized SIC. You may have to push the policy the first time after an upgrade.

Q: It doesn't seem like my Nokia is forwarding packets. How do I enable IP forwarding on a Nokia?

A: It should be enabled by default. If you believe that this may have been disabled, use the command *ipsofwd on admin* to enable IP forwarding in your Nokia. For help with the *ipsofwd* command, type **ipsofwd –help** to display the usage.

Q: What are the most important elements of a high-performance SecurePlatform configuration?

A: Of course, a fast CPU with ample cache (i.e. the Intel Xeon processor) is very important, but SecurePlatform can fully take advantage of multiple processors, so don't be afraid of installing two or more very fast processors. Extra memory is required for handling large numbers of connections. Most times, however, the limitation is the bus of the system. Multiple, fast PCI-X buses are the key to creating a very fast, high-throughput firewall. Refer to Check Point's Platform Selection Guide to view what different configurations of Dell, HP, IBM, and Sun systems running SecurePlatform yield with regards to throughput numbers. To get more out of your current Solaris or Linux installation, license and install the Performance Pack that will replace the stock kernel with a Check Point compiled (SunTone-Certified on the Solaris platform) kernel yielding tremendous gains in performance as well.

Chapter 3

Using the Graphical Interface

Solutions in this Chapter:

- Managing Objects
- Adding Rules
- Global Properties
- SmartUpdate
- SmartView Tracker
- SmartView Status

☑ Summary

☑ Solutions Fast Track

☑ Frequently Asked Questions

Introduction

Once the VPN-1/FW-1 software is installed and configured, you are ready to log into the graphical user interface (GUI) and start composing your objects and rule bases. This chapter walks you through all of the options available for creating various objects, and shows you some of the features that you can utilize in the SmartDashboard to manipulate your rules.

This chapter also shows you how to access the firewall's implied rules, and explains the global properties that affect every security policy you create. It is important to know why your firewall is allowing pings if you have not explicitly defined them in your rule base.

After examining your policy options, you are shown how to access your firewall logs and system status. The Track options you choose in your policy will affect the outcome of your logs. You may choose to log some rules and not others. This chapter also describes ways to make selections in your SmartView Tracker so that you can view only logs for a specific source Internet Protocol (IP) address or logs for a specific user. The Check Point SmartView Tracker has a high quality interface and is easy to understand.

Managing Objects

Managing objects is the most common task you will perform as a firewall administrator. Luckily, Check Point has made this task much easier. Every year, Check Point wins awards for its manageability, which is a large reason companies continue to choose Check Point Software. While there is a lot of information needed to set the foundation for your rule base, you do not have to put forth a great deal of effort to get that information into a useable format.

Your first task is to log into the FW-1 GUI management client (SmartDashboard). On a Windows system, simply start the SmartDashboard or your GUI client by double-clicking its icon. On a Unix system such as Solaris or AIX, execute the *fwpolicy* command found in *$FWDIR/bin*. You will be presented with a login window, as displayed in Figure 3.1. Note that if this is the initial connection from a GUI client, FW-1 will present the management server fingerprint. This is used as a security measure to enable you to validate the identity of that management server.

Once you have logged into the GUI, you will see a lot of information. Do not worry; you can easily customize this default view to show just what you need. You can also add or subtract from this view as needed. A couple of changes have been made from previous versions of the SmartDashboard (named the "Policy Editor" in previous versions). Figure 3.1 shows you the new default view.

Figure 3.1 SmartDashboard

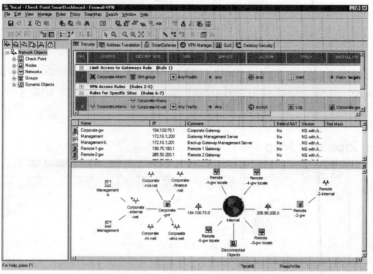

The window panes are called (from left moving clockwise) the Objects Tree, Rule Base, Objects List, and SmartMap. You can toggle which one is displayed by selecting **View** from the SmartDashboard menu, as displayed in Figure 3.2.

Figure 3.2 View Selection

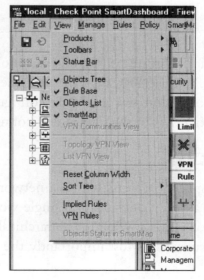

The Objects Tree gives a concise and orderly view of the defined objects of each available type. If you are asked which networks are defined, the Objects Tree will give you the quickest answer. The Rule Base enables you to instantly sum up the totality of what your firewall is enforcing, and also enables you to quickly view network address translation (NAT), Quality of Service (QoS), and Desktop Security rule information. The Objects List presents a little more detail than the Objects Tree about your defined objects.

SmartMap is new in FW-1. This gives you a network map showing the interconnections of all of your defined objects. Figure 3.3 shows that pane enlarged to full screen.

Figure 3.3 Topology Map

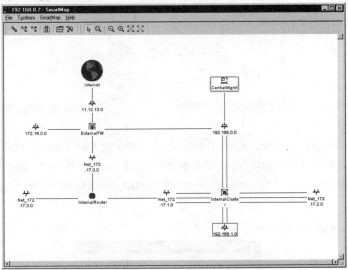

The map is automatically created based on the topology of your objects, and is completely interactive. You can rearrange the placement of the objects and even query them for information and alter their configuration. Click on any link to show the interface properties of the device it is connected to.

Network Objects

Network objects are simply the objects within a network. For example, an object can be a network range, a group of users, or a single workstation. Objects can also be groups of other objects, allowing for hierarchical layering and a more concise and descriptive rule base. Most importantly, the objects of interest within a network must be properly defined before using them in a FW-1 rule. As certain network objects are defined, they will automatically be added and arranged within the SmartMap.

Network objects can be defined in several ways, with the most common method being through the Network Objects Manager, which is shown in Figure 3.4. This GUI window enables you to create, delete, and alter all of the various types of network entities. To access this screen, select **Manage | Network Objects** from the SmartDashboard GUI.

Figure 3.4 Network Objects Manager

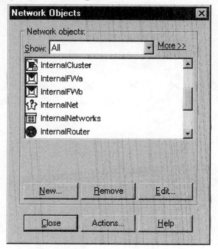

Check Point Gateway or Host Object

The Check Point gateway or host object defines a system with Check Point products installed on it, and contains many options. This computer may be a VPN-1/FW-1 system, a VPN-1 Net device, a Secondary Management Station, a log server, or any combination of those and more. This flexibility comes with a slight increase in complexity. The Check Point gateway or host properties page contains many more options than its counterpart in previous versions of FW-1, but luckily there is intelligence built in to the window. The branches on the left become visible as they are needed. A simple firewall gateway or host will have limited options, but the choices expand when dealing with Check Point installed products. Table 3.1 defines some of the more common configurations and their displayed options.

Table 3.1 Configuration Matrix

	FW-1	VPN-1 Pro	VPN-1 Net	Floodgate-1	Secondary Management Station	Log Server	UserAuthority Web Plugin
General	X	X	X	X	X	X	X
Topology	X	X	X	X	X	X	X
NAT	X	X	X	X	X	X	X
Authentication	X	X	X	X			
VPN	X	X	X		X		
Remote Access	X	X	X				
Logs and Masters	X	X	X	X	X	X	
Capacity Optimization		X	X	X			
UserAuthority Web Access	X	X		X	X	X	X
Advanced	X	X	X	X	X		

The General configuration window, as shown in Figure 3.5, enables you to associate a system name and IP address with this object. If the name is resolvable via Domain Name System (DNS) or Windows Internet Name Service (WINS), you can use the **Get Address** button to retrieve the IP address or you can type it in manually. If this system will have a dynamically assigned IP address (via dynamic host control protocol [DHCP]), check the **Dynamic Address** box, which will disable the IP Address field. The Comment field is optional. Like all FW-1 objects, you can assign a color to the object. The remaining fields have special meanings when selected, which impact the way VPN-1/FW-1 interacts with them. A gateway means that there are multiple interfaces on the device that will be routing traffic. A host can also have multiple interfaces, but will likely only be terminating connections, not routing them through.

If you accidentally define a system as a host instead of as a gateway, you can right-click on the object in the Object Tree and select **Convert to Gateway**. Similarly, you can convert a gateway to a host or even convert a node to a Check Point system. The difference between a host and a gateway is that it will be assumed that a host is an endpoint that will only receive traffic for itself (even if it has multiple interfaces), whereas a gateway will be routing traffic between the multiple interfaces it has.

Figure 3.5 Check Point Gateway Properties, General Properties Window

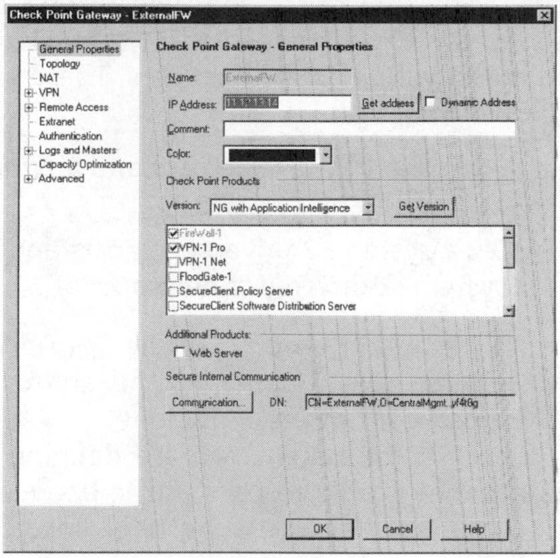

- **Check Point Products** This section designates the products and version of Check Point products installed on this system. As you select products, others become grayed out as they are not compatible. For example, VPN-1 Net and VPN-1 Pro are two separate licensing schemes for the same software and are not able to be mixed on the same system.

■ **Additional Products** Here, the Web Server option is available. This option is also available for Node objects. This defines whether or not the Cross Site Scripting inspection of SmartDefense will be applied to this system. By selecting this, you will also see a new option on the left-hand side of the window.

■ **Secure Internal Communication** This is where you define the activation key for setting up a secure channel between the enforcement module and management station. You can also verify that you are able to securely communicate with this host inside this section.

Configuring & Implementing…

What's in a Name?

Although the value in the Name field does not have to be anything but unique, it is strongly recommended that you use an actual resolvable name. It is also strongly recommended that you include the hostname to address mappings in your systems host files. These files can be found in the following locations:

■ For Unix systems, edit the */etc/hosts* and */etc/networks* files

■ For Win32 systems, edit the %SYSTEMDIR%\system32\drivers\etc\hosts and %SYS-TEMDIR%\system32\drivers\etc\networks

This will ensure the proper function of the Get Address function. Be careful to maintain these files. Hostname and address changes could lead to potential exposure if not properly done.

Also, if the Check Point system you are defining is a gateway (a multi-homed system that is able to pass traffic between its interfaces), and you are using Internet Key Exchange (IKE) encryption, be sure to specify the **outside** address. If you fail to do so, IKE encryption will not function properly. Remember that this address is the address that the Management Station communicates with, so this change may cause

Continued

some routing problems. In our example, we could either set ExternalFW (specifically the 192.168.0.2 interface) as our default route from the management station or set a static route for 11.12.13.14 to 192.168.0.2. Keep in mind that most of the problems engineers run into in the field are routing related, so when debugging a connectivity issue, check the routing first.

The Node Object

The node object is used to define a single system (host) or a system that will be routing traffic (gateway). A node is usually used to create a placeholder for a single IP address. To create a new node object, select **New | Node** from the Network Objects management window. This will present you with the panel shown in Figure 3.6.

Figure 3.6 Node Properties

The Network Object

The network object defines a group of hosts or, more specifically, a network range such as a subnet. When defining individual systems as workstations becomes too tedious or otherwise untenable, it is easy to arrange them with this object type. To create a new network object, select **New | Network** from the Network Objects management window. This will present you with the panel shown in Figure 3.7.

Figure 3.7 Network Properties: General Window

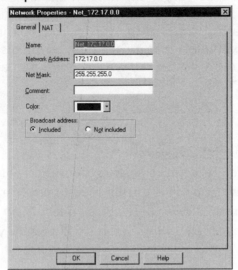

The General window allows some simple configuration information to be entered, such as an IP address, netmask, and a comment. You should already be familiar (at least slightly) with IP subnetting. In the example panel, the network is 172.17.0.X with a 24-bit subnet, producing a mask of 255.255.255.0. In this case, you enter the host portion as a zero. Keep in mind, though, that the host portion might not always be set at zero, and might not always fall on a tidy boundary. For example, you might have a network address of 10.3.4.128, with a subnet of 255.255.255.128. When in doubt, consult your local networking expert or become one. To ease your understanding, there are many subnet calculators available online such as the one at: www.telusplanet.net/public/sparkman/netcalc.htm

As with all object types, a color can be assigned as well. The Broadcast Address field denotes whether you desire the broadcast addresses to be included within the defined network. The broadcast address is defined as the first and last possible IP within that range. The NAT panel includes the option to establish automatic translation rules. (NAT is covered in detail in Chapter 5.)

For added simplicity, when you define interfaces on Check Point objects, it automatically shows each attached network as an "implied network" in SmartMap. You can right-click on any one of them and select **Actualize Network**. This will automatically create *Net_<network address>*, as shown above, as a naming scheme and fill in the network and subnet. Once an object has been actualized and an object has been created, it can be used in rules as well as in the other SmartConsole clients.

The Domain Object

The domain object is used to group hosts by commonly used techniques. A machine is determined to be within the domain if a reverse DNS lookup on the machine's IP address yields the proper domain information. Figure 3.8 illustrates this panel, which is accessed by selecting **New | Domain** from the Network Objects management window.

Figure 3.8 Domain Properties

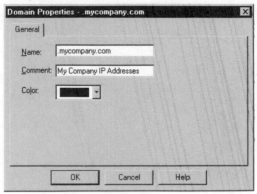

Notice that in the previous example the domain name begins with a period. You may be wondering how FW-1 knows what to do with a domain object. When a domain object is used in the rule base as a source or destination, FW-1 will attempt to do a reverse DNS lookup (that is, getting the name for a specified IP) on the appropriate portion of the incoming packet. If the lookup yields the domain information, you have a match. If there is no reverse record, the object will be useless. It is also possible that, through DNS poisoning, this sort of object could lead to a security breach. Furthermore, the performance overhead for looking up each address as well as the latency added on making a rule decision while waiting for a DNS resolution is significant. For these reasons and others, Check Point does not recommend the use of Domain objects in your rule base. If you decide to use them, use them as close to the bottom of the rule base as possible.

Open Security Extension Device

Open Security Extension (OSE) technology allows FW-1 to manage third-party devices that support these extensions. Most notable among these devices are Cisco routers running IOS version 9 and higher. The number of devices that you may manage depends on your license. The configuration for an OSE-compliant device features five windows. To create a new OSE device, select **New | OSE Device** from the Network Objects management window. Figure 3.9 illustrates the General window.

Figure 3.9 OSE Device: General Window

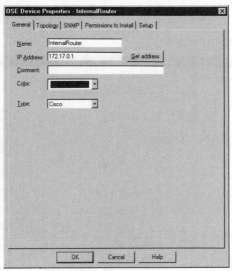

This window enables you to specify some of the basic information about the device, specifically the IP address, name, comment, and device type. The device type may be either of the following:

- Nortel

- Cisco

- 3Com

When a device from this category is managed by the firewall, access control lists (ACLs) are generated based on the security policy. As with other object types, the **Get address** button will attempt to resolve the specified name to an IP address, saving you that one step.

The Topology window is identical to that of its counterpart for the other devices. The main caveat is that at least one interface must be defined (as opposed to, say, a simple workstation) or the ACL entries will not be created successfully. Anti-spoofing and related topology information are also defined by editing the interface properties, just as with a workstation. If you choose to only allow certain administrators to manage the ACLs on this router, you can specify a group of administrators defined in the GUI (not in *cpconfig*) in the **Permissions to Install** page. However, there are some additional steps to take, which are accomplished by editing the information on the Setup window.

The Setup window differs depending on the OSE type specified on the General window. The window as displayed with a Cisco router, is shown in Figure 3.10.

Figure 3.10 Cisco OSE Setup Window

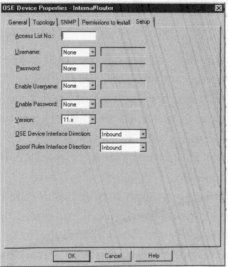

The following fields are displayed in this window:

- **Access List No.** The number of the ACL that will be applied.

- **Username** This is the exec mode username that will be used for initial access to the device. It, along with the remaining drop-down lists, can be set to None, Known, or Prompt. If set to Known, the gray box to the right will become active and allow the entry of a username.

- **Password** Enter the password associated with the exec mode username.

- **Enable Username** The name, if any, of a user with privileged exec access.

- **Enable Password** The password associated with the privileged username.

- **Version** The IOS version installed on this router.

- **OSE Device Interface Direction** The direction in which to enforce the security policy. This can be Inbound, Outbound, or Eitherbound.

- **Spoof Rules Interface Direction** The direction in which to enforce anti-spoofing behavior. This can be Inbound, Outbound, or Eitherbound.

The fields for the 3Com and Nortel devices are similar in their requirements, and the security policy is enforced in an identical manner.

Interoperable Devices

An interoperable device is used to define any third-party device you wish to establish a site-to-site virtual private network (VPN) to. This device could be a Cisco Router, a Netscreen Firewall, or one of literally hundreds of IKE-compatible products from as many vendors. In all actuality, you will not need to know the type of device on the other end, however, it can help you debug problems if you run into them, as not all vendors interpret the IKE Request for Comments (RFC) specifications the same.

The configuration is pretty straightforward, with the common rules applying. Define the name, IP address, and an optional comment. Then define the topology (VPN domain) of the remote object. Figure 3.11 illustrates the configuration panel. To open this panel, select **New | Interoperable Device**.

Figure 3.11 Interoperable Device General Properties

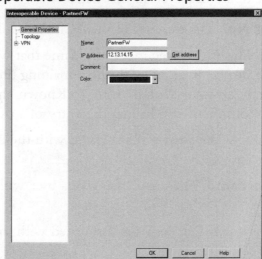

The Group Object

The group object can be used to manage other objects of dissimilar types. There are three types of groups that can be defined within FW-1. To create a new group, select **New | Group** from the Network Objects management window. The group types are as follows:

- Simple group
- Group with Exclusion
- UserAuthority Server group

A Simple group is a collection of network objects. A Group with Exclusion allows some granular control over the contents of a group. For example, if you are working in a network with a flat topology, you may be in a situation where there is not much physical separation within the network. A group of this type enables you to force some structure here. Figure 3.12 illustrates a Simple group.

Inside the **Manage | Network Objects**, you can only specify Network Objects. A Network Objects group is different than a User Group.

Figure 3.12 Group Properties

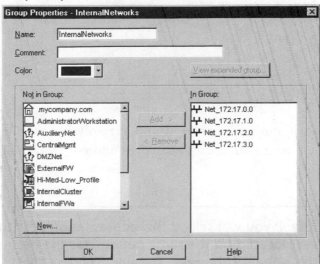

A Group with Exclusion is similar, with the difference being that you specify a major group, defined by Check Point as an "outer group." This will be the group that is included for this definition. You then specify minor, or inner, groups. These will be the groups culled out and excluded from the major group.

Logical Server

The Logical Server group (available by selecting **New | Logical Server** from the Network Objects window), enables you to group like servers (FTP, HTTP, SMTP, and so forth) to be treated as one and used in a sort of resource sharing or server pooling. Note that this is an optional feature and may not be included within your FW-1 installation. Workload is distributed among these servers in a user-configurable manner. Figure 3.13 shows the configuration options for this object type.

Figure 3.13 Logical Server Properties Window

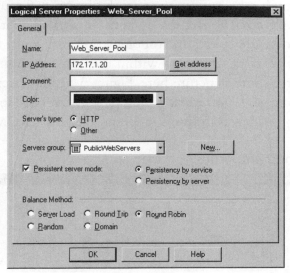

As usual, the name must be entered, and, if resolvable, the **Get address** button can be used to gather the associated IP address.

NOTE

Regarding the IP you will select; this address should be that of a non-existent server located on the same network as the destination servers, but can also be that of the FW-1 module. Think of this IP as a virtual IP address. It will be used by the clients to connect to the Logical Server group, and therefore cannot belong to any one member of that group.

The Server's Type feature defines the method of load balancing, or more specifically, the type of algorithm used. The two methods behave very differently. For example, with HTTP selected, only the initial connection will be handled by the logical server address. A redirection is sent to the client informing their browser of the new IP (that of the selected destination server), and the remainder of the conversation goes forth without the intervention of the firewall module. If **Other** is selected, address translation is performed and the conversation is balanced per connection, with the firewall module constantly involved, unless **Persistent server mode** is checked.

The **Servers** section enables you to select the server group that will make up this logical group. If selected, **Persistent server mode** allows some fine-tuning of the balancing mechanism. When enabled, you can enforce connection persistence, meaning you can force packets from an established flow to continue to a single destination. This is very useful for something like an HTTP conversation when using **Other** as the server type. You can select between two modes here: **Persistency by service** and **Persistency by server**. The main difference between the two is that, when the former is selected, only connections to a single server for a single service will have persistency enforced, while in the latter any service on a specific server will be impacted.

The final settings define the type of balancing to be performed. The Balance Method has several possible options.

- **Server Load** FW-1 sends a query using port 18212/UDP, to determine the load of each server. There must consequently be a load-measuring agent on each server to support this method.

- **Round Trip** FW-1 sends a simple Internet Control Message Protocol (ICMP) ping to each server. The fastest round-trip time is chosen as the preferred server. This lacks somewhat, in that the ping is from the firewall to the server, and may not be optimal from a remote client. (Remember, the servers need not be centrally located to participate in a server group.) Also, a ping does not tell you that the HTTP daemon has crashed on the server. As long as the server is up and on the network, regardless of the status of any of its services, traffic will be sent to it.

- **Round Robin** FW-1 selects sequentially from a list. This is among the simplest methods.

- **Random** FW-1 selects randomly from a list.

- **Domain** FW-1 attempts to select the closest server to the client, based on a domain naming convention. This method is not recommended.

Address Range

An address range defines a sequential range of IP addresses for inclusion with a rule base. In previous versions, the Address Range object usage was restricted to the Address Translation rule base only. Starting with Next Generation (NG), the ability to use an Address Range in the Security Policy has been enabled. An Address Range is similar in use to a Network object, with the major difference being that you specify a starting and ending IP address instead of a network number and subnet mask. Figure 3.14 illustrates the General panel for this object type, which is available by selecting **New | Address Range** from the Network Objects management window. As usual, the NAT panel features no special information and is the same as that found on most other object types.

Figure 3.14 Address Range Properties Window

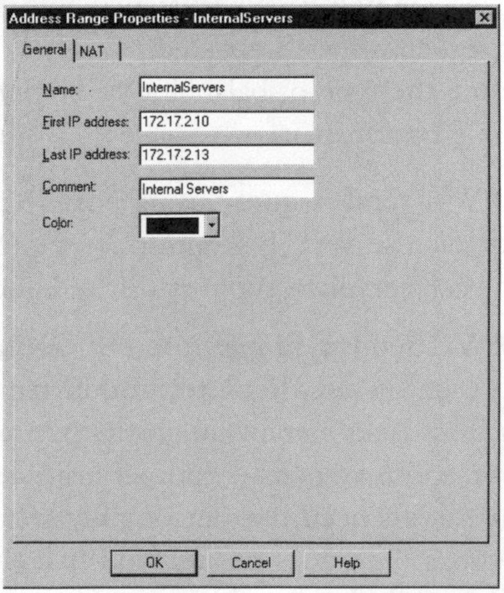

Gateway Cluster

A gateway cluster is a grouping of machines running VPN-1/FW-1 that is grouped together as a means of fail over or load sharing support. Clustering is a complex subject, and configuring it is much more detailed than the majority of other object types. (Detailed coverage of clustering is discussed in Chapter 12.)

The next step is to create your workstation objects. In order to support clustering, you must have at least three objects, two of which must be firewall modules, and one a manager. The workstation object should be created as normal for a machine with FW-1 installed. It is important that the interfaces are properly defined, as anti-spoofing is required for proper high-availability function. Next, you create a new gateway cluster object. The General panel is illustrated in Figure 3.15, and is accessed by selecting **New | Gateway Cluster** from the Network Objects management window.

Figure 3.15 Gateway Cluster—General Panel

This panel allows the initial configuration for the cluster. The name and IP address are defined here, as are the specific Check Point products that will reside within this cluster. Also, you can specify whether you or another party manage the cluster. You can specify on the topology panel which addresses reside behind this cluster. This is similar to the features on a workstation object's interface properties topology panel.

Dynamic Object

A dynamic object is perhaps the most interesting object type supported on FW-1. It is also one of the most useful in a large enterprise, when managing Safe@ appliances or when using dynamically assigned IP address firewalls. This object type enables you to define a logical server type, one in which the actual IP address will resolve differently on each FW-1 machine. This enables you to create rules referencing "mail server" and distribute that policy to several different FW-1 machines, all of which will resolve "mail server" as the proper machine within their realm. NG Application Intelligence (AI) comes with a number of dynamic objects pre-defined. Figure 3.16 shows the basic configuration window, which you can see by selecting **New | Dynamic Object** from the Network Objects management window.

Figure 3.16 Dynamic Object Properties Window

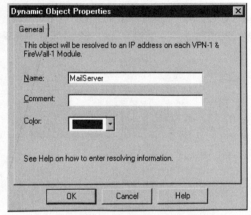

The real key to a dynamic object is the **dynamic_objects** command. This command is run on the firewall module where the name will be resolved, and enables you to specify the values to which it will resolve. Table 3.2 describes this command and its options.

Table 3.2 dynamic-objects Command Options

Option	Explanation
-o <object name>	Specifies the object name to work with. This option is often used with operators such as –a to add addresses to an existing object.
-r <from starting address> <to ending address>	Specifies an address range.
-a <from starting address> <to ending address>	Adds the address of <range> to the object.
-d <from starting address> <to ending address>	Deletes addresses from the object.

Continued

Table 3.2 dynamic-objects Command Options

Option	Explanation
-l	Lists all dynamic objects.
-n <object name>	Creates a new dynamic object; assuming the VPN-1/FW-1 process has been stopped.
-c	Compares the defined dynamic objects to those defined in the objects_5_0.C file.
-do <object name>	Deletes the specified object.
-e	Removes all dynamic object data

Services

The services objects give you a finer level of access control as compared to exclusive use of network entities. With the service object, you can define protocol-specific information like the protocol in use (Transmission Control Protocol [TCP], User Datagram Protocol [UDP], and so forth) and port numbers. FW-1 comes preconfigured with many of the more common services in use today, and further enables you to create custom services based on your unique needs. In addition, SmartDefense updates this list of objects as necessary.

To add, modify, or delete services, access the Services window by clicking **Manage | Services**. From here, you will be able to act on the following service types.

TCP

The TCP service object enables you to define a basic TCP service. Figure 3.17 illustrates this service type, using the DNS service as an example. To bring up this window, select **New | TCP** from the Services Management window.

Figure 3.17 TCP Service Properties

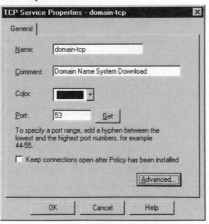

The information for this is very limited. Besides a name and comment, all you have to enter is the destination port number. This can be a specific port, as shown in Figure 3.17, a range (e.g., 1024 through 1028), or a greater-than/less-than definition (e.g., <56). The **Keep connections open after Policy has been installed** checkbox allows all control and data connections utilizing this service to continue until the session has ended, even if they are not allowed by the new policy. This overrides the related setting in Global Properties. There is also an **Advanced** button, which displays the window shown in Figure 3.18.

Figure 3.18 Advanced TCP Service Properties

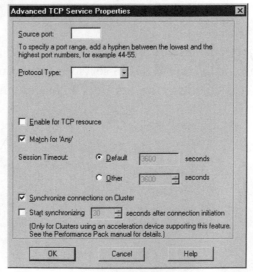

The advanced settings enable you to specify a source port, and allow for the same modifiers as in the General panel's port specification. You can also specify the protocol type that impacts which set of extended security definitions (INSPECT Code or Security Servers) will be applied for this service. . The checkbox marked **Enable for TCP resource**, if checked, enforces screening using a Content Vectoring Protocol (CVP) server, mitigating the intervention of a security server. The next item, **Match for 'Any'** allows connections using this service to be matched when a rule is crafted with 'Any' as the service. There can only be one service for each protocol (i.e., TCP) and port (i.e., 53), that uses the Match for 'Any'. The **Session Timeout** is a local setting meant to allow override of the global session timeout. FW-1 The option to **Synchronize connections on Cluster** enables connections matching this service to be synchronized with other members of a cluster. For connections that do not require synchronization, one can stop them from being synchronized. This reduces synchronization traffic on the synchronization network. Connections can also be synchronized after a certain period of time if utilizing a compatible SecureXL-enabled device. This is useful when a large number of connections are flowing through the firewall and are short-lived. The synchronization of connections of this nature (HTTP, for example) is less useful simply because synchronization consumes gateway resources and the connection will have probably finished by the time a failover happens.

UDP

The UDP service object enables you to define a basic UDP service. An example of this is the NTP service. UDP tracking poses a problem for many firewalls, especially circuit level gateways. Since UDP is connectionless, it is generally an all-or-nothing approach to security. Whole port ranges are often opened to allow UDP traffic, which is not a very nice notion. With FW-1, a second mechanism has been designed to keep track of a virtual "connection."

The General properties are identical to those for TCP, as seen in Figure 3.17. The Advanced options are slightly different, and are therefore depicted in Figure 3.19.

Figure 3.19 Advanced UDP Service Properties

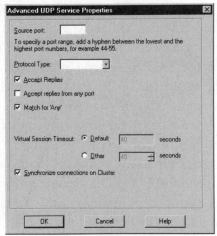

As with the TCP settings, you can specify a source port and a protocol type as well as the ability to selectively synchronize connections. Additionally, there are the familiar checkboxes, but this time with slightly different values. These are as follows:

- **Accept Replies** If checked, allows for a bidirectional communication to take place.

- **Accept replies from any port** Allows the server to reply from any port. An example of the need for this is the Trivial File Transfer Protocol (TFTP) service. This option is not enabled by default.

- **Match for 'Any'** Allows connections using this service to be matched when a rule is crafted with 'Any' as the service.

Remote Procedure Call

Remote Procedure Call (RPC) services are usually tricky for a firewall administrator. RPC-based connections do not use a fixed port number, so allowing these types of connections is either an all-or-nothing exercise. Usually, administrators choose to block all RPC connections on their external firewalls, while being far more permissive within their network boundaries.

To alleviate this potential risk, FW-1 transparently tracks RPC ports. Application information is extracted from the packet in order to identify the program used. FW-1 also maintains a cache that maps RPC program numbers to the assigned port numbers. The configuration panel, viewed by selecting **New | RPC** from the Service management window, is as shown in Figure 3.20.

Figure 3.20 RPC Service Properties

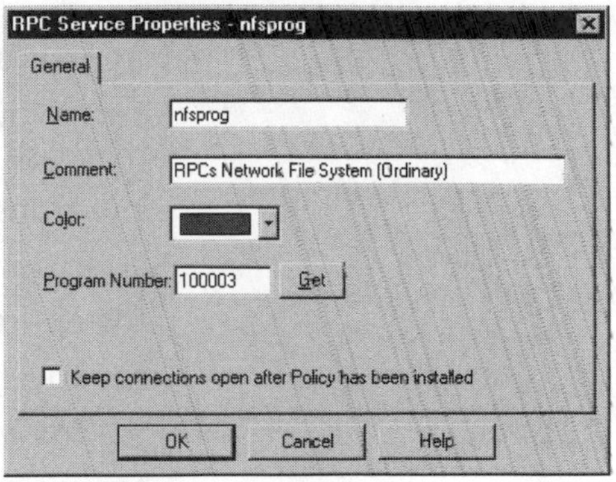

ICMP

ICMP is used for things like network troubleshooting and discovery. Unfortunately, attackers looking to gain information about you also use it. For this reason, many sites block all ICMP traffic. This is not necessary, and may cause more problems than it solves. Using FW-1, you can FW-1pick and choose the specific ICMP types (and even subtypes, or "codes") allowed. Table 3.3 details some of the more useful ICMP types, their associated codes, and their meanings, as defined by the Internet Assigned Numbers Authority (IANA) (www.iana.org/assignments/icmp-parameters). In Check Point NG AI, Stateful ICMP has been added to allow replies and errors to be returned to the requesting application, which removes the need to allow certain types of ICMP traffic into your network just to allow outbound ping and traceroute to function.

Table 3.3 ICMP Codes

ICMP Type	ICMP Code	Explanation
0		Echo (ping) reply
3		Destination unreachable:
	0	-network unreachable
	1	-host unreachable
	2	-protocol unreachable
	3	-port unreachable

Continued

Table 3.3 ICMP Codes

ICMP Type	ICMP Code	Explanation
	4	Dropped because DF (do not fragment) bit was set; fragmentation needed.
	5	Source routing not allowed or otherwise failed.
4		Slow transmission rate
5		Better network path available:
	0	-for entire network
	1	-for specific host
	2	-for tos and entire network
	3	-for tos and specific host
8		Echo (ping) request
11		Time exceeded for reason:
	0	-TTL reached 0 in transit
	1	-fragment reassembly time exceeded.
12		Bad IP header

Figure 3.21 shows the configuration panel for an ICMP service. Using Table 3.3, you can see how simple it would be to create services, and thus rules, to allow the beneficial types of ICMP while excluding those that may do harm.

Figure 3.21 ICMP Service Properties

```
ICMP Service Properties - echo-request              [X]

 General |

    Name:       echo-request

    Comment:    ICMP, echo request

    Color:      [███████]  ▼

    Type:       8

    Code:       [        ]

    □ Keep connections open after Policy has been installed


        [    OK    ]   [  Cancel  ]   [  Help  ]
```

Other

Often called "user-defined" services, **Other** {{FILL IN BLANK}} is a catchall
for whatever is missing. Its presence gives you a great deal of flexibility, but
requires at least a familiarity with the inspect language. The General panel is similar to that found in its cousin objects, allowing you to define a name, add a
comment, and assign a color. It also enables you to define the protocol identifier.
This is a very important field, as it is the key to matching against the incoming
traffic. Figure 3.22 shows the General panel for this service type.

Figure 3.22 User-Defined Service Properties—General Panel

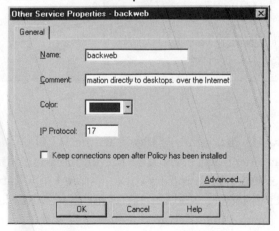

```
Other Service Properties - backweb                  [X]

 General |

    Name:        backweb

    Comment:     mation directly to desktops. over the Internet

    Color:       [███████]  ▼

    IP Protocol: 17

    □ Keep connections open after Policy has been installed

                                            [ Advanced... ]

        [    OK    ]   [  Cancel  ]   [  Help  ]
```

Clicking on the **Advanced** button brings up a screen that allows the entry
of the most crucial part of this object, the Match field. This field is a snippet of

inspect code that will be used to check the incoming packets. It can, therefore, be as complex as you can imagine. This makes the user-defined object a truly powerful tool for the enforcement of very specific requirements.

Group

The group object enables you to combine different protocols. For example, it can be used to define a service whose individual parts must also be separately defined, such as a ping. It consists of an echo request and an echo reply. These can be defined and then combined into a group, and that group used in the rule base. Figure 3.23 displays the configuration window, which is accessed by selecting **New | Group** from the Services Management window.

Figure 3.23 Group Properties

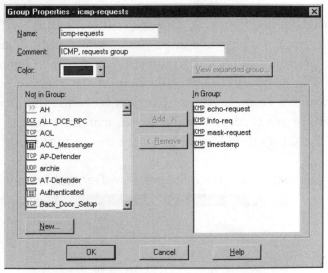

DCE-RPC

This service type works in a similar fashion to the RPC service, in that it tracks DCE-RPC based connections, extracting the information from the packet and creating a virtual session whose information is stored in a local cache. When you define the DCE-RPC service, you are asked for the Universally Unique Identifier (UUID) for the specific interface as well as the protocol type. In NG AI, a service of 0 was defined as a wildcard named ALL_DCE_RPC. This will log the UUID in the Information column in SmartView Tracker. Figure 3.24 illustrates this panel.

Figure 3.24 DCE-RPC Properties

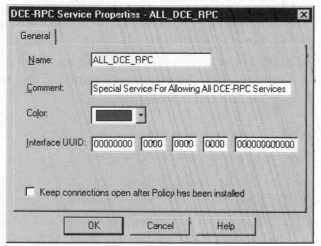

Many administrators define a service for port 135 to enable Microsoft applications (i.e., Exchange) to function through the firewall. This is very dangerous as it subverts for the granular filtering of DCE-RPC, which can have devastating effects. When granular inspection for DCE-RPC is enabled, attacks that do not follow the DCE-RPC specification (like the MSBlaster worm) will be blocked. If you do not know the UUIDs of your programs you can use the ALL_DCE_RPC service to accept the connections and the SmartView Tracker to view the UUIDs being used. It is highly recommended, however, to get the UUIDs from the software vendor directly.

Resources

Resource objects are used to configure content security on FW-1, and will be covered in greater detail in Chapter 7. Content security includes support for the HTTP, FTP, SMTP, and CIFS protocols. FW-1 provides part of this support by using the FireWall-1 Security Servers and the rest using its TCP Streaming technology. For each connection established through the FireWall-1 Security Servers, you are able to control access on a very granular level according to protocol-specific information unique to a specific service. This includes Uniform Resource Locators (URLs), file names, FTP commands, and so on.

Uniform Resource Identifier

A Uniform Resource Identifier (URI) defines how to access resources on the Internet. Most of us are familiar with the URI by another name: URL. A URI can contain HTTP, gopher, and mailto type addresses for specifying different applications to handle the resource. They are represented in the following form: www.syngress.com or mailto:user@mycompany.com

URI for QoS

Another type of URI object is the **URI for QoS**, which is used when defining a rulebase for FloodGate-1. This resource type allows the security administrator to classify certain URIs as part of a QoS policy. This object type is fairly simple to create. You will need to define a name and comment, and select the color for the object. Additionally, you will need to define a **Search for URL**. This specifies the URL that will trigger a match, and it can be as specific as a complete URL, or as general as *.JPG, which would match any JPEG file.

SMTP

The SMTP resource defines the methods used by FW-1 to handle incoming or outgoing e-mail. There are many options, including the ability to remove active scripting components, rewriting fields in the envelope (such as To: or From:), or filtering based on content. The configuration of this resource type is similar to that of the URI, including the ability to use a CVP server.

FTP

An FTP resource is defined in order to enforce content security for FTP connections. One function of an FTP resource is to define the verbs or methods that will be allowed through a firewall. For example, one can restrict downloading access to only a certain directory on the FTP server, adding a second layer of security over and above what security is enabled on the FTP server itself.

Open Platform for Security Applications

The Open Platform for Security (OPSEC) object defines a means of interacting with a third party-developed security application. These applications add extended functionality to the FW-1 installation. Some examples include virus scanning, content filtering, and intrusion detection. OPSEC allows FW-1 to send its data stream to other applications, and allows those applications to send data to the firewall (for example, log entries via the ELA or status via AMON interfaces). This is covered fully in Chapter 7.

Servers

A server is a host computer running a specific application or service. The server object is the representation of that relationship.

Remote Authentication Dial-In User Server

A Remote Authentication Dial-In User Service (RADIUS) server is used to provide authentication services. While originally used for remote access services, it is also now commonly used for various network devices such as routers and firewalls. To define a RADIUS server, select **Manage | Servers** from the SmartDashboard drop-down menu and then select **New | RADIUS**. The configuration appears, as shown in Figure 3.25.

Figure 3.25 RADIUS Server Properties

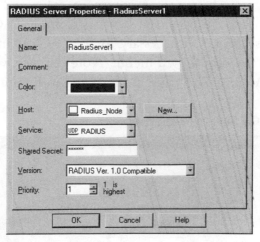

The RADIUS server object is configured in a way that is fairly common with the other server types. After defining the name, adding a comment, and selecting the associated color, you need to specify the **Host** that the RADIUS server is running on. You also need to assign a **Priority**. The priority is used to determine the preference for an individual server when more than one is available for contact, for example, when the server is assigned to a RADIUS group.

The next step is to define the **Service**, which is RADIUS. The **Shared Secret** must be entered in order to establish communication between the fire-walled object and the RADIUS server. Consequently, it must be the same on both devices. The final step is to select the proper version from the **Version** drop-down menu.

RADIUS Group

A RADIUS group is used to form a group of RADIUS servers to be used as one logical RADIUS server. These servers are then available for use as a single object, with authentication services being performed by the server with the highest priority (e.g., the lowest number). Unlike most other groups, server groups such as this may not contain any object of other types.

Terminal Access Controller Access Control Server

A Terminal Access Controller Access Control Server (TACACS) is another access control method. The definition of this object shares the same generalities of the other server entities, those being name, comment, color, and host. Once these are defined, you have only to specify if the server is running TACACS or a TACACS+, enter a secret key, if necessary, for TACACS+, and select the appropriate **Service** from the drop-down menu. (Note that you will not have to select a service with TACACS+.) This panel is illustrated in Figure 3.26.

Figure 3.26 TACACS Server Properties

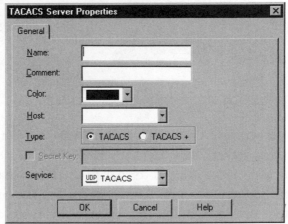

Lightweight Database Access Protocol Account Unit

Lightweight Database Access Protocol (LDAP) is used for a bevy of purposes. With regards to FW-1, this server object is used for the purposes of user management. A full discussion of the workings of LDAP is beyond the scope of this book but it is reasonable to assume if you are configuring an LDAP object, that you have access to an existing LDAP server and the necessary information. Figure 3.27 illustrates the **General** panel for LDAP configuration.

Figure 3.27 LDAP Account Unit Properties

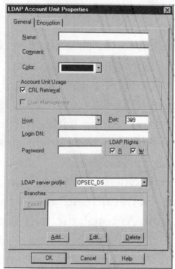

Certificate Authority

Even though Check Point builds has an Internal Certificate Authority (ICA), it will often not meet your Public Key Infrastructure (PKI) flexibility requirements when used outside the Check Point infrastructure. The inclusion of a Certificate Authority (CA) in your security infrastructure enables you to use certificate-based authentication and encryption that eases (or perhaps shifts) the administrative burden of VPN development.

There are three tabs for the CA object, with the first being the **General** tab. The associated panel allows the standard configuration information of name, comment, and color, as well as the ability to specify the CA vendor via a drop-down menu. Your choices in this drop-down will be determined by what you will be interoperating with. The contents of the second panel depend on the selection in this drop-down box.

The contents of the second panel will vary depending on your CA selection, but generally allow for the importing of a configuration from the PKI server and the importing of the CA's public certificate. You may also be able to specify the method of accessing the CAs certificate revocation list (CRL).

The **Advanced** panel deals with the CRL for this server; specifically, it configures the desire to cache the CRL and when to fetch a new CRL. You can also assign what branches are to be allowed.

SecuRemote DNS

SecuRemote DNS is an internal server type used to resolve private addresses to names. SecuRemote DNS replaces the need to create a *dnsinfo.C* file on the management server's *$FWDIR/conf* directory. You will, however, still need to edit *$FWDIR/lib/crypt.def*, adding the line *#define ENCDNS* to enable SecuRemote users to download this information along with their topology. This is not necessary if you are not using SecuRemote, but rather using SecureClient with Office Mode.

Configuration of this server type is fairly straightforward. You have two tabs: **General** and **Domains**. The **General** panel allows the configuration of the name, comment, color, and host. As usual, the host must have previously been defined as a workstation object.

The **Domains** panel lists the domains that are included for resolution, as well as something called a **Maximum Label Prefix Count**. This count defines the number of prefixes that will be allowed for the specific domain. For example, if the domain is *.edu*, then *troll.gatech.edu* has two prefixes. If the maximum prefix count were 1, this domain would not be resolved through the encrypted tunnel.

Internal Users

The ability to define users on the firewall is a nice feature, but is also administratively intensive. The benefit is that you can select specific groups of users as the source for traffic in a rule. The downside is you have to define these users. Fortunately, Check Point has simplified this process somewhat with the ability to define generic user templates. The use of LDAP as an external source of user information is also supported, which greatly decreases the workload redundancy of a firewall administrator. The user creation process is looked at in detail in Chapter 6.

The first step is to bring up the Users interface. This is accessed by selecting **Manage | Users** from the SmartDashboard menu. This window is used to define and modify users, and to install the user database to the VPN-1/FW-1 systems on which this policy is installed.

Time

Time objects are objects that enable you to schedule events, restrict connections, or simply quantify a time period. For example, you can restrict web browsing not only to specific sites, but also to specific times. There are three possible object types to select from. You can specify a time, a scheduled event, or a group of one or more of these types. To create a new time object, select **Manage | Time** from your SmartDashboard window.

The Time object is used to restrict the application of rules to specified times. There are two panels to this object: **General** and **Days**. The **General** panel allows the standard settings, as well as up to three time ranges. These ranges specify the time spans in which this object would be applicable. The **Days** panel enables you to enforce a finer-grained access control on the time object. You can specify days of a week, or a specific date, or a numbered day in each month. This is a very flexible tool. Figure 3.28 illustrates the **Days** panel.

Figure 3.28 Time Object—Days Panel

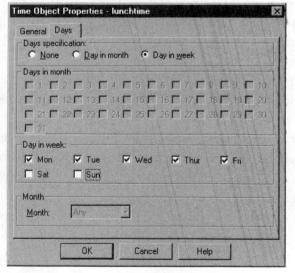

Group

A group is formed by the combination of several time object types, and can be used to simplify time-based rules. Instead of using multiple rules, you can create a group of time objects and assign this to a single rule. Creating a time group is similar to the other group types, and consists of assigning a name, comment, and color and then moving time objects from the **Not in Group** list to the **In Group** list.

Scheduled Event

A scheduled event is most often used for administrative purposes, such as scheduling log changes. Configuration is simple, with the only interesting field being the specification of the time at which the event will be triggered. As with the Time object, you can also schedule the repetition frequency of the object. For example, when you define the Management machine, you have access to the Management branch of the Workstation properties. The Schedule log switch to: field requires the use of a time object as its option.

Virtual Link

A virtual link is a path between two VPN-1/FW-1 modules or FloodGate-1 modules. Virtual links are defined in the SmartDashboard, and can be given Service Level Agreement (SLA) parameters. They can then be monitored using Check Point's SmartView Monitor GUI. To add a new virtual link, select **SmartView Monitor | Virtual Links** from the **Manage** menu in the SmartDashboard.

There are two panels to be configured. The **General** panel defines the name, comment, and color for the link, and also enables you to define the endpoints and to optionally activate the link.

The **SLA Parameters** panel, shown in Figure 3.29, enables you to specify the criteria that will be used to measure the integrity of the link. Thresholds are defined in three directions of traffic. You can specify the Committed Information Rate (CIR) for traffic point A to point B, and the reverse as well. You can also specify a maximum round trip time (RTT) for bidirectional communication, and optionally log the SLA statistics.

Figure 3.29 Virtual Link Properties—SLA Parameters

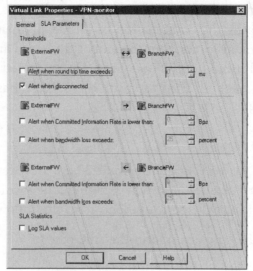

Adding Rules

The SmartDashboard is the main interface for all of your firewall needs. This is where you have been working to add objects, but it is also the interface to define rules. The next few sections briefly show how the SmartDashboard can be used to put your network objects into play in the form of firewall rules.

Rules

FW-1 is designed to enforce a set of rules, known as a rule base. This rule base defines the behavior of the firewall, and is configured by the firewall administrator. It is important that you carefully consider the underlying needs, related to both security and functionality, and make a measured application of both. You will probably never be able to strike a perfect balance, but the closer you come, the easier your life will be. Fundamentally, there are two models of firewall configuration. The first considers all traffic to be suspect, and only allows what is necessary (blocking all not explicitly allowed). This is commonly referred to as the "Least Privilege Principle" or "Principle of least privilege" and is considered a best practice when it comes to security. The second model is far more permissive, allowing all traffic that has not proven to be risky (allowing everything except what is explicitly denied). This model is typically seen when applying firewalling inside the network rather than at the edge. Which model you subscribe to is a decision that must be made at the policy level. Your firewall should be a technical implementation of the written corporate security policy.

A rule is made up by the combination of source, destination, action, tracking information, enforcement location, enforcement time, and an optional (but highly recommended) time fields. These fields are explained in the next few sections, along with the methods used to create them. Rule Base creation is covered in detail in Chapter 4.

Adding Rules

Adding rules in FW-1 is very straightforward. There are a few choices about rule placement you have to decide upon when adding a new rule. When you select **Rules | Add Rule** you will see a submenu with the following choices.

- **Bottom** After the last rule in the rule base.
- **Top** Before the first rule in the rule base.
- **After** After the currently selected rule.
- **Before** Before the currently selected rule.

After you insert the new rule, it will resemble the one shown in Figure 3.30. You will need to configure the specifics of each rule. In each field of the new rule, right-click to enter the necessary information.

Figure 3.30 New Rule

NO.	SOURCE	DESTINATION	VPN	SERVICE	ACTION	TRACK	INSTALL ON	TIME	COMMENT
1	✱ Any	✱ Any	✱ Any Traffic	✱ Any	◉ drop	− None	✱ Policy Targets	✱ Any	

Source

The Source field defines the IP address or hostname that is initiating the data stream. For the sake of your rule base, the source can be any of the properly defined network objects, as well as groups of users. When adding a source, you have the choice of adding an object or adding user access. You are not restricted in the number of sources for a rule, though it is a best practice to place numerous objects in a group and then use the group if they will be used together and have a logical grouping. This helps an administrator more easily understand the purpose of the rule and its need in the rulebase.

Destination

The destination can be any defined network object. When you right-click in the Destination field and select **Add**, you will see a window similar to that shown in Figure 3.31. Note that a rule can support multiple destinations.

Figure 3.31 Add Object

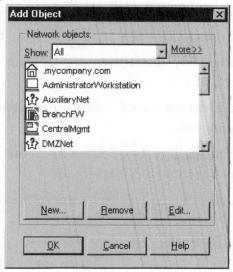

VPN

The VPN field is new in NG (previous to NG AI it was named "If Via"). This field is useful when using simplified mode VPNs. Simplified mode VPNs remove the Encrypt and Client Encrypt options (which are still available in traditional mode VPN policies) from the Action field and allow you to restrict this rule to only applying to traffic through a VPN community. VPN communities are covered more in Chapter 10.

Service

The Service field defines the service that must be present in order to generate a match. To add a service, right-click in the Service field and select **Add.** You will have the choice of adding a service or a service with a resource. You can define any number of services for a rule.

Action

The action is the way that FW-1 reacts when a rule is matched. You have a couple of choices when selecting an action, but only one selection is allowed. The available options are the following:

- **Accept** Accept the packet; allow the connection.
- **Reject** Reject the connection and notify the sender of the condition.
- **Drop** Reject the connection, but do not notify the sender.
- **User Authentication** Use User Authentication to authenticate users for this connection.
- **Client Authentication** Use Client Authentication to authenticate users for this connection.
- **Session Authentication** Use Session Authentication to authenticate users for this connection.
- **Encrypt** Encrypt outgoing packets; decrypt incoming packets. (Only available in Traditional Mode VPN policies.)
- **Client Encryption** Accept only if this connection originates from a remote access VPN client such as SecuRemote or SecureClient. (Only available in traditional mode VPN policies.)

Track

The Track column defines how information about this session will be recorded. There are several options in the menu when you right-click on this field. With the exception of the first two options which are pre-defined, the rest of these actions are actually defined in the **Alert Commands** section of the **Policy | Global Properties**.

- **Log** Write a log entry regarding this connection. This will be viewed with all the other logs in SmartView Tracker.
- **Account** Write an accounting log entry regarding this connection. This is similar to Log, but also includes the bytes transferred over the duration of the connection and the duration time itself.
- **Alert** Generate a pop-up alert in the SmartView Status GUI regarding this connection.

- **Mail** Send an e-mail regarding this connection.

- **SnmpTrap** Generate an SNMP trap based on this connection.

- **User-Defined** Execute the user-defined script as a result of this connection.

- **User-Defined 2** Execute the user-defined script as a result of this connection.

- **User-Defined 3** Execute the user-defined script as a result of this connection.

Install On

The Install On field defines which defined objects will have this policy installed on them. Although the entire policy is installed on each selected object, these objects only enforce the part of the policy that is relevant to them. If no rules are relevant, the system will not allow the policy to be installed.

- **Policy Targets** Enforce on all objects which will have this policy installed on them. This can be defined in the **Policy | Policy Installation Targets...**

- **Gateways** Enforce on all network objects defined as gateways.

- **Targets** Enforce on the specified target object(s) only, in the inbound and outbound directions.

- **Dst** Enforce in the inbound direction on the firewalled network objects defined as Destination in this rule.

- **Src** Enforce in the outbound direction on the firewalled network objects defined as Source in this rule.

- **OSE Devices** Enforce on all OSE devices.

- **Embedded Devices** Enforce on all embedded devices.

Time

In this field, use a time object to restrict the connection to certain specified intervals, or leave the default of **Any**.

Comment

This field is used to describe the rule, its purpose, and its functionality. It is highly recommended that you utilize this field to enable others (and yourself) to understand the purpose of this rule. Auditors typically also like to see this column utilized.

Global Properties

While the brunt of your security policy will reside in the rule base, there are other places you have to pay attention to. In order to fully secure your enterprise, you will need to be familiar with the Global Properties, and most likely you will need to alter them to fit your needs. You do this by accessing the Global Properties from the Policy menu. The next few sections discuss these properties. Figure 3.32 displays the initial panel of the Global Properties.

Figure 3.32 Global Properties

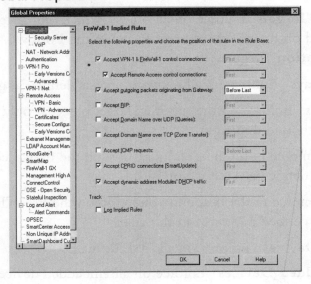

FireWall-1 Implied Rules

FW-1 has a feature called the "implied" rule base. This rule base is made up of settings in the Global Properties, as opposed to the one explicitly created by the firewall administrator, and is shown in Figure 3.32. What you select is up to your security policy, but we highly recommend that you enable the logging of these rules.

One important thing to understand is the implication of the option values. If you select a rule to be included within the implied rule base, you need to decide where to place that rule. You have three choices:

- First
- Last
- Before Last

You will need to select the location in the rule base where the selected rule will be placed. This is a critical decision, and you should understand how a packet passes through the rule base in order to assist your decision. Furthermore, not all implied rules are as simple as they may seem. The first implied rule, Accept VPN-1 and FW-1 control connections, for example, enables 32 services required for administrative tasks. Examples of connections allowed via the Accept VPN-1 and FW-1 control connections option include allowing a management station to push a policy to a firewall and allowing a firewall to query a RADIUS server to authenticate users. You probably do not need to worry about this too much, but it is a good thing to be aware of.

The reason for Last and Before Last is that it is a best practice for the last rule in your rule base to be a rule (referred to as "The Cleanup Rule") that drops all traffic if it has not been accepted by a previous rule. The Before Last option allows you to specify that this rule would be applied just before this rule. If you do not do this, the Last option would be appropriate to have applied at the end of your rule base.

Viewing Implied Rules

There are two methods of viewing implied rules. You can view them within the Global Properties window, but this is often cumbersome and difficult to do in a cohesive flow. When you want access to these rules while editing the rest of your rule base, the easiest way is to select the **View** menu and then select **Implied Rules**. You will see something like what is displayed in Figure 3.33. Note that the implied rules are unnumbered and are highlighted by their different color.

Figure 3.33 Implied Rules

NO.	SOURCE	DESTINATION	VPN	SERVICE	ACTION	TRACK	INSTALL ON	TIME	COMMENT
-	FW1 Module	FW1 Module o	Any Traffic	TCP FW1	accept	None	Policy Targets	Any	Enable FW1 Control Connections
	FW1 Manage	FW1 Module o	Any Traffic	TCP CPD	accept	None	Policy Targets	Any	Enable FW1 Control Connections
	FW1 Module	FW1 Managen	Any Traffic	TCP CPD	accept	None	Policy Targets	Any	Enable FW1 Control Connections
	FW1 Module	FW1 Managen	Any Traffic	TCP FW1_log	accept	None	Policy Targets	Any	Enable FW1 Control Connections
	Gui-clients o	FW1 Managen	Any Traffic	TCP CPMI	accept	None	Policy Targets	Any	Enable FW1 Control Connections
	FW1 Manage	RTM Module	Any Traffic	TCP CP_rtm	accept	None	Policy Targets	Any	Enable Real Time Monitor Connections
	Any	FW1 Module o	Any Traffic	TCP FW1_topo	accept	None	Policy Targets	Any	Enable FW1 Control Connections
	Any	FW1 Managen	Any Traffic	TCP FW1_key	accept	None	Policy Targets	Any	Enable FW1 Control Connections
	Gui-clients	Reporting Ser	Any Traffic	TCP CP_reportin	accept	None	Policy Targets	Any	Enable FW1 Control Connections to reporting tools

Other Global Properties

The following is a list of other Global Properties with brief descriptions.

- **Security Server** The Security Server panel allows the entry of welcome messages for many of the most common Internet services. This is accomplished by pointing to the appropriate file containing the message. You can also configure the HTTP Next Proxy, although this is better done in the workstation object, assuming a version of FW-1 of NG. Earlier versions still require entry in this field.

- **Voice over IP Protocols (VoIP)** The VoIP panel allows you to granularly define specifics of how VoIP will be inspected. This includes what you want to allow in regards to H.323 and SIP connections as well as whether to log VoIP-specific information such as phone numbers.

- **NAT** The NAT panel configures some general NAT behavior such as the Automatic NAT rules and NAT pools for SecuRemote connections. NAT is covered in Chapters 5 and 12.

- **Authentication** The Authentication panel enables you to specify the tolerance for failed login attempts. There are parameters for rlogin, telnet, client authentication and session authentication. There is also a section for configuring session timeout, wait mode, and logging/alerting for earlier version modules.

- **VPN-1 Pro** The VPN-1 Pro panel controls the behavior of SmartDashboard when creating new security policies with regard to whether they will be created as simplified mode, traditional mode, or to give an administrator the option.

- **Earlier Versions Compatibility** The Earlier Versions Compatibility panel controls the timeout configuration of IKE negotiations for pre-NG modules.

- **Advanced** This panel controls the multiple entry points and backup gateway functionalities for site-to-site VPNs as well as the CRL grace periods. Within this pane you will able be able to configure how gateways choose interfaces on other hosts to send VPN connections. The IKE denial of service protection is also defined on this panel.

- **VPN-1 Net** For gateways which only function as VPN endpoints and do not enforce specific firewalling rules, VPN-1 Net may be used. Because the administrator does not have granular control over the policy, the pre-defined policies for security, address translation, and logging are defined globally here. There are also options whether to allow Hypertext Transfer Protocol Secure (HTTPS) and Secure Shell (SSH) connections to the VPN-1 Net device within this panel.

- **Remote Access** The Remote Access panel contains information regarding the behavior of your firewall with regard to SecuRemote and SecureClient connections. The settings you select here are highly dependant on your own security policy, but it is strongly recommend that you log violation notifications and **not** respond to unauthenticated topology requests. Desktop security is covered in depth in Chapter 11.

- **Extranet Management Interface** In the event that you purchased Extranet Manager, there are two configuration parameters within this panel regarding how often to check the partner for updates and the grace period for Secure Sockets Layer (SSL) certificates from the partner. You also have the ability to view the local digital fingerprint.

- **LDAP Account Management** The LDAP account management panel allows the enabling of LDAP for account management. Here you can also set some session timeouts and password rules. LDAP is covered in depth in Chapter 6.

FloodGate-1

Though outside the scope of this book, specific configuration for what will be available in the QoS rule base is configured from the FloodGate-1 panel.

- **SmartMap** The SmartMap provides a very slick interface to view your objects and their interrelations. This panel enables you to display the SmartMap or conceal it from view. Note that if you disable the SmartMap, no topology calculations will take place within the firewall inner-workings.

- **FireWall-1 GX** FW-1 GX is used for firewalling GSM and GPRS networks. Configurations related specifically to GTP and other cellular networking options are able to be set globally here.

- **Management High Availability** Management High Availability is similar to that for gateways, except that it allows the management modules to exhibit some redundancy. This panel allows for you to select the synchronization time of the management servers participating in the High Availability configuration or what events trigger a synchronization, if any.

- **ConnectControl** The ConnectControl panel allows the configuration of this very handy feature. On this panel, you can set the interval that VPN-1/FW-1 will wait between server checks (commonly known as "heartbeat" checks) and the number of retries before a server is considered unreachable. You can also set the persistency timeout. This is the time within all connections from the same source IP will be forwarded to the same server. Finally, you can configure the listening address of the server agent used to measure server load and the pooling interval for that.

- **OSE** The OSE panel allows an administrator to define implied rules for rule bases installed on OSE-compatible devices.

- **Stateful Inspection** Stateful Inspection is the heart of FW-1. This panel enables you to specify some timeout settings for the TCP sessions and to configure stateful UDP and ICMP behavior as well as define how to handle Out-of-State TCP, UDP, and ICMP packets.

- **Log and Alert** This panel enables you to configure the responses taken when a packet matches a rule. This topic is covered in depth in Chapter 9.

- **Alert Commands** This panel enables you to configure the actual actions which happen behind the scenes for Mail, Alert, User Defined Alerts, and SNMP Trap operations. This topic is covered in depth in Chapter 9.

- **OPSEC** This panel defines whether to allow an OPSEC Roaming Administrator to complete the registration process without having to access SmartDashboard again.

- **SmartCenter Access** This panel defines how administrators are locked out based on failed logon attempts.

- **Non Unique IP Address Ranges** This panel defines any networks which may be used in multiple places in your security policy. This is important for VPN topology calculations and SmartMap. By default, it lists the RFC 1918 addresses.

- **SmartDashboard Customization** This defines how SmartDashboard itself will operate. For administrators managing a large number of firewalls or making a large number of changes, certain configuration changes such as defaulting to Classic Mode when creating new gateways or automatically selecting all gateways to install a policy on rather than having to check each check box, can have significant increases in productivity. There is also a button for Advanced Configuration, but it is highly recommended to **not** make changes in the Advanced area unless directed to by Check Point Technical Support.

SmartUpdate

SmartUpdate is a tool for the easy management of both software updates and licensing for both Check Point and OPSEC products. Chapter 8 covers the version management and upgrade features, but it will not hurt to touch on the licensing here. This component can be a real lifesaver, as you will understand if you have ever had to manually upgrade several dozens of licenses.

The GUI interface features two panels, one for **Products** and one for **Licenses**. These can be selected by clicking on the appropriate tab within the window. Figure 3.34 illustrates this GUI panel.

Figure 3.34 SmartUpdate GUI

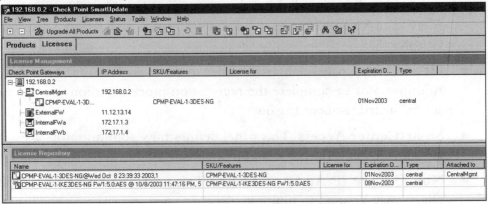

The real blessing of the SmartUpdate tool is that of centralized management and authority. Using this product, you can apply updates to your Check Point modules in a timelier manner, update licenses, and modify the currently licensed machines. Before you begin doing this, however, you should know about a new feature of FW-1 NG. This feature is called Central Licensing and uses what is known as a license repository.

In previous versions of FW-1 you had only one licensing option, that of a local license. Local licensing mandated that the license be tied to the IP address of the module. This model was not very flexible and made upgrades very difficult and migrations nearly impossible. Central licensing binds the license to the address of the management server and allows several benefits.

- When you change the IP address of the firewall module, the license remains useable. This has not always been the case.

- All licenses are bound to only one IP address. This allows great flexibility in your FW-1 deployment. Imagine the scenario where your network boundaries are migrated from one provider to another, and with that comes a new network block. Using central licensing makes that address change a much quicker operation. Licenses can be taken from one module and given to another and managed from this central location.

Note that while local licenses can still be used with FW-1 NG, you will not be able to use them like central licenses. This means that they cannot be detached from their module and reattached to another address after they have been installed.

Before you can begin using the functionality of SmartUpdate product, some common-sense things have to be in place. Obviously, there needs to be connectivity between the management module and the modules that are being maintained. For your purposes, connectivity implies both IP connectivity and FW-1 connectivity (SIC). Once this is all in place, you are on your way to licensing bliss.

Licenses can be added to the license repository in one of two ways. The first, more tedious method is to copy the license details by hand. This is annoying and can lead to typographical errors, (although support exists to paste the license details from the clipboard, removing the need to hand-type) so you probably will not want to add licenses in this way. The second method is to import a file created by the Check Point User Center. The option to **Add From User Center** is somewhat misleading as you do not actually use this option to add licenses, but rather to fetch them from User Center.

To begin, select **Licenses | New License** from the SmartUpdate tool bar. This will allow you the choice of adding manually, from User Center, or importing from a file. Figure 3.35 illustrates this menu option.

Figure 3.35 Adding a License

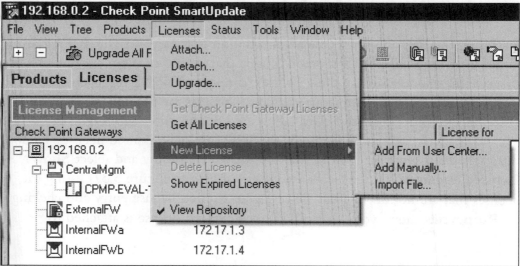

If you opt to add the license manually, you will see a window with a slew of fields that you will need to fill out, or as mentioned previously, you can paste the values from the clipboard. If you select **Import File**, you will see the standard file browse window. The option to acquire the new license from User Center will open a Web browser window. Also under the License menu option is the ability to view the License Repository. The Repository is a listing of all installed licenses and allows a filtered view. It can show you all licenses, all attached licenses, or all unattached licenses. This is a handy way to get a feel for what spare licenses you have, as well as enabling you to attach and detach central licenses. Remember that the old style licenses cannot be moved. (SmartUpdate automatically attaches them to the proper module when they are imported.) Figure 3.36 shows the license repository.

Figure 3.36 License Repository—View All Licenses

Name	SKU/Features	License for	IP Address	Expiration D...	Type	Attached to
License 6	CPVP-VIG-5...	VPN-1 Inter...	1.1.1.1	01Dec2001	central	Gateway1
License 7	CPVP-VIG-5...	VPN-1 Inter...	1.1.1.1	08Oct2001	central	
License 1	CPVP-VIG-5...	VPN-1 Inter...	1.1.1.1	05Oct2001	central	
License 2	CPFW-FIG-...	FireWall-1 In...	1.1.1.1	05Oct2001	central	Gateway3
License 3	CPTC-FGG-...	FloodGate-1...	9.3.1.8	05Oct2001	local	Gateway2
License 4	CPFW-ENC-...	Add-on VPN...	9.3.1.8	23Dec2001	local	Gateway2
License 5	CPFW-FIG-...	FireWall-1 In...	9.3.1.8	10Nov2001	local	Gateway2

Using the Repository, license administration is as easy as right clicking. In Figure 3.36, you will see all licenses. Notice that several of them are not attached to a specific module. To use these licenses, simply right-click on its entry and select **Attach.** At this point, you will see a listing of the defined workstations with Check Point modules. Select the desired system and select **OK.**

One other very helpful feature is the ability to view expired licenses. To do this, right-click anywhere within the **Repository** window and select **Show Expired Licenses.** This presents a window (shown in Figure 3.37) listing the licenses that are no longer valid. Selecting an expired license entry and clicking on **Properties** shows you what module the expired license is attached to.

Figure 3.37 Expired Licenses

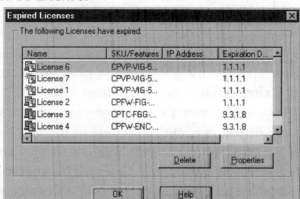

SmartView Tracker

The SmartView Tracker is your interface to the log data recorded by VPN-1/FW-1. Log data is created by the rule base, by firewall activities, by your own actions (accounting log), and by several other sources. Viewing this data regularly is a key to good security enforcement, and this GUI makes the task of observing the log data much more pleasant.

Upon startup, the SmartView Tracker begins display of the active security log. You can also use the GUI to view older logs, which may have been rotated out and placed into archive for later review. Note that the name of the log file being viewed is displayed in the upper-left portion of the window title bar, as shown in Figure 3.32. This is helpful in the aforementioned case where you are viewing archived data.

The SmartView Tracker has three modes of operation, which are accessed by the pull-down menu shown in the figure, or alternatively, via the **Mode** menu option. These modes are log, active, and audit. Active mode displays currently active connections being tracked by the firewall. The active mode is most often used when performing real time-monitoring of traffic, or when you wish to block a connection via SAM. (Block Intruder is discussed in Chapter 9.)

Audit mode is very handy for keeping track of who did what on your firewall. The "who" is your group of firewall administrators, and the "what" are administrative actions. Examples of these are logging in, creating or deleting objects, and so on. You can also view specific details for any log entry by right-clicking that entry and selecting **Show Details**. Note that the audit data is stored in a separate file, *fw.adtlog* which is stored in the *$FWDIR/log* directory of the firewall installation.

Log mode is the most common method of interacting with the log data, and is the most comprehensive way to view the security events. What events you actually see is entirely up to you, as FW-1 allows extensive customization of what is called **Selection Criteria**. This criterion defines what data is extracted from the log data and is displayed to you. You can save your favorite selections and reuse them frequently, or you may opt to use one of the built-in views. In Log mode, there is also an option to enable watching logs as they are generated in real-time. This can be enabled by selecting **Query | Autoscroll**.

Active mode allows the information about connections currently traversing the gateways to be retrieved and viewed in real-time. This is available regardless of whether or not the connections are being logged.

The default views are available via the toolbar or via the **View** menu. These views select some of the more commonly accessed information for display. For example, there is a predefined selection for VPN-1 data, which shows you such entries as Key IDs, encryption method, VPN peer gateway, and so forth. But the real power of the SmartView Tracker is in its ability for customization. The SmartView Tracker GUI is shown in Figure 3.38.

Figure 3.38 Check Point SmartView Tracker

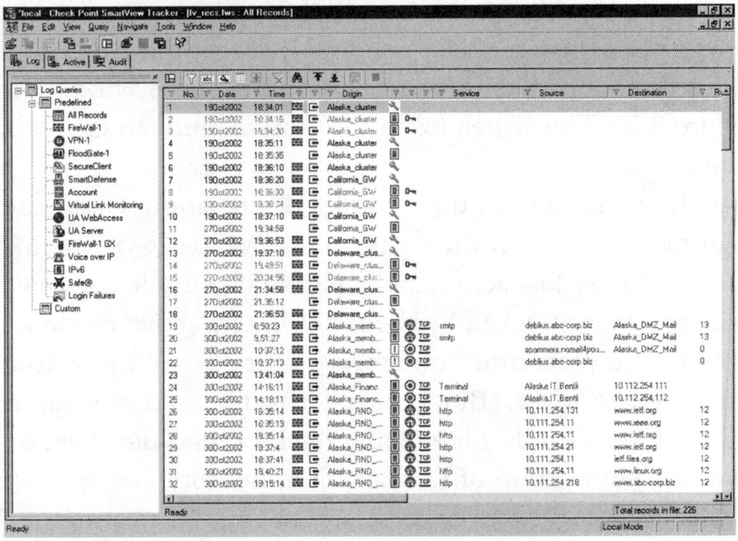

Column Selections

To alter the data displayed click **View | Query Properties**. You will be presented with the window shown in Figure 3.39. Using this window enables you to select or deselect any of the available data fields. You can also change the column width using this window. By pressing the **Selection** button, you have access to very granular methods of defining information. We highly recommend that you spend a few minutes looking into this feature on your firewall.

Figure 3.39 Column Options Window

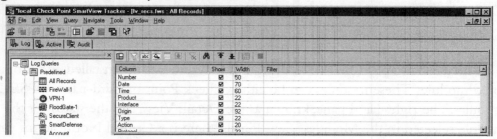

The SmartView Tracker is much like most common spreadsheet applications. You can resize columns not only from the options window, but also directly from the viewer main menu.

Right-clicking anywhere within the column you want to modify will bring up a context menu, which enables you to do things such as hide that column and resize the width. You can also resize the width by dragging the border of the title header. Once you have tailored the view to your liking, you can begin gathering the information.

The SmartView Tracker features a very handy search utility, accessed by selecting the **Navigate** menu and then **Find**. This enables you to specify the column or columns you want to search through, and the entry of the search criteria. You can also specify a search direction.

SmartView Status

The System Status GUI allows a quick peek at the overall health of your security infrastructure. Real-time monitoring, along with status alerting, is featured to assist in the integrity of your enterprise. The System Status viewer is a friendly, lightweight interface. You are presented with a three-pane window, with two of those shown in Figure 3.40.

Figure 3.40 System Status GUI

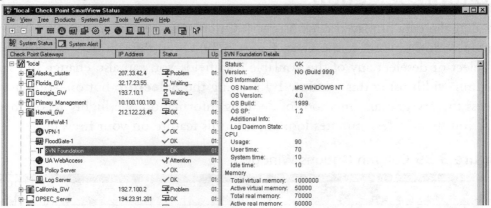

The left-hand pane, known as the Modules View, lists the installed and monitored modules. These modules can be either Check Point or third-party OPSEC modules. The right-hand pane, known as the Details View, lists the status for the module selected in the Modules View. Finally, there is a Critical Notifications pane (not shown in the figure) that keeps you updated on any status alerts generated.

The Modules View window is further broken down into three columns: Modules, IP Address, and Status. Their meanings are self-explanatory. You can also select specific components to query for status using either the Products menu or the button bar across the top of the window. You can query the following components for status (left to right on the button bar).

- SVN Foundation Details

- FW-1 Details

- VPN-1 Details

- FloodGate-1 Details

- High Availability Module Details

- OPSEC Application Details

- Management Details

Summary

This chapter discussed the GUI provided for access to VPN-1/FW-1. It looked at the process to create each of the possible object types available for use within an enterprise security policy, including network objects, servers, and resources. You should now feel comfortable creating objects to support your own implementations.

This chapter also discussed the SmartDashboard, and saw how to use these newly created objects to create rules. These rules will be the embodiment of your written security policy, and are the definitions that FW-1 enforces. It also demonstrated how FW-1 has included something called an "implied rule," how to edit them, and how to view them. With regards to editing, this chapter also covered the various methods of editing the rule base, including adding new rules, deleting existing ones, and rearranging the rule base with cut/paste functions.

Global Properties and how these settings impact the behavior of the firewall was also discussed. This chapter finished with a look into some of the additional tools provided with VPN-1/FW-1. The SmartView Tracker and the SmartView Status tools were introduced, as well as the SmartUpdate tool.

Solutions Fast Track

Managing Objects

☑ Do not be stingy: Create as many objects as necessary to support your rule base. You only need to do it once, but you can use them dozens of times.

☑ Save time and complexity by using groups of objects and users.

Adding Rules

☑ Remember that the order in which your rules are displayed is the order they are enforced.

☑ Save time by using cut/paste when creating similar rules. It is easier to edit one field than to create a new rule.

☑ Remember that your security policy is enforced on more than just your firewall modules. Routers and other OPSEC devices may also be impacted.

Global Properties

☑ Be aware of the default settings within the Global Properties and how these may impact the operation of your firewall.

☑ Make sure that you tailor the implied rules to suit your site's needs. Do not live with the default entries; they probably will not be just what you need.

Secure Update

☑ Use SmartUpdate to track license and version information enterprise-wide from a single point.

☑ Take advantage of the Check Point VPN-1/FW-1 central licenses to ease the crunch of enterprise management.

SmartView Tracker

☑ Do not live with the default view. Take advantage of the customizations offered to create views that suit your needs.

☑ Remember that the SmartView Tracker is also home to the Block Connection feature; keep it close at hand.

☑ Do not be afraid to try experiments with new and advanced features!

SmartView Status

☑ Make use of the features in this tool.

☑ System Status is as important to your enterprise as any other factor. This tool enables you to keep an eye on the health of your infrastructure, which is never a bad thing.

Frequently Asked Questions

The following Frequently Asked Questions, answered by the authors of this book, are designed to both measure your understanding of the concepts presented in this chapter and to assist you with real-life implementation of these concepts. To have your questions about this chapter answered by the author, browse to **www.syngress.com/solutions** and click on the **"Ask the Author"** form. You will also gain access to thousands of other FAQs at ITFAQnet.com.

Q: I see that there is a Read-Only option when I log into the GUI client. Is there a way to force a user to be read only all the time?

A: Yes. Using the cpconfig utility, you can add/delete/modify administrators. You can assign Read-Only permissions here. Note that, depending on the installed products, you may see a slightly different configuration panel. This panel also features a custom selection option, which allows different permissions for different Check Point components.

Q: I've installed my FW-1 inspection module on a separate machine as my Management module, and I'm having trouble connecting to manage it now.

A: Make sure that you have properly set up the communication infrastructure. To do this, access the General panel of the workstation properties and select the Communication button. Verify that the Trust State is indicated as initialized or communicating.

Q: In older versions of FW-1, I could manually edit the *objects.C* file to alter or add objects. Can I still do this on FW-1 NG?

A: The easy answer is no. Previously, there were two copies of the *objects.C* file. One existed with the management module, the other with the firewall module. This is no longer true. In Check Point FW-1 NG, the firewall module *objects.C* is created dynamically based on the objects_5_0.C file found on the management module. The preferred method of editing this file is through the use of the *dbedit* command (or the GUIdbEdit tool). Consult your documentation for the command reference.

## Chapter 4

Creating a Security Policy

Solutions in this Chapter:

- Reasons for a Security Policy
- How to Write a Security Policy
- Implementing a Security Policy
- Installing a Security Policy
- Policy Files

☑ Summary

☑ Solutions Fast Track

☑ Frequently Asked Questions

Introduction

This chapter discusses how to define a security policy, which needs to be done early on in order to find the right solution for your specific environment. Once you determine how you want to enforce security in your company, you will know whether you need to set up user authentication or whether you should use your existing Lightweight Directory Access Protocol (LDAP) server. Once you have created a security policy for your company and have planned to introduce security into your network, choosing your implementation strategy should be fairly straightforward.

Next is a discussion on how to implement your security policy into the Check Point SmartDashboard. If you are using private Internet Protocol (IP) addresses inside your firewall, you may need to read the chapter on network address translation (NAT) before you can put your firewall completely in place. This chapter shows how to get your firewall ready to enforce your policy and begin passing packets in your network.

You are then walked through the setup of a firewall object, and the step-by-step procedure for adding the services outlined in your Information Security Policy into the Check Point SmartDashboard interface. This chapter then discusses some additional ways in which to manipulate your rules as well as how to install your policy so that it is enforced.

Reasons for a Security Policy

You are probably deploying Check Point Next Generation (NG) with Application Intelligence (AI) to protect something. Do you know what you are protecting, what you are protecting it from, and how you are protecting it? Before you can effectively deploy any security control, especially a powerful tool like Check Point NG AI, you need to have an Information Security Policy. This is not to be confused with the Check Point Security Policy, which, according to Check Point, is "Defined in terms of a Rule Base and [FW-1 NG AI] Properties."(www.checkpoint.com/products/downloads/fw1-4_1tech.pdf) We are talking about an enterprise-wide information security policy that includes a written Security Policy accompanied by standards, guidelines, and procedures for implementing and maintaining an information security program. (This is explained in more detail in the next section.)

Many organizations now find the need to have an articulated information security policy. Having such policies makes organizations more effective in their preventative, detective, and responsive security measures. Moreover, as a result of government regulations, organizations in certain vertical industries are required to have formally documented information security policies.

In addition, an Information Security Policy is also extremely beneficial to the security manager because it provides, at an executive level, a mandated framework for ensuring the confidentiality, integrity, and availability of an organization's information assets. What this means is that the security manager has some weight in their corner for budget requests when they have an approved Information Security Policy.

For the security administrator, having a written and approved policy can ensure that they are able to deploy Check Point NG AI in a way that minimizes disruption to business but enforces the protection necessary to keep business functioning. Think of the written policy as a recipe to ensure that you configure everything correctly.

How to Write a Security Policy

To write an entire Information Security Policy can take months of work with involvement from the Legal and Human Resources departments, as well as various business units. In order to implement Check Point NG AI, you need at a minimum an Executive Security Policy and a Perimeter Network Security Policy. Typically, the Executive Security Policy is a high-level document of about three to five pages that points to relevant standards, procedures, and guidelines. Because the highest levels of management or the board of directors must adopt the Executive Security Policy, it should be written without details about technologies, people, or methods. This will ensure that as technology changes or as people change, the document will not become obsolete. Think of the Executive Policy as a declaration of the importance of security to your organization. However, choose your words carefully because it is a legal document in many respects.

The Executive Security Policy is important because without an executive endorsement of your security policy, enforcement may become difficult. In order to write an effective Executive Security Policy you must identify early on the departments with an interest in maintaining information assets, such as R&D, Finance, and IT. Approach the managers and request their involvement in drafting an executive-level security document. In addition, you will want to include the Legal department and an executive sponsor.

NOTE

Executive support and approval is critical to the success of your Information Security Policy. When the CEO has to follow the same rules as everyone else, it makes policy enforcement much simpler.

The final document should have language such as: "Because of the nature of our business, customer non-public information is frequently transmitted or stored on our information systems. As a result, we will employ appropriate controls and safeguards including encryption to ensure that non-public information is adequately protected against unauthorized disclosure while in storage or transit." At this point, that the policy seems rather vague and legal. However, resist the impulse to say, "We must use Triple DES encryption on all private data that is stored or transmitted." This is important because technology changes and this document will eventually be presented to management for approval. Management does not want to see you once a month asking for changes to the security policy. As a guiding principle, the Executive Security Policy should address why security is important and delegate the further implementation of appropriate standards, guidelines, and procedures to the appropriate individuals or groups.

Designing & Planning…

Get Trained

Use the Information Security Policy to help you do your job better and to get the things you need. For example, use the policy to ensure that you get security training. Include a statement in the policy that says, "To ensure that we are adequately controlling and anticipating current and new threats, the security manager and his or her team must attend security training on a semi-annual basis in the form of conferences, seminars, symposiums, and workshops." As you can see, the Security Policy can be your friend.

Drafting the second part of your overall Information Security Policy, the Perimeter Network Security Policy, is somewhat different. The Perimeter Network Security Policy is a document that includes specific standards, procedures, and guidelines for implementing and maintaining perimeter network security. The first step in drafting a Perimeter Security Policy is to obtain a network map. The network map will help you to better identify resources that need protecting and how to architect your security solution. Depending on the size of your organization, you may elect to do this yourself or to obtain the assistance of individuals with specific knowledge regarding their environment. Although there are a number of software tools to assist you in automatically mapping the network, it will still be necessary to manually validate.

After mapping the network, determine once again the departments or business units with a specific interest in network perimeter security, and assemble the representatives for a meeting. The best approach in this meeting is to identify what is needed and then, by default, disallow everything else. It is at this point that successful security managers recognize the purpose of security to meet business needs. Although it would be great from a security perspective to disconnect the business from the Internet, to stay in business the connection must be maintained. In this meeting, you need to specifically ask the representatives what would need to be changed and configured to allow the business to continue, if you were to put up a firewall today and block everything,. This step is called "defining requirements." For example, some of the requirements that might be voiced include the following:

- We *need* a Web site that has dynamic content

- We *need* to have an e-Commerce storefront

- We *need* to be able to get and send e-mail.

- We *need* to secure all of our internal information from external attacks.

- We *need* to be able to access the Internet securely using HTTP, HTTPS, and FTP from the local area network (LAN).

- We *need* to secure our critical information from internal attacks or destruction.

In addition, you will also want to identify any wishes the representatives have. Examples of wishes are as follows:

- We *would like* to have Instant Messaging

■ We *would like* to be able to have sales representatives connect remotely to download order status.

You may find that most needs are simple and can use further refinement. For example, the requirement to send and receive e-mail begs the questions, "From where do you need to send e-mail? Do remote users need to send and receive e-mail? Should there be any additional restrictions on e-mail?" In addition, you should ask questions about what types of communication to log and how long these logs are kept.

Often you will be faced with end users that ask for more access than they actually need. This is typically rooted in the fact that they do not know, or are not sure, of what access is actually necessary. This can prove to be a trying situation, but it is best to work with these users to investigate what is required and explain why it is important to only allow the minimum access required.

Designing & Planning…

Community Involvement

Make sure that everyone who has an interest in the implementation and maintenance of a security policy is involved in its creation. This may involve representatives from Human Resources or even the custodial staff. Involvement from these departments will ease acceptance of the new policy and make the actual implementation much smoother. Sometimes, however, this involvement is legally mandatory if your company falls under HIPAA or other government regulations.

The next stage in the drafting of the Perimeter Security Policy is risk assessment. Every requirement and wish has a risk attached to it. As a security professional, you must be able to identify those risks and communicate them to the involved parties so they can be weighed against the benefits.

Security Design

After identifying the requirements and risks you are willing to accept, you must design security solutions. Having knowledge of the features and abilities of FW-1 NG AI will help you to determine what you can and cannot do. In addition, be aware of the other types of controls that can be used to maintain perimeter network security. There are three main categories of controls: technical, physical, and administrative. Each category of controls has three functions including preventative, detective, and responsive, as shown in Table 4.1. The firewall is primarily a technical control of a preventative and detective nature. That is to say, the firewall prevents unauthorized access and can be used to detect unauthorized access. However, do not dismiss addressing physical and administrative controls in your Perimeter Network Security Policy.

Table 4.1 Categories of Security Controls

	Technical	**Physical**	**Administrative**
Preventative	Check Point NG AI VPN-1	Locked data centers Identification badges	User ID/password policy Change management
Detective	Check Point NG AI	CCTV	Log and report review Rule base audits
Responsive	Check Point NG AI	High availability	Incident response procedures

Other policies that FW-1 NG can help enforce are:

- NAT security
- Quality of Service (QoS) security
- Desktop security
- Monitoring

Firewall Architecture

Before writing the policy, one thing you need to explore is whether you will need to have different policies for different locations or if you will have only one. If you have one security policy, Check Point can enforce the same policy on all firewall modules from a central management station. Otherwise, you will have to maintain a different policy for different locations. Although for business reasons this might be necessary, it can add a level of complexity to your environment that could decrease your overall effective security. If it is necessary, make sure that it is thoroughly documented.

Writing the Policy

Now that you know what is necessary, you can write your Perimeter Network Security Policy. As you can see in Figure 4.1, writing a security policy is a logical progression of steps.

Figure 4.1 Steps to Writing a Security Policy

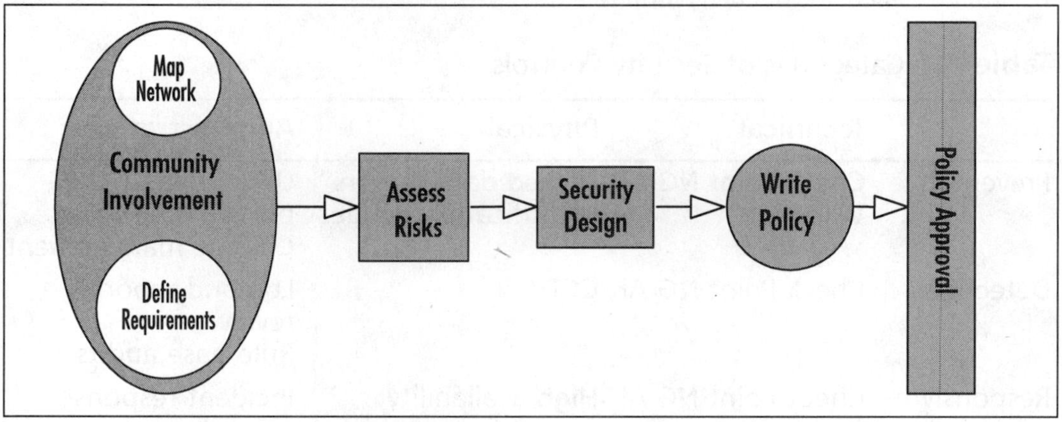

Briefly, the structure of the policy should include the following:

- **Introduction** In this section, state the purpose of this policy. What is the objective of the policy? Why it is important to the organization?

- **Guidelines** In this section, detail the guidelines for choosing controls to meet the objectives of the policy. These are the basic requirements. Typically, you will see the word "should" in these statements.

- **Standards** In this section, detail the standards for implementing and deploying the selected controls. For example, state the initial configuration or firewall architecture. This section tends to detail the requirements given in the meeting with the interested departments and business units. This section is written with the words such as, "It is the policy that…"

- **Procedures** In this section, detail the procedures for maintaining the security solution, such as how often the logs should be reviewed and who is authorized to make changes.

- **Deployment** In this section, assign responsibilities and specific steps for the implementation of the policy. Think of it as a mini project plan. In a Perimeter Network Security Policy, this is the section that translates the standards and guidelines into language that the security administrator can enforce on the firewall.

- **Enforcement** Many policies lack this component, however, all policies require a method for enforcement. A popular and effective method for enforcement is auditing. In this section you can state that the firewall rule base would be subject to an external audit yearly. In addition, this section should detail the enforcement and consequences if someone were to circumvent the firewall or its rules.

- **Modification or Exceptions** No policy is perfect, and may require modifications or exceptions. In this section, detail the methods for obtaining modifications to the policy or exceptions.

Following is a sample Perimeter Network Security Policy:

Introduction

Due to Company X's required connection and access to the public Internet, it is essential that a strong perimeter firewall exist that sufficiently separates the internal private LAN of Company X and the public Internet. The firewall should provide preventative and detective technical controls for access between the two networks.

Guidelines

The implementation of any firewall technology should follow these basic rules:

- The firewall should allow for filtering of communication protocols based on complex rule sets.

- The firewall should provide extensive logging of traffic passed and blocked.

- The firewall should be the only entry and exit point to the public Internet from the Company X LAN.

- The firewall OS should be sufficiently hardened to resist both internal and external attacks.

- The firewall should fail closed.

- The firewall should not disclose the internal nature, names, or addressing of the Company X LAN.

- The firewall should only provide firewall services. No other service or application should be running on the firewall.

- The firewall should provide read-only access for auditors.

Standards

The implementation of any firewall must follow these basic rules:

- Only the identified firewall administrator is allowed to make changes to the configuration of the firewall.

- All firewalls must follow the default rule: That which is not expressly permitted is denied.

In addition, the following standards for perimeter networks are as follows:

- The deployment of public services and resources shall be positioned behind the firewall in a protected service net.

- The firewall shall be configured to disallow traffic that originates in the service net to the general LAN.

- Any application or network resource residing outside of the firewall and accessible by unauthorized users requires a banner similar to the following:

> A T T E N T I O N! PLEASE READ CAREFULLY.
> This system is the property of Company X. It is for authorized use only. Users (authorized or unauthorized) have no explicit or implicit expectation of privacy. Any or all uses of this system and all files on this system will be intercepted, monitored, recorded, copied, audited, inspected, and disclosed to Company X management and law enforcement personnel, as well as authorized officials of other agencies, both domestic and foreign. By using this system, the user consents to such interception, monitoring, recording, copying, auditing, inspection, and

disclosure at the discretion of Company X. Unauthorized or improper use of this system may result in administrative disciplinary action and civil and criminal penalties. By continuing to use this system, you indicate your awareness of and consent to these terms and conditions of use. LOG OFF IMMEDIATELY if you do not agree to the conditions stated in this warning.

Procedures

The firewall will be configured to allow traffic as defined below.

- Transmission Control Protocol (TCP)/IP suite of protocols allowed through the firewall from the inside LAN to the public Internet is as follows:
  - HTTP to anywhere
  - HTTPS to anywhere
- TCP/IP suite of protocols allowed through the firewall from the inside LAN to the service net is as follows:
  - HTTP to Web server
  - Simple Mail Transfer Protocol (SMTP) to mail server
  - Post Office Protocol 3 (POP3) to Mail server
  - Domain Name System (DNS) to DNS server
- TCP/IP suite of protocols allowed through the firewall from the service net to the public Internet is as follows:
  - DNS from DNS server to anywhere
- TCP/IP suite of protocols allowed through the firewall from the public Internet to the LAN is as follows:
  - None
- TCP/IP suite of protocols allowed through the firewall from the public Internet with specific source, destination, and protocols is as follows:
  - SMTP to mail server
  - HTTP to Web server
  - FTP to FTP server

Deployment

The security administrator will define the rule base and configure the firewall as defined above, in addition to other industry standard properties (as appropriate).

Enforcement

Traffic patterns will be enforced by the firewall's technical controls as defined by the firewall administrator. Periodically, an external vulnerability assessment will be performed to assure the proper configuration of the firewall. Additionally, an independent third party will annually audit the configured firewall.

Modifications or Exceptions

Requests for modification to the firewall configuration must be submitted via e-mail to the security manager and firewall administrator, accompanied by justification and the duration of the requested change. The security administrator is allowed to make modifications outside the company's change control process in cases where they deem it necessary to prevent or contain disastrous events.

Implementing a Security Policy

Now that you have a written Information Security Policy and a Perimeter Security Policy, you can begin configuring and deploying Check Point NG AI by translating your organization's written security policies into a technical policy that can be enforced by Check Point NG AI.

Default and Initial Policies

The default and initial policies taken together comprise boot security for FW-1 NG AI. Unlike previous version of FW-1, FW-1 NG automatically applies the default policy upon restart. The default policy is intended to protect the firewall and the networks behind it by blocking all traffic while it is loading the firewall services. Additionally, boot security will disable IP forwarding to keep the operating system (OS) from routing traffic while the firewall is booting. However, there are some things that the default filter will allow. You can view the default filter by viewing the *$FWDIR/conf/defaultfilter.pf* file. Specifically, the default filter will allow the following:

- Outgoing communication from the firewall itself,

- Incoming communications that are a response to communications initiated by the firewall.

- Broadcasts.

Because the firewall is allowing something, the firewall also enforces anti-spoofing measures to ensure that the allowed FW-1 NG AI communications are not spoofed on any of its interfaces.

As FW-1 NG AI boots up and the default filter takes effect, the interfaces are configured and the FW-1 services are started. At this point, FW-1 applies an initial policy made up of implicit rules. The purpose of the initial policy is to add rules that will allow a graphical user interface (GUI) to be trusted and connect to the firewall. After the GUI is able to connect to the firewall, a new security policy can be installed. The initial policy is only installed on a module after *cpconfig* is executed and there is no security policy. The initial policy is replaced after a regular policy is written and installed by the administrator to the module. Thereafter, the enterprise Security Policy will follow the default filter and interface configuration. The enterprise Security Policy will be composed of the defined rule base and implicit rules. This process is illustrated in Figure 4.2.

Boot security ensures that at no time is the firewall left unprotected. Ensuring that FW-1 starts at boot will allow boot security to be enforced. It is possible to alter boot security and enable IP forwarding and disable the default filter. However, this is not recommended.

Figure 4.2 Boot Security

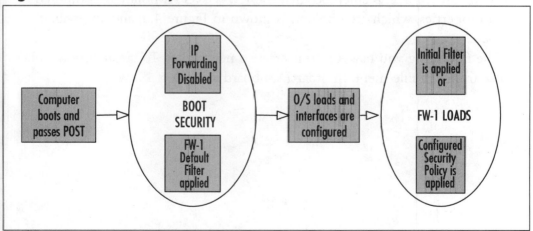

After the default policy is loaded, the firewall will attempt to fetch the policy from the management station or, in the case that it cannot load the policy from the management station, load the locally cached policy. In the event that this is a new installation and no policy has been pushed to it, the Initial Policy will be installed. The initial policies are defined in the *$FWDIR/conf* directory named *initial_management.pf* and *initial_module.pf* depending on whether the firewall is installed with or without a management station, respectively. There is no policy for systems that are only management stations, due to the fact that there is no firewall configured for the host. Each policy includes the following communications with the aforementioned default filter applied appended afterwards:

- GUI client connections to the management station (from addresses in the *$FWDIR/conf/gui-clients.def* file)

- HTTPS and Secure Shell (SSH) connections (if the system has any addresses in the *$FWDIR/lib/webgui-clients.def* file defined)

- CPD_Amon, FWD, CPD, and FW_ICA_Push from the management station to the firewall

- You can view the policy which is currently being enforced by typing **fw stat** at the command line.

Translating Your Policy into Rules

At this point you can take your written policy and your network map and start translating your documented security policy into a policy that Check Point FW-1 NG AI can enforce. Remember that the FW-1 NG AI policy is composed of global properties, which are implicit, as shown in Figure 4.3, and an explicit rule base.

The first thing you have to do is create a new policy. To create a new policy, choose from the File menu in SmartDashboard and select **New**.

Figure 4.3 Global Properties Implied Rules

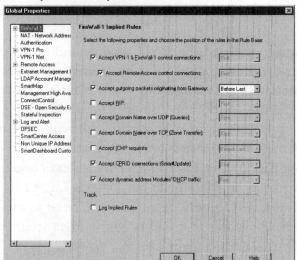

As shown if Figure 4.4, you have a few options in the new policy dialog window. First, type a name for the policy. Now select **Security and Address Translation** as your Policy Type. By default, you will be presented with a simplified mode security policy. If you wish to utilize Traditional Mode or be given the option, select your preference in the Global Properties.

Figure 4.4 New Security Policy Dialog

Defining A Firewall Object

The first step in translating the policy into an enforceable policy is to define the relevant network objects. The first object you will create is your firewall object. The firewall object must be defined before you can install your FW-1 Security

Policy. The setup process has been streamlined in NG AI to allow for the automatic creation of network objects known to the firewall. This requires that the appropriate routing is configured on the firewall.

If you have initially installed the FW-1 module and management server on the same box, then the firewall object will be created and partially configured. If the components are installed in a distributed environment, however, you will have to create the firewall workstation object. You start by logging into your management server via the SmartDashboard GUI. If you have not opened the Workstation Properties as shown in Figure 4.5, you may do so by selecting the firewall object from the Objects List, right-clicking, and choosing **Edit** by double-clicking the firewall object from the Objects List, or by going through the **Manage | Network Objects** menu. You will need to create one firewall object for each firewall module that will be enforcing a security policy and that will be managed by this management server.

If you are creating the firewall object for the first time, you can right-click on the **Network Objects** in the Objects Tree and choose **Check Point | Gateway** from the New menu. After selecting **Classic Mode** to configure the gateway, the first field you will be challenged with is the name of the firewall. This field should be the firewall module's TCP/IP host name. For better performance, it is recommended that DNS be configured to resolve this name to the firewall's external IP address, or better yet, have it set up in the host's file on the firewall and management module. By defining this in a hosts file, it removes the reliance on DNS functioning.

The next field should contain the external IP address of the firewall. If DNS is configured and you click **Get address**. DNS will be queried and the address will be filled in for you. Otherwise, you can just type in the value. In the Comment field, be as descriptive as possible. Using comments is a good way to document what you are doing so that others can understand more quickly and easily. The next decision is what color to give the object. This should be based on a scheme that will help you to read the rules and logs more easily.

Figure 4.5 Workstation Properties with Check Point Products Installed

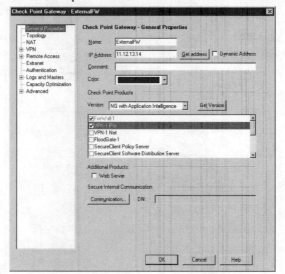

Now select the version as **NG with Application Intelligence**. This will enable the appropriate next list of product modules. From the list, choose the modules that are installed on this host. If the management server and firewall module are on different hosts, you will need to configure Secure Internal Communication (SIC) to establish communication between these two machines. To do so, click on the **Communication** button and enter a shared password. If this object was created for you, Check Point already knows which products you have installed and has made the selection for you. Double-check that the selection is correct before you continue. The second branch on the Workstation Properties is the Topology window. This enables you to define the networks reachable behind the internal and external interfaces that exist on your firewall object. Figure 4.6 illustrates this configuration window.

Figure 4.6 Topology Window

To define the interface, make sure that you have selected the right one. After selecting an interface to define, as shown in Figure 4.6, click **Edit**. This will open up the dialog box, as shown in Figure 4.7.

If you are configuring an interface manually, it is important to use the proper name. For example, the name as displayed by the *ifconfig -a* Unix command. Failure to properly define the interfaces may cause features such as anti-spoofing to not function, and may leave the network open to attack. The easiest way to define the interfaces is to use the **Get | Interfaces** feature, which will query the system (encrypted via SIC) for its interface information and is the recommended method of gathering this information. To make your job even easier, the **Get | Interfaces with Topology** option will also fill out your anti-spoofing definitions as well as create the necessary network, host, and group objects. This is dependent on your firewall having the correct host and network routes predefined, so make sure that they are configured before you get to this point.

When defining the interfaces manually, you are not only able to specify this interface as internal or external, but you can also specify the range of addresses that reside behind the interface for enforcing anti-spoofing and generating NAT rules. This is done while manually adding or editing interface information from the topology tab, as illustrated in Figure 4.7.

Figure 4.7 Topology Definition

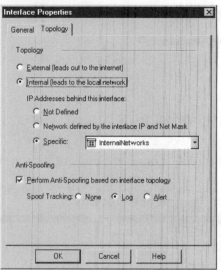

If the interface is internal, it is very important to define the addresses that reside behind the interface. The first option, **Not Defined**, generally should not be used unless the interface is present in the system but not connected to any network. If selected, anti-spoofing will be disabled on this interface. Generally speaking, it only makes sense to have anti-spoofing configured either for all or none of the interfaces. If you select the second option, these addresses will be calculated based on the address and subnet mask for this interface. Lastly, you can specify an explicit range of addresses or groups of networks. Anti-spoof tracking can also be defined on a per-interface basis. Anti-spoofing will stop someone from creating packets which, by address, seem to come from one network, though they are actually coming from another. A full discussion of address spoofing is available in Appendix B.

The Logs and Masters branch is important for your FW-1 configuration. The Logs and Masters window enables you to specify logging options. The options are broken down into three sections: Additional Logging, Masters, and Log Servers. This branch is covered in more detail in Chapter 8.

The Advanced window allows the configuration of Simple Network Management Protocol (SNMP) settings. If you expand out the **Advanced** branch, you will see five submenus as follows:

- SMTP

- Security Account Manager (SAM)

- Connection Persistence

- Permissions to Install

- SYNDefender

A new GUI option in Check Point NG AI is the Connection Persistence option. This defines how Check Point NG AI will treat existing connections when a new policy is installed. These options are displayed in Figure 4.8.

Figure 4.8 Connection Persistence Options

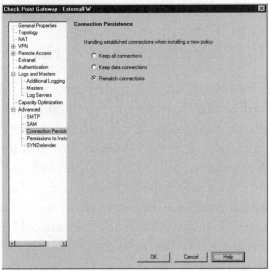

The three options have three discrete functionalities:

- **Rematch connections**, the default, is the safest selection. After a connection has been accepted, the connection is entered into the connections state table on the firewall. Upon a new policy installation, previously accepted connections are marked as "old". When a packet matching an "old" connection is received, it is matched against the security policy and, if it matches a connection that is allowed in the rule base, the state of the connection is changed back to its previous state and communications continues.

- **Keep all connections** represent a different stance to the question of how to deal with previously accepted connections. It does not mark any as "old" and allows any connections that were allowed to continue communicating.

- **Keep data connections** allows an administrator to have functionalities of the other two options. With "Keep data connections" all control connections will be rematched to the rule base, but data connections will function in the same way as "Keep all connections" operates.

The SMTP page enables you to set local options on how the SMTP security server handles mail. Typically, the defaults on this page are appropriate, although you may have to define the postmaster name. These values are stored in the firewall's *$FWDIR/conf/smtp.conf* configuration file.

The "Permissions to Install" page is a new addition as well. You can create groups of administrators and allow certain groups to install polices on certain firewalls. This functionality used to only be available with a large enterprise and managed service provider product Check Point produces called Provider-1.

On the SAM page, you will not need to modify anything unless your SAM server is external to your management server. In most cases, you will skip this section. Changing these values will affect the firewall's *$FWDIR/conf/fwopsec.conf* configuration file. SYNDefender options are discussed in more detail in Chapter 13, along with SmartDefense.

Define Rule Base

Now let's use the Perimeter Network Security Policy to create a Check Point FW-1 NG AI enforceable policy. The first step is to map things out and identify the objects that will compose the rule base. Below is the relevant excerpt from the policy.

- TCP/IP suite of protocols allowed through the firewall from the inside LAN to the public Internet is as follows:
  - HTTP to anywhere
  - HTTPS to anywhere
- TCP/IP suite of protocols allowed through the firewall from the inside LAN to the service net is as follows:
  - HTTP to Web server

- ■ SMTP to Mail server

- ■ POP3 to Mail server

- ■ DNS to DNS server

- ■ TCP/IP suite of protocols allowed through the firewall from the service net to the public Internet is as follows:

  - ■ DNS from DNS server to anywhere

- ■ TCP/IP suite of protocols allowed through the firewall from the public Internet to the LAN is as follows:

  - ■ None

- ■ TCP/IP suite of protocols allowed through the firewall from the public Internet with specific source, destination, and protocols is as follows:

  - ■ SMTP to Mail server

  - ■ HTTP to Web server

  - ■ FTP to FTP server

Reading through your policy, it refers to the LAN, the Internet, and a service net. These are all network objects that will need to be defined before you can continue. Next, traffic is flowing anywhere, to the Web server, the mail server, the DNS server, and through the firewall. These three servers on the service net will be defined as hosts or workstations. Now that you know what objects are needed, you can create them.

NOTE

For simplicity purposes, when creating this rule base disregard the cluster of firewalls shown in the diagram at the beginning of this book as well as the servers and networks (172.17.1.x and 172.17.2.x) attached to them. To reiterate, the service net is the 172.16.0.x network attached to the ExternalFW firewall.

Now that you have all of the objects defined, it is time to create the rule base. For your first rule, it is best to create the "Cleanup rule." By default, anything that is not explicitly permitted is dropped. This is called the Implicit Drop Rule. Anything not matching the rule base will be dropped and not logged.

However, it would be smart to log those events, and the only way to accomplish that is to define an explicit drop rule in the policy and enable tracking. For your first rule, select **Add rule** from the Rules menu in the SmartDashboard. This is your first rule, so bottom or top does not matter, although eventually this rule will be the last rule in the policy. From the rule that appears, confirm the following: source **Any**, destination **Any**, VPN **Any**, service **Any**, action **Drop**, and track **Log.** The only thing you will need to change is the track cell from **none** to **Log**, and add a comment in the Comment field of "Cleanup Rule." At this point, your rule base should consist of one rule and look like the example in Figure 4.9.

Figure 4.9 The "Cleanup Rule"

NO.	SOURCE	DESTINATION	VPN	SERVICE	ACTION	TRACK	INSTALL ON	TIME	COMMENT
1	✱ Any	✱ Any	✱ Any Traffic	✱ Any	⊙ drop	▤ Log	✱ Policy Targets	✱ Any	Cleanup Rule

Another good rule to have in your rule base is the "Stealth Rule." This rule is defined to protect the firewall and alert you of traffic that is directed to the firewall itself. This time, create the rule from the Rules menu by clicking **Add rule** and selecting **Above.** You can also achieve this by right-clicking on the rule number and selecting **Add Rule | Above**. From the newly created rule, change the destination field by right-clicking and selecting **Add** from the context menu. From within the Add dialog, select your firewall object. Next, in the Track field select **Alert.** This rule should read **Any**, **Firewall**, **Any**, **Drop**, and **Alert**, as illustrated in Figure 4.10. Add the comment "Stealth Rule" in the Comment field.

At this point, you may be wondering how you will be able to communicate with the firewall after this policy is installed. This communication is enabled through the implied rules in **Global Properties | FireWall-1 | Accept VPN-1 & FireWall-1 control connections**, discussed in Chapter 3.

Figure 4.10 The "Stealth Rule"

NO.	SOURCE	DESTINATION	VPN	SERVICE	ACTION	TRACK	INSTALL ON	TIME	COMMENT
1	✱ Any	▤ ExternalFW	✱ Any Traffic	✱ Any	⊙ drop	❗ Alert	✱ Policy Targets	✱ Any	Stealth Rule
2	✱ Any	✱ Any	✱ Any Traffic	✱ Any	⊙ drop	▤ Log	✱ Policy Targets	✱ Any	Cleanup Rule

Now you have the beginnings of a good rule base. Let's start adding some rules that are based on your policy.

The first element in the security policy states that you allow HTTP and HTTPS to anywhere. Because your policy does not call for any user authentication, you can leave your "Stealth Rule" at the top. Place this next rule beneath the "Stealth Rule." Click on the icon in the toolbar that represents **Add Rule below Current**. Your current rule will always be the rule that is highlighted in white, instead of being gray like all the other rules. You should see a new rule sandwiched between your two previous rules. There are many ways to create this rule. However, the best way is to select **LAN** (172.16.3.x) as the Source. For the Destination, select the **Service_Net**. Under the service field, add **HTTP**, then **HTTPS**, and finally **FTP**. Make sure you select **accept** in the Action field. The Track field will be changed to **Log** for this rule. Now right-click on the Destination **Service_Net** and choose **Negate**. A red "X" should now appear on the service net object in your rule base. What you have done is created a rule that allows LAN users the use of HTTP and HTTPS to everywhere *except* the service net. The reason you had to do this is because the policy does not allow HTTPS from the LAN to the service net, as you will see in the next couple of rules. In the Comment field, write in **Permits LAN access to HTTP, FTP, and HTTPS on the Internet**.

Second, you must define what is allowed to the Service_Net from the LAN. In these rules, you will allow the LAN access to the mail server for POP3 and Internet Message Access Protocol (IMAP), and the DNS server for DNS queries. Start creating the next rule by right clicking on the number **2** from the previous rule and choosing **Add Rule below**. Just like the previous rule, the Source is the LAN; however, the Destination is now the **Email_Server**. In the Services field, add **POP3 and IMAP** and select **accept** in the Action field. As far as the Track field is concerned, there are no requirements to log this traffic, and it might make the logs pretty large, but for debugging and forensic purposes, choose **Log**. If the logging is too much, it can easily be turned back to **None**. In the Comments field, write in **Permits LAN access to retrieve e-mail via POP3 and IMAP**. Since the next rule will probably generate a lot of traffic (DNS queries), place it just below your stealth rule. So, add a new rule below rule one, and enter **LAN** in the Source field, **DNS_Server** in the Destination, **domain–UDP** as the Service, and **accept** in the Action field. Again, you may not want to log this traffic because domain queries can be quite numerous, but it is a good practice and will help during the implementation when debugging problems. Enter "Permit LAN access to DNS server for DNS name resolving" in the Comment field.

Next, let's create a rule that allows your DNS server in the service net to perform queries to the Internet for domain name resolution. Add this rule beneath the rule you just finished. Set the rule to read Source-**DNS_Server**, Destination-**LAN** (Negate), Service-**DNS**, Action-**accept**, Track-**None,** and Comment, "Permits DNS server access to Internet for domain name resolving."

For your final rules, what will you allow in from the Internet? According to the policy you will allow SMTP to the mail server, and HTTP and FTP to the Web server. Create a new rule beneath the current rule. Rule number 4 should be defined as Source-**Any**, Destination-**Email_Server**, Service-**SMTP**, Action-**accept**, Track-**Log,** and Comment, "Permit anyone to send e-mail to the e-mail server via SMTP." Notice that this rule also permits your LAN users to connect to the mail server for SMTP. This will not only allow users on the Internet to send mail via SMTP to the mail server, but also users on the LAN. Rule number 5 should be defined as Source-**Any**, Destination-**Web_Server**, Service-**HTTP**, Action-**accept**, Track-**Log,** and Comment, "Permit anyone access to Web pages via HTTP on the Web server." This rule also allows access for your LAN. Add one more rule below 5, and define it as Source-**LAN** (negated), Destination-**Web_Server**, Service-**FTP**, Action-**Accept**, Track-**Log**, and Comment, "Permit anyone on the Internet access to FTP on the Web server." Since your policy does not allow your LAN to connect to the FTP server for FTP, you had to negate it in the source.

Now you are pretty much done. Your rule base will have nine rules and should look like the FW-1 rule base shown in Figure 4.11. You should do a **File | Save** or click on the floppy disk icon to save your finished policy.

Figure 4.11 Rule Base from Security Policy

NO.	SOURCE	DESTINATION	VPN	SERVICE	ACTION	TRACK	INSTALL ON	TIME	COMMENT
1	Any	ExternalFW	Any Traffic	Any	drop	Alert	Policy Targets	Any	Stealth Rule
2	LAN	DNS_Server	Any Traffic	UDP domain-u	accept	Log	Policy Targets	Any	Permit LAN access to DNS server for DNS name resolving
3	DNS_Server	LAN	Any Traffic	dns	accept	Log	Policy Targets	Any	Permits DNS Server access to Internet for domain name resolving
4	Any	Email_Server	Any Traffic	TCP smtp	accept	Log	Policy Targets	Any	Permit anyone to send email to the Email Server via SMTP
5	Any	Web_Server	Any Traffic	TCP http / TCP https	accept	Log	Policy Targets	Any	Permit anyone access to web pages via HTTP on the web server
6	LAN	FTP_Server	Any Traffic	TCP ftp	accept	Log	Policy Targets	Any	Permit anyone on the Internet access to FTP on the FTP Server
7	LAN	Service_Net	Any Traffic	TCP http / TCP https / TCP ftp	accept	Log	Policy Targets	Any	Permits LAN access to HTTP, HTTPS, and FTP on the Internet
8	LAN	Email_Server	Any Traffic	TCP pop-3 imap	accept	Log	Policy Targets	Any	Permits LAN access to retrieve email via POP-3 and IMAP
9	Any	Any	Any Traffic	Any	drop	Log	Policy Targets	Any	Cleanup Rule

With these rules, the ordering is critical. Keep in mind that the firewall matches packets on the first three columns (Source, Destination, and Service) by using top-down processing. Each packet starts at the top rule and moves down until a rule matches. When a packet is matched, no further processing is performed. This is called "top-down processing." If you wrote your rule base directly from a piece of paper, there may be a few problems to sort out. There will always be more than one way to define your policy; the trick is finding the best method for your organization.

As you fine-tune your policy, you can try to simplify the way you say things. By moving rules, consolidating rules, or just by stating rules differently, you can improve the effectiveness and performance of your rule base. (Performance implications and optimization is discussed in Chapter 8.) You will also need to install your rule base when you are satisfied that it is set up properly. Any changes that are made through the SmartDashboard do not take effect on the firewall module until the Security Policy is installed. The Policy menu is explained later in this chapter.

Manipulating Rules

FW-1 features a very flexible rule base. It provides the ability to alter both content and context very simply. The next few sections focus on manipulating the rule base.

Copy, Cut, and Paste Rules

Rules can be cut and pasted in a way that will be instantly familiar to most anyone. You simply select the rule (by clicking on its number), and either copy or cut the rule by right-clicking on the rule number or selecting the appropriate selection from the Edit menu, as shown in Figure 4.12. Alternatively, you can select from the Edit menu. Pasting a rule is just as easy, but there is one additional selection to make. When you select paste from the Edit menu, you will also have to decide on the placement of the rule. Your choices are top, bottom, above, or below, with the choices indicating a relation to the currently selected rule. Top and bottom are only available when using the Edit menu.

Figure 4.12 Context Menu for Manipulating Rules

Disable Rules

Disabled rules are one step from being deleted. They are not part of your security policy and are not installed when you install the policy. They are, however, displayed in the rule base window. Disabling rules is a handy method of troubleshooting, providing an easy way of recovering the rule's functionality. To disable a rule, simply right-click on that rule's number and select **Disable Rule** from the menu. To re-enable the rule, right-click the rule's number and deselect **Disable Rule.**

Notice the big "X" in Figure 4.13 signifying a disabled rule.

Figure 4.13 Disabled Rule

Delete Rules

Deleting a rule eliminates it from both the security policy and your rule base view. To delete a rule, simply select the rule's number and select **Edit | Cut.** You can also select **Cut** from the right-click menu. While it is true that you can delete a rule outright, it is recommended you get into the habit of cutting rules, since if you mistakenly delete the wrong rule, you can recover it quickly. It is also a good idea to use the database revision control to mitigate this possibility.

Hiding Rules

Sometimes, especially with a large rule base, you do not really need to see every rule all the time. Luckily, FW-1 allows you the ability to hide rules. These rules are still part of the security policy and are still installed when that policy is loaded, but they are not shown in the rule base window.

To hide a rule, select the rule by clicking on its number. The easiest way is to right-click and select **Hide** from the menu, or you may select **Hide** from the Rules menu. A hidden rule is replaced with a thick, gray divider line, giving you an easy visual indication that a hidden rule exists.

In Figure 4.14 you can see the thick, gray line between rules 4 and 6. Notice how the rule numbers stay the same. Rule 5 still exists; you just do not see it.

Figure 4.14 Hidden Rules

NO.	SOURCE	DESTINATION	VPN	SERVICE	ACTION	TRACK	INSTALL ON	TIME	COMMENT
1	* Any	ExternalFW	* Any Traffic	* Any	drop	! Alert	* Policy Targets	* Any	Stealth Rule
2	LAN	DNS_Server	* Any Traffic	UDP domain-u	accept	Log	* Policy Targets	* Any	Permit LAN access to DNS server for DNS name resolving
3	DNS_Server	LAN	* Any Traffic	dns	accept	Log	* Policy Targets	* Any	Permits DNS Server access to Internet for domain name resolving
4	* Any	Email_Server	* Any Traffic	TCP smtp	accept	Log	* Policy Targets	* Any	Permit anyone to send email to the Email Server via SMTP
6	LAN	FTP_Server	* Any Traffic	TCP ftp	accept	Log	* Policy Targets	* Any	Permit anyone on the Internet access to FTP on the FTP Server
7	LAN	Service_Net	* Any Traffic	TCP http, TCP https, TCP ftp	accept	Log	* Policy Targets	* Any	Permits LAN access to HTTP, HTTPS, and FTP on the Internet
8	LAN	Email_Server	* Any Traffic	TCP pop-3, imap	accept	Log	* Policy Targets	* Any	Permits LAN access to retrieve email via POP-3 and IMAP
9	* Any	* Any	* Any Traffic	* Any	drop	Log	* Policy Targets	* Any	Cleanup Rule

You also have the ability to both view and manage hidden rules. To view hidden rules, select **View Hidden** from the Rules menu. Managing hidden rules is even more flexible, as it enables you to create and apply masks to the rule base. These masks can be applied or removed to alter the view of the rule base. For example, suppose you have hidden all of the rules with a specific destination. You can store this view as a mask by selecting **Rules| Hide | Manage hidden** and then storing this view. Later, if you choose **Unhide All** from the Rules menu, you can easily reapply the filters via the same menu options. The options for working with Hidden Rules are shown in Figure 4.15. **View Hidden** will show all the hidden rules, but with a dark gray background.

Figure 4.15 Hidden Rules Options

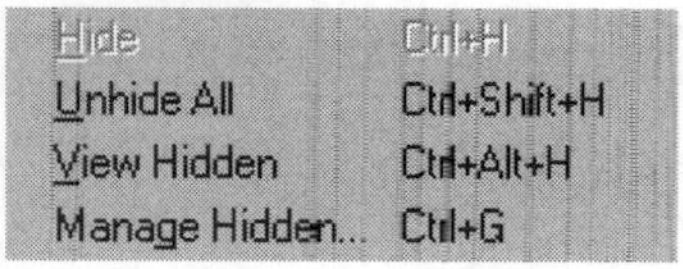

Hide	Ctrl+H
Unhide All	Ctrl+Shift+H
View Hidden	Ctrl+Alt+H
Manage Hidden...	Ctrl+G

Drag and Drop

There are several ways in which you can manipulate the rules by dragging and dropping within the SmartDashboard. You can move a rule to a new location in the rule base by simply clicking on its rule number and dragging it to the new position. You can also drag network objects and services into your rules from the Object List pane and drop them in the appropriate fields. You can even drag an object from one rule into another. This can save you time when adding new rules or editing your existing rule base. It is worth your time to become familiar with this feature. For practice, and for the next section, drag rule 7 to rule 8. This will place the LAN access to the Internet rule at rule 8.

Section Titles

When working with a large rule base, it can sometimes be beneficial to break it down into logical or functional groupings. Section Titles can add this functionality to a policy. Section Titles allow an administrator to visually collapse sections of rules together for concise viewing and quicker rule locating. Figure 4.16 shows the policy with some section titles added. Rules 2 and 3 can be easily shown by double-clicking the section title or clicking the + at the right of the section title. The information about which rules are encompassed by the section title is automatically added and updated by the GUI. Section titles can be added by right-clicking a rule number and selecting **Add Section Title**. You can go back and edit the text by right-clicking a section title and choosing **Edit Text**.

Figure 4.16 Policy with Section Titles

NO.	SOURCE	DESTINATION	VPN	SERVICE	ACTION	TRACK	INSTALL ON	TIME	COMMENT
	Stealth Rule (Rule 1)								
1	✱ Any	ExternalFW	✱ Any Traffic	✱ Any	drop	! Alert	✱ Policy Targets	✱ Any	Stealth Rule
	DNS Traffic (Rules 2-3)								
	Service Net Traffic (Rules 4-7)								
4	✱ Any	Email_Server	✱ Any Traffic	TCP smtp	accept	Log	✱ Policy Targets	✱ Any	Permit anyone to send email to the Email Server via SMTP
5	✱ Any	Web_Server	✱ Any Traffic	TCP http TCP https	accept	Log	✱ Policy Targets	✱ Any	Permit anyone access to web pages via HTTP on the web server
6	✖ LAN	FTP_Server	✱ Any Traffic	TCP ftp	accept	Log	✱ Policy Targets	✱ Any	Permit anyone on the Internet access to FTP on the FTP Server
7	✛ LAN	Email_Server	✱ Any Traffic	TCP pop-3 imap	accept	Log	✱ Policy Targets	✱ Any	Permits LAN access to retrieve email via POP-3 and IMAP
	LAN to Internet Traffic (Rule 8)								
8	✛ LAN	✖ Service_Net	✱ Any Traffic	TCP http TCP https TCP ftp	accept	Log	✱ Policy Targets	✱ Any	Permits LAN access to HTTP, HTTPS, and FTP on the Internet
	Cleanup Rule (Rule 9)								
9	✱ Any	✱ Any	✱ Any Traffic	✱ Any	drop	Log	✱ Policy Targets	✱ Any	Cleanup Rule

Querying the Rule Base

The rule base can be viewed in many different ways. Sometimes it is beneficial to view it in its entirety, while at other times you may need to see only specific items. This is especially true when dealing with a very large rule base on a very complex network. One way to achieve this narrower view is through the ability to query the rule base.

To query the rule base, select **Query Rules** from the Search menu. A query builder will appear. This window lists queries and allows for the addition, deletion, or modification of these queries. Select **New** to define a new query. A window will appear that enables you to strictly define the criteria to query against. Enter a name for your query and then click **New** again to begin entering search clauses. This window, the **Rule Base Queries Clause** window, is similar to that presented when creating a group. Simply select the column you wish to query and add the objects you wish to include in the query to the **In List** box. You also have the ability to create a negation, that is, a query that will match only if the specified criteria are not present. The final option is to enforce the query explicitly. What this means is that the match must be exact. For example, if you select **Explicit**, then a query that contained a workstation object would not match a rule that used a group containing that workstation.

Policy Options

Once you have created your Security Policy, you are ready to put it into action. The next few sections describe the options available for working with the policy you have built. Access to these options is available by selecting **Policy** from the Policy menu.

Verify

Verify is used to test the policy. It compiles the objects and prepares them for installation, but it does not actually perform the install. This is useful when you are in the process of editing and modifying your security policy and wish to make sure that you are not doing something wrong. Selecting **Verify** from the Policy menu would tell you that "Rule 1 blocks Rule 2 for service Telnet." This means that Rule 2 is redundant, and will never be matched on a packet, and therefore it is misplaced.

Install

This option actually performs the install. You will be presented with a list of possible firewall objects and can select the proper firewall or firewalls to install on from this list. The policy is then compiled and pushed out to the selected modules. You have a choice as to how these modules are treated.

- **Install on Each Selected Module Independently** This is useful when you are dealing with a large number of gateways. With this option, each module is treated as a single entity, and failure to install policy on one will not impact the others negatively.

- **For Gateway Clusters Install on All Members, If it Fails do not Install at All** This checkbox determines whether or not to allow the policy to be installed if it cannot be installed on all systems within the cluster.

- **Install on All Selected Modules, If it Fails do not Install at All** This is an all-or-nothing proposition. If you are concerned with configuration integrity, this is the option for you. Failure on any single module will preclude the installation on any module.

You will need to install your Security Policy whenever you make changes through SmartDashboard and wish for those changes to be enforced. Nothing you do in SmartDashboard will take effect until you push the policy to the appropriate firewalls.

The Database Revision Control section allows an administrator to create a new version of the policy, which can be viewed or restored at any time. This eliminates the need for saving a new policy each time a change is made. Saving a completely new policy each time a change is made leads to very large files (specifically rulebases_5_0.fws) and can lead to slow times loading the GUI and installing policies. In addition, the objects database does not get saved each time a new policy is saved, but changes are saved and can be restored using Database Revision Control. (Database Revision Control is discussed later in this chapter.)

Uninstall

This removes the policy from the objects that you select. The object selection method is identical to that when installing policy.

View

The View option enables you to view the compiled security policy; that is, it enables you to view the inspect statements, which allows you to view and save the actual inspect scripts. Saved files can be manually altered and loaded with the command-line interface (CLI) of FW-1, though it is not recommended and likely not supported by Check Point.

Access Lists

This is used to incorporate rules into an Open Security Extension (OSE)–compliant device, such as a router. When a rule is installed on a router, the firewall is actually generating an access control list (ACL) for that router and applying it as needed. You can also import the existing ACL entries for the OSE device and verify and edit them. This menu option allows for all three functions. When selected, the OSE Device Access List Operations window is displayed. This window enables you to select the OSE device you want to interact with and perform the specified operation. When fetching an ACL, you can further specify the direction you are interested in and the format you wish the ACLs to be presented in (ASCII or GUI). This requires additional licensing.

Install Users Database

This option, available from both the Policy menu and the User Management function, propagates the user database defined on the management server to the selected modules. Note that the user database is also loaded when a security policy is published (pushed/installed) to the modules, but this manual process allows the updating of user information without interfering with the firewall operations.

Management High Availability

This option of the Policy menu enables you to modify the behavior of your Management High Availability groups. This feature allows multiple management modules to synchronize and support each other, just as with HA FW-1 modules. This option loads a maintenance panel, which allows for both manual synchronization and preempting of the primary management server.

When performing a manual synchronization, you have two modes of behavior to select from.

- **Synchronize Configuration Files Only** If this is selected, only the database and configuration files will be synchronized between management modules.

- **Synchronize Fetch, Install and Configuration Files** This mode also synchronizes the Fetch and Install files, allowing the interaction with a standby management server.

You can also change the current state of the management module, from Primary to Standby and vice versa. Note that a Standby management module cannot be used to push or edit configurations until it is promoted to Primary status.

Installing a Security Policy

After you have defined all objects and composed the rule base, it is time to install the policy on your chosen modules so that it can be enforced. Remember that any time you modify network objects, rules, or Global properties, you need to install the policy for the changes to take effect. The install policy process does a few things before your rules get enforced.

When you select **Install** from the Policy menu, first Check Point saves your objects and rules. Next, Check Point verifies your rule base to ensure that you do not have any conflicting rules, redundant rules, or rules with objects that require definition. Alternatively, before you install, you can verify the policy by choosing **Policy** and then selecting **Verify**. Check Point NG AI will then parse your rule set. After the verify process returns the results that "Rules Verified OK!," Check Point NG AI asks you to select on which network object and module to install the compiled policy.

When you select the object that you wish to install this policy on, an installation window will come up. The progress of the compile and install will be displayed here. Note that in NG AI, installations are processed in parallel, dramatically improving the time required to install the policy on multiple modules. Previously, the installation process was done on each module one at a time. When the policy install is completed, you can click on the **Close** button at the bottom of the window, as shown in Figure 4.17. If you wish to cancel the installation, press the button while the **Abort** button is enabled If an error or warning occurs, you can press the **Show Errors** button to view which module and which errors were generated during the installation process.

Figure 4.17 Install Policy Progress Window

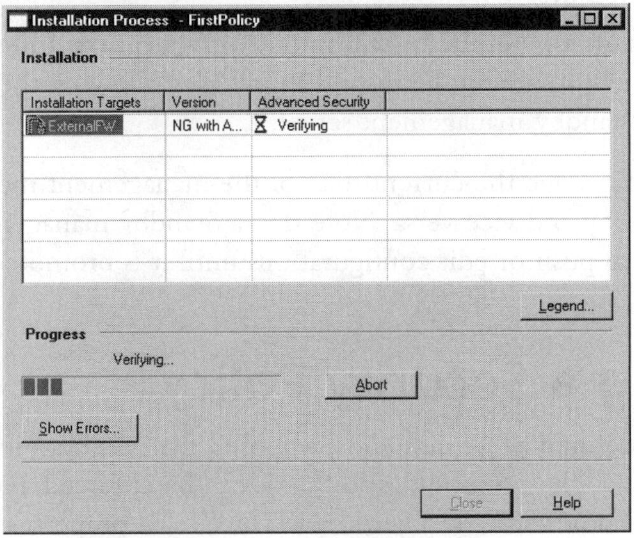

Alternatively, you can install the policy on the firewall modules at the command prompt with the using *$FWDIR/bin/fw load*. For example, if you want to install the policy named FirstPolicy on a firewall module defined with an object named Gatekeeper, you would run the following *load* command from the Management server's *$FWDIR/conf* directory:

```
$FWDIR/bin/fw load FirstPolicy.W ExternalFW
```

To confirm the installation of your policy at the command line, execute *$FWDIR\bin\fw stat*. This will display the host, policy, and time of install.

Policy Files

In the process of compiling your security policy, Check Point NG AI takes the contents of the rule base file *.W that you created through the SmartDashboard GUI, to create an INSPECT script with the same name adding a *.PF* extension. The *.PF* file is compiled into INSPECT code designated as a file called *.FC* (where the * represents the name given to your policy in the initial dialog). The INSPECT code is then applied to the network objects (firewalls) specified in the install. Keep in mind that when you install a policy on a module that has no rules to enforce, the policy will not install as it would default back to the implicit "deny all" rule.

To back up your policy, you should make and keep a separate copy of the files listed below:

- *$FWDIR\conf\objects_5_0.C*
- *$FWDIR\conf*.W*
- *$FWDIR\conf\rulebases_5_0.fws*
- *$FWDIR\database\fwauth.NDB**

The *objects_5_0.C* file stores all the network objects, resources, servers, services, and so on. The *.W* files are each individual policy files that you named via SmartDashboard. The *rulebases_5_0.fws* file is the master rule base file that holds each of the individual *.W* policies in one place. If you needed to restore your policies, you would not necessarily need to replace each *.W* file, but just the *rulebases_5_0.fws*. When you log in to SmartDashboard, this file will open and create the *.W* files that were not already in the conf directory. This *.FWS* file gets called whenever you do a **File | Open** from SmartDashboard, and you can rename or delete policies from this file via the **Open** window. Deleting a policy from here does not remove it from the hard drive; it simply removes it from the *rulebases_5_0.fws* file. The *fwauth.NDB** files contain the user database.

Configuring & Implementing…

Editing Files Manually

The *.W file can be edited with a text editor. Editing this code does not affect the GUI representation of rules. However, it will be used to create the INSPECT script and may introduce inconsistencies between the GUI interface and the installed policy. As an alternative, the *.DEF file can be edited instead.

NOTE

Editing files directly is not for the faint of heart. Similar to the registry on a Microsoft Windows system, it should not be attempted unless you have been directed to by technical support, as simple changes done incorrectly can introduce significant problems.

Summary

This chapter discussed the importance of a Security Policy and how to write one for your organization. Remember that the most important aspect of defining a Security Policy is involvement. Because the default policy of Check Point is to deny everything, with community involvement you can better define the requirements, and as a result, only permit communication that is necessary for business activities while denying all others. This is referred to as the "principle of least privilege."

As you implement and translate your written policy into something that can be enforced by Check Point NG AI, you will have to define network objects. Much of this information should have been gathered during the design of your policy and includes items like workstations, gateways, networks, applications, users, and services. Eventually, the rules you write will use these objects to match packets for processing and applying actions.

A firewall object must be defined for each firewall you are installing a policy on. In a simple, stand-alone installation where the management server and firewall module reside on the same machine, the firewall object is created for you during software installation. You will need to configure the interfaces topology and anti-spoofing within your firewall object definition.

FW-1 provides several tools to manipulate the security policy. You have several different methods of adding a rule to the rule base, disabling rules, cutting and pasting rules, and querying the rule base. Once you have the policy defined and you are ready to start the firewall enforcing the policy, you must install the policy onto the firewall objects that you have previously defined.

The installation of a policy is a process that converts the GUI rule base, which is represented as the *.W file, into an INSPECT script language *.pf file. The *.pf file is then compiled into INSPECT code, and is represented as a *.fc file that can be understood and enforced by the specified Check Point enforcement modules.

Solutions Fast Track

Reasons for a Security Policy

☑ A written Security Policy is becoming a requirement for some industries as mandated by government regulation, including financial and healthcare organizations. Parts of the Sarbanes-Oxley Act also apply to a corporation's Security Policy.

☑ Having a written Security Policy can help the security manager and administrator perform their jobs better and receive executive-level support for technologies and training.

☑ Developing a Security Policy before implementing security products will help to ensure that the deployed product meets the requirements of the business and is properly configured.

☑ A written Security Policy will provide an organization with direction and accountability in the implementation and maintenance of an information security program.

How to Write a Security Policy

☑ One of the most important aspects of writing a Security Policy is community involvement. Everyone with a stake or interest should be involved in the writing of certain aspects of the Security Policy.

☑ Writing a Security Policy should reflect your business needs and how you will manage the risks posed by those needs.

☑ An Executive Information Security Policy should be simple, readable, and accessible to users.

☑ An Information Security Policy is composed of an Executive Security Policy and specific standards, guidelines, and procedures. In addition to the Executive Security Policy, a Perimeter Network Security Policy or a Firewall Security Policy can detail specific standards for implementing a firewall and procedures for maintaining it.

Implementing a Security Policy

☑ The translation of a written policy to a Check Point NG AI policy is a step-by-step process. First, define your network objects. Then compose rules that enforce your written policy, specifying the actions to be taken when a packet matches the defined criteria.

☑ When creating a rule base, the ordering of rules is critical. Because packets are evaluated against the rules in the rule base from the top to the bottom, incorrect positioning can have undesirable consequences.

☑ The initial policy of Check Point NG AI is to deny everything. Use this to your advantage and configure your Security Policy from the perspective that you will only allow what is needed and everything else will be disallowed. This is much more secure than the approach to allow everything and only disallow that which you know is harmful.

☑ Consider putting the most-often-matched rules near the top of the rule base to increase performance.

Installing a Security Policy

☑ When you install a policy, it will be verified by Check Point NG AI and then compiled into INSPECT code.

☑ When you choose **install policy** from the GUI, it executes the **fw load** command.

Policy Files

☑ The *.W file is derived from the GUI rule base. It can be edited with a text editor.

☑ The *.PFfile is INSPECT script created from the *.W file in the install process.

☑ The objects_5_0.C file contains object definitions.

☑ The rulebases_5_0.fws file is an aggregation of all the *.W files.

Frequently Asked Questions

The following Frequently Asked Questions, answered by the authors of this book, are designed to both measure your understanding of the concepts presented in this chapter and to assist you with real-life implementation of these concepts. To have your questions about this chapter answered by the author, browse to **www.syngress.com/solutions** and click on the **"Ask the Author"** form. You will also gain access to thousands of other FAQs at ITFAQnet.com.

Q: Why can't I just write a policy? I know better than anyone does what our network needs.

A: Community involvement is essential. You cannot enforce a policy that is your personal opinion. Furthermore, it is likely you do not want the blame when something goes wrong. In addition, having too strict of a policy could encourage users to back-door the network and bypass the firewall.

Q: We are pretty small and do not have legal counsel on staff. Is legal counsel a necessity in writing the policy?

A: It depends on your potential liability. A security policy can be the standard you are held to in court, so if there is a possibility that may happen, you should seek legal counsel.

Q: My logs are filling up with a bunch of broadcast stuff. How do I filter it out?

A: You can write a rule that drops or accepts the broadcasts but does not log them. The rule will probably state that from any source to destination gateway with protocols NetBIOS, drop. However, make sure the rule appears before the rule that logs them. NetBIOS is a common protocol to filter out because it is so noisy.

Q: Where do I find all the firewall's configuration files?

A: They are located at *$FWDIR/conf.*

Q: We are using some protocols that are not listed in the Services menu. They are custom and I do not know anything about them. What can I do?

A: Find out from the vendor the protocol and destination port and source port number. If this does not work, then a search on the Internet will yield some results. Or you can just set up a sniffer such as TCP Dump or Ethereal to sniff the traffic. One final method is to initiate the connection from a known IP address and filter to see only those connections using the SmartView Tracker. Once the service information is found, you can then create the new service in SmartDashboard via the Services Management window.

Q: How do I know my policy is working?

A: Using vulnerability assessment tools or port scanners, you can check your firewall to ensure it is properly configured. Good tools include NMAP, Nessus, or LANguard network scanner. A third-party audit is not only recommended, but is required by the government for certain industries.

Q: What is the difference between a drop and a reject in the FW-1 rule base?

A: When the firewall drops a packet, it discards it into the bit bucket and does not respond to it in any way. When the firewall rejects a packet, however, it sends a "Connection Refused" back to the requesting client, thereby ending the connection attempt. If a Telnet connection is getting dropped, for example, the client will wait until the Telnet times out. If the Telnet connection is getting rejected, however, the client will get a "Connection refused" message right away and will not continue to try the connection. In most cases, it is best to use Drop because it is best that the firewall not respond to port scan requests, as opposed to letting the scanner know that a device is there and refusing the connections.

## Chapter 5

Applying Network Address Translation

Solutions in this Chapter:

Introduction

One method of securing your internal network or DMZ (demilitarized zone) network behind the firewall is to assign it a network or subnet from one of the reserved IP network numbers for private addressing. These address ranges were set aside by the Internet Assigned Numbers Authority (IANA) to conserve the limited amount of address space available as defined in RFC 1918. These numbers are assigned for reuse by any organization, so long as they are not routed outside of any single, private IP network. This means that they cannot be routed over the Internet, which provides you with a network more easily secured from outside attack.

Even if you are not using one of the IANA-reserved addresses for private networks, you can still utilize Network Address Translation (NAT) to hide your internal network and servers from the Internet. If you are using a private address internally, then you must use some external, Internet-routable network for Internet communications.

We will show you how to set up hiding NAT on your network objects and one-to-one NAT on your workstation objects in this chapter. We will also show you how you can set up some port address translation and other interesting NAT rules by manually adding rules under the Network Address Translation tab in SmartDashboard. If you read the previous chapter on creating your security policy, then once you're done with this chapter, you should have a fully functional Check Point VPN-1/FW-1 NG firewall to put on the wire and start passing packets. There are several other important topics in the chapters to come, such as user authentication and managing your policies and logs.

Hiding Network Objects

Because of the incredible and unpredictable speed at which the Internet has expanded, acquiring IP addresses for your organization has become more difficult over time. As a result, it has become increasingly important to use wisely the address space that is available. This is mostly due to the fact that there is very little unassigned public IP address spaced left and obtaining public addresses can be a very difficult and costly process. Ultimately, ICANN defines how addresses are allocated, but they delegate this responsibility to regional registrars who allocate addresses to Internet Service Providers (ISPs), who in turn delegate these addresses to companies. End-users can also request addresses directly from the regional registrar by following a process similar to what ISPs must do. In most cases, an end-user must be able to show 25 percent utilization immediately and 50 percent utilization by the end of the first year in order to receive public addresses directly from the regional registrar.

Using hide-mode NAT is one easy way to conserve address space while not limiting the functionality of your network. Hide-mode NAT enables you to hide an entire range of reserved address space behind one or more routable IP addresses.

The advantages of hiding network objects extend beyond simply conserving address space: hidden objects are not directly accessible from external hosts, and are therefore far less susceptible to attacks or unauthorized access attempts. Even though hidden objects benefit from this protection, you may still grant them full access to the Internet. FW-1 will translate packets originating from your hidden objects so that once their traffic leaves your firewall, they appear to be originating from a routable address. In turn, when the external host responds, the incoming packets are again translated by the firewall back to the original reserved address, allowing your hidden object to receive the response without knowing any translation took place. Because FW-1 translates source port as well as destination port, it is able to determine which internal host should receive an incoming connection, even if there are multiple connections destined for the firewall's external address. The firewall maintains a translation table, and from the source port in this table, it is able to direct incoming connections appropriately.

The following example will demonstrate how this process works, and how you can configure FW-1 to accomplish hide-mode NAT. One of the most common uses of hide-mode NAT, and where you will want to consider using it, is connecting your office workstations to the Internet. In order to accomplish this, you should assign your office workstations reserved IP addresses; we will use 172.17.3.0/24 for this example. This means that your workstations will use 172.17.3.1 as their default gateway, and you will configure this address on one of your firewall's internal interfaces. Then, each of your workstations will be assigned an address in the range of 172.17.3.2 to 172.17.3.254 (either manually or with a DHCP server).

One important issue to keep in mind is that your firewall must be licensed for sufficient hosts to encompass your DHCP scope, plus any statically assigned addresses. If you end up using more addresses than your FW-1 license contains, you will see repeated error messages in the system log on your firewall.

Now your workstations will be able to communicate with the internal interface of the firewall. Be sure to enable IP forwarding on your firewall; otherwise, packets will not be forwarded from one interface to another, and your workstations will not be able to gain connectivity from your internal network to the Internet, for example.

The next step is to look at the Address Translation tab in the Check Point SmartDashboard, as shown in Figure 5.1.

Figure 5.1 Address Translation Tab

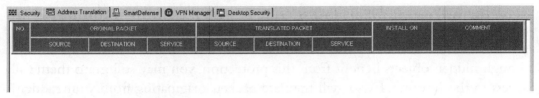

The rules in this tab can be generated automatically, as we will discuss later in this chapter, or manually. In this case, we are going to add a manual rule to take care of hiding your office network. First, add a new rule by selecting **Rules | Add Rule | Top** from the menu bar. This will insert a blank rule at the top of the current rule base.

The address translation rule base has two main sections:

- Original packet
- Translated packet

When a connection comes through the firewall, it compares the packet for a match with the source, destination, and service of the original packet section. If a match is made, the firewall then alters the source, destination, and service as specified in the translated packet section.

Just as in the standard rule base, rules in the translation rule base are processed in the order that they appear—top down, one at a time. This means that you have to be careful about where you insert new rules so that they are not overridden by rules that appear higher in the list. It is also recommended, for performance reasons, that you keep the most used NAT rules at the top of the NAT rulebase. This is discussed in more detail in Chapter 8.

Before you can configure the new rule you have created, you need to be clear on which network objects are involved. The first object you need is one representing your internal office network (172.17.3.0/24). This will be called "Net_172.17.3.0." The second object required is one representing the routable IP address that you are going to hide the office network behind. In this case, you are going to hide the internal network behind the external IP address of the firewall, so it is not necessary to create a separate object for this—you will use the existing firewall object called "ExternalFW." Note that you can hide a network behind other addresses besides that of the firewall's external interface. To do this, you would simply create another network object representing this address. However, you may have to deal with some routing issues that are discussed below.

Now that we know which objects we are going to use, it is time to create the NAT rule. To do this, start with the **Original Packet** section of the new rule you created. Add **Net_172.17.3.0** to the Source column, which indicates that this rule will apply to all traffic originating from any of your workstations. Destination should remain as **Any**, since we want to do translation no matter what destination the workstation is trying to reach. Service should also remain as **Any**, since we are not restricting this translation to any particular service type.

In the **Translated Packet** section, set the Source to **ExternalFW** by choosing **Add (Hide)** from the drop-down menu. This means that all traffic originating from your workstations will appear to external hosts to be originating from the firewall's routable external address. The **Add (Hide)** option is used for many-to-one translations. If we were translating this network to a network of the same size, we could apply the less commonly used **Static** option. Again, Destination and Service should be set as **Original**, since we are only concerned with translating source addresses here, not about destinations or services. Install On should be set to include any firewall which will be performing this translation (in this case it will be ExternalFW), and it is always a good idea to add a comment to describe the rule—"Hide rule for Office Network—172.17.3.0/24" is a good description. See Figure 5.2 for the completed rule.

Figure 5.2 Completed NAT Rule

NO.	ORIGINAL PACKET			TRANSLATED PACKET			INSTALL ON	COMMENT
	SOURCE	DESTINATION	SERVICE	SOURCE	DESTINATION	SERVICE		
1	⊹ LAN	* Any	* Any	ExternalFW	≡ Original	≡ Original	ExternalFW	Hide rule for Office Network--172.17.3.0/24

Security Address Translation | SmartDefense | VPN Manager | Desktop Security |

In addition to adding the translation rule, you must also ensure that the security policy will allow your workstations to pass traffic; the translation rule itself does not imply that packets going to and from your network will be allowed. Figure 5.3 displays what this rule should look like.

Figure 5.3 Rule to Allow Outbound Traffic

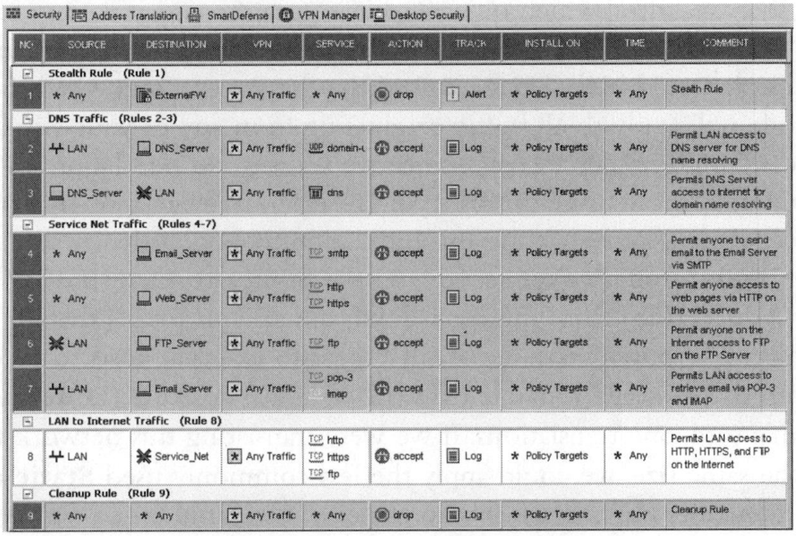

This rule, rule 4 in Figure 5.3, has source **LAN**, destination and service **Service_Net (Negate),** and action **Accept.** This means that all traffic originating from any of your workstations not directed to the Service_Net will be allowed outbound. Of course, because we have already configured the translation rule, once the firewall accepts traffic from any of these objects, it will then go on to translate the packets as specified.

Routing and ARP

Address Resolution Protocol (ARP) translates IP addresses to hardware MAC addresses, and vice-versa. In the example above, where we used hide-mode NAT to translate packets going to and from your internal network, we used the firewall's external IP address as the translated address. In this case, there are no ARP issues to consider because the firewall will respond to requests directed to its own external address.

However, if we were to use another routable address as the translated address, we would have to ensure that this address is published, so that when external hosts send traffic to this address, the firewall responds. To do this, you must add a static ARP entry to the host on which the firewall is installed. There is also an option, enabled by default on new NG installations but not upgrades, that enables the automatic addition of ARP entries by the firewall. This is discussed in more detail later in the chapter.

On a Solaris system, use the following syntax to add the static ARP entry:

```
arp -s <translated IP> <MAC address> pub
```

The MAC address to use here is the MAC address of the external interface of your firewall. You can determine this address using the *ifconfig -a* command. Note that this ARP entry will only exist until the system is rebooted. To make the ARP entry permanent, you will have to add it to the appropriate startup file on your system. For example, we will say that the public IP address for the Web Server is 11.12.13.10, and that the MAC address on the external interface of the firewall is 00:01:03:CF:50:C9. The ARP command you would use in this case is as follows:

```
arp -s 11.12.13.10 00:01:03:CF:50:C9
```

Similarly, in Windows NT, you would also need to add a static ARP entry. However, NT does not allow this via the arp command, and so you must edit the file $FWDIR\state\local.arp. In this file, add a line as follows:

```
<translated IP>        <MAC address>
```

Or, in our example:

```
11.12.13.10            00:01:03:CF:50:C9
```

On both Windows and Solaris, you can display a list of current ARP entries by issuing the command *arp -a*. This will include any manual ARP entries you have created, as well as all other ARP entries the system has learned. When entering the *arp* command, separate the fields with a space or tab. After editing this file, you will have to stop and restart the FW-1 service to activate your changes.

If you are using a Nokia to configure a static ARP entry, access the Voyager GUI select **Config | ARP**, and add the entry. You should select the **Proxy Only** type. Note that if you are using VRRP, and you use the virtual IP address as the hiding address, there is no need to add a static ARP entry because the firewall already knows that it should respond to the specified address.

In addition to ARP issues, you need to keep routing issues in mind when configuring any type of NAT. Our example above does not present any obvious routing issues, assuming the workstations are all directly connected to the firewall, and are used as a gateway. However, if there were a router or any other Layer 3 device between the workstations and the firewall, you would have to ensure that the router forwarded traffic between the workstations and the firewall properly.

One other routing issue to take into account is that if the IP address you are using as your hiding address is not part of your firewall's external interface, external routers may not know how to reach this address. If traffic does not reach the firewall, then the ARP entry you created for that address will do no good. To ensure that traffic reaches the firewall, you will have to ensure that the router responsible for announcing your networks also publishes the network you are using for NAT. This may involve contacting your Internet provider (if you do not manage your own router).

Configuring Static Address Translation

Static address translation translates an internal IP address to an external IP address on a one-to-one ratio. This is in contrast to hide-mode translation, which translates many internal IP addresses to one external IP address (many-to-one). Situations especially suited to static-mode translation include cases where external hosts on the Internet have to initiate connections with hosts on your protected network. Using hide-mode translation would not allow for this—internal hosts are hidden, as the name suggests, and therefore cannot be contacted directly from external sources. Static address translation is also useful in situations where hide-mode will not work, such as with certain VPN clients or other specialized applications.

Static address translation rules come in two flavors: static source and static destination. Rules are generally generated in pairs—you will want matching source and destination rules for each internal object involved with static-mode translation. If you have only static source or static destination, it will provide NAT for connections only in one direction. The NAT rulebase is similar to the Security Policy rulebase in that it works based on the connection, not the individual packet. Therefore, for incoming connections to a web server, it is *not* required that you define a static source NAT rule just to enable response packets to be translated on the way out to the Internet.

The following sections provide more detail about the two types of static-mode translation rules and describe an example configuration. In the example, there is a Web server sitting behind the firewall, called "Web_Server," on an internal IP address, 172.16.0.10. Our objective here is to use static address translation to allow external users to access this Web server. To do this, we will first create a static source rule to allow the Web server to connect to the Internet with its public IP address. We will then configure a static destination rule that will allow others on the Internet to contact the Web server.

Static Source

The first step in configuring static address translation for your Web server is to ensure that connections originating from the Web server are able to exit your network and reach their destinations on the Internet. This is the purpose of static source mode.

In both hide-mode address translation and static source mode translation, reserved IP addresses are translated into a routable IP addresses before they leave the firewall. The difference is that in static source mode there is a one-to-one relationship between reserved addresses and routable addresses. That is, each reserved address is translated into a unique routable address.

Static source rules, like hide rules, can be configured either automatically or manually. While this example will focus on manual rule configuration, you can refer to the "Automatic NAT rules" section for information on how to generate these rules automatically.

To configure a static source rule, open SmartDashboard, and select the **Address Translation** tab. Select **Rules** | **Add Rule** | **Top**. Again, depending on which rules are already present, you may need to add the rule elsewhere in the rule base. The next step is to configure this rule; see rule 1 in Figure 5.4.

Figure 5.4 Static Source Rule

⊞ Security	⊞ Address Translation	🖳 SmartDefense	🚇 VPN Manager	🗖 Desktop Security				

NO.	ORIGINAL PACKET			TRANSLATED PACKET			INSTALL ON	COMMENT
	SOURCE	DESTINATION	SERVICE	SOURCE	DESTINATION	SERVICE		
1	🖳 Web_Server	✱ Any	✱ Any	🖳 Web_Server_External	≡ Original	≡ Original	✱ Policy Targets	NAT outbound connections to the web server
2	⊹ LAN	✱ Any	✱ Any	🖩 ExternalFW	≡ Original	≡ Original	✱ Policy Targets	Hide Rule for Office Network--172.17.3.0/24

Before you configure the new rule, you will need to add an object representing the routable IP address that will translate the Web server's internal address. Create a standard workstation object with a valid routable IP within your address space, and call it "Web_Server_External," as in Figure 5.5.

Figure 5.5 Web Server External Object

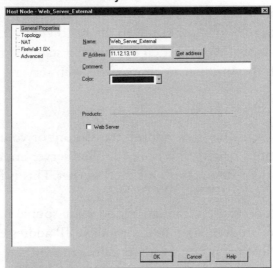

Now, back to the translation rule. In the Original Packet section, under
Source, add the **Web_Server** object—double-check that this object has an
internal address. Leave the **Destination** as **Any**, since we want to apply this rule
no matter what external host the Web server is attempting to contact. Also leave
the **Service** as **Any**, since we are not going to restrict the destination port for
this rule. Note that you could specify HTTP or HTTPS here, depending on
your specific application, but it's easier to allow all services in case you ever have
to use another service like ICMP to test connectivity.

In the Translated Packet section, set Source to **Web_Server_External**, and
double-check that this object is set to the routable address you are using for
translation. Again, leave **Destination** and **Service** unchanged, as **Original**, since
we are only interested in translating the source address, not in the destination or
service.

Set **Install On** to **All,** or if you are only planning to use this rule on a subset
of your available firewalls, set this to match that set. Be sure to add a descriptive
comment, such as "Static source for Web_Server," so that you will be able to
identify this rule later.

The last step to enable static source translation is to ensure that your standard
rule base will allow traffic from the Web server outbound if necessary. See rule 9
in Figure 5.6.

Figure 5.6 Outbound Rule for Web Server

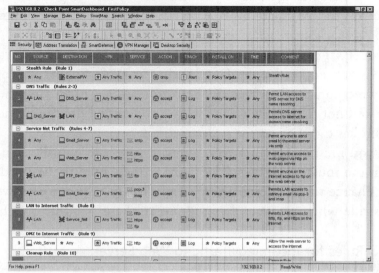

Set the **Source** to **Web_Server**, **Destination** to **Any**, and **Service** to **HTTP**. **Action** will be **Accept**, and **Track** should be **Log**.

Once you install the policy, you will have a working static source translation rule for this Web server. Remember that this rule only takes care of allowing the Web server to reach external hosts; without any further configuration there is no means by which inbound traffic can reach the server. In general, the functionality of a Web server requires external traffic to reach the server, and so static source rules are usually created in pairs with static destination rules, which are described next.

Static Destination

Creating a static destination rule is very similar to creating a static source rule, except for the order of the objects. See rule 2 in Figure 5.7.

Figure 5.7 Static Destination Rule

Again, add a rule to the translation rule base by selecting **Rules | Add Rule**. Here you should place this rule above or below the static source rule. In this case, in the Original Packet section, set the **Destination** to **Web_Server_External**, and leave **Source** and **Service** as **Any**. In the Translated Packet section, set the **Destination** as **Web_Server**, and again leave the other two columns as **Original**. The reason we are modifying the destination in this case and not the source is that we are concerned only with incoming traffic, which has the Web server as destination.

Finally, you must ensure that your standard rule base will allow incoming traffic to hit the routable address. If not, this traffic would be dropped before it even had a chance to go through your translation rule. In our case, we already created this rule when we were defining our rulebase. See rule 5 in Figure 5.8.

Figure 5.8 Rules for Incoming Traffic to Web Server

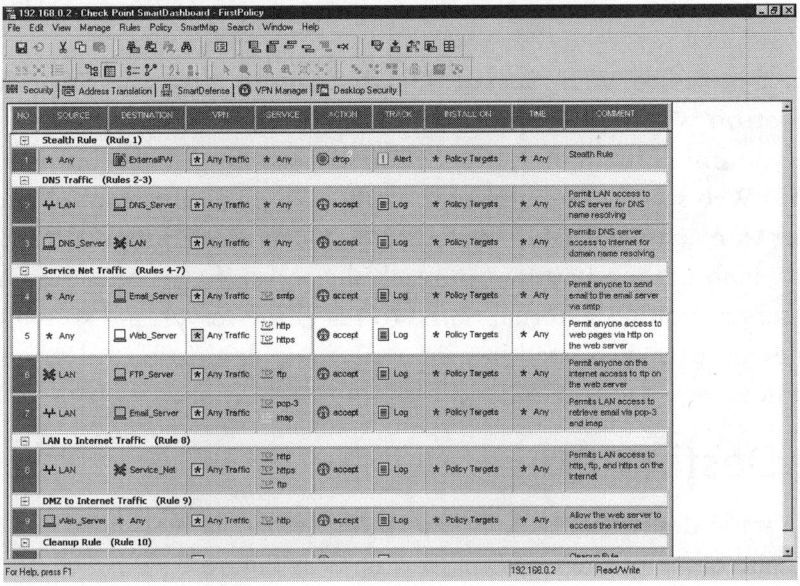

Here, set **Source** to **Any**, **Destination** to **Web_Server**, **Service** to **Any**, and **Action** to **Accept**. Note that you could specify specific services, such as HTTP or HTTPS, and you could also narrow down the acceptable remote hosts that can access the Web server by adding them to the destination.

After you install the policy, you will have a working static destination setup. What you can do then is configure DNS so that the name by which you want people to access this Web server, for example www.mycompany.com, points to the address you have assigned to Web_Server_External.

When this name is accessed on the Internet, traffic will be directed to your firewall, which will then translate and forward the packets to your Web server's internal address (the same one assigned to the object *Web_Server*). The Web server will recognize these packets as belonging to itself, and will respond to the request. When the response reaches the firewall, the firewall will again translate the packets back to the routable address, and forward them back toward the client. The client will see the response as originating from the same address to which they sent the request, and will not even know translation took place.

Routing and ARP

Just as in hide-mode address translation, there are ARP and routing issues to take into account for static source and static destination modes.

Static-mode NAT requires the same ARP configuration as hide-mode; the routable address you are using (in this case the one assigned to Web_Server_External) must be configured on the firewall host. This is necessary so that incoming traffic bound for this address is recognized by the firewall as belonging to itself, and processed rather than forwarded elsewhere.

On a Solaris system, use the following syntax to add the static ARP entry:

```
arp -s <translated IP> <MAC address> pub
```

On a Windows NT system, edit the file $FWDIR\state\local.arp. In this file, add a line as follows:

```
<translated IP>        <MAC address>
```

In both cases, use the translated IP assigned to Web_Server_External and the MAC address of your local network card. Be sure to stop and restart the firewall process after making these changes.

If you are using a Nokia, add an ARP entry in the Voyager GUI under **Configure | ARP**. Here, add a permanent ARP entry with type **Proxy Only**.

Static destination mode requires that you take into account routing the packets destined for the Web server. Specifically, the firewall will not know which interface to use to transmit the packets unless told explicitly. This may seem confusing, since you may think the translation rule will take care of routing the packet properly. However, if you upgraded your firewall to NG from a previous version (for instnace v4.1), then translation takes place *after* the packets are routed. You can think of this as the packet header being rewritten just as the packet is on its way out of the firewall's interface. So, it must be going out of the correct interface before the address is translated. New installations of NG will translate *before* the packets are routed. See the section NAT Global Properties for more information.

To add a static route on a Solaris system, use the following command:

```
route add <routable address> <internal adress>
```

Note that in Solaris, this route, as well as any ARP entries you have added statically, will only remain present until the system is rebooted. You will need to ensure that you add this route to the appropriate startup file prior to the next reboot.

To add a static route on a Windows NT system, use the following command:

```
Route add <routable address> <internal address> -p
```

Here, the route will remain intact following a reboot due to the *-p* option, which stands for persistent. In both cases, the *routable address* is the address assigned to *Web_Server_Ext*, and the *internal address* is the address assigned to *Web_Server* or the next hop router.

To add a static route on a Nokia, open the Voyager GUI and select **Configure | Routing Configuration | Static Routes**. Add the route here, and then apply and save your changes.

Now that you have taken care of all outstanding ARP and routing issues, you can be sure that your static source and static destination translation rules will allow the Web server to function normally, while still being protected by the fire-wall.

Automatic NAT Rules

In additional to creating translation rules manually, FW-1 gives you the ability to generate these rules automatically. Generating automatic translation rules saves you time, and reduces the opportunity for error. You can create both hide-mode and static-mode translation rules automatically. Manually defined NAT rules can be more efficient, but Automatic NAT rules are easier for novice users and are typically used for simplicity when possible.

Automatic Hide

As above, we will use the example of configuring hide-mode translation to hide your LAN network, 172.17.3.0/24, behind one routable address. To configure automatic hide-mode translation, open the SmartDashboard and select **Manage**

| **Network Objects**. Edit the properties of LAN and select the **NAT** tab, as shown in Figure 5.9.

Figure 5.9 NAT Tab of Network Object

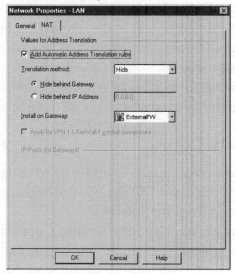

Select **Add Automatic Address Translation Rules**. Select **Hide** from the **Translation Mode** drop-down list. To specify a routable IP address to hide the network, enter the address in the **Hide behind IP Address** field (enter **0.0.0.0** to configure the firewall to use its external IP address). Alternatively, you can use the external IP address of the gateway by selecting the **Hide behind Gateway** option. Use the **Install On** drop-down list to specify the firewalls that will require this rule, or select **All** to apply this rule to all existing firewalls.

Click **OK**. FW-1 will automatically generate the required rules for this hide-mode translation. See Figure 5.10.

Figure 5.10 NAT Rule Base with Generated Rules

NO	ORIGINAL PACKET			TRANSLATED PACKET			INSTALL ON	COMMENT
	SOURCE	DESTINATION	SERVICE	SOURCE	DESTINATION	SERVICE		
1	LAN	LAN	Any	Original	Original	Original	ExternalFW	Automatic rule (see the network object data).
2	LAN	Any	Any	LAN (Hiding Address)	Original	Original	ExternalFW	Automatic rule (see the network object data).
3	Web_Server	Any	Any	Web_Server_External	Original	Original	Policy Targets	NAT outbound connections to the web server
4	Any	Web_Server_External	Any	Original	Web_Server	Original	Policy Targets	NAT incoming connections to the web server

Rules 1 and 2 above have been generated by the *LAN* object's automatic translation settings. Rule 1 ensures that traffic traveling within LAN will not be affected by translation; this traffic does not require translation since it is not leaving your network. Rule 2 resembles the manual translation rule we created earlier. It translates all traffic originating on your network into the routable IP address you specified, and then translates the destination of incoming packets back into their original addresses.

The final step to activating hide-mode translation is to ensure that your general rule base will allow traffic to flow as expected. These are the same rules you created when you configured manual hide-mode translation.

Automatic Static

Configuring static rules automatically is similar to creating hide-mode rules automatically. In this example, we will again be configuring translation to allow *Web_Server* to be accessed from the Internet.

To configure automatic static-mode translation, open SmartDashboard and go to the properties of the object you are configuring, in this case *Web_Server*. See Figure 5.11.

Figure 5.11 NAT Tab of Web Server

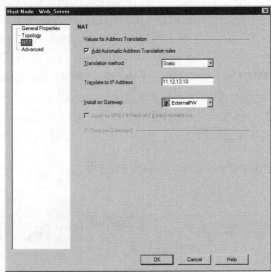

Access the **NAT** tab and enable **Add Automatic Address Translation rules**. Select **Static** from the **Translation Method** drop-down list, and for Valid

IP Address, enter the routable IP address you are going to use in this case. The Install On field should include the firewalls for which this rule is appropriate, or be set to **All**.

Click **OK**. FW-1 will automatically generate the required rules for this static-mode translation. See rules 1 and 2 in Figure 5.12.

Figure 5.12 Generated Address Translation Rules

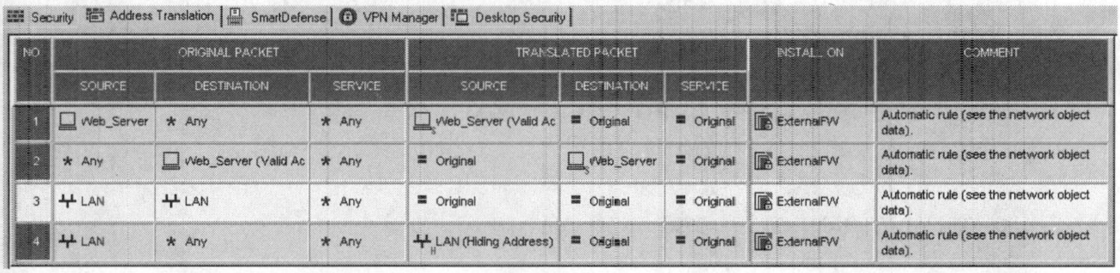

Here, rules 1 and 2 have been generated by the *Web_Server* automatic translation settings. These rules will resemble the static source and static destination rules we created earlier. Rule 1 translates traffic originating from the Web server to the routable IP address, and rule 2 translates incoming traffic from valid, routable address back to the internal address for incoming traffic.

Again, the final step is to ensure that your general rule base will allow traffic to flow to and from the Web server. These are the same rules you created when you configured manual static-mode translation.

Routing and ARP

With automatic NAT, you also need to keep routing and ARP issues in mind. The procedures for ensuring packets reach their intended destination are the same as with manual NAT.

Configuring & Implementing…

Automatic ARP

A new feature to FW-1 is automatic ARP configuration. This feature eliminates the need for manual ARP entries. When enabled, via the NAT tab in global policy properties, FW-1 will automatically create ARP entries for all required addresses. This includes single IP addresses and address ranges, but applies only to automatic NAT.

Note: in earlier versions (pre-FP3), automatic ARP did not work with clusters. In NG AI, ARP only works with ClusterXL implementations, not third party implementations such as Nokia IPSO's VRRP.

If there is a router or multiple routers on your internal network and you are using reserved address space, you need to ensure that static routes (and default routes) exist on the router, or that dynamic routing protocols are configured correctly, so that packets will reach the firewall. For static source and hide-mode NAT, you must ensure that proper ARP entries exist on the firewall for the hiding or static source address. If you have upgraded to NG from a prior version of FW-1, then for static destination you need to add a static host route on the firewall to direct the traffic out the proper interface, since routing will take place before NAT.

You can configure individual ARP and routing tasks using the same techniques that you use when you configure NAT manually. Alternatively, you can configure ARP and routing tasks by enabling some of the options available in the NAT Global Properties, which we will talk about next.

NAT Global Properties

FW-1 has some global NAT settings that affect the firewall's behavior. To access these settings, open SmartDashboard and select **Policy | Global Properties**. Select **NAT – Network Address Translation,** shown in Figure 5.13.

Figure 5.13 NAT Global Properties

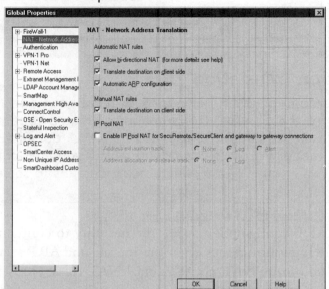

The **Automatic rules intersection** setting, when checked, will apply when there is more than one automatic NAT rule that applies in any given situation. Automatic rules intersection means that in this case the firewall will combine or intersect the rules, thereby applying them both. When this box is not checked, the firewall will only apply the first matching NAT rule, and will ignore any subsequent matching rules.

For example, if a packet matches one translation rule's source and other rule's destination, the firewall would translate both the source and destination.

When **Perform destination translation on the client side** is checked, the firewall will perform static destination mode NAT on the client side of the connection, as opposed to the server side. With this option enabled, the need to add static host routes on the firewall is eliminated since address translation will take place before routing.

Configuring & Implementing...

Destination Translation

Previous versions of FW-1 performed destination mode NAT on the server side of the firewall. This sometimes created routing and anti-spoofing issues. As a result, this version of FW-1 defaults to handling destination mode NAT on the client end, unless you are upgrading from a previous version of FW-1, in which case it defaults to server side.

Automatic ARP configuration avoids the necessity to configure ARP entries manually on the firewall, as discussed in the routing and ARP sections. This applies only to automatic NAT, not to manual NAT rules. This setting causes the firewall to automatically generate ARP entries for all configured translated IP addresses, enabling the firewall to respond to these addresses. This occurs on the firewall module that is enforcing the translation policy, and you can view the ARPs the firewall is generating with this command: *fw ctl arp*

Summary

Network address translation is an effective way to protect your network, while at the same time conserving valuable IP address space. Hosts that are protected by NAT are far less vulnerable to attack or compromise by external threats, since they are not directly accessible from the Internet.

FW-1 provides you with two main methods of doing NAT: hide-mode and static-mode. Hide-mode translation is most useful for situations when you need to translate an entire range of private IP space into one routable address. A common example is an office LAN: multiple office workstations, none of which need to be accessible externally, can be hidden with hide-mode NAT.

Static-mode translation, divided into static source and static destination, is suited to cases when the device you are hiding must be accessible from the Internet. In static-mode, there is a one-to-one relationship between internal and external addresses.

For both hide- and static-mode translation, FW-1 enables you to define NAT rules manually, or to have them generated automatically. The end result is the same—which method you use to define rules is up to you, and will depend on the situation and on how comfortable you are with the NAT rulebase.

Now that you understand how to configure network address translation with FW-1, you have a powerful tool available that will enable you to create a highly secure, yet functionally uninhibited environment. Using NAT effectively is a key to building an optimal security policy.

Solutions Fast Track

Hiding Network Objects

☑ Hide-mode NAT is used to hide an entire range of private addresses behind one routable address.

☑ With hide-mode NAT, internal hosts are not accessible from external hosts, but internal hosts can still retain full access outward.

☑ When configuring hide-mode NAT, you need to take ARP issues into account, and may have to add manual ARP entries to your firewall.

Configuring Static Address Translation

☑ Static-mode NAT is used when internal hosts need to be accessible from the Internet.

☑ With static-mode NAT, there is a one-to-one ratio between internal and external addresses.

☑ There are ARP and routing issues to take into account when configuring static-mode NAT. You may need to add static routes if you have a router between your workstations and firewall, as well as static ARP entries.

Automatic NAT Rules

☑ NAT rules in FW-1 can be created manually via the NAT rulebase, or automatically via each network object's NAT tab.

☑ Configuring FW-1 rules automatically may simplify your configuration tasks, and allow you to more easily visualize your environment.

☑ Even when configuring NAT automatically, you need to keep the same ARP and routing considerations in mind.

NAT Global Properties

☑ FW-1's global NAT properties help you to configure rule intersection behavior, determine where to perform destination translation, and perform automatic ARP configuration.

☑ Automatic ARP configuration is an especially useful feature that eliminates the need for manual ARP entries on the firewall. FW-1 will create ARP entries for all required addresses.

Frequently Asked Questions

The following Frequently Asked Questions, answered by the authors of this book, are designed to both measure your understanding of the concepts presented in this chapter and to assist you with real-life implementation of these concepts. To have your questions about this chapter answered by the author, browse to **www.syngress.com/solutions** and click on the **"Ask the Author"** form. You will also gain access to thousands of other FAQs at ITFAQnet.com.

Q: Should I configure NAT rules manually, or use FW-1 to generate them automatically?

A: No matter how you configure NAT, the end result should be the same. In fact, if you configure NAT automatically, you should still check the NAT rule base to ensure that the rules ended up as you expected. So, the answer to this question really depends on your familiarity and comfort level with NAT and with FW-1 in general.

Q: How do I know when to use hide-mode and when to use static-mode NAT?

A: As a general rule, use static-mode NAT only when the internal device must be accessible from the Internet. This includes devices such as Web servers, FTP servers, or any other server you want external users to have access to. Also, some forms of VPN and some other specialized applications require static-mode NAT. Hide-mode translation should be used when the internal device needs access outbound, but does not need to be reached externally.

Q: When will the firewall use an ARP entry as opposed to a route?

A: ARP entries are used for devices that are on the same network as the firewall, while routes are used otherwise. For devices on the same network, when the firewall tries to reach an IP address, it first checks to see if it already has an ARP entry for that host. If not, it sends out an ARP broadcast, received by all devices on the same network, requesting the MAC address for the given IP. For devices not on the same network, the firewall simply checks its routing table for a route to that host, and uses the default route if none is found.

Q: I have a lot of NAT rules, and it takes a long time to compile my security policy. What can I do to speed things up?

A: If you have several sequential networks or subnets defined for your hiding NAT networks, you can combine these into one network object with a subnet that will cover all (or as many as possible) of your networks. For example, if you have 10.1.1.0, 10.1.2.0, 10.1.3.0…10.1.128.0, and you have automatic NAT turned on for each of these networks, you could have 256 NAT rules. Instead, you can create one object with address 10.1.0.0 and subnet mask 255.255.128.0 and add the automatic NAT to this one object.

Q: My management console is managing several firewalls, and we have an assortment of 10.x.x.x networks on our internal network networks spread out across different locations. How can I keep my NAT rule base simple?

A: Create one network object for 10.0.0.0 with netmask 255.0.0.0, and add hide NAT with a translation address of 0.0.0.0 or select **Hide behind Gateway**. Using this address will hide the traffic behind the firewall's IP address that the traffic is leaving.

Q: I can't access my remote network over our Virtual Private Network because the firewall is hiding our local network. What should I do?

A: Sometimes it is necessary to create manual address translation rules that *do not* translate. If you should not be translating your internal network to your remote office, then you could add a rule where the Original Packet fields match these VPN packets, and the Translated Packet section keeps all three columns (Source, Destination, and Service) as **Original.** This rule would have to be added above any rules in the rulebase that translated this source or destination. Note: you can only use one object in each cell in the NAT rulebase. As a result, it may be necessary to create a group of objects between which you will not be NATing.

Q: How can I troubleshoot my NAT configuration?

A: Perform these steps to verify that you have things configured properly for static address translation. You may need to add a security policy rule for this to report correctly. If you cannot determine a problem with ping, check your Log Viewer for dropped or rejected packets as well as look at the following columns in the Log Viewer: NAT rule number, NAT additional rule number,

XlateSrc (Xlate is short for Translate) for the translated source IP address, XlateDst for the translated destination IP address, XlateSPort for the translated source port, and XlateDPort for the translated destination port. Don't worry if they are blank, they are only recorded if the particular part of the packet is being changed.

1. From the firewall, ping the internal IP address of the host/server. If you cannot, then check the cabling.

2. From the firewall, ping the routable, external IP address of the host/server. If you cannot, then check the host route on the firewall. If the host route looks right, then check the network object for your workstation; the IP address or Address Translation may be incorrect.

3. From the host, ping the internal IP address of the firewall. If you cannot, then check the cabling.

4. From the host, ping the firewall's external IP address. If you cannot, then check the default route on the host, and the default route of any intervening routers.

5. From the host, ping your Internet router (or the firewall's default gateway). If you cannot, then check the address translation on the workstation's network object in SmartDashboard. If that looks fine, then check the ARP on the firewall (local.arp in NT).

Q: Why can't I get to any servers on my DMZ that are configured with static NAT after rebooting the firewall?

A: If you are using a Windows firewall, check that the static host route was added with a –p switch, which stands for persistent or permanent. This ensures that the routes are added into the registry and restored whenever the system is rebooted. If you are using a Solaris firewall, ensure that your ARP and route statements are added in a startup file. If you have a Nokia firewall, make sure that you make any route and ARP change through the Voyager GUI, and that you SAVE your changes after you apply them.

## Chapter 6

Authenticating Users

Solutions in this Chapter:

- FireWall-1 Authentication Schemes
- Defining Users
- User Authentication
- Client Authentication
- Session Authentication
- LDAP Authentication

☑ Summary

☑ Solutions Fast Track

☑ Frequently Asked Questions

Introduction

There are many reasons that your organization may decide to implement user authentication at your firewall. Perhaps you want to allow different departments access to various resources on your de-militarized zone (DMZ), or maybe you are using Dynamic Host Control Protocol (DHCP) inside your network, and Internet Protocol (IP) addresses are changing every week when their leases expire. If you want to keep track of who is going to what Internet Web sites for whatever reason, then you could authenticate your users at the firewall, so that it can accurately log the user's login identity. Then you don't have to rely on IP addresses to determine who is going where. Authentication is also necessary when utilizing client-to-site or Remote Access Virtual Private Network (VPN) connections to ensure only authorized users are able to access resources inside your network.

VPN-1/FW-1 Next Generation provides you with several different authentication schemes and user authentication methods, and you should be able to choose one of them to suit your organization's needs. This chapter will describe the various options and provide some examples of how you might implement them into your current security policy structure.

Some of the options available for authenticating your users are SecurID, RADIUS, TACACS, OS password, and VPN-1/FW-1 authentication. You can choose to authenticate your users by one of these methods, and then you can pick from several authentication options in the policy, which we will cover in this chapter. Though not the complete Single Sign-On solution provided by User Authority, the information this chapter provides will include useful capabilities in the base firewall installation.

FireWall-1 Authentication Schemes

Authentication is a major component of any firewall. Without authentication, we would not be able to distinguish authorized users from unauthorized users, requiring the access to always be based on IP addresses. FW-1 gives you the option of several different authentication schemes. Some of these schemes make use of external products or servers, while others are purely internal to FW-1.

All of these schemes can be used in conjunction with user, session, and client authentication, which will be discussed later in this chapter. Note that to use any of these schemes, you must enable them in your firewall object's Authentication tab (Figure 6.1).

Figure 6.1 Firewall Object Authentication Tab

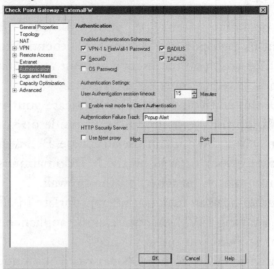

Turning on each of the schemes merely gives you the option of using them for a particular user; it does not force you to use this scheme. You can also use this tab to configure **User Authentication session timeout**, which is the amount of time that must pass before a user is required to authenticate again. The **Enable wait mode for Client Authentication** option will be discussed below, under Client Authentication.

SecurID

SecurID is a two-factor authentication method, meaning two pieces of information are required before access is granted: a password and a token. The token is generally generated by a SecurID token—a small electronic device created by RSA Security that the user keeps with him or her that displays a new number every 60 seconds. Combining this number with the user's password allows the SecurID server to determine whether or not the user should be granted access.

In order to configure SecurID, your FW-1 server must be configured as an ACE client. A separate server is required to run the ACE Server software. Please refer to your ACE server documentation for further information. To enable SecurID authentication in FW-1, ensure that it is first enabled in the firewall object's Authentication tab. There are no settings for SecurID in the Policy Editor; you simply need to set the authentication scheme for the user you are configuring to "SecurID" in the user's Authentication tab.

OS Password

Authentication via operating system (OS) password means that FW-1 will refer to the user's account in the operating system for authentication. This may be a convenient method for you if all the users you want to configure for firewall authentication already have accounts on the system.

One example of this is if you want to authenticate your users with their domain passwords. To do this, your firewall must reside on your NT domain so that the firewall can access the domain user database. Be aware of the possible security risks of locating your firewall on the NT domain; if security is breached on the domain, it may also be breached on the firewall.

OS password authentication may not be appropriate in all situations. For example, if you are running FW-1 on a standalone appliance, it is unlikely that users will have local accounts on the appliance.

In order to configure FW-1 to use OS password authentication, ensure that it is enabled in the firewall object's Authentication tab, and simply choose it as the authentication scheme for the user you are configuring; there are no other settings for this scheme.

Designing & Planning…

OS Password Authentication

If you are using OS password authentication, be careful about users who have OS accounts that you do not want to grant access to through the firewall. If you have defined a default "generic*" user, you may inadvertently grant access to more users than you intended. If this is the case, you can create users with authentication schemes set to "Undefined", which will deny those users access. If a significant amount of your OS users should not have access, consider using a different authentication scheme.

VPN-1 & FireWall-1 Password

If your users do not have accounts on the local FW-1 server, but you do not want to use an external authentication scheme such as SecurID, then your best option is FW-1 password. Using a FW-1 password simply means that you assign the user a password within FW-1, and the user must enter a matching password to authenticate.

To configure VPN-1 and FW-1 password authentication, ensure that this option is enabled in the Authentication tab of your firewall object. Access the **Authentication** tab of the user you are configuring and choose **VPN-1 & FireWall-1 Password.** Enter a password of eight characters or less. FW-1 will ask you to confirm the password.

RADIUS

RADIUS, which stands for Remote Access Dial In User Service, is a convenient way of managing usernames and passwords. In order to use this authentication scheme, you must have a functional RADIUS server that contains a database of all the users you would like to authenticate.

To configure RADIUS authentication in FW-1, the first step is to add a workstation object to represent your RADIUS server. To do this from SmartDashboard, click **New** or go to **Manage | Network Objects | New | Node | Host**. Create the object with the IP address of your RADIUS server.

The next step is to add a RADIUS server object. To do this, open the SmartDashboard, and select **Manage | Servers and OPSEC Applications**. Click **New** and select **RADIUS**, (see Figure 6.2).

Figure 6.2 RADIUS Server Configuration

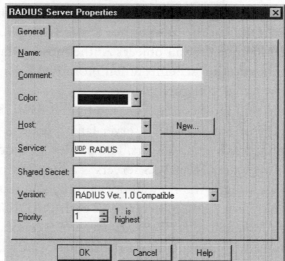

Enter the following information:

- **Name** A descriptive name for your RADIUS server.

- **Comment** A descriptive comment about your RADIUS server.

- **Color** Select the color that will identify your RADIUS server icon in the user interface.

- **Host** The physical server on which your RADIUS server is running. Note that you need to define this host as a network object prior to completing this configuration.

- **Service** Select **RADIUS**. If the RADIUS Server is listening for queries on a different port, select the service object that represents that port.

- **Shared Secret** Enter a secret password. You also need to configure this password on the RADIUS server; see your RADIUS server documentation for details.

- **Version:** Select either version 1.0 or 2.0 compatible, depending on the version of your RADIUS server.

- **Priority:** Specify **1** if you only have one RADIUS server. If you have more than one RADIUS server, then you have the option of ranking them by priority so that certain servers are always contacted first. See below for a discussion about configuring multiple RADIUS servers.

Now that you have configured your RADIUS server and have told FW-1 about it, enabling RADIUS authentication for a user is simple. Ensure that **RADIUS** is enabled in your firewall object's Authentication tab, and then select **RADIUS** as the authentication scheme. When prompted for a RADIUS server to use, select the server you configured above.

You also have the option of configuring multiple RADIUS servers. The advantage of this is that if one RADIUS server fails, users will continue to be able to authenticate via the backup servers. The process of synchronizing usernames and passwords between RADIUS servers is a function of the RADIUS server package you are using—the firewall does not handle this.

To configure multiple RADIUS servers, add each RADIUS server to FW-1 under the **Manage** menu and select **Servers**. Be sure to configure each server with an appropriate priority, depending on the sequence in which you want the servers to be queried; lower numbers indicate higher priorities.

Once you have all your RADIUS servers configured, create a RADIUS Group in your list of servers, and add each RADIUS server to this group. Then, when configuring each user, select this group in their Authentication tabs after choosing RADIUS authentication. You will see that you also have the option of selecting **All,** which means all available RADIUS servers will be queried. This has the same effect as adding all your servers to a RADIUS group and using that group.

TACACS

TACACS, which stands for Terminal Access Controller Access Control System, is another external authentication scheme you can use to authenticate your users. Configuring TACACS is similar to configuring RADIUS.

First, you need to ensure that your TACACS server is set up and configured correctly. Then, add a workstation object to the firewall with the TACACS server IP address. Next, in FW-1's Policy Editor, select **Manage | Servers and OPSEC Applications**. Choose **New | TACACS** (see Figure 6.3).

Figure 6.3 TACACS Server Configuration

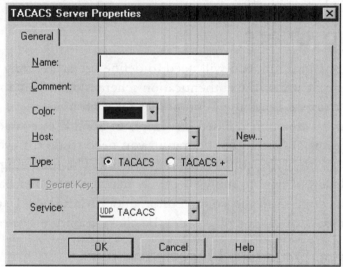

Enter the following information:

- **Name** A descriptive name for your TACACS server.
- **Comment** A descriptive comment for your TACACS server.

- **Color** Choose a color for the icon that will represent your TACACS server.

- **Host** Choose the physical server on which your TACACS server is configured. Note that this server should already be configured as a firewall object prior to this configuration.

- **Type** Choose **TACACS** or **TACACS+**, depending on the version of your TACACS server.

- **Secret Key** This option is only available for TACACS+ servers. If you have configured a secret key on your TACACS+ server, check this box and enter the same key here.

- **Service** Choose **TACACS.** Note that if you select **TACACS+** for **Type**, this option is not available.

Now that your TACACS server is defined, you need to ensure that TACACS is enabled in the Authentication tab of your firewall object. Next, choose **TACACS** in the Authentication tab of the user you are configuring, and select the TACACS server you defined.

Defining Users

To perform authentication, you will need to define users. Defining users enables you to make use of any of the authentication schemes described above, as well as to decide upon several other useful properties for each user.

In FW-1, users are defined based on templates. Templates enable you to reduce the amount of custom configuration you need to do for every user, by predefining as much of the configuration as possible. The following sections describe the details of how to most effectively manage your user base. All user configuration is done from the Policy Editor, under **Manage | Users and Administrators…**, or via the object tree, by clicking on the **Users** tab.

Creating a Default User

All of abovementioned FW-1 authentication schemes can be categorized as either internal and external. Internal schemes, including FW-1 password and OS Password, have all of their users defined within the FW-1 user database. External schemes, including SecurID, RADIUS, and TACACS, inherently have their own user management systems. It would therefore create an unnecessary amount of overhead if you were required to add all users using external authentication schemes to FW-1's user database, too.

To avoid this, FW-1 enables you to define a default user that will be used for external authentication schemes. As long as you have a default user defined for a particular external scheme, you do not need to define all users within the FW-1 user database.

To create a default user, open the Policy Editor, and select **Manage | Users and Adminitrators | New | External User Profile | Match all users...** (see below for more information on templates). In the **General** tab, you will notice that there is a predefined User Profile called "generic*". This will enable you to make use of external authentication schemes without duplicating your work in defining users. This functionality replaces the definition of a user named "generic*" and the limitations of having only one external user profile. If you require the use of multiple external user profiles, you can use the **Match by domain...** option to add a prefix or suffix to the login name to correlate a user to a specific external user profile.

Creating and Using Templates

All users in FW-1 are defined via templates. Templates are also a convenient way to eliminate having to define the same user properties repeatedly; you define the user properties once, and create subsequent users with the same settings by simply choosing that template.

It is important to note that templates do not restrict you from changing individual users' settings. Even though you may define two users based on the same template, you are free to change any of the properties of one user without affecting the other user or the template itself.

To create a new template, open the SmartDashboard, and select **Manage | Users and Administrators... | New | Template** (see Figure 6.4).

Figure 6.4 User Template General Properties

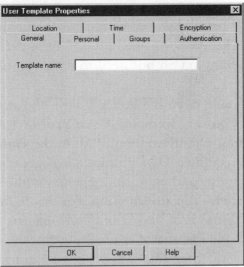

Enter a descriptive name for this template, such as "Accounting Department template." Next, let's look at the Personal Tab, shown in Figure 6.5.

Figure 6.5 User Personal Properties

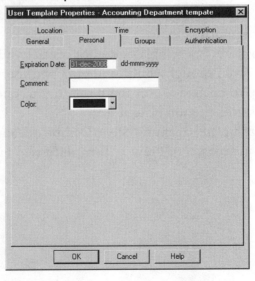

Here, you can define an **Expiration Date** for users defined with this template. When a user's account expires, FW-1 will no longer allow him or her to authenticate. This is useful in scenarios such as when you know a user will only require access for a limited amount of time, and you don't want to worry about remembering to disable their account. The **Comment** field enables you to enter any additional information regarding this user that might be useful to you, and **Color** enables you to define a unique color for the icon that will represent this user.

The Location tab, shown in Figure 6.6, enables you to restrict both the sources and destinations that are acceptable for this user. Defining a source means that the user will only be permitted to authenticate if their connection originates from the network object(s) you define. Defining a destination means the user will only be permitted to access the object(s) you specify. Note that you can also control the objects a user is permitted to access via the standard rule base.

Figure 6.6 User Location Tab

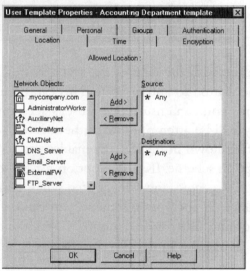

If you would like the user to have access to all objects, be sure to specify **Any** for both **Source** and **Destination**. Otherwise, by default, the user will not have access to anything if these are left blank.

In addition to location-based restrictions, you also have the option of defining time-based restrictions via the Time tab, shown in Figure 6.7.

Figure 6.7 User Time Tab

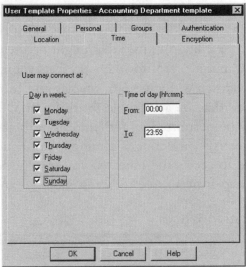

Here, you can define both the days of the week as well as the times of the day that the user is permitted to authenticate. This can be useful to provide increased security, since you can ensure that a user's account is only available when you know they will be attempting to authenticate.

The Encryption tab, shown in Figure 6.8, enables you to choose to enable the available client encryption scheme, IKE. The option for FWZ was removed, as IKE is a much more proven, accepted, and widely used scheme, and is also a published public standard. For the IKE encryption scheme, you can define various properties of that scheme by choosing **Edit.** By default in NG AI, the advanced properties are part of the Global Properties in the Remote Access section.

Figure 6.8 User Encryption Tab

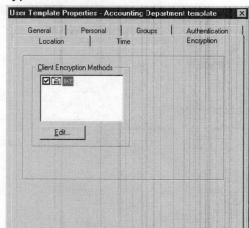

Now that you have defined a template, you can easily create new users. Back on the main Users screen, simply choose **New** and then the name of your template, in this case **Accounting Department template**. You will see a User Properties screen that is identical to what you configured for the template. Feel free to change any settings that are unique to this user, or if this user follows the template exactly, then all you have to do is enter the login name and a password, and you're done.

Creating Groups of Users

Grouping users is an effective way of aligning users into categories when adding them to rules. Users are not added to rules individually, but as part of a group, which can consist of one or more users. To create a group of users, open the Policy Editor and select **Manage | Users and Administrators**. Select **New | User Group** (see Figure 6.9).

Figure 6.9 Group Properties

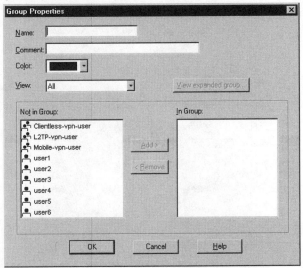

Here, you see a list of all your current users. Select each user that you want to add to the group, then click **Add**. You will see that user move from the left side—**Not in Group**—to the right side—**In Group**.

In addition to adding users to a group, you can also add other groups to a group. When you do this, you will be asked by FW-1 whether or not you want to add each member of the group individually. Adding each user individually means that if you make a change to the group you are adding, that change will *not* be reflected in the group being added to. If you do not add users individually, then changes to the group you are adding *will* be reflected in the group being added to.

User Authentication

User authentication is one of three FW-1 authentication types, used to authenticate users for HTTP, telnet, FTP, and rlogin only. This type of authentication can be used in-line, meaning that the user is not presented with any separate authentication challenge when using one of the available services; it is all handled using the client you are already using within the methods provided by the protocol. No additional software is required, nor is there any additional operation the user must remember in order to be authenticated.

One important aspect of user authentication to note is that there is no facility to restrict authentication based on source address. This means that if a user's login credentials are compromised, unauthorized users could use this information to gain access to your network.

User authentication is available only for HTTP, HTTPS, telnet, FTP, and rlogin because FW-1 proxies all of these connections. This means that you can only set up user authentication for services for which FW-1 has built-in server.

To configure user authentication, first define your users in SmartDashboard, under **Manage | Users and Administrators**, as discussed above. Your users can be configured with any type of authentication scheme—internal or external—as long as that scheme is enabled in the Authentication tab of your firewall object's properties.

Once your users are defined, and before you can add the users to a rule, you must place them in groups. This is because FW-1 does not allow you to add individual users to rules—only groups. If you want to add just one user, simply create a group with only that user as a member.

To configure user authentication, create a new rule in your rule base, right-click on the **Source** section, and choose **Add User Access** (see Figure 6.10).

Figure 6.10 User Access

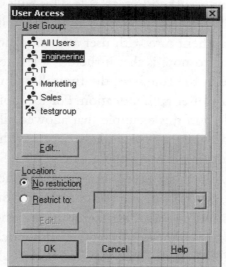

Here, you will see a list of your current user groups. Choose the group you want to add to this rule. You also have the option of setting location restrictions, which will limit the sources from which the user can connect. Figure 6.11 displays the completed rule.

Figure 6.11 User Authentication Rule

NO	SOURCE	DESTINATION	VPN	SERVICE	ACTION	TRACK	INSTALL ON	TIME	COMMENT
Stealth Rule (Rule 1)									
1	Any	ExternalFW	Any Traffic	Any	drop	Alert	Policy Targets	Any	Stealth Rule
DNS Traffic (Rules 2-3)									
2	LAN	DNS_Server	Any Traffic	Any	accept	Log	Policy Targets	Any	Permit LAN access to DNS server for DNS name resolving
3	DNS_Server	LAN	Any Traffic	Any	accept	Log	Policy Targets	Any	Permits DNS server access to Internet for domain name resolving
Service Net Traffic (Rules 4-7)									
4	Any	Email_Server	Any Traffic	smtp	accept	Log	Policy Targets	Any	Permit anyone to send email to the email server via smtp
5	Any	Web_Server	Any Traffic	http https	accept	Log	Policy Targets	Any	Permit anyone access to web pages via http on the web server
6	LAN	FTP_Server	Any Traffic	ftp	accept	Log	Policy Targets	Any	Permit anyone on the Internet access to ftp on the web server
7	LAN	Email_Server	Any Traffic	pop-3 imap	accept	Log	Policy Targets	Any	Permits LAN access to retrieve email via pop-3 and imap
LAN to Internet Traffic (Rule 8)									
8	Engineering@LAN	Service_Net	Any Traffic	http https ftp	User Auth	Log	Policy Targets	Any	Authenticates LAN access to http, ftp, and https on the Internet
DMZ to Internet Traffic (Rule 9)									
9	Web_Server	Any	Any Traffic	http	accept	Log	Policy Targets	Any	Allow the web server to access the Internet
Cleanup Rule (Rule 10)									

Here, rule 9 is our user authentication rule. This rule states that all users in the Engineering group, when connecting to anywhere with services, HTTP, HTTPS, or FTP must authenticate with user authentication.

One important thing to note is that if there is a less restrictive rule above the user authentication rule in the rule base, the firewall will use the less restrictive rule and will not perform user authentication. For example, if you had an "accept" rule above rule 3 in this example that allowed all traffic from the user's source to any destination, the user would have access without being required to authenticate. This is the case for users going to the Web_Server on the Service_Net in rule 5. Also, if the user is not yet authenticated, it will not match the authentication rule, skip past it, and see if the user would still be allowed even if he or she is not authenticated. In the event that there is a rule that would allow the user to make the connection after the authentication rule (for example, Source: LAN, Destination: Service_Net (negate), Service: http, Action: Accept) it will not prompt the user for authentication because it is not required to gain access. An easy way to think of this behavior is to think that the firewall will check all the rules first for an accept and when it does not match one before it matches a drop, it will then scan the rulebase again to the position of the drop for an authentication rule.

To continue configuring user authentication, right-click **User Auth**, and choose **Edit properties** (see Figure 6.12).

Figure 6.12 User Authentication Action Properties

The purpose of the **Source** and **Destination** fields is to resolve any conflicts in configuration between the user database and the rulebase. Remember earlier, when we discussed defining users, you had the option of restricting a user's access to certain source and destination addresses. You also have the ability to control this aspect of a user's access via the standard rulebase. What happens if the two conflict? This setting decides how the firewall should react.

Choosing **Intersect with User Database** means the firewall will *combine* the settings in the user definition with the standard rule base. Choosing **Ignore User Database** means that the firewall will use the settings defined in the standard rule base alone. For example, if a user has the source defined as LAN and is attempting to authenticate from the Internet, if **Intersect with User Database** is selected, the user will not be granted access because the username is not valid from that location. Conversely, if **Ignore User Database** is selected, the user will be able to be authenticated—assuming that the user is allowed in the Source column of the rule (like "All Users@Any").

In addition, you have the option here of providing HTTP access to all servers or predefined servers. The **Predefined Servers** setting relates to the predefined servers in the Security Server section of Global Properties.

Under Authentication Settings in the properties of each individual firewall, the value for **User Authentication session timeout** defines how much time may elapse before a user is forced to reenter their login credentials, as shown in Figure 6.13. Back in the User Authentication Action Properties window, setting HTTP access to be to all servers essentially disables the User Authentication session timeout setting. Setting HTTP access to be only to predefined servers activates the timeout.

Figure 6.13 Firewall Object Authentication Tab

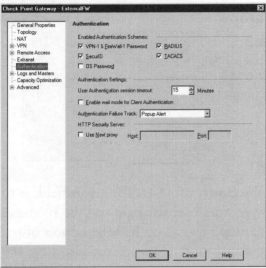

Note that these settings apply to both inbound and outbound authentication. If you are going to have users authenticate to external servers on the Internet, which is likely, your only option here is to set the HTTP access in the authentication action properties window to **All servers**, since it is not practical to define each external server that users may access.

Once you have configured these settings, you are ready to have your users authenticate with user authentication. In order to have the users authenticate in-line using their client (Web browser, ftp client, telnet client), they will need to add the firewall as a proxy server within their Web browser's configuration. This will cause their Web browser to first hit the firewall, which will challenge the user for their authentication credentials, and if they authenticate successfully, it will then pass the user on to the Web server.

If users do not configure the firewall as a proxy in their Web server's configuration, they can still use user authentication, but they will be asked to authenticate multiple times even when accessing one site (unless the **All servers** option is checked). This is because, unless the Web browser uses the firewall as a proxy, it does not cache the authentication data. The advantage to this is that if other users gain access to the authorized user's workstation, they will not have unprotected access to the site the original user was accessing. However, the continuous re-authentication may be time consuming and tedious for authorized users.

Configuring user authentication for other services, such as FTP or telnet, is done in the same manner. In these cases, since the user will not use a Web browser to connect, the FTP or telnet client, when transmitting usernames and passwords, will actually be sending these to the firewall first, allowing it to verify authentication parameters, before passing the connection on to the real destination.

When logging in to an FTP server, users will have to use a special username and password format, so that the firewall understands which username and password is to be used for what purpose. The username is of the format "remote_user@FireWall-1_user@remote_host." For example, to use a remote username of "anonymous," a local username of "Joe," and a remote host of "ftp.checkpoint.com," the user would enter "anonymous@Joe@ftp.checkpoint.com" as the username. When prompted for a password, the password format is "remote_password@FireWall-1_password." Check with your FW-1 documentation for the syntax for Telnet logins.

Client Authentication

In contrast to user authentication, client authentication is used to grant access based on source address rather than users. Client authentication is also not restricted to any particular service—it can be configured to work with all applications and services. The downside to client authentication is that it will associate a username with an IP address for a given period of time. For example, if a user from your network uses client authentication to authenticate to a firewall on the other side of the Internet, any other users coming from your network will also be allowed because the connection will be coming from the same IP address (because hide-mode NAT was configured for the LAN). This is also a valid concern if a user abandons his IP address (shuts down his system, for example) and it is reassigned to or reused by another system before the firewall times out the authentication.

In order to authenticate via client authentication, users must connect to the firewall with either telnet (port 259) or HTTP (port 900). Access via HTTPS is also an option; see skI5130 in Check Point's SecureKnowledge Database. The firewall will challenge the user with username and password prompts, and will use the response to determine whether that user is authorized to connect from their source address.

Configuring client authentication is similar to configuring user authentication. Again, the first step is to define your users in the user manager. Then, create a rule in the rule base, as in rule 8 in Figure 6.14.

Figure 6.14 Client Authentication Rule

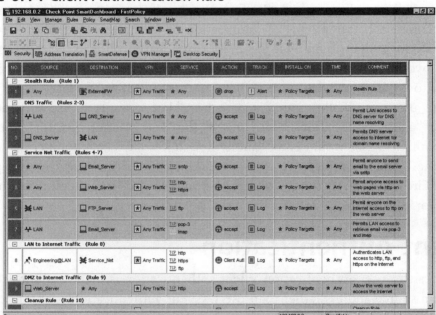

Again, we are allowing all users in the Engineering department, when originating from the "LAN," to connect via HTTP, HTTPS, and FTP to systems on the Internet. Just as in user authentication, there are action properties for client authentication, accessed by right-clicking **Client Auth** and choosing **Edit Properties** (see Figure 6.15).

Figure 6.15 Client Authentication Action Properties

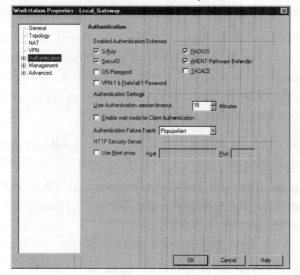

The source and destination options behave the same as they do in user authentication. **Verify secure configuration on Desktop** only applies to users who are using the Secure Client VPN client, which will be covered in chapter 11. This setting ensures that the user's desktop settings are secure. Specifically, it ensures that only TCP/IP is used, and that the desktop policy has been applied to all available network interfaces.

Required Sign On, when set to **Standard**, means that once a user has authenticated one time, they are permitted to access all services, as long as they are allowed to do so according to the rulebase. When set to **Specific**, users must authenticate again for each new service they attempt to access.

Sign-On Method has the following five options:

- **Manual** Users must use either telnet to port 259 of the firewall, or use a Web browser to connect to port 900 on the firewall to authenticate before being granted access. Access via HTTPS is also an option; see skI5130 in Check Point's SecureKnowledge Database.

- **Partially Automatic** If user authentication is configured for the service the user is attempting to access, and they pass this authentication, then no further client authentication is required. For example, if HTTP is permitted on a client authentication rule, the user will be able to transparently authenticate since FW-1 has a security server for HTTP. Then, if this setting is chosen, users will not have to manually authenticate for this connection. Note that this applies to all services for which FW-1 has built-in security servers (HTTP, FTP, telnet, and rlogin).

- **Fully Automatic** If the client has the session authentication agent installed, then no further client authentication is required (see session authentication below). For HTTP, FTP, telnet, or rlogin, the firewall will authenticate via user authentication, and then session authentication will be used to authenticate all other services.

- **Agent Automatic Sign On** Uses session authentication agent to provide transparent authentication (see session authentication below).

- **Single Sign On** Used in conjunction with UserAuthority servers to provide enhanced application level security. Discussion of UserAuthority is beyond the scope of this chapter.

Client Authentication versus User Authentication

Table 6.1 compares various aspects of user authentication and client authentication:

Table 6.1 Client Authentication versus User Authentication

Authentication Property	User Authentication	Client Authentication
Based on Source IP	No	Yes
Restrict on Username	Yes	Yes
Transparent	Optional	Depends on Sign On Method
Services Available	HTTP, HTTPS, FTP, telnet, rlogin	All

Session Authentication

The third type of authentication available is session authentication. Session authentication enables you to grant users access to any service, without requiring them to originate from the same source IP.

In order to accomplish this type of authentication, the user must run a session authentication agent. This agent is responsible for receiving the authentication request from the firewall, prompting the user for his or her login credentials, and transmitting that information back to the firewall. The session authentication agent can be found on the Check Point installation CD, and does not require any special licensing.

Configuring session authentication is similar to configuring client or user authentication. First, ensure that your users are configured in the user manager. Then, add a rule to the standard rule base as in rule 8 in Figure 6.16.

Figure 6.16 Session Authentication Rule

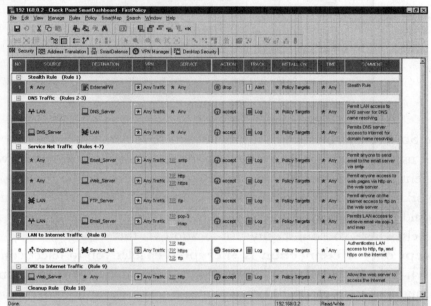

Here, the rule is similar to our previous rule for client authentication. Note that it is not required that you restrict session authentication to a service. Again, there are action properties available for session authentication, accessible by right-clicking on the **Session Auth** icon and choosing **Edit properties** (see Figure 6.17).

Figure 6.17 Session Authentication Action Properties

The **Source** and **Destination** properties behave here just as they do in client or user authentication. **Contact Agent At** enables you to specify where the authentication agent is running. In general, the agent will be running on the user's workstation, which is located at the source of the connection, so this setting should be left as **Src**. In special cases, when the authentication agent is installed elsewhere, you can specify that location via this setting.

Accept only if connection is encrypted enables you to reject connections, even if the authentication information is valid, unless the user is connecting over through an encrypted VPN connection.

Query user identity from UserAuthority enables you to integrate session authentication with a UserAuthority server for Single Sign On.

Session Authentication versus Client and User Authentication

Table 6.2 compares various aspects of session, client, and user authentication:

Table 6.2 Session Authentication versus Client and User Authentication

Authentication Property	User Authentication	Client Authentication	Session Authentication
Based on source IP	No	Yes	No
Restrict on Username	Yes	Yes	Yes
Transparent	Optional	Depends on Sign On Method	Yes
Services Available	HTTP, HTTPS, FTP, telnet, rlogin	All	All
Agent required	No	No	Yes

LDAP Authentication

LDAP, or the Lightweight Directory Access Protocol, is used for a bevy of purposes. With regards to FW-1, this server object is used for the purposes of user management. A full discussion of the workings of LDAP is beyond the scope of this book, but it is assumed that if you are configuring an LDAP object, then you have access to an existing LDAP server and the necessary information.

LDAP Account Unit

In NG AI, the concept of having multiple LDAP servers with a single shared database is supported more directly and the configuration is streamlined. An LDAP Account Unit can now be defined to include multiple servers that provide access to the LDAP database.

To configure LDAP in FW-1, you need to set up an LDAP account unit. To do so, open the Policy Editor and select **Manage | Servers and OPSEC Applications | New | LDAP Account Unit**.
Figure 6.18 illustrates the General panel for LDAP configuration.

Figure 6.18 LDAP Account Unit Properties

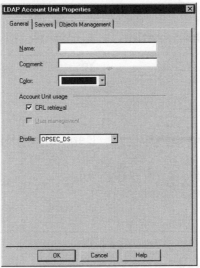

Aside from the common **Name**, **Comment**, and **Color** fields, there some specific options to select. First, define whether this LDAP account unit will perform queries for digital Certificate Revocation Lists (**CRL retrieval**). This is most important when used in conjunction with an external Certificate Authority. Next, define the **Profile** that the LDAP server will be defined to use. This will take into account any special nuances of Microsoft's Active Directory, Novell's NDS, and Netscape's Directory Server. All other OPSEC-certified LDAP servers should use the OPSEC_DS option.

On the **Servers** tab, you are presented with a place to list the LDAP servers that will serve the LDAP database defined for this LDAP account unit. Additionally, you can choose one of the servers from the list to be queried by pre-NG AI enforcement modules. The **Earlier Versions Compatibility server** allows for compatibility with NG FP3 and earlier versions that did not have the capacity to define multiple servers per account unit.

When adding a server to the list, as shown in Figure 6.19, you will be prompted for the **Host** on which this server will be running, as well as the **Port** it will be listening on, and the credentials used to connect and query the server. This page is also used to define which permissions are granted (and will be utilized) by the enforcement modules. In the event that the LDAP server is capable of encrypting communications using SSL technology, the **Port** on the General page will be disabled and the port is defined in the Encryption page of the

LDAP Server Properties. Also on the Encryption page is the server's digital certificate fingerprint and the minimum/maximum encryption strength.

Figure 6.19 LDAP Server Properties

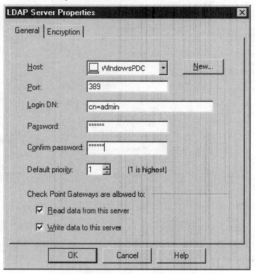

Back in the LDAP Account Unit properties, the Objects Management tab allows an administrator to define which server will be updated (and presumably the update will get synchronized to all other servers in the account unit) in the **Manage objects on** selection as well as the **Branches in use**, how many entries to return from a query, and finally whether to automatically log in to the server from the GUI or to **Prompt for a password when opening this Account Unit** in SmartDashboard. Note: if you do not define the branches in use, you will not be able to manage any users in the account unit.

Account Management Client

The Account Management Client, or AMC, is how FW-1 interacts with an LDAP server. There are several steps to complete before you can make use of the AMC. In the Policy Editor, select **Policy | Global Properties | LDAP Account Management** (see Figure 6.20).

Figure 6.20 LDAP Properties

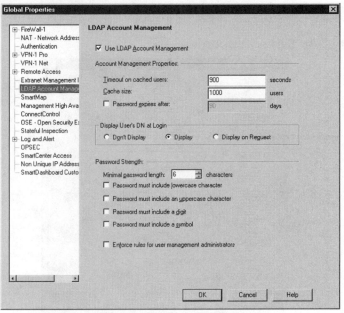

Here, enable the **Use LDAP Account Management** field, which indicates that you plan to use the integrated AMC. If required, you can adjust the **Timeout** and modify the **Cache size** depending on the number of users you plan to have. If you would like to force users to change their passwords periodically, enable **Password expires after**, and specify a number of days.

Only normal passwords will expire. Pre-shared secret passwords, such as those used with the IKE encryption scheme, do not expire, no matter what you choose for this setting.

For **Display User's DN at Login**, choose one of the following:

- **Don't Display** If you *do not* want the distinguished name (DN) to be displayed to users after they log in.

- **Display** If you *do* want the DN to be displayed to users after they log in.

- **Display on Request** If you only want the DN to be displayed to users if they request this information.

Displaying a DN at login is important if you would like your users to verify that the account they are attempting to log into actually belongs to them. There may be some cases where, because of duplicate names, users may be confused unless they are permitted to see the full DN.

The Password Strength settings enable you to specify how secure your users' passwords must be. It is always a good idea for users to choose hard-to-guess passwords, and these settings force them to do so by using uppercase, numeric, and symbolic characters.

Enabling the **Enforce rules for user management administrators** option means that all the previous settings also apply to administrators, in addition to normal users. This is a good idea; administrators should not be exempt from proper security practices!

Now that you have configured the general LDAP settings, you need to create an LDAP account unit object, as described in the previous section. You will then be able to use the AMC to manage remote users directly from the Policy Editor.

Summary

Authenticating users in a reliable, consistent, yet straightforward manner is key to the success of your security policy. No matter how secure the rest of your policy is, without the power of controlling who is authorized to access your network, you will not have succeeded in securing your environment.

The various authentication schemes we discussed provide you with different ways of challenging users for their credentials, providing the firewall with a means of determining if they are who they say they are. Some of the schemes are very simple, such as FW-1 password, which simply requires a username and password for successful authentication. Others, such as SecurID, present more elaborate challenges to the user before granting access.

Schemes can also be divided into internal and external. Internal authentication schemes, such as FW-1 password, are based entirely within FW-1; they do not interact with any external servers to provide their services. In contrast, external authentication schemes, such as RADIUS or TACACS, query servers outside the firewall to obtain the information they require to authenticate users.

To use these authentication schemes, you must create a database of users. This can be done within FW-1, as we discussed when we looked at the FW-1 user manager, or you may choose to integrate FW-1 with an LDAP server. Using LDAP to integrate an external database of users is especially useful in cases where other components of your network also require access to the user database.

FW-1 provides three types of authentication: user, client, and session. User authentication is used to authenticate users transparently for HTTP, HTTPS, FTP, telnet, and rlogin. Client authentication is more flexible—it works for all services—but is not necessarily transparent. Users must manually authenticate via telnet or HTTP before they are granted access. Session authentication also works for all services, and is transparent, but requires an extra piece of software on the client's end: the session authentication agent. Single Sign On is also available from Check Point with its UserAuthority software, but is not covered within this book.

Now that you are familiar with all of FW-1's authentication schemes, user-management functions, and authentication types, you will be able to ensure that authorized users have straightforward access to your network, while protecting your environment from the rest of the Internet.

Solutions Fast Track

FireWall–1 Authentication Schemes

☑ FW-1 authentication schemes include FW-1 Password, RADIUS, TACACS, and SecurID.

☑ Each user you want to authenticate uses one of these authentication schemes.

☑ Before you can use any scheme, it must be enabled in your firewall object's Authentication tab.

Defining Users

☑ Defining users enables you to make use of the authentication schemes mentioned at the beginning of this chapter, as well as to decide upon several other useful properties for each user.

☑ All users in FW-1 are defined via templates. Templates are also a convenient way to eliminate the need to define the same user properties repeatedly; you define the user properties once and create subsequent users with the same settings by simply choosing that template.

User Authentication

☑ User authentication works only for HTTP, HTTPS, FTP, telnet, and rlogin.

☑ It can be transparent, and does not require any additional software on the client end.

Client Authentication

☑ Client authentication works for all services, but is not transparent.

☑ Users must use telnet or HTTP to authenticate prior to being granted access. No additional software is required on the client end.

Session Authentication

☑ Session authentication also works for all services and is transparent.

☑ The session authentication agent must be running on the client end. It communicates with the firewall and provides authentication credentials.

LDAP Authentication

☑ LDAP can be integrated into FW-1 to enable you to have an external user database for authentication.

☑ To configure LDAP, set up your LDAP server, ensure that it is operating properly, and then add an LDAP Account Unit to your list of Servers.

Frequently Asked Questions

The following Frequently Asked Questions, answered by the authors of this book, are designed to both measure your understanding of the concepts presented in this chapter and to assist you with real-life implementation of these concepts. To have your questions about this chapter answered by the author, browse to **www.syngress.com/solutions** and click on the **"Ask the Author"** form. You will also gain access to thousands of other FAQs at ITFAQnet.com.

Q: I don't want to use a single-phase authentication scheme—what are my options?

A: You may want to consider using SecurID. Outfitting your users with SecurID tags will simplify their authentication process, while still providing a dual-phased authentication approach. Other vendors developing tokens include Secure Computing and Aladdin.

Q: I am using external authentication schemes, and it seems redundant to have to define all my users in FireWall-1. How can I get around this?

A: In earlier versions you would create a default user, called *generic**. This avoids the requirement of creating all users locally as well as externally. Now in NG AI, you can use the External User Profiles option.

Q: With user authentication, how can I authenticate users transparently?

A: Transparent user authentication requires that the username and password on the target server and the firewall be identical. When this is the case, the firewall can intercept the authentication attempt before it reaches the target server, authenticate the user itself, and then pass the connection on to the target server without prompting the user again, since the credentials are the same.

Q: If session authentication is supposed to be transparent, why is the user prompted for a username and password?

A: Transparent, in this case, refers to the perspective of the target server. Since session authentication allows a direct connection between the user and the target server, assuming that connection is allowed, the connection is said to be transparent.

Q: I'm using User Auth in the rule base, so why do my users keep getting prompted for authentication over and over again in their Web browsers?

A: Configure your users' Web browsers to point to the firewall as a proxy server for HTTP connections or change the User Auth properties in the rule to All Servers.

## Chapter 7

Open Security (OPSEC) and Content Filtering

Solutions in this Chapter:

- OPSEC Applications
- Content Vectoring Protocol
- URI Filtering Protocol
- Application Monitoring
- Client Side OPSEC Applications
- Other Resource Options

☑ Summary

☑ Solutions Fast Track

☑ Frequently Asked Questions

Introduction

Check Point's Open Platform for Security (OPSEC) model enables you to implement third-party vendor applications into your firewall environment. Based on open protocols, the OPSEC model enables vendors to easily design their applications to conform to this standard, and therefore interoperate with the VPN-1/FireWall-1 product.

You may be asking how this can benefit you? The most notable examples are your content filtering options. You can use other vendors' virus scanners that support the Content Vectoring Protocol (CVP) (for example, Aladdin's eSafe Protect Gateway) to easily implement virus scanning of Simple Mail Transfer Protocol (SMTP) mail, Hypertext Transfer Protocol (HTTP), and/or File Transfer Protocol (FTP) traffic, just by adding some objects and rules to your Security Policy.

Other content-filtering applications use Website databases, which are broken into categories, so that you can easily block your users from going to specific sites, such as adult entertainment, shopping and chat sites, while on the job. Several schools that provide Internet access for their young students utilize this technology to prevent them from accessing certain categories that are considered inappropriate for children.

We will talk about other OPSEC applications, and show you how to configure CVP and UFP (Universal Resource Identifier (URI) Filtering Protocol) applications in this chapter, and also how you can use the resources available in Check Point VPN-1/FireWall-1 (CP VPN-1/FW-1) to implement limited content filtering without needing a third-party application.

OPSEC Applications

Realizing that no single product or vendor could address network security completely and do it well, Check Point designed the OPSEC standard to enable security managers to easily extend the functionality of VPN-1/FW-1 with best-of-breed third-party applications designed for specific security requirements. By using a standard set of Application Programming Interfaces (APIs) and open protocols, OPSEC applications are able to easily move data in and out of the VPN-1/FW-1 infrastructure.

An OPSEC session is a *dialog between two OPSEC entities using one of the OPSEC APIs*, and usually is between VPN-1/FW-1 and a third-party application that performs a specific task on the data received from the firewall. For a list of available applications, check the OPSEC Alliance Solutions Center at www.opsec.com.

The properties of the OPSEC session are defined in the OPSEC application's object properties in the Security Policy Editor database. As you can see in Figure 7.1, there are three major types of OPSEC servers using the CVP, UFP, and AMON (Application MONitoring) protocols, as well as six client options using the following APIs:

- Event logging API (ELA)

- Log exporting API (LEA)

- Suspicious activities monitor (SAM)

- Check Point management interface (CPMI)

- Object management interface (OMI)

- UserAuthority API (UAA)

Each one of these protocols is a specific interface used to extend the capabilities of the firewall to another application. This tight integration provides functionality exceeding what would be available with each piece operating individually.

Figure 7.1 OPSEC Application Properties–General Tab

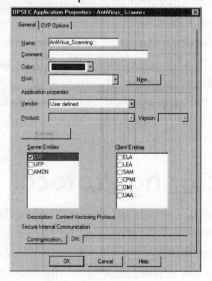

Besides the required naming information, the General tab of the OPSEC Application Properties window requires you to specify the host that this server is running on. You must create the host object before creating a new OPSEC application object, as you will not be able to create a new workstation object while application properties window is open. You must then define the application properties, located in the section of that same name. To set the application properties you can select **User defined** from the **Vendor** drop-down menu, and then manually select both the server and client entities, or you can select a specific vendor, product, and version here. Vendors and products available from the Vendor menu include the following: Computer Associates' SafeGate product, Finjan Software's SurfinGate, as well as a variety of solutions from Trend Micro, F-Secure, Aliroo, and Aladdin Knowledge Systems. Over 70 vendors are predefined and listed in Next Generation Application Interface (NG AI), some with multiple products listed. A complete list of OPSEC certified CVP vendors and products can be found at www.opsec.com/solutions/sec_content_security.html. After selecting a predefined vendor and product from the list, the appropriate Server and Client Entities sections will be filled in automatically.

If you selected **User Defined** from the **Vendor** menu, the next step in defining a new OPSEC application object for use in your security policy is to select the **Client** or **Server** entry that matches how the application functions. As shown in Figure 7.1 with **CVP** checked, once you select the appropriate application type, the second tab of the OPSEC Application Properties window, which contains application-specific communication configuration information, will change to match your selection. Your final step on this tab is to configure SIC, or Secure Internal Communication, by clicking the **Communication** button. Setting up SIC for OPSEC applications is identical to setting up SIC for firewall modules.

The next few pages will discuss each of these communication methods in detail and give you a sense of the flexibility and ease of integration that the OPSEC standard offers.

Content Vectoring Protocol

Content Vectoring Protocol is normally used to move data, such as Web pages or e-mail messages, from VPN-1/FW-1 to another server for validation. Though a CVP server (such as an antivirus server) could reside on the same physical server as a firewall module, it is not recommended as this would add a significant amount of overhead to the firewall (in the case of an antivirus server, looking through a database of known viruses for each HTTP connection would likely slow down the firewall). For example, CVP could be used to move all inbound SMTP e-mail messages to a content-scanning server that will check for malicious Active-X code. Most commonly, CVP is used to virus-scan file data from e-mail messages or files downloaded from the Internet as they pass through the firewall. However, it has also been used to monitor and filter incoming traffic to a SQL database from the Internet by Log-On Software's SQL-Guard application.

Defining Objects

There are three steps involved in creating a new CVP object to use in your Security Policy.

1. Create a standard *workstation* object for the server. The workstation object enables you to assign an Internet Protocol (IP) address and name to the server that hosts the application you will be sending data to.

2. Create a new *OPSEC application* object to define the properties of the service you're enabling. This can be done by selecting **Servers and OPSEC Applications** from the **Manage** menu, and then clicking **New,** or by right-clicking in the **OPSEC Applications** tab of the **Object Tree** and selecting **New**, and then **OPSEC Application**. When you complete the General tab of the OPSEC Application Properties window, you will be using the workstation object you created for the resources' host. Figure 7.1 shows the completed General tab.

3. Configure the *CVP* properties. This is done on the CVP tab that appeared when you checked the **CVP** option under the **Server Entities**. The CVP tab is used to define how this application communicates with the firewall. As shown in Figure 7.2, CVP applications only require a few options, consisting only of a **Service** drop-down list and an optional directive to use backward compatibility.

Figure 7.2 OPSEC Application Properties—CVP Options Tab

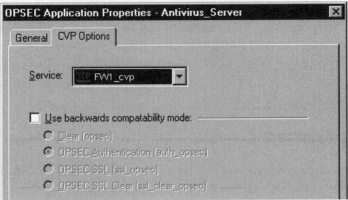

The **Service** selected on the CVP Options tab defines the port on which this application will be listening for connections from the firewall, and is almost always set to FW1_cvp (Transfer Control Protocol port 18181). The **Use backwards compatibility mode** section replaces the function of the fwopsec.conf file that was used in the version 4.*x* of FireWall-1. If your OPSEC vendor has supplied instructions relating to that file, then this is the area where you implement them. Generally, applications based on the OPSEC Software Development Kit (SDK) version 4.1 or lower will require that you use backward compatibility. Typically when applications use backward compatibility they also require the legacy **fw putkey** command to be used on both sides to establish trust instead of SIC.

Creating a CVP Resource

Now that you've defined your OPSEC application server, you'll want to start sending it data from your security policy through a *resource* definition. There are five resource types that can be used in your security policy to send data to a CVP server:

- **URI** URI resources are mostly used to manipulate HTTP requests.

- **SMTP** SMTP resources enable you to filter and modify e-mail message data as it passes through your firewall.

- **FTP** FTP resources provide the tools needed to control you users' FTP sessions.

- **TCP** The Transfer Control Protocol resource enables you to work with other TCP services that are not covered by the other resources.

- **CIFS** The Common Internet File System resource enables you to granularly filter CIFS file and printer sharing connections.

The previously listed resources are implemented by the VPN-1/FW-1 security servers. Each security server is a specialized module that provides detailed control for specific services. Located just above the Inspection Module in the firewall daemon, the security servers have the ability to monitor and manipulate SMTP, Telnet, FTP, and HTTP traffic, providing highly tunable access control and filtering capabilities.

Since each security server has full application awareness of the protocols it supports, it is capable of making control decisions based on the data and state of the session similar to how proxy firewalls function. In addition to performing specific content filtering, the security servers provide a conduit to send and retrieve data to and from third-party severs, allowing VPN-1/FW-1 to use other security applications in the traffic control process.

When invoked by a resource, the security servers will proxy the affected connections. Aside from the possibility of adding latency to the session (normally only measurable on very busy firewalls or with servers that are improperly equipped to run the OPSEC application) and additional load to the firewall, Network Address Translation (NAT) cannot be used with data allowed (or dropped) using resources. Since the firewall must proxy the connection, all data will appear from the address of the firewall that is closest to the server. This means that any applicable NAT rules will not be used because the firewall itself will function as the server the client is connecting to. Then, once the content is approved, the firewall will create a new connection to the actual server that will service the request. This is probably not a big deal when using hide-mode NAT, but it can be a bit confusing when debugging a problem between networks where NAT is not used. In this case, you would expect the traffic to be coming from the server's IP address, but it would actually be coming from an IP address on the firewall.

To help understand how CVP servers can be used as part of the security policy, let's look at how to integrate virus scanning into the security policy. Later on, we'll examine in detail how FTP and other resources match data streams that we can send to our CVP server, but for now let's just look at how to set up a simple FTP resource that enables users to retrieve files from the Internet and scans those files for viruses before sending them to the user. There are three steps involved in setting up this simple resource:

1. Create the resource object by selecting **Resources** from the **Manage** menu. Click **New**, then **FTP**. Set up the object name, comment, and color on the resulting FTP Resource Properties window. The other two tabs of this window will allow you to specify the details for the resource's filter and allow you to send data to the CVP server.

2. On the **Match** tab, set **Method** to **GET**. This instructs the VPN-1/FW-1 FTP security server to only allow users to download files via FTP, since uploading would require the use of the **put** command.

3. Use the **CVP** tab, shown in Figure 7.3, to select the antivirus server object and define how it will function for this resource.

Figure 7.3 FTP Resource Properties—CVP Tab

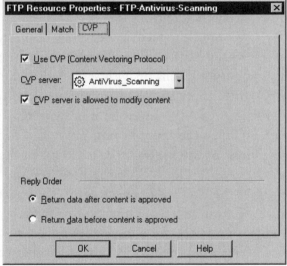

Aside from the **Use CVP** checkbox, which enables the **CVP server** drop-down list where you select the server to use, the CVP tab has two other important options that control how the CVP server functions in your resource. The **CVP server is allowed to modify content** checkbox controls whether or not VPN-1/FW-1 will pass on data that has not come back from the CVP server in its original form. This option is particularly useful for virus scanning where an infected file may be sent to the antivirus server and cleaned before being returned. This option would allow the VPN-1/FW-1 security server (which enforces the FTP Resource definition) to accept the cleaned file and send it on to its destination. If the **CVP server is allowed to modify content** option was not enabled, the antivirus software would only be allowed to report that the file was infected, causing the security server to discard the file completely.

The **Reply Order** options control when and how the CVP server will scan data being passed to the user. The options for controlling how data is scanned are:

- **Return data after content is approved** This option sends the entire file or data stream to the CVP server to be checked after the security server has validated the content. In our example, the GET request would be validated before the file was checked for viruses.

- **Return data before content is approved** Some packets are returned to the security server before the CVP server has approved them. This option is especially useful for resources that may deal with large files. Continuing to send the data stream before it has been approved may help stop problems with FTP or HTTP sessions timing out while the CVP server downloads and then checks the requested file. With this option the CVP server will allow all packets to be sent back to the security server and on to its destination, but the final packet will be held pending approval from the CVP server. This means the file will be incomplete and unusable at the end of the transfer if it is disallowed.

The method you select will depend greatly on what function your CVP server performs on the data, and on how the application is designed. In the antivirus server example, the CVP server controls the reply order. This allows the antivirus software maximum flexibility for scanning files and raw data differently if desired, since the application could decide to assemble a complete binary file before scanning, but scan HTML packets individually. Note that your CVP application must support this option, so check the documentation that came with your application before creating the resource to ensure compatibility.

Using the Resource in a Rule

The final step in using a CVP server, after creating the OPSEC application object and using it in a resource definition, is to build it into a rule in your security policy. Creating a security policy rule to use a resource is almost identical to creating a normal rule. The only exception is in the service column where, instead of selecting **Add** after right-clicking, you will select **Add With Resource**. Figure 7.4 shows the Service with Resource window that enables you to configure the resource to be used in the security policy.

Figure 7.4 Service with Resource Window

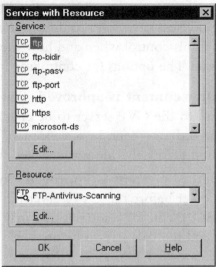

The Service with Resource tab allows you to select from the supported services and define which resource to use with that service. In the case of our virus-scanning example, we'll be using the FTP service with the ftp_get resource. Figure 7.5 shows the completed rule that allows local network traffic to FTP data from the Internet using the resource that limits access to FTP GETs only, and will use the CVP server we defined to scan all files for viruses before passing them to the user. Notice that the Service_Net is negated in the destination. This enables the user to control access to known networks separate from access to the Internet as well as to strictly adhere to the security principle of least access. If the destination field had been set to **Any**, it would have inadvertently opened FTP access to the network represented by the Service_Net object even though the intention was just to allow FTP GETs from the Internet. You will also notice that the icon used in the Service column indicates that we're allowing the FTP service with the ftp_get resource.

Figure 7.5 Security Policy Rule Using Resource

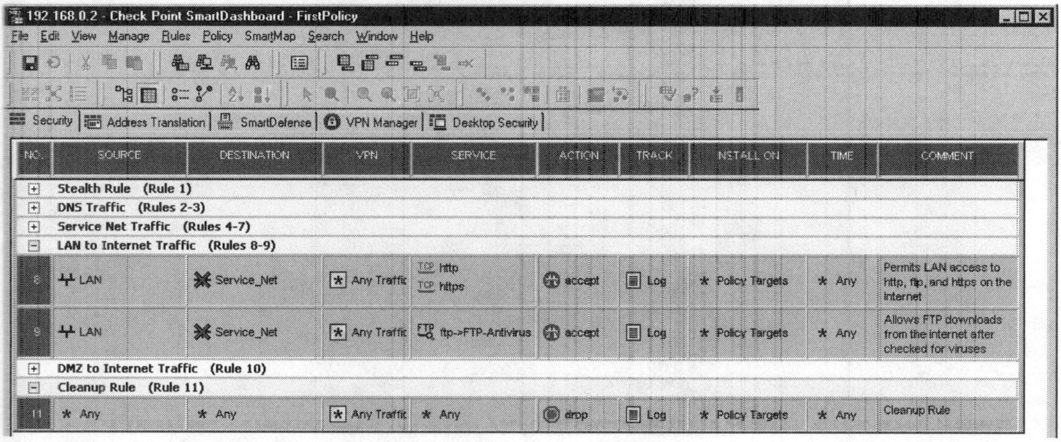

The important thing to remember when using resources is that data is matched or denied on a per-packet basis. You could, for example, select to scan only files of type "*.exe" downloaded via HTTP, with an *accept* rule that uses a CVP resource. However, this will only accept the downloaded files, not the pages you must browse to find the file you want. To make this work, you must specify a rule to match all other HTTP traffic, otherwise the HTTP-browsing traffic will fall through to the *cleanup rule* and be discarded.

CVP Group

As with most other objects in the Security Policy, CVP objects can be grouped. When you combine two or more OPSEC applications into a group, additional options for load balancing and chaining become available. Figure 7.6 shows a CVP group configuration tab being used to enable load balancing across two antivirus servers.

Figure 7.6 CVP Group Properties

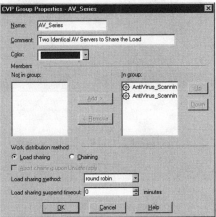

Creating a new CVP group can be done easily by right-clicking in the
Servers and OPSEC Applications tab of the object list. Next, select **New** and
CVP Group. After defining the group's name, adding a descriptive comment,
and assigning the color you want for this object, you'll need to select the servers
that will be members of this group. Note that groups don't have to be of identical object types. You can have a group consisting of a UFP server (which we'll
look at next) and a CVP server to enable application chaining.

Once the components of the group have been defined, you'll have to select
the function of this group by making the appropriate selection in the **Work distribution method** section. You have two choices:

- **Load sharing**   When selected, the workload is distributed among the
  servers in the group. There are two distribution methods allowed: round
  robin or random.

- **Chaining**   Chaining allows a data stream to be inspected by several
  servers that perform different functions. For example, a chaining group
  consisting of an antivirus scanner and a Web content scanner could be
  employed to check your incoming e-mail traffic for viruses and appropriate language. If you select chaining, you'll have an option to abort the
  chain when any individual server detects a violation, or to allow all the
  servers to inspect the data before making a control decision.

Once you have the CVP group created, it can be used in the security policy
to create a resource rule, just like any other group object would be used to create
a standard rule.

Configuring & Implementing...

Load Balancing Chained Servers

CVP chaining enables you to tie servers with different functions together to apply multiple levels of control to a single data stream. For example, you may chain an antivirus and content filtering server together to inspect and clean files downloaded by your users. Load sharing enables you to spread the work to be done across multiple servers for efficiency and redundancy, but what happens if you want to do both?

You cannot apply load balancing to chained servers since load balancing must be done between two or more servers with similar functions, and a chain contains multiple servers all doing different functions. You can, however, chain multiple load balanced servers, enabling you to achieve a similar effect.

Consider that you have two antivirus servers and two content filtering servers that you want to load balance and chain. To do this, you first must create two URI groups that use load sharing, one for the antivirus servers, and one for the content filters. Then all you need to do is create a third URI group that chains the first two groups together. This provides load sharing between similar servers and enables you to chain the servers together.

URI Filtering Protocol

A Uniform Resource Identifier most commonly defines how to access resources on the Internet. URI Filtering Protocol is used to enable passing data between VPN-1/FW-1 and a third-party server for URI classification.

The most common example of UFP is to pass HTTP Uniform Resource Locators (URLs) to a server running Websense, SurfControl, or a similar product, to check that the requested URL is allowed by your organization's acceptable Internet usage policy. Since the term URI (described in RFC 1630) and URL (RFC 1738) essentially deal with the same thing (especially when discussing HTTP), it is common to see the terms interchanged. Which term you use (URL or URI) is more a matter of preference than being technically correct, as there seems to even be disagreement between the industry standards organizations as to which is correct in which circumstances.

Defining Objects

Creating a UFP server object is almost identical to creating a CVP object. Both objects require that you define a workstation object with at least a name and IP address for the server and that you use that workstation in the OPSEC application object. Figure 7.7 shows the General tab of the UFP server object, which enables you to define the application you are using. You can choose from the predefined list, which includes vendors such as WebSense, Symantec, SurfControl, Secure Computing, and 8e6_Technologies, or you can use the **User Defined** option to customize your UFP server object. A complete list of UFP applications from OPSEC-certified vendors is available atwww.opsec.com/solutions/sec_content_security.html.

Figure 7.7 UFP Server Object—General Tab

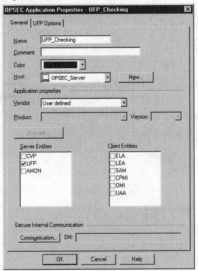

The difference in setting up a CVP server compared to a UFP server starts when you select **UFP** (as seen in Figure 7.7) in the **Server Entities** section of the OPSEC Application Properties window, which makes the UFP Options tab (Figure 7.8) available.

Figure 7.8 UFP Server Object—UFP Options Tab

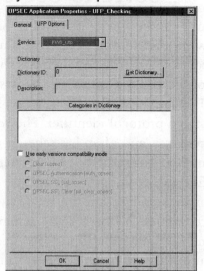

The **Service** drop-down menu defines which port the UFP service will be listening on; for most UFP applications, this is set to FW1_ufp (TCP port 18182). The backward compatibility options for UFP servers are the same as for the CVP server you looked at earlier, enabling you to configure options that, in previous versions of VPN-1/FireWall-1, were set in the now nonexistent fwopsec.conf file.

The **Dictionary** section of the UFP tab will show the category list from the UFP server. In order for the UFP server to function with VPN-1/FW-1, the servers' **Dictionary ID** and category list are required. The dictionary is basically a list of categories and the dictionary ID is the version of the list. This is useful if you are using a dictionary that is updated often. Once you've set up the server object on the General tab and set the service to match your UFP server, you can click the **Get Dictionary** button to retrieve the category list and ID number from the UFP server. The category list is displayed to help you verify that the connection to the UFP server is established and to show you which categories are available on that server. Note, however, that the categories in this window cannot be manipulated here. To select which categories you would like to filter incoming URLs against, you must create a URI resource that uses UFP.

Creating a URI Resource to Use UFP

Unlike a CVP server, which can be used with SMTP, TCP, FTP, and URI, a UFP server can only be used with URI resources. A URI is made up of two basic parts: a scheme or protocol, and a path. The scheme is the first portion of the URI, located to the left of the colon. Common schemes are HTTP, FTP, Trivial File Transfer Protocol (TFTP), Lightweight Data Access Protocol (LDAP), and so on, and can be thought of as a protocol identifier. The remainder of the URI specifies the path to the resource, and often has scheme-dependant syntax. Part of the path may contain a method, such as GET, POST, or PUT, which the UFP server may use to make filtering decisions.

Although the UFP server actually scans the URL and makes a control decision, it's the URI resource that tells VPN-1/FW-1 where and how to send the URI to be scanned. Figure 7.9 shows the URI Resource Properties window that is used to create the resource that will enable you to validate URLs through the UFP server created above.

Figure 7.9 URI Resource Properties–General Tab

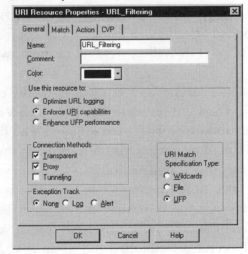

Aside from the generic object identifiers, there are some interesting URI resource options to select from. The first is the **Use this resource to** radio button set, which affects how the URI resource functions. If you select the first option, **Optimize URL logging**, all of the remaining options will gray out, and the object will only be used to log HTTP URLs into the VPN-1/FW-1 log. This option will not require the use of a security server to proxy the connection.

In order to use this resource as a conduit to an UFP server, you must select the **Enforce URI capabilities** or **Enhance UFP performance** option. The former utilizes the security server and provides extended options for filtering traffic, while the latter allows the firewall to retrieve the URL deep in the INSPECT engine (without the use of a security server), and to query the UFP server with the URL. Unfortunately, if you select the **Enhance UFP performance** option, UFP caching, CVP, certain HTTP header verifications, and authentication will not be available. For the rest of this section, we will use the **Enforce URI capabilities** option.

The **Connection Methods** section defines which modes VPN-1/FW-1 will use to examine traffic. If **Tunneling** mode is selected, you will not have access to the CVP tab and will not be able to use any URI filtering or UFP servers, since tunneling only allows the security server to inspect the port and IP address information, not the URI that you're interested in. **Transparent** mode is used when users' browser configurations do not contain proxy server information. In this configuration, the firewall must be the network gateway that handles Internet traffic. As your users request resources from the Internet, the firewall will send the URIs to the UFP server to be checked as part of the security policy. In **Proxy** mode, the firewall must be specified in each user's browser as a proxy server. This configuration is very useful if you want to direct Internet service requests (such as FTP and HTTP) to a firewall that is not the default gateway for your network, as the security server will provide proxy services to Internet requests. Using the **Proxy** option also enables you to manually load balance your Internet traffic by directing users' traffic to different firewalls, or to separate traffic based on type (for example FTP to one firewall, HTTP to another) if required.

The **URI Match Specification Type** section specifies how you want to inspect the URIs matched by this object. We'll be examining the **File** and **Wildcards** options later in the chapter, but for now we're only interested in the **UFP** option. Once you select the **UFP** option, then the **Match** tab, as seen in Figure 7.10, will provide you with additional UFP options needed to enable the UFP server.

Figure 7.10 UFP Options for URI Resources

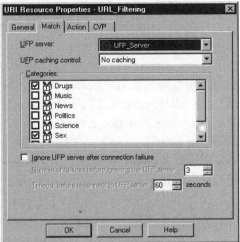

The **Match** tab enables you to select which **UFP server** to use, as well as to set operating parameters to control the interaction between the firewall security server and the filtering application. The **UFP caching control** field allows you to increase the performance of the URI resource by reducing the number of URLs sent to the UFP server. There are four caching options.

- **No Caching** With caching disabled, the UFP server is used to check each URI. Typically, turning off the cache has a negative impact on performance, as every request must be checked by the UFP Server. However, this option is useful if your UFP server configuration changes frequently and you want to ensure that each request is filtered using the newest options. However, when using the **Enhance UFP performance** option, the overhead of a security server is removed, providing better performance than even a security server, which caches UFP requests.

- **UFP Server** This option allows the UFP server to control the caching. The UFP server may choose to check each URL or it may maintain its own cache to speed up the checks.

- **VPN-1 & FireWall-1 (one request)** The VPN-1/FW-1 security server controls UFP caching. Unique URIs will be sent to the UFP server only once before being added to the cache. This option provides the greatest performance by significantly reducing the number of URIs sent to the UFP server.

- **VPN-1 & FireWall-1 (two requests)** URIs previously checked by the UFP server will be sent a second time before being added to the cache. Reduced performance is traded for the added security of checking each URL twice.

The **Ignore UFP server after connection failure** option controls how the security server will react if the UFP server is not available to service requests. Leaving this option unchecked can have a severe impact on performance if your UFP server fails, since the security server will attempt to send each URI to the failed server and will not allow traffic to pass until the server responds with an accept message. If this option is not enabled and your UFP server fails, then you most likely will experience a Denial of Service (DoS) condition, since even acceptable sites cannot be checked. The telltale sign of this condition will be messages in your logs that read, "Unknown error while trying to connect to UFP," and users calling your help desk complaining of a lack of access. Enabling the **Ignore UFP server after connection failure** option enables you to specify the **Number of failures before ignoring the UFP server** option, which controls how many attempts are made before considering a UFP server offline. The **Timeout before reconnect to UFP server** value instructs VPN-1/FW-1 on how long to wait before considering the connection to the UFP server lost.

WARNING

The **Ignore UFP server after connection failure** option is not to be used lightly. By checking this box, if the UFP server fails, all access would still function without the added security the UFP server provides. This could be a circumvention of your overall security policy. Make sure to check what value the company (specifically the Human Resources and Legal departments) places on Web access and the inspection capabilities UFP provides. Because Internet access impacts the ability of users to do work, it must be balanced against any relevant legal ramifications, which means this decision typically needs to made at an executive level by someone with the authority to decide if lost productivity takes a higher priority than content security.

Finally, the CVP tab enables you to hand data off to a third-party server for validation. In addition to the antivirus example we looked at earlier, CVP servers like Symantec's Igear Web content scanner can provide you with fine-tuned con-

tent control for Web applications. Note that the CVP tab is not available if the
Tunneling or **Enhance UFP performance** options are selected. The Action
tab in the URI Resource Properties window is discussed later in this chapter.

Using the Resource in a Rule

Using a UFP server to validate URIs as part of your security policy is similar to
using a CVP server in a resource rule. To follow the example used earlier, the
UFP server can be used to scan URL requests to Internet sites. In doing so, the
final step is to add the URI resource, which uses the UFP server object, as the
resource in a new (or existing) rule. As with the CVP rule we created earlier, the
only difference between a rule that uses a resource and a normal security policy
rule is what is defined in the service column. Instead of selecting the **Add**
option for the service, use the **Add with Resource** option to select the URI
resource that contains the UFP server configuration you need. Figure 7.11 shows
the final rule in the security policy being used to reject unacceptable data
requests. Notice that the Service column shows both the scheme being used
(HTTP) and the name of the URI resource (URL_Filtering).

Figure 7.11 Security Policy Rule Using UFP Server in URI Resource

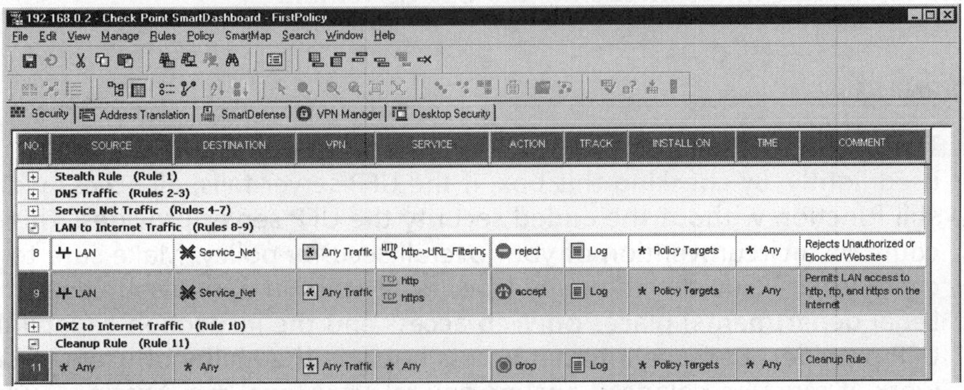

As with CVP resources, it is necessary to remember that a match is made on
the packet, not the session. For example, with UFP, you will typically create a
drop or reject rule to match on the categories you want to disallow. As you can
see in Figure 7.11, you must have another rule that will accept the traffic that
you want to allow, or else it will be dropped on the *cleanup* or *Drop All* rule. This
second rule is necessary because the resource rule only deals with dropping
traffic, not with allowing it. You could, of course, use a UFP resource in the rule

base to allow traffic based on category rather than drop it to get around this second rule requirement. The only problem with this approach is that the allowed list is often longer that the drop list, and is therefore is harder to maintain. The difference between drop and reject in these two cases is that drop will silently drop the packets, whereas reject will quickly tell the user that his connection is not allowed by returning an error or redirecting the user to another Website if defined in the Action tab. Reject is typically a more useful configuration because it will allow you (and your helpdesk) to distinguish between network connectivity problems and disallowed Websites.

UFP Group

A UFP group is similar to a CVP group except that it does not support chaining. The configuration of a UFP group is similar to the other generic group configuration screens, in that you enter a name, comment, and select the appropriate color and then simply move UFP servers from the *Not in group* section to the *In group* section.

Your choices for load balancing between servers in a UFP group are either **Random** or **Round Robin**. Using **Up** and **Down** buttons will enable you to change the order in which servers are used in the round robin configuration, but since the server being used will change with each incoming session, changing the order will only slightly affect how the object performs. The final option, **Load sharing suspend timeout**, enables you to configure the time to ignore a failed server before attempting to reestablish communication with it. You can set this time to anywhere from 0 (ignore the failure, attempt to use server normally) to 10,000 minutes.

Application Monitoring

Using OPSEC applications as CVP and UFP resources in your security policy makes those servers an integrated part of your security environment. To allow for easy monitoring of OPSEC products that function alongside VPN-1/FW-1, Check Point developed the AMON API.

AMON is the third tab in the OPSEC Application Properties window (as shown in Figure 7.12). It allows supported applications to report status information to VPN-1/FW-1. This status information is then available in the Check Point System Status Viewer alongside the real-time status of your Check Point applications. This is very useful for monitoring all devices interoperating within the security infrastructure, but another solution would probably be more useful for monitoring your entire network.

Figure 7.12 AMON Application Properties—General Tab

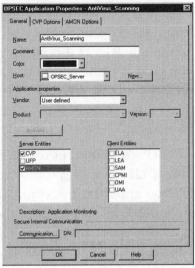

Enabling AMON is as simple as selecting the **AMON** option under **Server Entities**, and then setting the **Service** and **AMON Identifier** information on the AMON tab. As seen in Figure 7.13, the **Service** option is usually set to FW1_amon (TCP port 18193), but you should check the documentation that came with your application to ensure that this is the port the application is listening on. The **AMON identifier** field contains the Management Information Base (MIB) identifier, which also must be provided by your application's vendor.

Figure 7.13 OPSEC Application Properties—AMON Options Tab

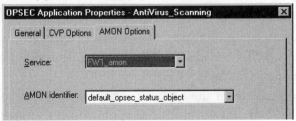

Client Side OPSEC Applications

In addition to the UFP and CVP application servers and the AMON monitoring service, there are six client application APIs that extend the functionality and management of VPN-1/FW-1 to third-party applications. Although complete configuration and implementation details for each of the six APIs will be dependent on which third-party application you're using, this section will give a quick look at each to discuss the capabilities of the API and to show the integration options possible for OPSEC-certified products.

Event Logging API

The Event Logging API allows third-party applications to send log data to the VPN-1/FW-1 log database. Sending log data to the central log has two main advantages: log consolidation and alert triggering.

In many networks, the firewall gateways are the security focal point, making the VPN-1/FW-1 logs the primary data source for security auditing. By extending the log to third-party products with the ELA, Check Point has enabled you to collect your security logs into a single location, making it easier to analyze and trend your security infrastructure's performance. An added benefit of consolidating logs from other products into the central log is that products using ELA will be able to trigger the VPN-1/FW-1 alert mechanism. This allows products like Stonesofts' StoneBeat high-availability solution to send logs and alerts to the Check Point Management Console when a FireWall-1 product has failed over to a standby machine.

Log Export API

To securely and efficiently access the Check Point log database, third-party products can use the Log Export API. The LEA allows access to the log in both real-time and historical access modes. In order to use LEA, the product vendor must write an LEA client that will access data from the Management Console that is running the LEA server. Using the LEA client/server model, OPSEC applications reduce the need to try to access the locked, proprietary formatted logs directly or having to export the Check Point logs out to plain text before being able to work with the log data.

For example, products like the WebTrends Firewall Suite can set up a secure connection to the VPN-1/FW-1 log database to pull in historical information for report generation. Since LEA supports encryption, you can be assured that the information used to generate the reports was not copied or corrupted during the transfer from one application to another.

Real-time data retrieval using LEA is most useful for generating alerts, based on firewall events, with a non–Check Point application. For example, LEA could be used to funnel firewall events into an Enterprise security manager (ESM) product that could correlate data with other security products, to generate trends and alerts based on a bigger view of the security infrastructure.

Suspicious Activities Monitoring

The Suspicious Activities Monitor was designed to provide a method for intrusion detection system (IDS) software to communicate with VPN-1/FW-1. This provides a method for an IDS application to create dynamic firewall rules to block traffic that the application believes is malicious.

Using a SAM-enabled application allows you to add some level of reflexive access to block previously allowed traffic. The key is in remembering that the access can only be granted with the static security policy rules, not the SAM application's dynamic rules. For example, if an IDS system detected something suspicious like a connection attempt to a closed port, it would be able to close all access to all resources from the IP address in question for a configurable period of time. This would block traffic, such as browsing your Internet Website, which may be explicitly allowed in your security policy. The action taken by the firewall is configurable and can include anything from making an entry in the logs, disconnecting a session in progress, or blocking all further access from the offending host. You need to be especially careful when allowing SAM applications to create firewall rules. If not configured properly, you can inadvertently create a denial of service situation on your own servers. For example, if you block all data from any host that has tried to connect to a closed port for one hour, an attacker may send connection requests to your servers with spoofed IP addresses in order to cause your own firewall to block traffic from your customers.

SmartDefense can be used to block attacks it recognizes them (as discussed in Chapter 13), but other solutions may notice traffic that is also unauthorized. The SAM API allows other devices to tell the firewall to block connections as appropriate. The SAM protocol is discussed in more detail in Chapter 9.

Object Management Interface

The Object Management Interface allows OPSEC applications to interact with the management server. The OMI has been replaced by the Check Point

Management Interface, and has only been kept in NG for backward compatibility. New applications being developed with the NG OPSEC Software Development Kit (SDK) will use CPMI.

Check Point Management Interface

Replacing OMI in the NG OPSEC SDK, the Check Point Management Interface allows OPSEC applications access to the management server's security policy and objects database. This can enable you to use objects already defined with the Policy Editor in other applications. Additionally, this secure interface can provide other applications access to create objects in the VPN-1/FW-1 database. The CPMI has three main benefits that OPSEC applications can take advantage of:

- CPMI can allow access to authentication information, enabling vendors to design single sign-on security solutions that take advantage of the authentication information already known to the firewall.

- Access to the Check Point object database can allow for report generation and alerting based on changes to monitored objects.

- Some management tasks can be automated, allowing software products to modify VPN-1/FW-1 in response to a security event.

UserAuthority API

The UserAuthority API is designed to extend the firewall's knowledge of users' VPN and local area network (LAN) authentication to other applications. In addition to providing the information that applications need in order to enable a single sign-on model, the UAA can also be used to provide information needed to develop billing and auditing applications that track individual users instead of just sessions.

The UAA also allows third-party applications to take advantage of the secure virtual network's (SVN) openPKI infrastructure for authentication. This reduces the vendor's need to develop their own authentication methods, which not only speeds development time for new applications, but also ensures compatibility with and leverages the investment in your existing infrastructure.

Other Resource Options

When we examined CVP and UFP resources, we touched on the basics of URI and FTP resources to show how to use the third-party servers in the security policy. URI resources can be used to filter based on wildcard matches and can be configured using specially formatted files, which you could create or purchase. After covering the remaining URI filtering methods and functions, we'll have a closer look at the FTP resource that we used in the virus-scanning example earlier, and we will examine SMTP and TCP resources.

The URI, SMTP, FTP, TCP and CIFS resources can be used in the rulebase in the same fashion as a normal service (such as HTTPS). The difference is in how the firewall handles the resource. When a packet matches a rule that uses a resource, the connection is handed off to the appropriate security server (if necessary) to make a control decision after inspecting the connection's content. This means that the packet must be approved by the resource before the rule's action will take effect. This is important to keep in mind when creating your rules, as you don't want to waste time virus-scanning files with a resource that will be dropped by the rule that caused the scan to be performed.

URI Resources

In addition to the resource we examined earlier (Figure 7.9) to use a UFP server in the security policy, there are two other types of URI resources. URI file resources allow you to use a specially formatted file to load complete URL strings, while wildcard resources allow you to create completely custom-match strings that may be as simple as looking for all executable files.

When you select a type of URI resource on the General tab, the Match tab will change to offer specific options for that type of object (Wildcard, File, or UFP). We've already looked at the UFP Match tab (Figure 7.10), and will examine the File and Wildcard tabs next, but it's worth noting that regardless of which **URI Match Specification Type** you choose, the Action and CVP tabs remain unchanged.

As we saw when we looked at CVP servers, the CVP tab (Figure 7.3) enables you to configure the resources' interaction with the CVP server. The Action tab, shown in Figure 7.14, enables you to specify some interesting things to further control and filter URI requests. Here you can enter a **Replacement URI**, which redirects the user's session to a site of your choice if the rule that matches this object sets the action to reject. Many companies use this option to redirect users to the corporate acceptable Internet-use policy when certain blocked URLs are requested.

Figure 7.14 URI Resource Properties—Action Tab

Limited content filtering is available through the use of **HTML Weeding** on the **Action** tab. You have five options for removing Active X, JAVA, and JAVA Script code from the HTML data.

- **Strip Script Tags** Remove JavaScript information from the selected Web page.

- **Strip Applet Tags** Remove Java Applet information from the selected Web page.

- **Strip ActiveX Tags** Remove ActiveX information from the selected Web page.

- **Strip FTP Links** Remove links destined for an FTP site from the selected Web page.

- **Strip Port Strings** Remove port strings from the selected page.

Although removing this data from the HTML code before the user sees it does reduce the risk of malicious code being sent to your users, the data stripping is non-selective, so all tags are removed. In addition, you have the option, under **Response Scanning**, to block all Java execution. You need to consider how these settings may reduce the functionality of some pages and have a negative impact on your users before enabling this type of filtering. To achieve more

granular control over these data types, you need to look into the services provided by a good CVP or UFP application.

URI File

After selecting **File** on the URI Resource Properties General tab (Figure 7.15),
the Match tab will display the import and export options, as seen in Figure 7.16.
These options enable you to load the match string definitions from disk rather
than having to create complicated match strings manually.

Figure 7.15 URI Resource Properties—General Tab

Clicking **Import** will enable you to specify the directory and filename of the
file that contains the URIs you want to apply the filter to. The **Export** option
will create a file containing the currently filtered URIs.

Figure 7.16 URI File Configuration

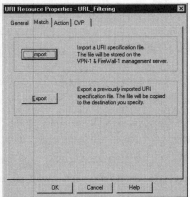

A URI specification file can be bought from companies that specialize in URL classification, or you can create your own. When creating a URI specification file, be sure to use an ASCII editor that uses a **\n** as the new line character, as this is the character the security server expects at the end of each line. There are three parts to each line in the URI specification:

- The IP address of the blocked server.

- An optional path to filter.

- A category number. Typically, each line is set to 0 (zero), but you can pick any number you like. Be careful when applying service or feature packs to your firewall, as it is possible that Check Point may start using this field in the future, so you may need to adjust it to an acceptable value.

The completed line will look similar to this: **192.168.0.1   /home   0**, which will deny any data request for information under the /home directory on the 192.168.0.1 server. Your firewall will require access to a domain name service (DNS) server if you use the name of the blocked resource rather than the IP address. Also, note that you could be generating a considerable amount of DNS traffic if you have a busy firewall and are using names rather than IP addresses, since each URI must be resolved before being checked.

URI Wildcards

When you select the **Wildcards** option from the General tab on the URI Resource Properties window (Figure 7.17), you are offered several options on the Match tab that will help you build a customized string to search for. You'll also notice that a new tab, SOAP, is created.

Figure 7.17 URI Wildcard Resource General Tab

Figure 7.18 shows the predefined checkbox options available on the Match tab. As well as the commonly used schemes and methods provided, the **Other** option can be used to provide even greater flexibility.

Figure 7.18 URI Wildcards Match Specification

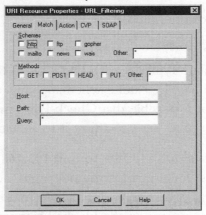

Under the **Schemes** section, you can select from the predefined common schemes of HTTP, FTP, Gopher, mailto, NEWS, and WAIS. If what you're looking for isn't among the six schemes provided, you can specify exactly what you need in the **Other** field. Most commonly, you'll be entering complete schemes to catch such as HTTPs, but this field also supports wildcards, so you can, if needed, specify something similar to ⋆tp in this field. This would enable you to catch any scheme that ended in the string 'tp' such as FTP, NNTP, SMTP, and HTTP, among others. You need to choose your wildcards carefully to ensure that you're not blocking or allowing something that you hadn't intended with a poorly written search string.

The **Methods** section provides the most common HTTP methods in a predefined set of options:

- **Get** The GET method is used to retrieve all the information specified by a URI. It is commonly used to download a complete HTML file as part of a Web browser session.

- **POST** Used to ask the server to accept a block of data, and is usually found in forms to send input from the user back to the server for processing.

- **HEAD** This method functions almost exactly like GET, except that the entire requested resource is not returned. HEAD is commonly used to validate URL links and to check time and date stamps for modification (normally to see if a cached copy is still current).

- **PUT** This method is used to place data (normally files) into the location specified by the URI, and is unlike the POST method, which sends data to an application as input.

The **Other** field in the **Methods** section supports the following less-common methods as well as wildcards that can be used to specify a custom pattern to match.

- **OPTIONS** This method can be used to determine the parameters available and supported at a specified URL. The OPTIONS method is commonly used to retrieve information about the server or specific resources without using a method like GET or HEAD, which would attempt to retrieve the actual object.

- **PATCH** Functions like PUT except that only a list of changes or differences between the file specified in the URL and the client's copy is sent. This method is most likely to be used when dealing with large files that only receive small updates, so sending only the changes is more efficient than sending the entire file again.

- **COPY** The COPY method specifies a second URL in the request headers and instructs the server to place a copy of the specified resource at the location defined in the headers. This would enable the user to copy data from one server to another without having to download a copy of the data first, and is commonly used if the network between the servers is faster than between the client and the servers.

- **DELETE** Instructs the server to delete the resource (normally a file) specified in the URL.

- **MOVE** The MOVE method will first copy the data to another specified URL then delete the original.

- **LINK** Allows you to create relationships between resources and is similar to the **ln** command on UNIX systems.

- **UNLINK** Deletes the relationships created by LINK.

- **TRACE** The TRACE method is normally used for testing and will cause the server to echo back the information it receives from the client. This allows the client to analyze the information that was received by the server and compare it to what was sent.

The final section of the Match tab allows you to specify the host, path, and query options to match. The **Host** option can be specified by name (such as www.syngress.com) or by IP address. If you specify the host by name, you will need to ensure that the firewall has access to a DNS server to resolve the name to an IP address. You can use wildcards to help build the pattern to match if needed.

The **Path** option must include the directory separation character (normally /) in order for a match to be made. When you define the path to match, you must specify the complete path, down to the individual file, or use wildcards to match all files or directories. Table 7.1 shows common strings used in the path field and how they will match to incoming data.

Table 7.1 Path Field Search Examples

String	Results
/home	Will match a file called home in any directory. For example: /home and /mysite/mydir/home would both be matched. In either case, if home was a directory, no match would be found.
/home/*	This pattern will match all files and directories under the home directory. For example, /home/index.htm and /home/files/index.htm would be matched.
/home/	This will match any URI that contains the directory home, so files in /home would be matched as well as files in /mydir/home/mysite.
*/index.htm	This will match the file index.htm in any directory.
/.mp+	This pattern will match three character file extensions that start with "mp," such as mp3 and mpg.
/.{exe,zip,gz}	Will match all files that end in .exe, .zip, and .gz in any directory.

The **Query** field can be used to match on any string of characters found after a question mark (?) in a URL. Since wildcards are supported here as well, it is not necessary to know the exact placement of the key words you are looking for in the query. For example, this will allow you to block or redirect searches for keywords that are in violation of your Internet acceptable-use policy.

When working with URI resources, it is common to use a single asterisk in the three match fields so that all possible requests can be matched. However, when using CVP servers, it is often useful to do specific file matching with wild-cards in the patch field to ensure that only supported data types are sent to the server to be scanned.

The final tab is the SOAP tab. SOAP stands for Simple Objects Access Protocol. It is a lightweight protocol used in the exchange of information in a decentralized, distributed environment. SOAP messages are encoded in XML (extensible markup language). A full discussion of SOAP and XML is well outside the scope of this book. More information can be found in other books or at http://www.w3.org/TR/SOAP/.

The SOAP option can only be used with HTTP connections that are accepted. It is not usable if the action is drop or reject. The additional checking that VPN-1/FW-1 does when **Allow all SOAP requests** is selected is to confirm that the SOAP requests conform to RFC standards (see Figure 7.19). When selecting **Allow SOAP requests as specified in the following file**, a file named scheme1 through scheme10 in the management station's $FWDIR/conf/XML directory will specify the namespaces and methods used for the exchange. The namespace and XML methods being passed can be viewed in SmartView Tracker by setting the Track SOAP connections option. An example can be seen in $FWDIR/conf/XML/SchemeSample.dat. The syntax for the file is as follows:

```
namespace method
```

Example:

```
http://tempuri.org/message/ EchoString
http://tempuri.org/message/ SubtractNumbers
```

Figure 7.19 URI Wildcards SOAP Specification

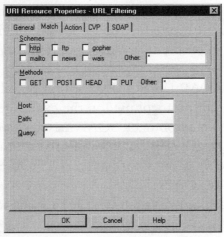

SMTP Resources

The SMTP resource defines the methods used by VPN-1/FW-1 to control and manipulate incoming and outgoing e-mail. There are many options, including the ability to remove active scripting components, rewriting fields in the envelope (such as to: or from:), or filtering based on content. The configuration of an SMTP resource is similar to that of URI resources, including the ability to use a CVP server to provide third-party content filtering. Figure 7.20 shows the General tab of the SMTP Resource Properties window that is used to set basic operational parameters for the resource.

Figure 7.20 SMTP Resource Properties—General Tab

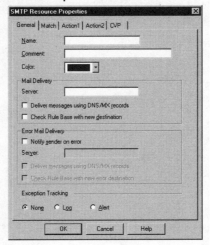

This tab includes the standard initial object setup of name, comment, and color. If you want to forward all messages to another server, specify its name or IP address in the **Server** text field. Enable the **Deliver messages using DNS/MX records** option to have these messages delivered directly to the specified server rather than to a group of servers used for redundancy purposes. The **Check Rule Base with new destination** option can be used to instruct the security server to recheck the SMTP message's destination server against the security policy after being modified by the SMTP resource. Identical settings are available for the handling of error mail messages if the **Notify sender on error** option is selected.

The Match tab, shown in Figure 7.21, has only two option fields that control how to match messages being examined by the security server. The **Sender** and **Recipient** fields are used to define the addresses you want to work with. Wildcards are supported in these fields to provide the ability to specify all addresses (using ★) or all users in a specific domain (with ★@domain.com) if needed. The example shown in Figure 7.21 shows how an administrator would allow incoming mail to mycompany.com, but not allow relays or outgoing mail. In most cases an administrator would configure two resources, one for inbound mail and another for outbound mails.

Figure 7.21 SMTP Resource Properties—Match Tab

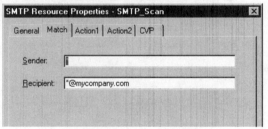

When you create a new SMTP resource, the **Sender** and **Recipient** fields are blank and must be filled in before the resource will function. You need to be careful with these options, though; it's common to just set the **Recipient** field to an asterisk to save time. You need to keep in mind that the resource defines how the security server will function, and by placing an asterisk in both of the available fields, you could be allowing external hosts to bounce mail off your firewall. This makes your firewall an open relay for SMTP traffic, and aside from the possibility of your server being used to send unsolicited bulk e-mail (spam), many domains and even some ISPs may refuse to accept SMTP traffic from your domain if it's found that you have an open relay. For information on blocking open relays from your domain, or checking to see if you've become blacklisted, check an open relay database site such as www.ordb.org and check your Postmater@yourdomain.com mailbox.

The Action1 tab has a few simple options that allow you to re-address messages and change limited content. The **Sender** and **Recipient** fields allow you to re-address messages on a single-user basis, or by using wildcards, to translate addresses for an entire domain. The **Field** option allows you to modify data in any of the other standard SMTP fields such as the carbon copy (cc), blind carbon copy (bcc), or subject. Once you've specified the field to change, you need only specify the string to look for, and what to replace it with. Shown in Figure 7.22, this tab is very useful if you have recently changed your SMTP domain name but still have a few messages coming to the old domain. Using the simple rewrite options shown, you could easily translate an address joe@olddomain to joe@newdomain.com. The **Help** button for this section has some useful information in the section entitled *Using wildcards and Regular Expressions in Resources*. It also defines how you can specify multiple rewriting rules even though you see only one text box.

Figure 7.22 SMTP Resource Action Tab Showing Address Rewrite

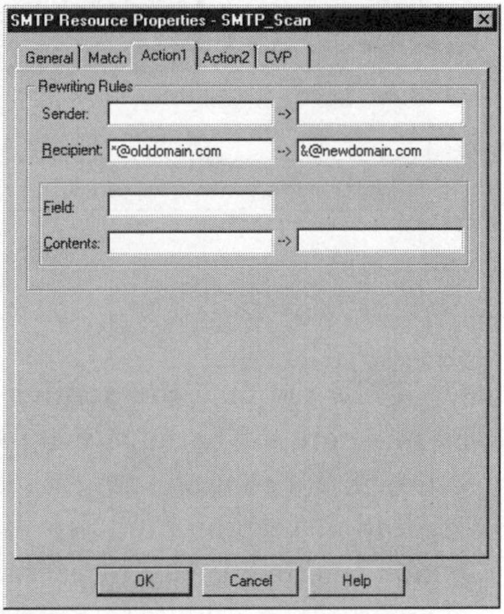

The Action2 tab allows the removal of information found within the body of the message. The **Attachment handling** section provides two simple methods

of discarding attachments from messages. In Figure 7.23, the resource is configured to strip attachments of the message/partial type. There are seven supported options, as defined in RFC 2046, for removing specific file.

- Text
- Multipart
- Image
- Message
- Audio
- Video
- Application

You can use the **Strip file by name** field to remove files based on a pattern, using wildcards if needed, rather than by Multipurpose Internet Mail Extension (MIME) type. This field is often used to stop "zero day" or new viruses and worms that spread via e-mail. It's often faster to start filtering out viruses by their specific attachment names (once known), than it is to update the virus signatures throughout your entire enterprise. In Figure 7.23, files ending with the extension .exe, .vbs, or .scr will be stripped. If nothing else, this function will buy you enough time to update your signatures properly while you block new infections from entering (or leaving) your network.

Use the **Do not send mail larger than** field to specify the maximum allowable message size. Use the **Allowed Characters** options to specify whether the security server will accept messages in either 7- or 8-bit ASCII. The **Weeding** section allows you to remove JAVA, JAVA Script, Active X, FTP URI links, and Port strings from the message's headers and body.

Figure 7.23 SMTP Resource Properties—Action2 Tab

One common mistake made when creating SMTP resources is not checking the **Do not send mail larger than** field. By default, the messages larger than 10,000 KB will be dropped. Note that in NG AI the default maximum message size has been raised to 10,000 KB, compared with 1,000 KB in its predecessor. This is because many attachments are larger than the previous limit of just under one megabyte. Aside from irritating users, failing to check this option often resulted in e-mail administrators spending hours troubleshooting lost SMTP messages, since the security server would discard the entire message.

The CVP tab of the SMTP Resource Properties window provides the standard options we discussed when examining CVP servers. The only exception, as shown in Figure 7.24, is the addition of a single SMTP-only option to **Send SMTP headers to CVP server**. This option instructs the CVP server to scan messages' full headers in addition to the message body.

Figure 7.24 SMTP Resource Properties—CVP Tab

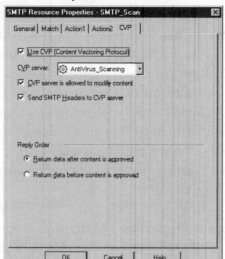

FTP Resources

We looked at FTP resources briefly when we first examined CVP servers. In addition to enabling you to send FTP data streams to another server for content filtering, FTP resources can be used without a CVP server to just control FTP sessions.

The General tab in the FTP Resource Properties window (Figure 7.25) allows you to specify the normal VPN-1/FW-1 object information, but the interesting options (aside from the CVP tab) are on the Match tab.

Figure 7.25 FTP Resource Properties–General Tab

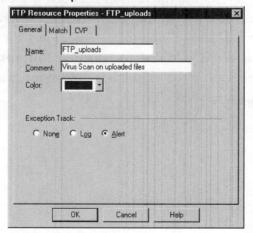

The Match tab, shown in Figure 7.26, contains three options that allow you to control the actual FTP session. The **Path** field allows you to specify specific file paths, using wildcards if desired, to perform actions on. The most interesting and useful part of the FTP resource is the use of GET and PUT, since they enable you to control FTP functions. Using these options will allow you to control the commands that your users can issue to remote servers. Allowing your users to GET but not PUT will prohibit them from pushing data out of your network, while still allowing them to download files as needed. Allowing PUT but not GET would be a good solution for a publicly accessible FTP server used to receive files from your business partners, since they could upload files to you, but could not download anything.

Figure 7.26 FTP Resource Properties—Match Tab

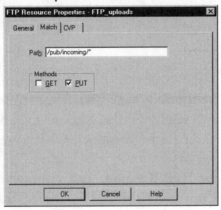

The FTP Resource CVP tab enables you to specify a CVP server to send matched data to, and defines the interaction between the FTP security server and the CVP server. Similar to the example you looked at when examining CVP server objects, Figure 7.27 shows how to scan incoming files for viruses. By enabling the **CVP Server is allowed to modify content** option, you can specify that infected files are to be cleaned. If this option was unchecked, all infected files would be discarded.

Figure 7.27 FTP Resource Properties—CVP Tab

TCP

The TCP resource allows you to work with services not handled by built-in security servers, and has only two methods of operation. You can use the TCP resource as a generic daemon, providing an alternative to the HTTP security server, for interaction with a CVP server.

Additionally, you can use the TCP resource to screen URLs via a UFP server without the intervention of the security server. Note that the UFP server must support this sort of interaction, as the format of its incoming data stream will not be in full URI format, since only the IP-based URL is available without the security server. The TCP resource has three possible tabs, only two of which are displayed at any time. The **Type** option on the General tab (Figure 7.28) enables you to select either **UFP** or **CVP,** and this dictates which other tab (UFP or CVP) is offered for configuration.

Figure 7.28 TCP Resource Properties—General Tab

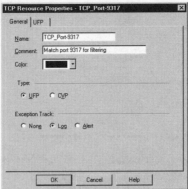

After checking **UFP** on the General tab, you can then access the UFP tab (shown in Figure 7.29) and configure the associated tab. The UFP configuration on this tab is similar to other resources that use UFP servers. You need only to select the UFP server that this resource will be using, configure the caching method, and select the categories against which this data stream will be checked from the supplied list.

Figure 7.29 TCP Resource Properties—UFP Tab

If you select **CVP** on the General tab, you will be presented with the CVP tab (Figure 7.30), which will allow you to configure the resource's interaction with the CVP server. You will need to specify which **CVP server** to use from the drop-down list on the CVP tab. The other options here are identical to the CVP objects you've looked at before, and will enable you to configure options such as whether the CVP server is allowed to modify the content passed to it, and to specify the method in which data is returned to the security server.

Figure 7.30 TCP Resource Properties—CVP Tab

CIFS

With a CIFS resource, an administrator can grant granular access to shares on a server to different user groups or to everyone. CIFS resources are most common when controlling access to internal servers from the LAN or controlling access to a file server across a site-to-site VPN.

CIFS is the protocol used for file and print services between clients and servers on the network. Legacy CIFS connections (implemented over NetBIOS) run over port 139. In Windows 2000 and later, the Microsoft-DS protocol (running over port 445) is used. A single CIFS resource can be used with both ports to ensure consistent enforcement across both file-sharing protocols. In Figure 7.31, the resource could be used in a rule to grant access to the shared for only certain source address, to certain users, or to deny access to the shares to the entire LAN. It all depends on how the resource rule is created.

Figure 7.31 CIFS Resource Properties—General Tab

Summary

Check Point's OPSEC standards program certifies that third-party applications meet minimum integration and compatibility requirements with the VPN-1/FW-1 products. This, in essence, extends the reach of your VPN-1/FW-1 security infrastructure to encompass areas where highly specialized or customized solutions are required to meet the needs of your network.

Through the use of CVP and UFP application servers, you are able to extend the information used by VPN-1/FW-1 to make data control decisions to include input from third-party solutions. In addition to providing you with greater flexibility, this enables you to build best-of-breed solutions into your firewall from vendors that specialize in the task you need to perform.

CVP is used to send an entire data stream, such as a downloaded file, to another server to be validated either as a whole or in parts. This validation can be as simple as checking the file for viruses or using image recognition software to discard images that may not be acceptable in your environment. In many cases, such as when using a virus scanner, the CVP server may modify the data before returning it to the security server to be passed along to its final destination. CVP objects can be grouped together to share load among servers performing a similar function, or servers can be chained together to perform multiple actions and validation checks on the data before returning it to the firewall.

UFP is used to check the scheme and path of data resource requests. UFP is most commonly used for HTTP traffic to control access to sites that may not be appropriate in a corporate setting, but can also be used with other protocols. UFP servers enable you to choose from predefined categories to specify which sites are to be filtered or denied from the data requests passing through the firewall. UFP applications often come with a subscription service that will provide updates to the database of sites and categories known to the product, as well as enabling you to specify your own so that your protection is kept up to date. As with CVP resources, you can group UFP servers together to provide high availability and load sharing among servers providing the same service. You cannot, however, chain UFP servers together.

AMON is new to the NG version of VPN-1/FW-1 and provides a method for third-party servers to report status information to the firewall products. This allows you to monitor the status of other security devices using the tools from Check Point, or other vendor tools that you're already using to keep an eye on your firewalls.

OPSEC applications can also access VPN-1/FW-1 information and resources by using LEA, ELA, SAM, OMI, CPMI or UAA. These client applications are not normally used in the data control process as OPSEC servers are, but often make use of the status, log, and object databases to report on and manipulate VPN-1/FW-1 devices and applications.

There are five major types of resources in VPN-1/FW-1: URI, SMTP, FTP, CIFS, and TCP. URI is the most common and offers the greatest flexibility, since URI resources can be created using wildcards or from specially formatted files that define the pattern to match on. Most commonly, URI resources are used with CVP or UFP servers as a method to move data between the security policy and third-party servers.

SMTP resources allow you to manipulate e-mail messages and provide a method to replace or substitute information in certain fields as messages pass through the firewall. FTP resources allow you to control FTP sessions down to the level of being able to specify whether users can issue GET or PUT commands, as well as the ability to stop users from accessing specific paths on the server. Both SMTP and FTP resources support using CVP servers to validate data coming into or leaving your protected networks. The TCP resource enables you to use either a UFP or a CVP server with TCP data that is not handled by one of the built-in security servers. A CIFS resource is used to granularly control access to file and print servers based on user, server, or share name.

Solutions Fast Track

OPSEC Applications

☑ Using third-party OPSEC-certified applications enables you to build onto your existing Check Point security infrastructure to address specific security needs, while ensuring compatibility and interoperability.

☑ There are three types of OPSEC server applications: CVP, UFP, and AMON. UFP and CVP servers interoperate with VPN-1/FW-1 by passing data back and forth and participating in the control process, whereas AMON is used by other applications to report status information back to the firewall management server.

☑ OPSEC client applications, as a general rule, either send data to or pull data from VPN-1/FW-1, and generally do not affect the control process directly as servers do. There are six methods for OPSEC clients to send or receive data from VPN-1/FW-1: LEA, ELA, SAM, OMI, CPMI, and UAA.

☑ ELA allows third-party applications to send log data to the VPN-1/FW-1 log database for consolidation and alerting functions.

☑ LEA provides a method for applications to extract log data from the central log database, either historically or in real time.

☑ SAM provides a conduit for IDS devices to signal and make changes to the current security policy, such as blocking traffic from a specific host.

☑ The OMI provides support for legacy applications that need to access the VPN-1/FW-1 object database.

☑ CMPI replaces OMI in the NG version of VPN-1/FW-1. CPMI allows applications to access the object database as well as authentication information known to the firewall. CPMI also provides the needed APIs to allow third-party applications to make limited changes to the security policy.

☑ The UAA can be used to access VPN and LAN authentication information from VPN-1/FW-1. This allows applications to be designed to use existing logon information to provide single sign-on capabilities.

Content Vectoring Protocol

☑ CVP is normally used for sending data, such as binary files or e-mail messages from VPN-1/FW-1, to a third-party server to be scanned. The results of the scan have a direct impact on the control decision for that data, which can include blocking the data entirely or just modifying it to an acceptable format (in the case of removing a virus).

☑ CVP resources are created using an OPSEC Application object as the server to send data to, and contain configuration settings for what actions the CVP server is to perform on the data.

☑ CVP groups allow you to load share between servers or chain multiple CVP servers together to perform different tasks one after another.

☑ Load sharing splits the incoming work to be done evenly among the defined servers, using the method that you specify.

URI Filtering Protocol

☑ A URI describes how to access a resource and is made up of two parts. The scheme defines which protocol (such as HTTP) to use and is separated by a colon from the path to the desired resource.

☑ UFP can be implemented through the use of URI resources in the security policy, and allows you to examine and filter URIs passed from the VPN-1/FW-1 security servers as part of the control decision.

☑ UFP is commonly used to verify that requested or returned URLs conform to an acceptable standard, by classifying URLs into categories and enabling you to choose which categories are permissible in your environment.

☑ UFP groups enable you to share load between multiple UFP servers to increase efficiency and provide availability, if a UFP server should fail.

Other Resource Options

☑ URI file resources allow you to use a specially formatted file to define the URIs that you want to filter on. This option is commonly used when you have many URIs to filter but do not want to use a UFP server.

☑ URI wildcards allow you to build a completely customized URI string to match to incoming data. The flexibility of wild cards enables you filter on a specific file extension or even specify entire IP address blocks.

☑ SMTP resources enable you to inspect and modify e-mail traffic passing through your firewall. You can, for example, modify sender or recipient information in addition to the data within the body of the message. It is also possible to perform limited screening for potentially malicious content by removing Active X and/or JAVA code from the messages. For more granular screening capabilities, the SMTP Resource enables you to send e-mail messages, with complete headers, to a CVP server to be analyzed.

☑ FTP resources allow you to control FTP data streams. In addition to looking for certain paths or file names being requested, you can control when and where your users can use the FTP GET and PUT commands to control data moving into or out of your network.

☑ The TCP resource allows you to send data from TCP protocols not covered by the normal security servers to a CVP or UFP server for inspection.

☑ The CIFS resource enables an administrator to very granularly define access to file and print sharing servers over NetBIOS and Microsoft-DS protocols.

Frequently Asked Questions

The following Frequently Asked Questions, answered by the authors of this book, are designed to both measure your understanding of the concepts presented in this chapter and to assist you with real-life implementation of these concepts. To have your questions about this chapter answered by the author, browse to **www.syngress.com/solutions** and click on the **"Ask the Author"** form. You will also gain access to thousands of other FAQs at ITFAQnet.com.

Q: My URI specification file looks okay, but it doesn't work properly. What should I look for?

A: There are three major parts to each line in the URI specification file. After you've entered the IP address, path, and category, you must end each line with a new line character (\n). If you use a Windows-based computer to build your file, ensure that you use an editor that uses only \n when you end a line. The WordPad application or Edit (run from a cmd.exe window) will create the file properly, whereas the Notepad application may not. When in doubt, add an extra new line character at the end of the file.

Q: What are the valid wildcard characters?

A: There are only four characters that can be used as wildcards in resource definitions, such as a URI wildcard object:

- The asterisk (*) can be used to match any number of characters.

- The plus sign (+) can be used to match a single character only. For example, '+tp' will match 'ftp' but not 'http.'

- The ampersand (&) can only be used with SMTP addresses and allows you to manipulate information on either side of the @ symbol for address replacement objects. For example, changing from "jim@yoursite.com" in an object to "&@yournewsite.com" results in "jim@yournewsite.com."

- A list of strings may be separated with commas (,) to match any one of the specified strings. The case of "hr,sales," "@yoursite.com" will match "hr@yoursite.com" and "sales@yoursite.com."

Q: What OPSEC applications are available?

A: The list of OPSEC-certified applications grows everyday. At the time of this writing, there are over 300 certified OPSEC vendors, each with one or more certified applications. This means that when you're looking for a third-party product to fill a specific security need in your organization, odds are that there is an OPSEC-certified product available. The current list of OPSEC-certified products and vendors can be found at www.opsec.com.

Q: How do I block the latest virus that is spreading today?

A: In addition to the capabilities of SmartDefense discussed later in this book, if the virus is spread through http/ftp downloads and/or through e-mail attachments, then you can use VPN-1/FW-1 resources to block these connections. Using the Nimda virus as an example, you could use the SMTP file and/or MIME stripping to match MIME attachments of type *audio/x-wav* and the filename of *readme.exe*. Then use a URI wildcard resource to match HTTP, GETs to any host and any query match. Fill in the **Path** field with the following string: **{*cmd.exe,*root.exe,*admin.dll,*readme.exe, *readme.eml,default.ida}**. Then just use these resources in rules that drop or reject the connections. For more information on blocking Nimda, see Check Point's public knowledge base (support.checkpoint.com/public) article sk7473.

Q: Why do my users receive the error, "FW-1 Unknown WWW Server," intermittently?

A: If your firewall cannot resolve the Website name to an IP (DNS), then it will present this error when a Web browser has the firewall defined as a proxy. Sometimes other problems with the HTTP security server may result in this error as well. You may want to try some of the objects_5_0.C changes or contact support for assistance.

Q: My users are complaining that they cannot connect to certain sites and they are receiving the following message: "Web site found. Waiting for reply..." All of these sites seem to include a double slash in them. Is there a problem with the firewall?

A: If the site your users are trying to access contains a double slash within in the URL GET command, then the GET command does not conform to RFC 2616 standards (according to Check Point), and the security server will not allow a connection. Your only option (if you must pass the site) is to bypass the security server by creating an HTTP accept rule specifically for this destination above any HTTP resource rules defined in your VPN-1/FW-1 security policy. See Check Point's public knowledge base article skI3834 for more information.

Q: In FireWall-1 4.1, there were several objects.C file modifications for the HTTP security server that resolved several problems. Are the same changes available in NG?

A: Yes, most of the changes that you implemented in 4.1 can be used in NG as well. To edit the objects_5_0.C file, you need to use the dbedit utility in NG. Some changes are as follows.

```
:http_disable_content_type (false)
:http_disable_content_enc (true)
:http_enable_uri_queries (false)
:http_max_header_length (8192)
:http_max_url_length (8192)
:http_avoid_keep_alive (true)
```

These are the default settings that are in the objects.C file in NG HF1:

```
:http_allow_content_disposition (false)
:http_allow_double_slash (false)
:http_allow_ranges (false)
:http_avoid_keep_alive (false)
:http_block_java_allow_chunked (false)
:http_buffers_size (4096)
:http_check_request_validity (true)
:http_check_response_validity (true)
```

```
:http_cvp_allow_chunked (false)
:http_disable_ahttpdhtml (false)
:http_disable_automatic_client_auth_redirect (false)
:http_disable_cab_check (false)
:http_disable_content_enc (false)
:http_disable_content_type (false)
:http_dont_dns_when_star_port (false)
:http_dont_handle_next_proxy_pw (false)
:http_failed_resolve_timeout (900)
:http_force_down_to_10 (0)
:http_handle_proxy_pw (true)
:http_log_every_connection (false)
:http_max_auth_password_num (1000)
:http_max_auth_redirect_num (1000)
:http_max_connection_num (4000)
:http_max_header_length (1000)
:http_max_header_num (500)
:http_max_held_session_num (1000)
:http_max_realm_num (1000)
:http_max_server_num (10000)
:http_max_session_num (0)
:http_max_url_length (2048)
:http_next_proxy_host ()
:http_next_proxy_port ()
:http_no_content_length (false)
:http_old_auth_timeout (0)
:http_process_timeout (43200)
:http_proxied_connections_allowed (true)
:http_query_server_for_authorization (false)
:http_redirect_timeout (300)
:http_servers (
        :ers ()
        :Uid ("{6CAC812A-202F-11D6-AB57-C0A800056370}")
)
:http_session_timeout (300)
:http_skip_redirect_free (true)
```

```
:http_use_cache_hdr (true)
:http_use_cvp_reply_safe (false)
:http_use_default_schemes (false)
:http_use_host_h_as_dst (false)
:http_use_proxy_auth_for_other (true)
:http_weeding_allow_chunked (false)
```

## Chapter 8

Managing Policies and Logs

Solutions in this Chapter:

- **Administering Check Point VPN-1/FW-1 NG AI for Performance**

- **Administering Check Point VPN-1/FW-1 NG AI for Effectiveness**

- **Administering Check Point VPN-1/FW-1 NG AI for Recoverability**

- **Performing Advanced Administration Tasks**

- ☑ **Summary**

- ☑ **Solutions Fast Track**

- ☑ **Frequently Asked Questions**

Introduction

In this chapter we strive to give you some basic firewall administrator knowledge and show you how to administer the enterprise security software package VPN-1/FW-1 Next Generation with Application Intelligence (NG AI) so that it doesn't get too big for you to handle. It's very easy for several administrators to be involved in policy development and manipulation, but if you have too many people involved in a security system such as a firewall, you need to keep strict vigilance and record who is making changes when and why. Otherwise, you could end up with a misconfigured firewall, which could compromise the security it is meant to provide.

Besides monitoring administrator activities, you should also keep software up to date. You should frequently check Check Point's Web site for the latest security patches and software updates. Sometimes these updates require you to modify configuration files or to stop and start your firewall services, and we discuss how to go about performing those tasks in this chapter.

This chapter covers performance related to your security policy and logs and discusses what to do when you have multiple firewalls in various locations. It tells you about your firewall's log files and some ways to administer your logs so that you don't run into disk space issues. This chapter also equips you with several command-line options that you can use to perform maintenance or troubleshoot your firewall.

As a Check Point NG AI administrator, you have three main goals with respect to administration. They are as follows:

- **Performance** Because the Check Point NG AI firewall is the point through which all traffic to or from the unprotected to protected network flows, performance is critical. A poorly performing firewall will quickly bring complaints from users and eventually from your boss.

- **Effectiveness** The effectiveness of the firewall is a vital concern. If the firewall isn't doing its job at controlling and monitoring access, it isn't any good. In fact, an ineffective firewall could open up your organization to multiple vulnerabilities.

- **Recovery capability** Because the Check Point NG AI firewall is such a crucial piece in your network architecture, forget about rebuilding a firewall from scratch to its pre-crash state, duplicating the many rules and properties from memory. You need to be able to recover your configuration and security policy quickly and effectively should disaster strike.

Administering Check Point VPN-1/FW-1 NG AI for Performance

With FW-1 NG AI, Check Point has made a number of improvements over previous versions. One major improvement is with INSPECT XL, which is responsible for evaluating packets based on rules. The new version of INSPECT XL is supposed to be optimized and much more efficient because it uses only one state table, as opposed to earlier implementations that used multiple state tables. Despite these improvements, ensuring that your firewall is performing up to your expectations as well as everyone else's is important. There are a number of "best practices" that you should keep in mind when configuring and administrating your firewall to ensure that Check Point NG performance is at its optimum.

Configuring NG for Performance

There are a number of things that you can do when you're initially configuring FW-1 NG AI so that it provides optimum performance for your environment:

- Use hosts files on management servers and remote enforcement modules.
- Disable decryption on accept.
- Modify logging Global Properties.

The recommendation to use hosts files should be part of every installation. To clarify, every time you install a policy, the management station must resolve its name to an IP address and each of the enforcement modules onto which it is installing policy. In the event that a DNS server cannot be contacted or the name is not found in DNS, policy installations can fail or take a very long time—both undesirable consequences. Using hosts files, the host will parse the hosts file first for IP address mappings and not make a network query. This will speed up the install of security policy and ensure that it will install even during times when DNS servers are unavailable. On UNIX systems, the hosts file is located at /etc/hosts. On Windows NT/2000, the hosts file is located at %SystemRoot%\System32\drivers\etc\hosts.

For example, if the name of your FW-1 object in the Rule Base GUI is ExternalFW, you must be sure that the name ExternalFW is mapped to an IP address in the hosts file. Additionally, let's say that part of your policy installs policy onto a remote firewall named RemoteFW. The mapping of RemoteFW must also be defined in the hosts file. Here is a sample hosts file:

```
127.0.0.1 localhost
11.12.13.14 ExternalFW
15.16.17.18 RemoteFW
```

Configuring & Implementing…

NT Name Resolution

Windows NT 4 uses NetBIOS name resolution to find services on the network. WINS is a dynamic name registration service that a workstation can use to resolve NetBIOS names to IP addresses. Additionally, the LMHOSTS file located at %SystemRoot%\System32\drivers\etc can be used to statically map NetBIOS names to IP addresses. The NetBIOS name and TCP/IP host name can be two different names on an NT 4 workstation, although this is not recommended. Despite Microsoft's dependence on NetBIOS names, your FW-1 NG AI relies on TCP/IP host names.

Windows 2000 uses host name resolution to find services on the network. DNS is the network service that a Windows 2000 workstation can use to resolve name to IP addresses. However, the hosts file will always be parsed first; if there is no mapping, the host will attempt DNS resolution.

Another setting you can change right off the bat is *decryption on accept*. If you are not using encryption, you should uncheck **Enable decryption on accept**. This option can be found in Global Properties under the VPN-1 tab, as shown in Figure 8.1. This setting prevents FW-1 NG from attempting decryption of packets even when the rule doesn't require it. This setting allows FW-1 NG to free some resources for other tasks, but it should be noted that this setting is relevant only if you are using Traditional Mode policies.

Figure 8.1 Global Properties

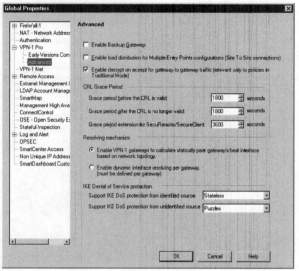

Other Global Properties that you should consider changing are related to logs and alerts, as shown in Figure 8.2. Although the default settings are generally effective, you might need to make changes, depending on your environment. For example, you can limit the amount of activity that gets logged to the log file by decreasing the **Excessive log grace period**. This is the period in seconds that FW-1 NG AI will not log the same activity multiple times. Decreasing this number will probably reduce the number of resources that the Log Unification Engine uses to consolidate activity into the log view.

There are also a couple of performance tweaks that will not affect firewall throughput but that do have an effect on overall performance. One such setting is the **SmartView Tracker resolver timeout**. Decreasing this value will decrease the amount of time in seconds that FW-1 NG AI spends resolving IP addresses to names for log entries. If names are not critical to your understanding of the logs and if DNS queries frequently timeout, this option would be good to decrease. Doing so increases the Log Viewer but not the firewall throughput.

And finally, you can decrease the **Status fetching interval** to decrease the frequency in seconds that the management server queries the modules that it manages for status. If your environment is pretty static, this setting could be reduced. Again, this decrease will not affect firewall throughput and will not even be an issue if the System Status window is not open and querying modules.

Figure 8.2 Log and Alert Global Properties

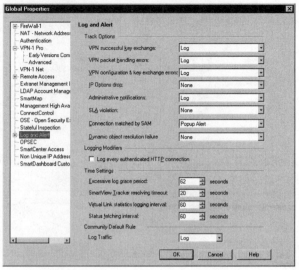

Administering NG for Performance

In addition to the initial configuration of FW-1 NG AI, you should keep in mind a number of administration "best practices" to ensure that the firewall is performing up to expectations and its capabilities:

- Keep the Rule Base simple.
- Put the most frequently applied rules near the top of the Rule Base.
- Keep accounting to a minimum.
- Use the Active Log mode sparingly.
- Use logging wisely.
- Consider limiting the use of security servers.
- Implement NAT wisely.
- Avoid the use of domain objects.

The first recommendation, to keep the Rule Base simple, will probably have the greatest impact on overall performance. Unfortunately, it is the most difficult to define and control. The reason this is so important is that every packet that isn't a part of an existing connection must be evaluated against the Rule Base sequentially, from the top to the bottom, until a match is found. A long, complex policy will introduce latency into the processing of packets, not to mention that a long, complex policy is hard to administer. When making modifications to the Rule Base, you should consider the best way to write the rule and where to place it. For example, instead of writing an extra rule to give FTP to the internal network, if you already have a rule for HTTP, simply add FTP to the HTTP rule. Just remember that there is almost always a simpler way to write rules. Keep the number of rules as low as possible.

Designing & Planning…

Top Performers

On the top end, Check Point has posted a number of top-performance numbers for throughput, concurrent firewall connections, and other data. According to Check Point, it is possible to have up to 4+ Gbps in a software installation. A firewall appliance optimized installation can see throughput upward of 8 Gbps, as shown in Table 8.1.

Table 8.1 FireWall-1 Throughput

Platform	Mbps
Windows 2000/NT Dual Xeon 2.4 GHz	625
Solaris Dual UltraSPARC-III Cu 750 MHz	900
Linux Dual Xeon 1.7 GHz	1,000
SecurePlatform Dual Xeon	4,000
Nokia IP740	2,000
Nortel Alteon Switch Firewall System 5710	4,200
Crossbeam X40	8,000

Putting this in perspective, keep in mind that the average Internet connection is around T1 speeds of 1.54 Mbps. Unless your firewall is protecting enclave networks internally running at Gigabit speeds or an OC12 connection to the Internet, the firewall will not be a performance bottleneck.

Another statistic, concurrent connections, is the number of connections maintained between hosts on either side of the firewall. The

Continued

number of connections is highly memory dependent. On an installation with 512 MB of memory, Check Point NG AI can support 1,000,000 concurrent connections. That same installation with 512 MB of memory can support 20,000 VPN tunnels. You will probably run out of bandwidth before you exceed one of these limiting factors. Hopefully this proves to some extent that FW-1 architecture can meet the most demanding environments. In fact, performance issues are typically a result of administration or configuration issues. If you would like more performance information, you can visit www.checkpoint.com/techsupport/documentation/FW-1_VPN-1_performance.html.

It's also interesting to note that Check Point has released VPN-1 Edge devices, which are hardware/software combinations that produce very high speeds for small offices at a very low price.

Remember in Chapter 4 we looked at a security policy that allowed our internal users the use of HTTP to anywhere and the use of HTTPS everywhere but the local service net. We chose to write the rule as Source-**LAN,** Destination-**Service Net,** Service-**HTTP/HTTPS,** Action-**Accept,** and Track-**None** with the Destination-**Service Net Negated.** And because another element of our policy allowed everyone HTTP access to the Web server in the service net, we wrote a second rule as Source-**Any,** Destination-**Web Server,** Service-**HTTP,** Action-**Accept,** and Track-**Log.** This rule could have been much more complicated. For example, we could have written our Rule Base to look like Figure 8.3.

Figure 8.3 A Bad Example

NO	SOURCE	DESTINATION	VPN	SERVICE	ACTION	TRACK	INSTALL ON	TIME	COMMENT
1	* Any	ExternalFW	* Any Traffic	* Any	drop	! Alert	* Policy Targets	* Any	Stealth Rule
2	LAN	Web_Server	* Any Traffic	TCP https	reject	Log	* Policy Targets	* Any	Stop LAN access to the public web server
3	LAN	* Any	* Any Traffic	TCP http / TCP https	accept	Log	* Policy Targets	* Any	Allow LAN access to http and https on the Internet
4	* Any	Web_Server	* Any Traffic	TCP http	accept	Log	* Policy Targets	* Any	Allow unrestricted access to the public web server
5	* Any	* Any	* Any Traffic	* Any	drop	Log	* Policy Targets	* Any	Cleanup Rule

Translating our policy this way, we used three rules instead of two. If we repeated this process over and over while writing the Rule Base, we would have one-third more rules than we need!

In addition to keeping the Rule Base simple, put the most frequently applied rules near the top. This will get packets through inspection more quickly and routed by the OS. Remember that a packet is processed from top to bottom until a match is made on the Rule Base; so, when optimizing, be aware of the effect of reordering rules. As an aid to optimization, monitoring your logs using the FW-1 predefined selection criteria can help you determine the most frequently applied rules. Take a look at Figure 8.4. Here you will see the most activity on Rule 12, which allows HTTP traffic outbound. Although this isn't enough information for you to decide that Rule 12 should be moved up, it is the kind of monitoring you should undertake. Keep in mind that you need to log all rules to see what is going on and that some rule order can't be changed or else it weakens the security policy.

Figure 8.4 Logs and Optimum Rule Placement

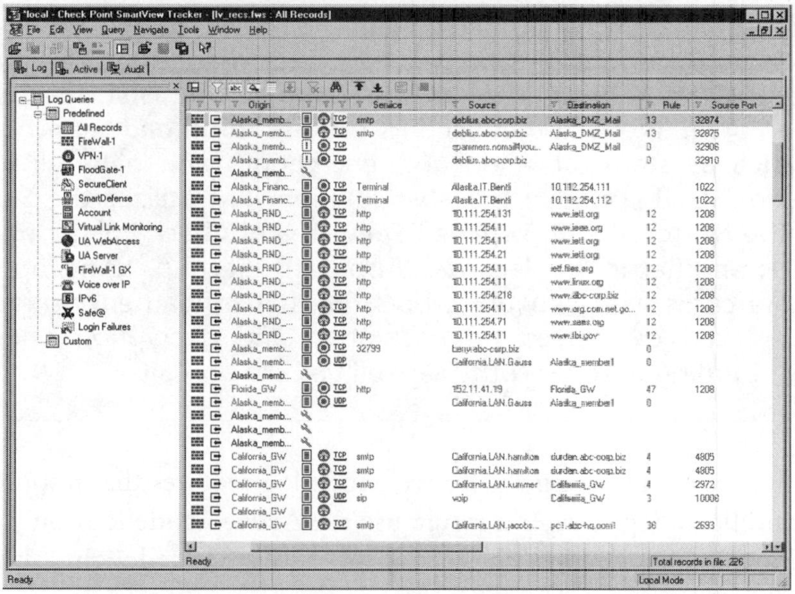

Accounting is an improved feature in FW-1 NG AI. In previous versions, accounting decreased performance 10 to 15 percent. However, because of NG AI's consolidation of connection tables, accounting information need only be pulled from one table and written to one log. Although this makes accounting in

NG AI much more efficient, the accounting data is still pulled from the logaccount.fwl file and consolidated into the fw.log by the Log Unification Engine. Obviously, this extra work requires resources. Unfortunately still, rules that use *Account* as the *Action*, such as Figure 8.5, have a price and should be implemented only as required by policy and when it is worth the performance hit.

Figure 8.5 Rules That Perform Accounting

| 3 | ⊥ LAN | ★ Any | ★ Any Traffic | TCP http TCP https | ⚙ accept | ▦ Accoun | ★ Policy Targets | ★ Any | Allow LAN access to http and https on the Internet |

Designing & Planning…

Extreme Performance

If you need even greater performance or need to maintain a high number of concurrent VPN tunnels, you should consider Check Point's SecureXL API technology and hardware acceleration. First, the SecureXL API is an open interface that vendors can use to offload security operations such as state table lookups, encryption, and network address translation. One currently available solution that utilizes the SecureXL API is the Nortel Alteon Switched Firewall and Check Point's own FW-1/VPN-1; another is the SecureXL Turbocard. Second, using optimized hardware cards with network processors that offload encryption from the CPU, you can speed up encryption and decryption operations without burning in the security capabilities like an ASIC.

As with accounting, using the Active Mode log requires that resources be used to consolidate log data. As a result, use the Active Mode logs only when actively blocking connections. The section on Active Mode logging discusses this topic in further detail.

Although one of the primary functions of the firewall is to monitor and log connections, carefully consider what is being logged. Over-logging not only decreases performance, it also may make it hard to review the logs. One hint is to create a special rule that drops and doesn't log noisy services such as NetBIOS or DHCP.

If you decide to use security servers for HTTP, FTP, SMTP, Rlogin, or Telnet, realize that the kernel may divert all packets that meet the Rule Base demand for content checking or authentication to the security servers for processing. The security servers then perform any authentication or content checking as required, and then, if allowed, they establish a second connection to the destination host on behalf of the originating source host. Both the connection from the source to the security server and from the security server to the destination are maintained in the connections table. You can open the fwauthd.conf file in a text editor to view which security servers are running. Security servers are turned on automatically when a rule requires content checking or authentication unless the Performance Pack is enabled or SecureXL is being used. With NG AI, more inspection capabilities have been added to the INSPECT engine, enabling options that previously required a security server to be handled in the kernel without the significant performance overhead. A good example of this is the option to select **Enhance UFP performance** in a URI resource that uses kernel inspection instead of a security server.

In addition, if you are using the HTTP security server, you can improve performance for your users by increasing the number of concurrent processes. Setting this number too high can degrade overall performance, so a good number is usually 4. Keep in mind, however, that Check Point recommends that you have multiple processors if you intend to modify this value. To make the change for additional HTTP processes, in the fwauthd.conf, modify the corresponding line for HTTP to the following:

```
80      in.ahttpd    wait    -4
```

Another recommendation is to consider limiting the number of NAT rules in your Address Translation Rule Base. Although this is probably something you will just have to live with, realize that NAT requires considerable resources. Fortunately, NAT performance is one of the things that Check Point claims to have improved in NG due to the single connection table. Moreover, you can further optimize your usage of NAT by limiting rules and combining objects intended for NAT. For example, if you or the network engineers have efficiently laid out the IP addressing scheme, you can use a subnet mask to combine multiple networks. For example, if you have several internal networks that are sequential, such as 172.16.1.0, 172.16.2.0, 172.16.3.0, … , 172.16.128.0, all with 255.255.255.0 subnet masks, you can create these objects separately for use in the Security Policy Rule Base if you need specific access restrictions for each network. However, if you don't need separate restrictions for each network, you can *supernet* them by creating one object with the subnet mask of 255.255.128.0 subnet mask. This will cover all the networks 172.16.1.0 through 172.16.128.0 as mentioned.

And finally, try to avoid the use of *domain objects*—network objects based on the TCP/IP domain name. Using them is unwise because every time a packet is matched up with a rule that has a domain object, FW-1 NG must do a domain name lookup. This slows the overall processing of packets. If you must use domain objects, place them as far down in the policy as possible so that connections that do not require that name resolution be accepted can be processed more quickly.

Monitoring NG for Performance

Memory is probably the most important commodity to Check Point FW-1 NG—or any other firewall, for that matter. According to Check Point, the formula for determining your required amount of memory is as follows:

```
MemoryUsage = ((ConcurrentConnections)/(AverageLifetime))*(AverageLifetime +
50      seconds)*120
```

ConcurrentConnections is the number of connections for hosts at one moment in time. Remember that the use of security servers will make what seems to be one connection really two. *AverageLifetime* of a connection is defined as the number of seconds a session will typically last from handshake to termination. You can use your accounting log to determine this figure.

No matter what the platform, you can use tools specific to FW-1 to monitor your firewall for performance. The easiest is to take a quick look at the System Status Viewer, an application that will show you the license status, alerts, and details from the different modules deployed in your enterprise.

By selecting the **SVN Foundation** object, you can see some performance-related details in the right windowpane, as shown in Figure 8.6. From SVN Foundation details you can view CPU usage, memory usage, and disk space. Obviously, high CPU usage that is consistently above 60 percent should be a concern, as should as a low amount of free real memory or free disk space.

Figure 8.6 SVN Foundation Details

A final method for checking the amount of memory available to the kernel is by executing at a command line:

```
FW ctl pstat
```

Executing this command will show you internal statistics of FW-1.

You can modify the amount of memory available to the kernel by changing the parameters in the **Capacity Optimization** section of the firewall's object.

There are also command utilities that help you understand how well the firewall is performing internally. An example is *fw tab*. Issuing the command *fw tab −t connections −s* will show you the connections table as specified by the *−t*, and in short format, as specified by the *−s*. This command will tell you how many connections are in the state table. Because the state table has a limit of 25,000 items by default, if the results are near 25,000 or if you know that you have 10,000 concurrent connections, you should increase the size of your state table. Changing the size of your state table in Check Point NG is a different process from changing it in previous versions of FW-1. In Check Point NG AI, the size of the state table is defined in objects_5_0.C, not $FWDIR/lib/table.def. Remember that new to Check Point NG AI is the use of *dbedit* to modify objects_5_0.C and other system files. To alter the size of the table, follow these easy steps:

1. Close all GUI clients that are connected to the management server.

2. Execute *dbedit*.

3. You will be prompted for the server name. (Enter the name of the local-host.)

4. Enter your Check Point NG AI administrator user ID, followed by the password.

5. At the Enter the Command prompt, type **modify properties firewall_properties connections_limit** *[Value]*.

6. After pressing **Enter**, on the next line, type **update properties firewall_properties**.

7. After entering the preceding line, you can end your *dbedit* session by typing **Quit**.

8. Next you must reboot the machine. Any time you modify a table with the *Keep* attribute, you have to reboot the machine. You can tell if a table has the *Keep* attribute by typing *fw tab -t 'table name'* as shown in Figure 8.7.

9. Finally, for changes to take effect, you must install the policy.

Figure 8.7 Viewing the Keep Attribute for Tables

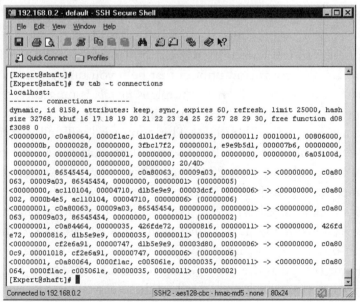

As you are modifying the connections table, you will probably need to modify the hash size as well. The hash size value should be a power of 2 that is as close as possible to the limit on the connections table. As you can see in Table 8.2, if you have modified the connection limit to 50,000, you should set your hash size to 65536.

Table 8.2 Relevant Powers of 2

	Hash Size	Connection Limit
2^{14}	16384	4097–24576
2^{15}	32768	24577–49152
2^{16}	65536	49153–98304
2^{17}	131072	98305–196608

NOTE

Check Point does sell a product called SmartView Monitor (formerly the Real-Time Monitor) that integrates nicely into the Check Point framework. SmartView Monitor is included with SmartCenter Pro, SmartCenter Express Plus, or SmartView. It enables you to monitor bandwidth, bandwidth loss, and round-trip time in end-to-end VPNs.

Platform Specific Tools

In addition to the Check Point NG AI tools provided for measuring performance on Windows NT, a number of FW-1 specific counters are installed to the Windows NT Performance Monitor. The counters provided include the following:

- Number of packets accepted
- Number of packets dropped
- Number of current connections
- Number of packets decrypted
- Number of packets encrypted
- Number of packets that fail encrypt/decrypt

- Amount of hash memory currently in use
- Amount of system kernel memory currently in use
- Number of packets logged
- Number of packets rejected
- Number of total packets processed
- Number of packets undergoing address translation

These counters can be invaluable in further tuning your firewall.

Performance Conclusion

And finally, if none of these suggestions improves the performance of your FW-1 NG, consider upgrading your hardware based on the recommendations in Table 8.3 and on your own observations of CPU, memory, and I/O usage:

Table 8.3 Quick Recommendations

If you require a large amount of...	Then you need...
Encryption/decryption	CPU
Network address translation	Memory
Logging	Memory and I/O
Sessions	Memory
Security servers	CPU and I/O

Administering Check Point VPN-1/FW-1 NG AI for Effectiveness

Although performance is important, if a firewall doesn't do what it's supposed to do, it is of no use. In fact, it is easy to trade increased performance for decreased effectiveness or security. In this section we talk about how to make sure your FW-NG is doing its job and securing your network.

Quality Control

One of the best ways to test a firewall's effectiveness is to assume the role of attacker. Although it is not only possible but also advisable to hire a third party to do penetration testing, the initial testing is your responsibility. The simplest way to test the firewall is by using a simple port scanner. Some popular and free port scanners you may want to try include the following:

- **Nmap** A favorite of security professionals and hackers alike. Nmap allows different types of scans, spoofing, decoys, and timing changes. It can be found at www.insecure.org.

- **Languard Network Scanner** A very noisy but full-featured scanner. This tool will pull SNMP information as well as attempt to connect to open services and gather banners. It can be found at www.gfisoftware.com/languard/lanscan.htm.

- **Hping2** An advanced tool that runs on *nix that allows the crafting of custom TCP/IP packets. Hping2 can be used to test firewall rules and even transfer files. You can download Hping2 from www.hping.org.

If you would like to further assess your configuration, you can use a full-featured vulnerability assessment tool. Most even have modules that enable you to test known vulnerabilities. For recommendations and more descriptions, you can visit www.insecure.org/tools.html.

This sort of quality control has multiple benefits. It helps you see what ports are open or not filtered from the outside. In addition, it may help you see what patches you might be missing or vulnerabilities you are exposed to. It enables you to test your logging and monitoring. Finally, it enables you to see what an attack might look like and help you detect one from your monitoring.

War Games

Don't underestimate the value of auditing your firewall configuration. Assign someone (another employee or an auditing firm) to periodically audit the configuration with scans from the outside or even simulated attacks. This will enable you to test your monitoring and incident response procedures. It will be much easier to hone your incident response skills under simulation than to respond ineffectively to a real attack—or worse yet, to not detect a real attack at all.

Patches and Updates

As a security professional, make sure you sign up to a few security mailing lists (such as *bugtraq*) to stay abreast of new developments in security. Especially make sure you get the Check Point e-mail newsletter, which will notify you of support issues and relevant patches when they're available. You can sign up for Check Point's newsletter at www.checkpoint.com/newsletter.html.

To obtain updates to your FW-1 NG AI installation, you can use SmartUpdate, as shown in Figure 8.8. From the **Products** menu, select **New Product | Add From Download Center**. After you agree to the licensing agreement, this choice will connect your computer to the Check Point download site. It will get a list of software available for download up to the version you have installed on the management station. Select the products you want to add to your repository, and click **Download**.

Figure 8.8 SmartUpdate Utility

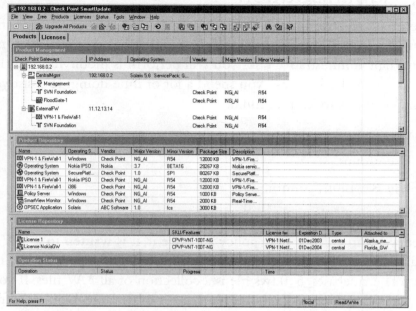

To use SmartUpdate to do remote installations and updates centrally, you must be licensed. Beyond that basic requirement, SmartUpdate tries to make it easy. The first step is to obtain a SmartUpdate package from the Internet or CD. The Product Repository is managed using *cppkg* commands. The command to add a new package is the following:

```
cppkg add <package-full-path | CD directory>
```

Next, you must put the package into the Product Repository. After the package is in the Product Repository, you can literally drag and drop packages onto modules from the SmartUpdate GUI interface or select **Upgrade All Products**.

As an alternative, if you are not licensed to use SmartUpdate, you can download updates from www.checkpoint.com/techsupport/downloads_ng.html. You will want to pay particular attention to the hotfixes. Download the appropriate hotfix just as you would any other file. After extracting it to a directory, you can install the hotfix. Make sure that the SVNFoundation (*cpshared_hf*.tgz*) hotfix is installed first, and then you can follow with the particular hotfix for the products you are running.

Policy Administration

The core of an effective firewall is policy. To help you manage and administer your firewall, you will want to implement a number of best practices. One of the most important administrative tasks you will perform is modifying security policy. This could also be a task you spend a lot of time doing. To assist you, here are a number of tips to keep in mind:

- Clean up old policies.
- Use groups.
- Use Revision Control.
- Use comments.

Whenever you create a new policy and save it, it is written to a *.W file and to the rulebases_5_0.fws file. The asterisk in the *.W file represents the name of the policy. The rulebases_5_0.fws file is a collection of all *.W files. If you have a lot of policies, the rulebases_5_0.fws file can get quite large. Don't be afraid to clean up some of the old policies if you no longer need them. The best way to do this is through the SmartDashboard interface. Choose **File** from the menu, and select **Delete | Entire Policy Package**. This will open a dialog box that will enable you to choose the policy you would like to delete. When you delete policies this way, the actual *.W file is deleted as well as the reference within the rulebases_5_0.fws file.

Second, try to arrange network objects into groups. This will help in administration and make the Rule Base easier to read. As you add new objects to groups, they are automatically included in any relevant rules.

Next, if you are making modifications to a production policy, before you begin ensure an updated version is saved in **File | Database Revision Control**. If something goes wrong or gets misconfigured, you can then restore the saved policy. Previous to Database Revision Control, it was suggested to save a new policy package. This resulted in enormous rulebases_5_0.fws files that would cause the GUI to take a long time to open, save, or push policies. This situation is discussed in the next section and is no longer an issue.

And finally, it cannot be emphasized enough: Use comments. Using comments in your FW-1 Rule Base will help you understand what certain rules are doing, whom they are for, and when they should expire. Comments are even more important when multiple administrators are managing the firewall policy.

The comments can help explain the purpose of the rule. This will help you keep the Rule Base fit and trim. There is nothing worse than making a modification on the fly and forgetting about it. Making appropriate comments will help you audit your Rule Base and network objects from time to time.

Managing Multiple Policies

Although possibly confusing at times, it may be necessary to have multiple policies for multiple firewalls. If this is the case for you, here are a couple of pointers to help you effectively administer your policies:

- Use meaningful policy names.

- Use the Policy Installation Targets setting for each policy.

- Delete old policies.

- Properly configure the Install On field.

When naming a policy, use a name that is indicative of its function and enforcement points. This is helpful so that you don't accidentally overwrite the wrong policy. Note that the GUI will alert you if you will be installing a policy package of a different name on a firewall. You can also set by which firewalls each policy will be enforced using **Policy | Policy Installation Targets** or **Select Targets** from the Install Policy dialog box. By defining the modules this policy will be enforced by, you will no longer be prompted to install the policy on the other systems.

Deleting old policies will also improve performance because the GUI downloads all policies from the management server. This could slow the GUI's response. Deleting old policies will decrease the amount of data that must be sent to the GUI. As recommended before, delete policies by selecting **Delete** from the **File** menu in the Policy Editor.

Finally, when working with multiple policies, be sure that the Install On field is properly configured. By installing a policy on FW-1 modules that will not enforce any of the policy, you do two things:

1. You will slow the install of the policy due to the process a policy goes through when it is installed.

2. FW-1 modules that have a policy installed to them but that enforce no rules in that policy will enforce the default rule and reject all communications.

Editing Files

One of the most powerful features of FW-1 is the ability to customize or change virtually everything about the way FW-1 operates. However, to do so requires that you manually edit certain files. Before we discuss how to go about that, let's identify some of those files and their purposes.

After you create a Rule Base in a new policy, it is written to a *.W file upon saving or installing the policy. This file can be edited, though that's not recommended, with a text editor, since it contains the information displayed graphically in the GUI regarding the Rule Base.

The objects_5_0.C file was formerly called objects.C in earlier versions of FW-1 (although objects.C still exists). The purpose of the objects_5_0.C file is to contain network objects, properties, and configuration information for the management server. It is a global file. The objects.C is pushed to the modules and is created from the master objects_5_0.C when a policy is installed. It is possible to edit the objects_5_0.C with the new DBEDIT utility, which is illustrated as Figure 8.9. The advantage of this utility is that it enables an administrator to search the file based on type and attribute. Moreover, the tool will keep an audit trail of modifications. This is the recommended way to edit objects_5_0.C. Remember to close all GUI clients and back up your objects_5_0.C before you use *dbedit* to make modifications. If you are an administrative user on the management station and are running *dbedit* on the local system, you can use the command *dbedit –m* to skip the authentication. All login data can be done as part of the *dbedit* command, and commands can be run from a file for easy scripting and automation if necessary. For a full listing of options, type **dbedit –help**.

Figure 8.9 Introduction to dbedit

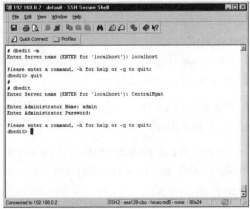

Another file you should become familiar with is the ⋆.pf. The ⋆.pf is the packet filter or Inspection script that results from the ⋆.W file and the objects_5_0.C file when you perform a policy install. It is not recommended that you attempt editing this file. You can view the Inspection script for a policy by selecting **View** from the **Policy** menu in the Policy editor.

During a policy install, the ⋆.pf file is compiled into a ⋆.fc file. The ⋆.fc file is the Inspection code that is installed onto enforcement modules. It is not recommended that you edit this file, either. The process of compiling the ⋆.W file into the ⋆.pf and subsequent ⋆.fc is begun by the command *fw load*. This command compiles and installs a policy to the firewall. The whole process of installing a policy is illustrated in Figure 8.10.

One ⋆.pf file that is of particularly importance is the defaultfilter.pf. This file is responsible for implementing security during the boot process. In FW-1 NG, **IP** forwarding is always disabled until a policy is loaded. This is the function of the default filter (default.pf). This policy protects the firewall until the initial policy can be loaded.

The boot process can be summarized as follows:

1. Machine boots up.

2. Default filter loads and IP Forwarding is disabled.

3. Interfaces are configured.

4. FW-1 services start.

5. Initial policy is fetched from the local module if this is the first boot and there is no policy; otherwise the configured policy is installed.

Figure 8.10 The Policy Installation Process

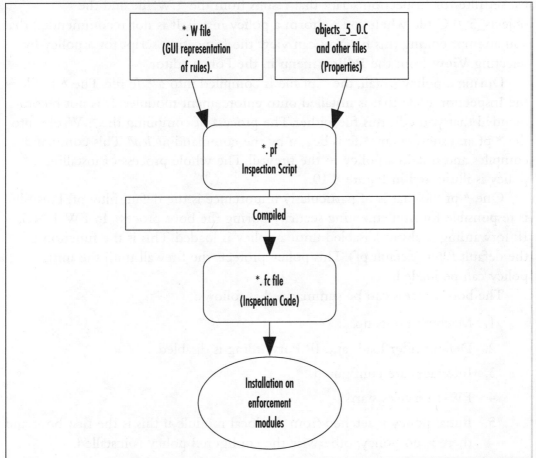

Managing Firewall Logs

Monitoring logs is an important job for administrators. Logs not only help you ensure that the firewall is effective—they can help you detect an attack. You should probably review your logs on a daily basis at a minimum. Understanding the different types of logs available to you and their purposes will help you review them.

There are basically three Log modes in FW-1 NG AI. The three modes are these:

- Log mode
- Active mode

■ Audit mode

Log mode is the basic log file that contains all logging information. It is the default Log mode. To assist you in reading the log, there are 15 predefined log views. They are as follows:

- General
- FW-1
- Account
- FloodGate-1
- VPN-1
- Virtual Link Monitoring
- SmartDefense
- UA WebAccess
- UA Server
- FW-1 GX
- Voice over IP
- IPv6
- Safe@
- Login Failures
- SecureClient

Obviously, each predefined view contains information specific to the view title. The new Log Unification Engine in FW-1 NG is responsible for bringing information from all these modules into one log (fw.log). The other two logging modes are Audit and Active:

- Audit mode files are named *.fwo. Audit mode provides an audit trail of administrator actions. This can be helpful for seeing what administrative actions have been performed.

- Active mode files are named *.fwa. Active mode is used primarily for monitoring current connections and blocking connections. When blocking connections, it doesn't modify the Rule Base and remains in effect until manually removed or until the enforcement module is unloaded. Your choices in blocking, as illustrated in Figure 8.11, include the following:

- Block only this connection.

- Block access from this source.

- Block access to this destination.

You can also specify how long the block should last and if the blocking should be enforced by the FW-1 that is currently processing the connection or on any other FW-1.

Figure 8.11 The Block Intruder Dialog Box

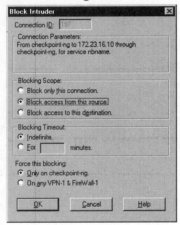

Log Rotations

Rotating your logs will prevent them from getting too big and eating up all your hard drive space or becoming too cumbersome to understand. You have two options in performing log rotations from within the Log Viewer application: Switch Active File and Purge Active File. If you select **Switch Active File** from the **File** menu, you will save a copy of the current log and start a fresh one. If you select **Purge Active File**, the current log file are deleted, and a new log is started. New to NG is the ability to schedule log rotation. Under your firewall object's workstation properties, displayed in Figure 8.12, you can create a logging policy and specify to perform a log switch when the log reaches a certain size or at a certain time. (The default time is midnight, though the option to schedule a log switch is off by default.) These options are explained in detail in Table 8.4.

Simply rotating your logs will not eliminate the problem of using up all available hard drive space. You need to have a separate process (a script, perhaps) to move the old log file to another drive, server, tape, or the like.

Figure 8.12 Setting Firewall Logging Policy

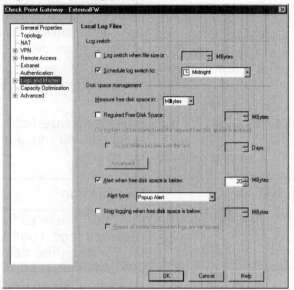

Table 8.4 Logging Options

Local Logging Options	Explanation
Log switch when file size is	Specifies a size, in megabytes, that the log file shall not exceed. When this size is met, the current log file will be closed and a new one created.
Schedule log switch to	Schedules a time (as defined by a pre-defined time object) when the current log will be closed and a new one created.
Alert when free disk space is below	Sends an alert when free disk space falls below this threshold. This also enables you to specify the alert type.

Continued

Table 8.4 Logging Options

Local Logging Options	Explanation
Turn on QoS logging Required Free Disk Space	Specifies a minimum amount of space on the log partition. If this minimum is exceeded, old log files will be removed until space is available. The Advanced button defines a command to run before deleting the old log files.
Do not delete log files from the last	Specifies the minimum length in days to keep logs. This overrides the deletion of logs.
Stop logging when free disk space is below	Specifies a threshold that, when reached, will cause log recording to cease.

Additional Logging	Explanation
Forward log files to Management Server	Specifies where to forward locally recorded logs. Logs are recorded locally when the defined log servers are unavailable. Logs will be forwarded according to the log forward schedule. A log switch can also be performed before sending the logs to the log server.
Update account log every	Specifies the time interval for accounting messages to be logged. Accounting messages contain the information about a connection, such as packets sent. When the accounting message is sent, those counters are reset. Each subsequent message is therefore a recording of the change since the last message.
Turn on QoS logging	Enables logging of QoS-related events. This option requires FloodGate-1.

Continued

Table 8.4 Logging Options

Additional Logging	Explanation
Detect new Citrix ICA application names	When utilizing FloodGate-1, Citrix ICA application names can be detected as it changes inside a single connection and QoS rules applied appropriately. This option defines whether to detect the new names and log the information.
Accept Syslog messages	If this option is selected, syslog messages will be accepted. This is often necessary when the source of the log data is not an OPSEC-compliant device. Note that the firewall must be configured to accept syslog data on UDP port 514 for this option to function. Also, the CPSyslogD daemon must have been started prior to the start of FW-1.

In previous versions of FW-1, the automation of log rotation required some configuration outside FW-1. As an alternative, a security administrator can still schedule a *cron* or *at* job, depending on the operating system, to execute the *fw logswitch* command. Additionally, you could also perform an export on the log files, such as copy or move the log files to another partition or disk drive or even to another machine.

The following is an example of *logswitch* script for Solaris:

```
#!/bin/sh
#
# Set variables
#
FW_BIN_PATH=/etc/fw/bin
BIN_PATH=/usr/bin
LOG_PATH=/etc/fw/log
TODAY='$BIN_PATH/date +%d%b%y'
#
# Switch the log files
#
$FW_BIN_PATH/fw logswitch $TODAY
```

```
#
# Export the logs
#
$FW_BIN_PATH/fw logexport -d ";" -i $LOG_PATH/$TODAY.alog -o
    $LOG_PATH/$TODAY.alog.txt -r 1000
$FW_BIN_PATH/fw logexport -d ";" -i $LOG_PATH/$TODAY.log -o
    $LOG_PATH/$TODAY.log.txt -r 1000
#
# Compress log files to conserve disk space, and delete pointer files.
#
$BIN_PATH/rm $LOG_PATH/$TODAY.*ptr
compress $LOG_PATH/$TODAY.*log
# EOF
```

This script could be placed in the *crontab* file and run at midnight every day or as often as required.

An example batch file for NT is as follows:

```
c:\bin\fdate /Ff /o"ddmn3yy" /P"@SET TODAY=" > c:\temp\_tmpfile.bat
call c:\temp\_tmpfile
del  c:\temp\_tmpfile.bat
cd c:\winnt\fw1\5.0\log
c:\winnt\fw1\5.0\bin\fw logswitch %TODAY%
c:\winnt\fw1\5.0\bin\fw logexport -r 1000 -d ; -i %TODAY%.alog -o
    %TODAY%.alog.txt
c:\winnt\fw1\5.0\bin\fw logexport -r 1000 -d ; -i %TODAY%.log -o
    %TODAY%.log.txt
:end
```

In this batch file, we are using a script called *fdate* to set the date for *TODAY* on the system. If you do not specify the format of the date for the *logswitch* command, the log files will be saved based on the date and time that the switch occurred. This can be tricky if you want to call the log file for an export, but if you are just performing a *logswitch* and are not manipulating the log files after the switch, the default format is sufficient. To use this script in NT 4, the scheduler would have to be enabled and an *at* job created to run the file every night at midnight or as often as necessary. To use this script in Windows 2000, the administrator would only have to create a task within the Task Scheduler application.

Log Maintenance

It is possible to see log corruption. If log corruption happens, the log can easily be rebuilt from the fragments of logs used to build fw.log. Executing the command *fw repairlog [-u] <logfile name>* will unify the log, replacing the corruption.

Administering Check Point VPN-1/FW-1 NG for Recoverability

Recoverability is an important issue for most organizations. In some organizations, a downed firewall can have a serious impact on business. Being able to recover quickly is essential.

Making Backups

Making backups of your FW-1 configuration is relatively easy. In fact, we have already identified most of the critical files you should back up:

- objects_5_0.c
- rulebases_5_0.fws
- fwauth.NDB★
- All ★.W files (not required)
- All ★.pf files (not required)
- fwmusers and gui-clients (not required)

You should back up these files to a secure and safe location after any modifications are made as well as after any files that have been manually modified such as the base.def or table.def. Restoring a firewall is as easy as copying these files. The ★.W and ★.pf files are not required because FW-1 will recreate them.

In addition to having your configuration backed up, you should consider how to recover if the hardware fails completely. Make sure that if you have a four-hour service response contract, you can live without a firewall for four hours. If this isn't the case, you should purchase a hot-swap server or invest in a high-availability solution.

If your firewall does go down and you need to move the installation, follow these easy steps:

1. If your IP address is changing or if your license is based on a host ID, request a license change from Check Point's Licensing User Center. If you need additional licensing features, contact your Check Point VAR.

2. Install the operating system on the new hardware and patch it, implementing any OS-recommended hardening measures.

3. Install the FW-1 software from a downloaded file or via CD, and install your license.

4. Patch the FW-1 software to the same build level as the machine you are copying files from.

5. Copy the files objects_5_0.c, rulebases_5_0.fws, and fwauth.NDB* files into the $FWDIR/conf directory.

6. If you do not want to add your administrators and GUI clients again by hand, you can also copy the files fwmusers and gui-clients in $FWDIR/conf.

7. You will need to redo any SIC configuration.

8. Install the policy and test connectivity.

9. Upgrade the firewall and add any new patches beyond the build you were duplicating.

In addition, some operating systems (such as SecurePlatform and Nokia's IPSO) have built-in backup utilities that can be used to back up and restore configurations of Check Point as well as the OS. A full discussion of proper backup and restore procedures appears in *Check Point NG VPN-1/FireWall-1: Advanced Configuration and Troubleshooting* (Syngress Publishing, ISBN: 1-931836-97-3).

Performing Advanced Administration Tasks

In this section we talk about performing some of the more advanced administration tasks that are possible with FireWall-1 NG. These are some of the "tricks of the trade" that can make life easier for you.

Firewall Controls

Sometimes the best way or *only* way to do something is at the command line. Fortunately, many of the things that you can do with the GUI you can also do at the command line. In fact, in case you haven't noticed, many GUI actions invoke command-line functions. In this section, we discuss some of the most common command-line options and their purposes.

fwstop

At times you may need to stop and restart the firewall for maintenance or just to bounce it. The easiest way to do this is with the *fwstop* command. Executing *fwstop* will kill the following:

- The FW-1 daemon (fwd)
- The management server (fwm)
- The SNMP daemon (snmpd)
- The Authentication daemon (authd)

It is possible to unload FW-1 processes but to maintain security by loading the default filter. This enables the FW-1 administrator to take down the FW-1 processes for maintenance without exposing the firewall machine to attacks while unprotected. The commands to stop FW-1 NG and load the default filter are these:

```
fwstop -default
fwstop -proc
```

fwstart

fwstart will load FW-1 and start the processes killed by *fwstop*:

- The FW-1 daemon (*fwd*)
- The management server (*fwm*)
- The SNMP daemon (*snmpd*)
- The Authentication daemon (*authd*)

No options are needed with *fwstart*.

cpstop

Not to be confused with *fwstop*. In fact, *cpstop* is inclusive of the *fwstop* function. Executing *cpstop* will stop all running Check Point applications. One exception is the *cprid,* which is a Check Point process that is invoked at boot time and runs independently of other Check Point applications.

cpstart

Executing *cpstart* will start all Check Point applications. Similar to *cpstop*, executing *cpstart* implies that *fwstart* performs its function.

cpconfig

The command *cpconfig* is used to configure FW-1/VPN-1. In Windows NT, executing this command opens the Check Point Configuration Tool GUI. In *nix environments, the command displays a configuration screen with options that depend on what is installed. In both environments, executing *cpconfig* enables you to install and update licenses, create administrators, view the management server fingerprint, specify remote clients that can log into the management server, configure SNMP, and register PKCS#11 cryptographic tokens.

cpstat

Executing this command will provide you with the status of the target hosts. In NG, *cpstat* is intended to replace *fw stat*.

fw Commands

A number of *fw* commands are helpful for controlling the FW-1 daemon. *fw* commands follow this basic syntax:

```
fw [action] [target (default localhost)].
```

- **fw load** This command will convert the *.W file from the GUI to a *.pf file and compile into Inspection code, installing a security policy on an enforcement module. A sample *fw load* command is as follows:

  ```
  fw load Standard.W all.all@localgateway
  ```

  This command will load the Standard.W policy onto the firewall object named *localgateway*.

- **fw unload** The *fwunload* command will uninstall security policy from the specified target(s). It is obsolete and has been moved to a subcommand of the *fwm* executable. An example of usage is as follows:

  ```
  fw unload ExternalFW
  ```

  This command will actually call *fwm unload ExternalFW* and uninstall the policy from the ExternalFW firewall. The common command *fw unload localhost* has also been taken into account and has changed to the following command.

- **fwm unloadlocalfw fetch** *fw fetch* is used to fetch Inspection code from a specified host and install it to the kernel of the current host. An example of usage is as follows:

```
fw fetch 192.168.0.2
```

This will fetch the security policy from the management station located at 192.168.0.2. You can also use the name of the management station's object or a DNS resolvable name.

- **fw putkey** The *fwputkey* command is helpful if you are integrating an NG Management Server with 4.*x* enforcement modules. Executing *fw putkey* will install an authenticating password. The password is used to authenticate SIC between the management server and the module the first time the two communicate. For an example of a remote firewall module, type the following:

```
fw putkey -n 192.168.0.2 192.168.0.1
```

The *-n* option specifies the dotted IP address that will be used to identify this host to other hosts. The second part of the syntax that specifies 192.168.0.1 is the closest interface on the target to which the password will be installed. Additionally, by not specifying the password to be used, you will be prompted for it.

- **fw ctl** *fw ctl* is a utility for controlling the FW-1 kernel. In addition, *fw ctl pstat* will provide you with internal FW-1 statistics. It can also be used for obtaining interface information.

- **fw tab** *fw tab* is used for displaying the contents of FW-1's various tables INSPECT tables. For example, to display the connections table, you would type the following:

```
fw tab -t connections
```

- **fw logswitch** The *fw logswitch* command will save the current log and start a new one. This is particularly helpful in rotating logs on remote machines from the Management server:

```
fw logswitch -h localgateway +old_log
```

This command will rotate the logs on the remote firewall named *localgateway* and copy the log to the management server with the name of *localgateway.old_log*.

- **fw logexport** The *fw logexport* command dumps the log to an ASCII file. Log files in this format can be processed by third-party tools or imported into databases for further analysis. For example, to export your logs with a semicolon that delimits the output fields and to give the file the name 4analysis, you would type the following:

```
fw logexport -d -o 4analysis.txt
```

- **fw ver** The *fw ver* command returns the version of FW-1 that's currently running. By adding the *-k* option, you can learn the kernel build as well:

```
fw ver -k
```

Firewall Processes

You can use a number of operating-specific commands to list the processes running on your bastion host:

- ***nix** In *nix, executing *ps −ef* will display all currently running processes and full information, including their process ID.

- **Nokia** For Nokias, using the command *ps −aux* will display running processes.

- **Windows** In Windows NT, you may view the running processes and their allocated memory by executing the Task Manager. Be aware that all FireWall-1 processes will appear as fw.exe. It is not uncommon to have five or more fw.exe processes running.

- **$FWDIR\tmp** FW-1 writes the process IDs of FW-1 processes as they are started and writes them to *.pid files that correlate with the processes started, as you can see in Figure 8.13. For example, opening the file fwd.pid in a text editor would display the process ID assigned to the fw.exe process. This is extremely helpful in Windows when each process is named fw.exe. This process-to-process ID mapping will help you figure out which fw.exe goes with what firewall process.

Figure 8.13 Process ID Mapping in SecurePlatform

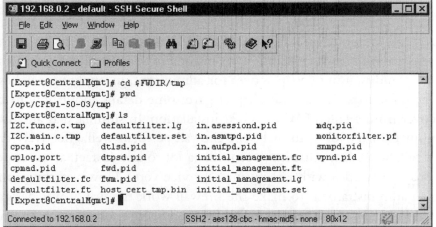

- **fwd** The FW-1 daemon.

- **fwm** The management server.

- **in.ahttpd** The name of the process assigned to the HTTP security server.

- **in.asmtp.d** The name of the process assigned to the SMTP security server.

- **in.atelnetd** The name of the process assigned to the Telnet security server.

- **in.arlogind** The name of the process assigned to the Rlogin security server.

- **in.aftpd** The name of the process assigned to the FTP security server.

- **in.aclientd** The process responsible for client authentication on port 259.

- **in.ahclientd** The process responsible for client authentication on port 900 through a Web browser.

- **fw kill** Can be used to terminate any running FireWall-1 process. The syntax is *fw kill [process name]*. For example, you can terminate the HTTP security server and restart it to resolve problems with the HTTP proxy by executing the following:

```
fw kill in.ahttpd
```

Summary

This chapter covered a lot of ground to help you administer Check Point FW-1 NG AI. It talked about ways you can tune and monitor the firewall's performance. Additionally, it discussed how to maintain the firewall's effectiveness by performing audits, using best practices for administration, applying patches, and monitoring the logs. Finally, this chapter gave some details about how to back up and recover from a failed FW-1 NG AI installation. In summary, as an administrator, your primary job is to make the firewall perform well, effectively, and without fail. Sometimes that may seem like a lot to ask. In fact, at times performance may be at odds with effectiveness, or vice versa. However, the primary goal of an administrator is to make the firewall work the way it was designed in the security policy. The best way to ensure the effectiveness of your firewall is daily administration through log review and performance monitoring.

Solutions Fast Track

Administering Check Point VPN-1/FW-1 NG AI for Performance

☑ Keep the Rule Base simple. Enough said.

☑ Keep the most frequently matched rules near the top. Because FW-1 uses top-down processing of all packets against the Rule Base, packets that are matched early on are kicked out to the OS for routing sooner.

☑ Monitor performance periodically using FW-1 built-in tools. There are also a number of platform-specific utilities, such as the NT Performance Monitor, to gauge the firewall's level of performance.

Administering Check Point VPN-1/FW-1 NG AI for Effectiveness

☑ Audit your firewall using assessment tools. This will not only test your configuration, it will also show you in the log how it looks when attackers perform reconnaissance on your firewall. Third-party audits of your network are also an advisable course of action, and in some cases, such as healthcare and financial industries, they are a legally required procedure.

☑ Subscribe to Check Point's mailing lists to be alerted to new patches and SmartDefense updates. Additionally, monitor general security lists for pertinent vulnerabilities.

☑ Monitor your logs on a daily basis, and develop a plan for log rotation. Leverage the filtering capabilities of SmartView Tracker to create customized views of the logs for more efficient auditing.

Administering Check Point VPN-1/FW-1 NG AI for Recoverability

☑ Save a backup copy of your policy in the Database Revision Control before you modify it. This will enable you to fall back should something go wrong or not work the way you planned.

☑ Back up FW-1's configuration files after modifications are made. The files you should back up include objects_5_0.c, rulebases_5_0.fws, all *.W files, all *.pf files, and fwauth.NDB*.

☑ Evaluate your hardware support contract to see if the specified time period would be acceptable if the firewall hardware were to fail.

Performing Advanced Administration Tasks

☑ The commands *fwstop* and *fwstart* can be used to stop and start FW-1, respectively.

☑ The *.pid files in $FWDIR\tmp can be used to determine the process ID assigned to FW-1 processes.

☑ The security server binaries are named in the format in.a*[application]*d. For example, HTTP is called in.ahttpd and FTP is in.aftpd.

☑ When the security servers are running in Windows, they show up as fw.exe processes.

Frequently Asked Questions

The following Frequently Asked Questions, answered by the authors of this book, are designed to both measure your understanding of the concepts presented in this chapter and to assist you with real-life implementation of these concepts. To have your questions about this chapter answered by the author, browse to **www.syngress.com/solutions** and click on the **"Ask the Author"** form. You will also gain access to thousands of other FAQs at ITFAQnet.com.

Q: Users are complaining that the firewall is slow. How do I know if I need a bigger, better, faster box?

A: After making sure that the firewall is appropriately tuned and has a good Rule Base, the best way to determine your need for new hardware is to monitor the CPU, memory, and I/O of the firewall.

Q: If I block a connection, how long will it last?

A: Blocked connections will persist based on what was specified when the blocking action was performed.

Q: How is NG AI different from previous versions with respect to performance?

A: Performance is one of the big improvements in NG AI. One of the new performance enhancements is the consolidation of state tables into one. This speeds up the processing of packets. The overhead of SmartDefense is negligible unless you are invoking the use of security servers.

Q: Why don't I see any security server processes running?

A: This is because they haven't been manually invoked in the fwauthd.conf or by a rule that requires authentication or content checking.

Q: How do I know when my Rule Base is too complex?

A: That is a difficult question. What is complex in one environment may be very appropriate in another. It appears that a medium-sized organization should have around 20 rules. The fewer the better is the rule, but get the job done first.

Q: How do I get these command-line options to run?

A: You must run them from $FWDIR\bin. Alternatively, you can add $FWDIR\bin to your path statement. To add $FWDIR/bin to your path statement, perform the following steps:

In UNIX:

1. You must edit the path statements in your .cshrc or .profile files. (Remember that these are hidden files.) The file you edit will depend on which shell you use when you log on.

2. If you are editing your .cshrc, add the following line:

```
set path=(. /usr/bin $path etc/fw/bin /usr/etc /etc /local/etc)
```

3. To activate your change, type the following:

```
source .cshrc
```

4. Now type **echo $PATH** to confirm your change. You should see etc/fw/bin in your path statement.

In Windows NT and Windows 2000:

1. Select **Start | Settings | Control Panel**.
2. Double-click the **System** applet, and select the **Environment** tab.
3. Select the **Path** variable from the **System Variables** window.
4. Verify that the Variable field at the bottom of the **Environment** tab shows **Path**, as follows:

```
Variable: Path
Value: %SystemRoot%\system32;%SystemRoot%
```

5. Add the FW-1 \bin directory path to the current Path variable value, in the following manner.

```
For FireWall-1
5.0:%SystemRoot%\system32;%SystemRoot%;C:\winnt\fw1\5.4\bin
```

Once you've added the FW-1 \bin directory to the Path variable, you can check the value of the Path variable by running the following command in the command prompt:

```
set
```

7. The value of the Path variable will be displayed in the following manner:

```
Path=C:\WINNT\system32;C:\WINNT;C:\WINNT\fw1\5.4\bin
```

Chapter 9

Tracking and Alerts

Solutions in this Chapter:

- **Alerts Commands**
- **User-Defined Tracking**
- **Suspicious Activities Monitoring Protocol (SAMP)**

☑ Summary

☑ Solutions Fast Track

☑ Frequently Asked Questions

413

Introduction

One important part of firewall security is being aware of what traffic is going through your firewall. For instance, in the event that you are under an attack, you will be able to react appropriately. Check Point VPN-1/FireWall-1 (CP VPN-1/FW-1) provides you with the ability to set up alerts based on certain criteria, and you can add some of these alerts directly into your rulebase under the **Track** column in your SmartDashboard. You can even decide what action to take if a certain alert is raised.

Check Point is continually praised for the usability and richness of its logging. Using SmartView Tracker, an administrator can easily track down problems, misconfigurations, or simply audit and analyze the network traffic in a concise manner from a single location. You can also receive, consolidate, and correlate logs from other devices, increasing the overall effectiveness of the logs shown in SmartView Tracker.

Alerts Commands

Your main day-to-day interaction with the firewall will be the handling of the alerts that it generates and creating new rules. These alerts are generated by the rules you have configured, and are also customizable. Using the SmartDashboard graphical user interface (GUI), you can customize the various alert types. Select **Policy | Global Properties** and then select the **Log and Alert** branch from the left. You'll see a screen like the one shown in Figure 9.1.

This panel contains a significant amount of information, but it is all pretty straightforward. The default settings are shown in Figure 9.1, but these settings may be altered to be any of the valid responses (including **Log**, **Popup Alert**, **Mail Alert**, and so on).

Figure 9.1 Log and Alert Main Menu

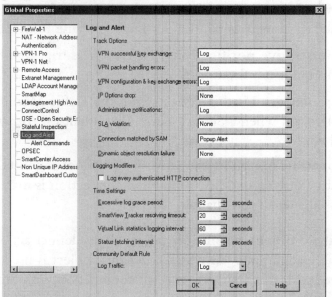

Using Track Options

The Track Options are very useful for seeing information about administrative happenings, such as virtual private network (VPN) information, as well as for a couple of security related issues, such as connections matched by suspicious activity monitoring (SAM). Say, for example, that your organization has placed the burden of configuring a VPN on your lap, and now you must troubleshoot while you attempt to establish this VPN with your parent organization. These options could be useful to you while you are in the first stages, by logging or alerting based on the criteria you select here.

- **VPN successful key exchange** This event is triggered by the successful exchange of VPN keys.

- **VPN packet handling errors** This denotes an error in a VPN connection, such as a method mismatch.

- **VPN configuration and key exchange errors** This field defines the behavior that FW-1 will exhibit when a VPN configuration or key exchange event fails.

- **IP Options drop** This is triggered by an Internet Protocol (IP) packet with options set. Since options are rarely (if ever) useful in a valid connection, CP VPN-1/FW-1 will always drop these packets. You may, however, do something when you see such a packet. Often, such packets are used to probe a network, so it might be wise to at least log them.

- **Administrative notifications** This action is triggered by a FW-1 administrative notification.

- **SLA violation** Used in concert with the Traffic Monitor, this event will alert you when a Service Level Agreement (SLA) has been breached.

- **Connection matched by SAM** This defines action taken when a packet belonging to a SAM inhibited connection is matched. SAM is discussed later in this chapter.

- **Dynamic object resolution failure** This defines action taken when a firewall loads a policy in which a dynamic object is used but it cannot resolve it. Most often this is used in conjunction with SmartLSM.

Logging Modifiers Options

The Logging Modifiers section features only a single option, **Log every authenticated HTTP connection**. This option instructs CP VPN-1/FW-1 to log each HTTP (Hypertext Transfer Protocol) request when a user has been authenticated. Because with the HTTP 1.1 protocol specification more than one request can be made in a single TCP connection, the firewall will only log the first request for brevity.

Time Settings Options

The Time Settings options can help decrease the amount of data that you see in your Log Viewer. You can accomplish this by setting thresholds on the packet flows, and recording only the data that is unique within that threshold.

- **Excessive log grace period** This defines the time in which packets belonging to an established Transfer Control Protocol (TCP) flow are considered uninteresting to CP VPN-1/FW-1 for logging purposes. Increasing this value has a proportionate decreasing impact on your log volume. Packets are considered part of the same flow if they have an identical packet header, meaning that they contain the same source address, source port, destination address, and destination port (for example, Telnet), and that they use the same protocol (for example, TCP=protocol 6). You can find a list of commonly used protocol numbers on most UNIX systems in the /etc/protocols file. Note that packets will still be inspected and acted on, but the logging of the packet will be suppressed.

- **SmartView Tracker resolving timeout** This indicates the amount of time that CP VPN-1/FW-1 will attempt to resolve Internet Protocol (IP) addresses into hostnames before quitting. If this time is reached, the IP address will be displayed in the Log Viewer instead. If the CP VPN-1/FW-1 Log Viewer GUI is slow in being displayed, you could adjust this setting to increase the Viewer's speed.

- **Virtual Link statistics logging interval** Specifies the amount of time between Virtual Link informative packets. This is meaningful if you are using SmartView Monitor and if you have properly defined virtual links between modules you manage.

- **Status fetching interval** Specifies how often your management station will query other systems it manages for status information. This can be any value between 30 and 900 seconds.

There is also a sub-panel, which is shown in Figure 9.2. This panel enables you to configure your response programs. Generally, most of the information on this panel does not require any altering, with the exception of the pointers for user-defined scripts.

Community Default Rule

Similar to the Logging Modifiers section, the Community Default Rule section features only one option: **Log Traffic**. This option specifies whether or not to log connections established through the VPN community. This is only meaningful if you select **Accept all encrypted traffic in the community**. The selection you make here will be shown (read-only) in the General page of the Community's configuration as well as the **Track** column in the VPN community's Accept rule in the rulebase.

Alerts Commands

The default alert, **fwalert** from the command line, is enabled by default for both the normal alert handling as well as the three optional user-defined alerts (a nice increase from the single user-defined alert offered by pre-NG installations). As you can see in Figure 9.2, each field enables you to interact with the SmartView Status component by sending the information for the log to the SmartView Status GUI as well as run a custom executable or script.

Figure 9.2 Alert Commands Sub-Menu

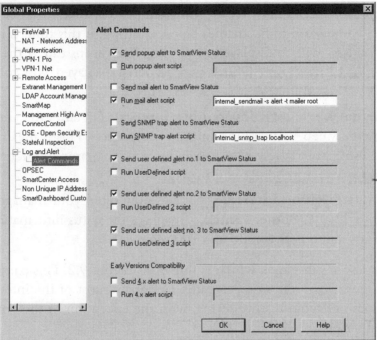

Keep in mind that the event is acted on by the machine that records the logs. While in the majority of cases this is the management machine, it does not necessarily have to be. Also note that the actual executables and scripts reside in the $FWDIR/bin directory on the system recording the log, which is typically the *Management* module. This is also where you would need to save your user-defined alert programs. You will also need to remember to copy your programs to the new $FWDIR/bin directory after an upgrade if you choose to use other utilities. Below is a brief description of how each scripting option may be used.

- **Pop-up alert script** This is the script that will be executed when you select Popup Alert as the action for a matched rule. Generally, this option should not be changed. One item of special note here is the actual function of a Popup Alert. When you are running the SmartView

Status GUI, and a rule is matched whose action is alert, and **Send popup alert to SmartView Status** is selected, you will be notified with a window containing details of the alert. These details include the packet information as well as items such as the component generating the alert. The pop-up window enables you to delete single events or all selected events.

- **Mail alert script** This specifies the command that will be run to send an e-mail alert regarding the matched event, assuming that this action is the specified one. You will need to change this and the command will be specific to your system. The syntax for the command is:

```
internal_sendmail [-s subject] -t mailserver [-f sender_email]
recipient_email [recipient_email ...]
```

- **SNMP trap alert script** Defines the action when a rule with the Simple Network Management Protocol (SNMP) trap action is matched. You may decide to alter this to send your traps to alternate locations, such as to a network management station instead of the default system, localhost.
- **User defined script (No. 1, 2, and 3):** These allow for you to write your own programs to handle a matched rule, and are very handy. User-defined alerts are covered later in this chapter.

Configuring Alerts

Once you have properly configured the commands to be run, you are ready to begin using them as an action. Your most frequent interaction with them will be in the rules you create for your firewall. When you create a new rule, or wish to modify an existing rule, simply right-click on the **Action** column and you'll see a Context menu, as shown in Figure 9.3.

Figure 9.3 Alert Context Menu

You also may interact with the alerting function within various network objects. For example, Figure 9.4 shows us the Firewall Object's Interface Properties window with the Topology panel active. Note the field labeled Spoof Tracking. In this field you'll be able to configure alerting for this event.

Figure 9.4 Alerting in Use

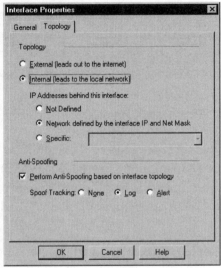

User-Defined Tracking

CP VPN-1/FW-1 features very robust event handling, but it isn't always able to do exactly what you want. In some cases you need to send multiple alert types, or need to send them to many different people. Check Point foresaw this need and has included the user-defined alert type. With this alert type, VPN-1 /FW-1 NG AI provides you the ability to create your own event-handling scripts to suit your needs. You also don't have to learn a new programming language to do so. If you are proficient in C, C++, Perl, WSH, the various UNIX shell-scripting languages, or even writing BAT files, then you are well on the way to creating a user-defined response. You also might be able to find an existing script via the Internet that would suit your needs.

The process of writing your own script is fairly simple; however; there are a number of ways to go about it. Initially, you may be more inclined to use user-defined alerts to generate multiple alert types. Suppose, for example, that you want to send an SNMP trap to a network management console, to a security console, and also mail an alert to yourself. Writing a simple Windows batch or

UNIX shell script will get this done for you with minimal effort, as shown in Figure 9.5.

Figure 9.5 Simple "Batch" Script

```
snmp_trap 172.17.2.15
snmp_trap 172.17.2.16
mailx -s Warning admin@security.mycompany.com
```

Advanced User-Defined Alerts

If you want to move into more advanced realms, the first step is to understand what VPN-1/FW-1 NG AI will be sending as input to your script. The format for this input is as seen in this example:

```
10Nov2003 15:00:12 drop    ExternalFW    >eth1 proto tcp
    src 172.17.3.2 dst 172.17.2.10 service 1234 s_port 2345
    len 40 rule 5
```

The various fields are described in Table 9.1.

Table 9.1 Basic User-Defined Alert Input

Field	Example
Date	10Nov2003
Time	15:00:12
Action	Drop
Originating firewall	ExternalFW
Traffic direction and interface	>eth1
Protocol in use	proto tcp
Source address	src 172.17.3.2
Destination address	dst 172.17.2.10
Service in use	service 1234
Source port	s_port 2345
Length of data captured	len 40
Rule matched	rule 5

Note that values these are the basic log input values. The values will change depending on your use of network address translation (NAT), VPN encryption, or the alerting of Internet Control Message Protocol (ICMP) packets. For example, an ICMP packet will include field information for the *icmp-type* and *icmp-code*. These additional fields are detailed in Table 9.2.

Table 9.2 ICMP and NAT User-Defined Input

Field	Explanation
icmp-type	ICMP type
icmp-code	ICMP code
Xlatesrc	When using NAT, this indicates the address to which the source IP was translated.
Xlatedst	When using NAT, this indicates the address to which the destination IP was translated.
Xlatesport	When using NAT, this indicates the port to which the source port was translated.
Xlatedport	When using NAT, this indicates the port to which the destination port was translated.

Once you understand what VPN-1/FW-1 NG AI will be sending your program, you can then make logical decisions as to what to do with the data. User-defined alerting can be very useful as a method to inform various people based on what the rule detects. For example, the script could parse out the destination IP address or system name, compare that information to a database and then, from the database, locate the proper contact information for the individual responsible. Once this person is located, he or she can be notified via any of several means, allowing the person a more rapid response to the attack. Some other common examples use the global WHOIS database to attempt to locate the administrator of the source of the event, and attempt to notify that person as well. Figure 9.6 includes a partial script as an example of how to get started. It's written in Perl, but, as mentioned earlier, the choice is yours.

Figure 9.6 Beginnings of a User-Defined Alert

```perl
#!/usr/bin/perl -w
#
# Here we'll request strict pragma checking and import a module to
# assist in sending a mail message.
use strict;
use Net::SMTP;


# Good programming practice mandates security!
$ENV{'PATH'} = '/bin:/usr/bin:/sbin:/usr/sbin:/usr/local/bin';
umask (0177);


# Get the log entry and break it up into smaller, useable bits.
my $log = <STDIN>;
my @elements = split (/[ ]+/, $log);


# Identify the most commonly used elements and assign them for frequent #
use.
my $date        = $elements[0];
my $time        = $elements[1];
my $source      = $elements[9];
my $destination = $elements[11];


# The array element to use can vary depending on the use of NAT, among
other factors. Be sure to test.
my $service     = $elements[13];
(...)
```

You can see that it is actually very simple to get the log data. Any program that can gather one line of input and parse it up will do the trick. The only remaining tasks are to install your program in $FWDIR/bin on the machine running the firewall management module, and point to it within the Global Properties. The fact that the alert script runs on the management module makes deploying this user-defined script much easier, especially in a large network. And, since it runs in one central location with access to all the firewall logs, you can also perform simple event correlation. OPSEC partners provide packages that provide more complex event correlations to suit your needs.

Designing & Planning…

Intrusion Detection?

While this book is about CP VPN-1/FW-1, you probably also have Intrusion Detection Systems / Intrusion Prevention Systems (IDS/IPS) on your mind as well. When coupled with SmartDefense, an IDS/IPS greatly adds to the overall effectiveness of a firewall when deployed properly. But what if you can't deploy an IDS/IPS suite because of something such as budget limitations?

The usual solution is to cross one's fingers and hope for fair weather, but with CP VPN-1/FW-1, you have better solutions. As we'll detail in Chapter 13, you can use Check Point SmartDefense to alert you to the presence of some simple probes and attacks, but this feature isn't all that extendable. Another solution is to use user-defined alerts.

Lance Spitzner maintains a guide on how to use user-defined alerts to create a lightweight IDS and honeypot based on the data collected by CP VPN-1/FW1 alerts, and even has a script that will do the trick for you. You can visit this guide and download the script (it's distributed under terms of the GPL license, free of charge) by pointing your Web browser to http://secinf.net/info/unix/lance/intrusion.html.

Suspicious Activities Monitoring Protocol (SAMP)

Check Point, along with their OPSEC alliance partners, has introduced a very powerful feature into CP VPN-1/FW-1. This feature, known as Suspicious Activity Monitoring, or SAM, enables the firewall to interact and block traffic as specified by other network devices. Most notable among these OPSEC partners is ForeScout Technologies, with their ActiveScout product. Using the Suspicious Activity Monitoring Protocol (SAMP) a scout can dynamically update VPN-1/FW-1 rules. These changes can be either permanent or time-based.

For you, as a firewall administrator, the most interesting element of SAMP is not the ability of other devices to restrict connections, but your own ability to block, or *inhibit*, a connection. This can be a very powerful reactive measure, and, if properly employed, can greatly enhance your site security. Imagine the ability to block a connection for five or ten minutes while you do some quick research on the nature of the suspicious connection. Teamed with a user–defined alert script, this can even be done in an automated way.

Connection inhibiting is enabled using the **fw sam** command. This command has some very useful options, most of which are detailed in Table 9.3. The usage of the **fw sam** command is as follows:

```
fw sam [-v] [-s sam-server] [-S server-sic-name] [-t timeout] [-l log] [-f
fw-host] [-C] -((n|i|I|j|J) <criteria>
```

```
fw sam [-v] [-s sam-server] [-S server-sic-name] [-f fw-host] -M -ijn
<criteria>
```

```
fw sam [-v] [-s sam-server] [-S server-sic-name] [-f fw-host] -D
```

Table 9.3 fw sam Command Options

Option	Explanation
-v	Enable verbose mode. In this mode of operation, SAM writes a message to STDERR on each firewall module that is enforcing the action. The message indicates the success or failure.
-s server	The address or registered name of the VPN-1/FW-1 system that will enforce the action. The default is localhost. This should be your management station, which will contact one, multiple, or all firewalls to actually block connections.
-S server_sic_name	The SIC name for the SAM server to be contacted. It expects that the system being contacted will have this SIC name. If it does not, the connection will fail. If this option is not used, it will proceed without comparing the name to the certificate that is presented to it.
-f <fw host>	The firewall that will actually block the connection(s). By default, your SAM server will contact all firewalls it manages. The <fw host> can be localhost, the internal object name (that is, ExternalFW), Gateways (only systems defined as Check Point Gateways, not hosts), or All.

Continued

Table 9.3 fw sam Command Options

Option	Explanation
-t timeout	The time period during which the action will be blocked, specified in seconds. If no value is specified, the action will be in effect indefinitely, or until canceled by you.
-C	Cancel the blocking of the connection specified by the parameters.
-D	Cancel all inhibit and notify directives.
-n	Notify (by recording a log entry) and alert (but do not block) based on the specified criteria.
-I	Inhibit the connection meeting the specified criteria. Connections will be *rejected*.
-I	Inhibit the connection meeting the specified criteria. Also close all existing connections that match the criteria. Connections will be *rejected*.
-j	Inhibit the connection meeting the specified criteria. Connections will be *dropped*.
-J	Inhibit the connection meeting the specified criteria. Also close all existing connections that match the criteria. Connections will be *dropped*.
-l	Specifies the log format to use when recording an event. Options are *nolog*, *long_noalert* and *long_alert*, with the latter being the default.

\<criteria\>	Used to match connections with a combination of various parameters. Criteria may be one of the following:
	
	`src <ip>`
	`dst <ip>`
	`any <ip>`
	`subsrc <ip> <net mask>`
	`subdst <ip> <net-mask>`
	`subany <ip> <net-mask>`
	`srv <src-ip> <dst-ip> <service> <protocol>`
	`subsrv <src-ip> <net-mask> <dst-ip> <net-mask>`
	`    <service> <protocol>`

Continued

Table 9.3 fw sam Command Options

Option	Explanation
	`subsrvs <src-ip> <net-mask> <dst-ip> <service>` `<protocol>`
	`subsrvd <src-ip> <dst-ip> <net-mask> <service>` `<protocol>`
	`dstsrv <dst-ip> <service> <protocol>`
	`subdstsrv <dst-ip> <net-mask> <service>` `<protocol>`
	`srcpr <ip> <protocol>`
	`dstpr <ip> <protocol>`
	`subsrcpr <ip> <net mask> <protocol>`
	`subdstpr <ip> <net mask> <protocol>`

This command is very useful if you are writing user-defined scripts, and you should really become comfortable with that process if you intend on writing user-defined scripts and being proactive.

Another way to interface with SAM is via the SmartView Tracker GUI. From SmartView Tracker, select the **Active** tab. You will then see entries representing the active connections for the firewall. Each connection will be assigned a Connection ID, as indicated in Figure 9.7.

Figure 9.7 Active Connections—Connection ID

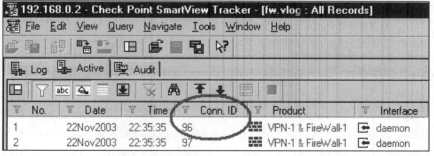

Once you have noted the connection that you wish to remove, select the connection and then choose **Tools | Block Intruder** from the menu. You will then see a screen as illustrated in Figure 9.8.

Figure 9.8 Specify the Connection ID

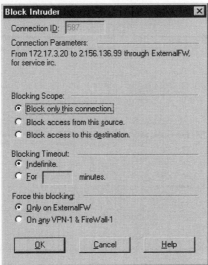

This is the panel used to block the connection. You have a couple of options to select from on this screen, and they are shown in Figure 9.9.

- **Blocking Scope** Enables you to block this specific connection, all connections from the source noted in the log, or all connections to the destination noted in the log.

- **Blocking Timeout** Enables you to specify either indefinite blocking or a time period for this block.

- **Force this blocking** Enables you to enforce blocking this connection on all firewalls or just the firewall that has recorded the event.

You see that the command-line arguments, while a bit more complicated, do allow a greater degree of flexibility. The ease of use of the GUI makes up for this, as scripted execution can be used when you want to be very specific.

So, what do you do when you've blocked a connection that shouldn't be blocked, or wish to unblock an existing block? Here's where it gets odd. The GUI only enables you to unblock *en masse*. It's an all-or-nothing proposition. From the menu bar, select **Tools | Clear Blocking**. You will be presented with a pop-up message, like the one in Figure 9.9, telling you that ALL the connections that were blocked via SAM are no longer blocked. If you've made a mistake and blocked the wrong connection (assuming you have other, valid blocks in place) your only real recourse is to use the command-line syntax to clear a specific block using the **–C** option with the **fw sam** command.

Figure 9.9 Clear Blocking Confirmation

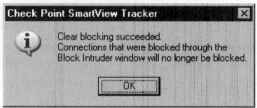

Summary

This chapter looked at some of the options you have when dealing with an event recorded by CP VPN-1/FW-1. It examined, in some depth, the ability for you to exercise some strong control over these settings and how their judicious use can greatly enhance the security of your network.

Also examined were the alert commands configuration panels, the default settings, and how to alter them to better suit your security policy. You saw that you can modify not only the data that is logged, and when it is recorded, but also what action to take based on event criteria.

The chapter then went on to discuss the process of defining your own programs to handle an event and some of the increased flexibility this allows you when designing your security policy. We even saw how user-defined alerts can be a sort of *lightweight* IDS system.

Finally, this chapter also showed the GUI interface to SAM, how to interface with the SmartView Tracker GUI to block connections, and how to use the command-line interface to SAM. All in all, the additional features and function added by the ability to define your own alerts, SAM and SmartDefense make Check Point FW-1 NG AI a real standout in the firewall.

Solutions Fast Track

Alerts Commands

☑ Do not change the default program for a pop-up alert.

☑ Be very cautious when changing the time parameters, specifically Excessive Log Grace Period. Your company may have a log retention policy that mandates verbose logging.

☑ Remember that if you're using multiple log hosts, you'll run the possibility of getting multiple alerts.

User-Defined Tracking

☑ Make every attempt to put the power of user-defined alerts to work for you.

☑ Be sure that you test any user-defined script against all the rules in the rulebase set to run it as an action. NAT, ICMP (and NAT'ed ICMP), and VPN traffic will have different formats sent as input to the script.

Suspicious Activities Monitoring Protocol

☑ Use SAM to enhance the power of your user-defined alert scripts.

☑ Be sure that you double-check the connection information before performing a block, and consider using the time restrictions.

☑ Remember that the GUI method to unblock a connection cannot specify which connection to unblock; it's all or nothing!

Frequently Asked Questions

The following Frequently Asked Questions, answered by the authors of this book, are designed to both measure your understanding of the concepts presented in this chapter and to assist you with real-life implementation of these concepts. To have your questions about this chapter answered by the author, browse to **www.syngress.com/solutions** and click on the **"Ask the Author"** form. You will also gain access to thousands of other FAQs at ITFAQnet.com.

Q: I installed my user-defined script on my firewall, but it isn't doing anything when the rule is matched. What's the problem?

A: Remember that the *alertd* process is running on the machine acting as the management server. Place the script in the $FWDIR/bin directory of that system and begin testing from there.

Q: I'm trying to block a connection with SAM, but I don't see a Connection ID field in SmartView Tracker, and when I click on **Tools**, the **Block Intruder** option is grayed out. Am I doing something wrong?

A: Remember that to use the SAM feature, SmartView Tracker must be in **Active Mode**.

Q: Is there a way to see which IP addresses are currently blocked on my firewall?

A: Yes and no. The blocked IP addresses are maintained in the FW-1 table, sam_blocked_ips. The firewall command **fw tab –t sam_blocked_ips** will show you the contents of that table, but it isn't the easiest thing on earth to read since it is all in a hexadecimal format.

Q: I'm no programmer, but I'm really excited by the user-defined alert idea. Does Check Point supply any preconfigured user-defined alerts?

A: No, but fear not—the Internet is full of helpful people, and a quick search might reveal what you need. You can also employ OPSWAT to assist you. OPSWAT is a consulting company specializing in creating customized OPSEC-compliant solutions for companies. More information about OPSWAT is available at www.opswat.com.

## Chapter 10

Configuring Virtual Private Networks

Solutions in this Chapter:

- **Encryption Schemes**

- **Simplified-Mode vs. Traditional-Mode VPNs**

- **Configuring an IKE VPN in Traditional Mode**

- **Configuring an IKE VPN in Simplified Mode**

- **Configuring a SecuRemote VPN**

- **Installing SecuRemote Client Software**

- **Using SecuRemote Client Software**

- ☑ **Summary**

- ☑ **Solutions Fast Track**

- ☑ **Frequently Asked Questions**

Introduction

Many organizations are using virtual private networks (VPNs) over the Internet in order to have a secure channel for remote offices, business partners, and mobile users to access their internal networks. For many, the VPN is replacing dedicated Frame Relay circuits or dial-in VPN services for their organizational needs.

For example, let's say that your office headquarters is in Hartford, Connecticut, but you have a small, remote office located in Tampa, Florida. You could set up a gateway-to-gateway VPN between these two offices so that they can share each other's resources on the network through an encrypted channel over the Internet. The communication between these two branches is secured by the endpoints of the connection, which are the firewalls at each location.

This chapter discusses the different types of encryption available to you in VPN-1/FireWall-1 Next Generation with Application Intelligence and explains this technology to you so that you'll understand how it is working. Check Point makes it easy to set up a VPN using its SmartDashboard, and this chapter will show you how to configure VPNs between gateways and to mobile clients. Then we will demonstrate how to install the SecuRemote client software. (If you are interested in desktop security for the client, we cover that topic in the next chapter.) Even though they will use the same installation binary, much has to do with the licensing you have purchased and a few configuration options on the server-side.

A bit of theory is necessary before beginning the process of describing how to set up VPNs with Check Point NG AI. You should first understand the basics of encryption algorithms, key exchange, hash functions, digital signatures, and certificates so that you can feel comfortable troubleshooting and deploying VPNs.

Encryption Schemes

Encryption is the process of transforming regular, readable data, or *plaintext*, into "scrambled," or unreadable, form, called *ciphertext*. *Decryption* is the reverse process—transforming ciphertext into plaintext. The process of encryption can be used in various ways to ensure privacy, authenticity, and data integrity:

- **Privacy** No one should be able to view the plaintext message except the original sender and intended recipient.

- **Authenticity** The recipient of an encrypted message should be able to verify with certainty the identity of the message sender.

- **Data integrity** The recipient of the message should be able to verify that it has not been tampered with or altered in any way while in transit.

Encryption is accomplished using an encryption algorithm, typically a pair of closely related mathematical functions that perform the actual encryption and decryption on the data provided to them. Modern encryption algorithms, including the ones used in Check Point NG AI, utilize what is called a *key* (or keys) to aid in the encryption or decryption process. There are two types of encryption algorithms: symmetric and asymmetric.

Encryption Algorithms: Symmetric vs. Asymmetric Cryptography

In what is called *symmetric encryption*, the encryption algorithm itself is public while the key is a secret. Anyone who discovers the key and has knowledge of the algorithm can decrypt any messages encrypted with that key. Since both the sender and recipient need to know the secret key before they can communicate, you must have a secure method of exchanging the key. Sometimes you will hear the term *sneakernet* used to describe this key exchange process, meaning that the exchange takes place via phone, fax, or in person, since an online exchange cannot be encrypted prior to the sharing of the key. Sometimes you will hear this key referred to as a *shared secret*. Symmetric encryption is typically very fast, but it has some disadvantages:

- As stated, anyone discovering the secret key can decrypt the messages.
- Since each sender/recipient pair (we will call them *users*) needs a separate secret key, the number of separate keys that need to be managed increases rapidly as the number of users increases. Mathematically, we need $n (n-1) / 2$ keys for a network of n users. Using this formula, a network of 500 users, for example, requires 124,750 unique keys.

Asymmetric encryption was developed to solve the problem of secure key exchange and to improve key management. It is called *asymmetric* because the encryption and decryption keys are different. In one form of asymmetric encryption, called *public key encryption*, the sender and recipient each have two keys, one of which is public and can be openly shared and another of which is private and is kept secret and never shared. If Alice wants to send an encrypted message to Bob, for example, she and Bob only need to exchange their public keys. The method used for the exchange need not be private in this case. Alice encrypts the plaintext message to Bob using Bob's public key. When Bob receives the message, he decrypts it using his private key. This method of public key encryption, invented in 1976 by Whitfield Diffie and Martin Hellman, is sometimes called the *Diffie-Hellman algorithm*.

Another form of asymmetric encryption, called RSA encryption, is used by Check Point NG AI for generating digital signatures.

As we can see, asymmetric encryption solves the problem of key exchanges needing to be done in private. Users need only share their public keys to encrypt messages to one another. Asymmetric encryption does suffer one serious drawback, however: It is much, much slower than symmetric encryption (on the order of 1,000 times slower). For this reason, real-life encryption schemes tend to use a "hybrid" form of public key exchange and private (symmetric) key encryption. Check Point NG AI is no different in this regard. A Diffie-Hellman key pair is used to generate and exchange a shared secret key, which is used for all encryption and decryption after the initial public key exchange. The shared secret key in this case is sometimes called a *session key*. The shared key can be regenerated at periodic intervals to lessen the chance of its compromise.

An encryption algorithm's security is completely dependent on its keys and how they are managed. Strong encryption that has a flawed key management algorithm is actually weak encryption. You will often hear of an encryption algorithm described as using a 128-bit key, for example. What this means is that, if the algorithm is implemented properly, someone who tried to enumerate every possible key in order to break your encryption (called a *brute-force attack*) would have to try 2^{128} different key combinations to be guaranteed success. This is not computationally feasible for the foreseeable future. In practice, cryptanalysts typically attack an algorithm's key generation or key management scheme instead, attempting to find a flaw such as a predictable sequence of keys to exploit. An example of this is a very technical but small flaw that enables an attacker to dramatically reduce the number of possible keys when decrypting WEP used for wireless networks.

The moral of all this is that you should pay attention to an algorithm's implementation rather than to its key size exclusively. The latter will not guarantee your security. Note that asymmetric encryption schemes typically have key sizes that are much larger than symmetric ones (1024 bits, for example). The strength of these keys cannot be equated to the strength of symmetric keys, since they use different mathematical principles. The original Diffie-Hellman public key scheme, for example, was based on the difficulty of factoring very large prime numbers.

Check Point makes available several encryption algorithms. They are enumerated in Table 10.1, along with their shared key sizes and whether they are based on a public standard or are proprietary.

Table 10.1 Check Point Encryption Algorithms

Algorithm	Key Length in Bits	Standard
CAST	40	Public
DES	56	Public
3DES	168	Public
AES	256	Public

IKE and ISAKMP

The Internet Security Association and Key Management Protocol (ISAKMP), or Internet Key Exchange (IKE), is an Internet encryption, authentication, and key exchange standard put forth by the Internet Engineering Task Force (IETF). In today's Internet, it is widely used for implementing VPNs. Because ISAKMP is a standard, a Check Point firewall utilizing it will be able to interoperate with other third-party VPN products. Check Point firewalls are known to interoperate with Linux gateways (Free/SWAN), OpenBSD, SonicWall, and Watchguard firewall products, as examples. The ISAKMP key exchange process is divided into two phases and utilizes what are called *security associations* (SAs) to facilitate encryption and key generation. Keys and SAs are regenerated on a periodic basis.

IKE uses what is called *tunneling-mode encryption*. This means that each packet that is to be sent over a VPN is first encrypted in its entirety (both header and data payload are encrypted) and then encapsulated with a new header. The new header will differ based on whether the packet is just being encrypted, just being authenticated, or both. This tunneling mode slightly degrades network performance because it increases the size of each packet, reducing the amount of actual data transferred per packet, but it is more secure than in-place encryption.

Before standards for VPN technologies were available, Check Point developed the first widely used encryption scheme for encrypting network traffic. Though no longer used, FWZ was a Check Point proprietary key exchange scheme that utilizes another proprietary protocol, Reliable Datagram Protocol, or RDP (not the same as the RDP described in RFC 1151), to negotiate encryption and authentication methods between gateways.

FWZ used what is called *in-place encryption*, in which packet bodies are encrypted, leaving the original TCP/IP headers in place. This method of encryption is faster (because it does not inflate the size of the packets by encrypting the headers) than tunneling mode but at the expense of security, since original header information is left in a readable state, including IP addresses, which are internal to an organization. Note that because FWZ does not encapsulate packets before sending them through a VPN, FWZ could not be used in situations in which any networks participating in the VPN domain have nonroutable addresses.

Hash Functions and Digital Signatures

A *hash function*, also known as a *one-way function*, is a mathematical function that takes a variable-length input and generates a fixed-length output, which is typically much smaller than the input. If we pass a plaintext message through a hash function, we produce what is called a *message digest*. A good hash function is one that, if we are given the message digest, is impossible to "reverse" and deduce the original message. It is also one in which for any two different function inputs (two different messages, in this context), the output should be unique to the input. To put it another way, the message digests for two different messages should also be different. As we will see, this principle can be used to ensure the integrity of a message. If a hash function generates the same message digest for two different inputs, we call this a *collision*. A good hash function will minimize collisions. When we talk about hash functions, we usually specify the length of the message digest in bits. This roughly corresponds (strength-wise) to the length of a symmetric encryption key. For example, a commonly used hash function, MD5, produces a 128-bit message digest for any size input it is given.

The output to a hash function is usually much smaller than the original message as well. MD4 and MD5 are good examples of hash functions. You may have heard of an MD5 checksum. This checksum is the result of sending a file through the MD5 hash algorithm.

Another important note about hash functions is that the output is unique to the message. If the original message were tampered with in any way, a different message digest would result. Since you cannot "decrypt" a message digest, you run the algorithm against the message and compare the two digests to verify that the message is intact. This is how data integrity is achieved.

A *digital signature* is an attachment to a message that utilizes a hash function and enables the receiver to authenticate the sender and verify data integrity. Digital signatures can be attached to encrypted messages. Check Point NG generates digital signatures using an RSA private key and a hash function, as shown in this example, where Alice wants to send a digitally signed message to Bob:

1. Alice sends the (unencrypted) message through a hash function, producing a fixed-length message digest.

2. Alice encrypts the message digest with her private RSA key and sends it on its way, along with the encrypted message. The encrypted message is now "signed" by Alice.

3. Bob decrypts the message as usual and passes it through the same hash function Alice used when it was sent. Bob compares this message digest he just generated with the decrypted message digest sent to him, making sure they match. Alice's public key is used to decrypt the message digest in this case.

A match in this case means that Bob can be sure that Alice sent the message and that no one tampered with it in transit. We are assuming here that Bob trusts that he is using Alice's public key; this trust is usually provided by a certificate authority who will certify public keys.

The two hash functions offered by Check Point are MD5 and SHA-1. MD5 is a 128-bit hash function; SHA-1 is considered more secure, with a 160-bit message digest length.

Certificates and Certificate Authorities

A *certificate authority* (CA) is a trusted third party from which we can reliably obtain a public key. A certificate is issued by a CA and contains reliable information about the entity that wants to be "certified" authentic. This entity could be a person's or a firewall's public key or a secure Web server host name and domain.

In the case of Check Point VPNs, certificates can be used by encrypting gateways to exchange public keys and to authenticate one another. Typically, the gateways themselves act as CAs in this regard.

Types of VPNs

There are logically two types of VPN: site-to-site and client-to-site. *Site-to-site VPNs* are what we normally think of when we think of a VPN: two gateways communicating across an insecure network (usually the Internet), with encrypted traffic passing between them.

Client-to-site VPNs, on the other hand, have a fixed gateway at one end and a mobile client on the other, perhaps with a dynamic IP address. This type of VPN is implemented by Check Point's SecuRemote or SecureClient products.

VPN Domains

We can define a *VPN domain* as a group of hosts and/or networks behind a fire-walled gateway that participate in a VPN. In a site-to-site VPN, each gateway has its own VPN domain defined and is also aware of the other gateway's VPN domain. Any traffic coming from one VPN domain and going to the other (behind the opposing gateway) will be encrypted outbound and then decrypted inbound at the other end.

VPN domains are defined on each gateway's firewall object and must be set up with certain rules in mind. We talk about this concept in more detail when we discuss VPN implementation.

Designing & Planning…

VPN Domains

It is important not to include either peer's gateway object in their respective VPN domains; otherwise, traffic to or from each gateway will be encrypted, which is not what we want, nor can it work, since key exchange has not yet taken place. Contrast this with *single entry point* (SEP) configurations, in which gateways must be a member of each VPN domain. Furthermore, for nonroutable VPN domains, make sure opposing subnets are not identical. In large deployments in which you may have more than one gateway, each with a unique VPN tunnel, make sure the VPN domains don't "overlap" or include the same hosts/networks in both domains. Both gateways will want to encrypt traffic in cases where traffic passes through more than one gateway on the way to its destination. It is better to use a SEP configuration for this, with some dynamic routing protocol inside you local network.

Simplified-Mode vs. Traditional-Mode VPNs

There are two methods to configuring VPNs in Check Point NG AI: traditional and simplified. If you upgraded from an earlier version, your policy will use Traditional mode by default. On new installations, Simplified mode is the default. Just as their names seem to state, Traditional-mode VPNs are configured the way they were in previous versions. Simplified-mode VPNs, by comparison, still provide the same VPN functionality, but the configuration is easier and quicker, as you will see. The type of VPN configuration mode you use for a new policy is defined in the VPN-1 Pro section of Global Properties, as shown in Figure 10.1. If your policy is in Traditional mode and you want to move it to Simplified mode, select **Policy | Convert To | Simplified VPN**.

Figure 10.1 VPN Configuration Method

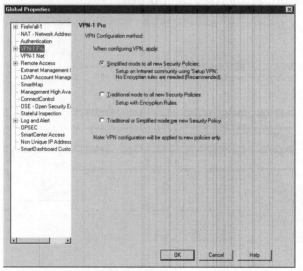

Configuring an IKE VPN in Traditional Mode

Here we will create a VPN from ExternalFW to our branch office firewall, BranchFW. The two firewalls are managed by the same management station. Be sure to define network objects for the networks that will be participating in your VPN domain. We will use LAN and BranchNet (10.0.0.0/24) for these networks. In this example, we use Simplified mode to configure the VPNs.

Defining Objects

For any site-to-site VPN, you need to create and properly configure certain network objects, including both gateways and the networks or group objects representing your VPN domains.

Local Gateway

Under the **VPN** tab of ExternalFW's **Properties** window, select **Traditional mode configuration**. The Traditional mode IKE properties dialog box comes up (see Figure 10.2). Select any and all of the encryption and data integrity methods you want your gateway to support, and check **Pre-Shared Secret** under **Support authentication methods** (you would check **Public Key Signatures** if you were using certificates). You will not be able to edit this secret until you define your remote gateway's encryption properties.

Figure 10.2 The IKE Properties Dialog Box

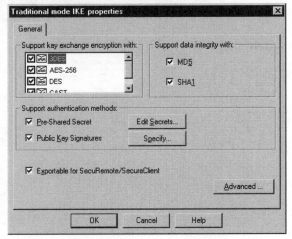

Next, open the **Topology** tab of the **Check Point Gateway** Properties window (see Figure 10.3). This is where you will define the VPN domain for your local gateway. Under **VPN Domain**, select **Manually Defined**, and choose your local network (LAN) from the drop-down list. Selecting Manually Defined also allows you to restrict the networks that are accessible via a VPN in the event that you do not want your entire network to be available through the VPN. If you have your topology configured correctly, you can instead choose **All IP Addresses behind Gateway based on Topology information**. This option summarizes all the networks behind interfaces defined as internal and dynamically creates the VPN domain for you.

Figure 10.3 VPN Domain Configuration

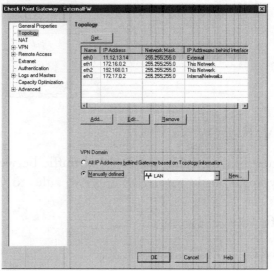

Remote Gateway

Configuration of the remote gateway is a nearly identical process—you just need to make sure that you support at least one of the same methods of encryption and data integrity methods as you did on the local gateway. When you check **Pre-Shared Secret** this time, you can click **Edit Secrets**, where you should see your peer, BranchFW, in the Shared Secrets List window (see Figure 10.4). You can edit the shared secret by highlighting the peer gateway in the list and clicking **Edit**. Enter the agreed-on shared secret in the **Enter secret** text field, and click **Set** to define it. Don't forget to define your VPN domain under the **Topology** tab, by opening the **Topology** tab of the **Check Point Gateway** Properties window (refer back to Figure 10.3). You can see very quickly that defining a secret for each and every gateway could get very cumbersome in a large deployment. This is solved by Simplified-mode VPNs, discussed later in this chapter. Under **VPN Domain**, select **Manually Defined**, and choose your remote network (BranchNet) from the drop–down list.

Figure 10.4 Shared Secret Configuration

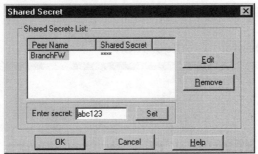

Adding VPN Rules

You will want to modify your Rule Base so that traffic between LAN and BranchNet is encrypted. You do this by adding two rules to your Rule Base (see Figure 10.5).

One rule specifies the following:

- **Source** LAN
- **Destination** BranchNet
- **Service** Any
- **Action** Encrypt
- **Track** Log

The other specifies the following:

- **Source** BranchNet
- **Destination** LAN
- **Service** Any
- **Action** Encrypt
- **Track** Log

Figure 10.5 IKE Encryption Rules

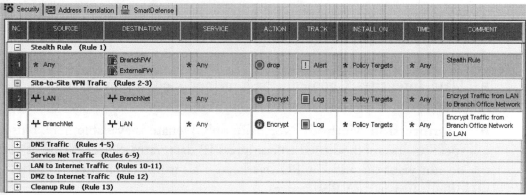

Note that we do not have a rule to allow the IKE traffic to talk from one firewall to the other. This is because it is part of the Global Properties. A rule to allow IKE between the two gateways is necessary only if you have **Accept VPN-1 & FireWall-1 control connections** unchecked in your security policy's Global Properties window (see Figure 10.5). This is checked by default, so in most cases you won't need a rule to be manually defined.

If you double-click the **Encrypt** action in either encrypt rule, you will open the **Encryption Properties** dialog box, from which you select **IKE** and click **Edit**, which pops up another box (see Figure 10.6).

Figure 10.6 IKE Properties Dialog Box

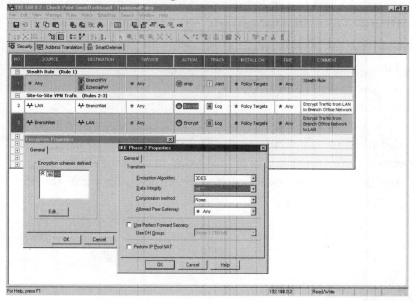

There are many options here. Go through the options one at a time:

- **Encryption Algorithm** Choose an encryption algorithm from the list. Strong encryption (e.g., Triple-DES or AES) is available, and recommended, with IKE.

- **Data Integrity** Choose the hash method used to provide authentication. SHA1 is available here, in addition to MD5.

- **Compression Method** Normally, only Deflate is available here. This specifies the method used to compress IP datagrams. Select **None** if you do not want the added CPU overhead. This is not often supported by other third-party VPN devices.

- **Allowed Peer Gateway** Specifies exactly which gateways with which this one is prepared to establish a VPN. Defaults to **Any**, meaning that you will allow VPN traffic from or to any gateway if the packet's source or destination IP address is in the other gateway's VPN domain. If this policy is to be installed on both firewalls, we would create a group with both firewalls in it. This is because each rule would be used for encrypting on one end and decrypting on the other.

- **Use Perfect Forward Secrecy (PFS)** PFS adds another measure of security to key exchanges, with some additional overhead.

- **Use DH Group** This enables you to select the Diffie-Hellman group you would like to use for encryption. Selecting a "longer" group means better key security but, again, more overhead.

- **Perform IP Pool NAT** Allows the use of a predefined "pool" of IP addresses that are assigned to incoming VPN connections. This is typically used to prevent or fix asymmetric routing conditions in which inbound and outbound VPN traffic follow different routes.

You may also need to add a rule to the NAT Rule Base to disable NAT between these networks if you are using NAT for your network objects.

Now that the rules have been created, push the policy and test the VPN.

Configuring an IKE VPN in Simplified Mode

Here we will create a VPN from ExternalFW to our branch office firewall, BranchFW, using Simplified mode. The two firewalls are managed by the same management station. Be sure to define network objects for the networks that will be participating in your VPN domain. We will use LAN and BranchNet (10.0.0.0/24) for these networks. In this example, we use Simplified mode to configure the VPNs. Remove the Traditional mode configurations, if any, that you defined previously.

Defining Objects

For any site-to-site VPN, you need to create and properly configure certain network objects, including both gateways and the networks or group objects representing your VPN domains.

Local Gateway

In ExternalFW's Properties window, select the **Topology** tab, as shown in Figure 10.3. This is where you will define the VPN domain for your local gateway. Under **VPN Domain**, select **Manually Defined**, and choose your local network (LAN) from the drop-down list. Selecting Manually Defined also allows you to restrict the networks that are accessible via a VPN in the event that you do not want your entire network to be available through the VPN. If you have your topology configured correctly, you can instead choose **All IP Addresses behind Gateway based on Topology information**. This option summarizes all the networks behind interfaces defined as internal and dynamically creates the VPN domain for you.

Remote Gateway

Configuration of the remote gateway is an identical process. Don't forget to define your VPN domain under the **Topology** tab, by opening the **Topology** tab of the **Check Point Gateway** Properties window (refer back to Figure 10.3). Under **VPN Domain**, select **Manually Defined**, and choose your remote network (BranchNet) from the drop-down list.

Creating the VPN Community

A VPN community is the way multiple VPN gateways communicate with, and encrypt between, each other. Three types of VPN communities are available in Check Point NG AI:

- **Remote access** Used for easily defining client-to-site VPN connections. Only one is allowed throughout the entire management infrastructure.

- **Meshed** This type of site-to-site VPN topology allows all participating gateways to communicate directly with any other gateway in the community. This is the simplest way of configuring site-to-site VPNs because it allows "everything to VPN to everything else." A meshed VPN is used most often when multiple corporate offices all need to VPN with each other directly.

- **Star** A star configuration, also known as a hub-and-spoke configuration, is a site-to-site VPN topology consisting of central gateways and satellite gateways. The satellite gateways, or spokes, communicate with only one or a few gateways, which are defined as central gateways. Satellites are typically remote or branch offices. The central gateways are typically headquarters, regional offices, or data center sites that communicate with all the satellite sites. Satellite gateways that need to encrypt data to other satellite gateways can do so through the central gateway(s) using VPN Routing. Satellites can also route all outbound traffic (including traffic destined for the Internet) through the hub gateway if necessary.

Select the **VPN Manager** tab in SmartDashboard to see the VPN communities. Predefined is the **MyIntranet** VPN Community. This is a meshed community. In Figure 10.7, a star community is used to explain the additional configuration options. You can select **Manage | VPN Communities** or simply right-click in the top pane of the VPN Manager and select **New Community** to create a new community. After creating a star community, you will be presented the pane shown in Figure 10.7.

Figure 10.7 Star VPN Community Properties

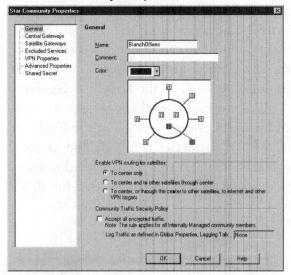

Here you can define the traffic that will be sent from the satellites to the central gateways. Your options for enabling routing for satellites are as follows:

- **To center only** Allows connectivity from the Branch to the Corporate Office and back.

- **To Center and to other satellites through center** Allows one branch to communicate with another via each satellite's individual VPN to a central gateway.

- **To center, or through center to other satellites, to Internet and other VPN targets** Allows all access, including access to the Internet, to occur through the central gateway. This final option is not often used, but it can be very handy, depending on your needs.

The other configurable element on this page is the Community Traffic Security Policy. By checking the **Accept all encrypted traffic** check box, you do not have to create any rules in the Rule Base. It will emulate a Frame Relay network in that no access controls will need to be defined in the security policy Rule Base. An implied rule will be added to the top of the Rule Base. All traffic will be accepted on Rule 0 in SmartView Tracker, though only if you define it to be logged in the Global Properties Logging tab. You can see these rules by selecting **View | VPN Rules**. Keep in mind, however, that even though the all traffic will be accepted, it will still be subject to the enforcements of the firewalls, including three-way TCP handshake, SmartDefense, and more.

Next, select **Central Gateways** from the tree on the left and add ExternalFW. If we had multiple firewalls acting as central gateways, we could also select to mesh all the central gateways together, removing the need for another meshed VPN community. Now select the **Satellite Gateways** option on the left and add the BranchFW. You can also exclude certain services from being encrypted as part of the VPN community using the Excluded Services option from the left. When **VPN Properties** is highlighted, as shown in Figure 10.8, define the IKE (key exchange) and IPSec (encrypted network traffic) encryption algorithms and data integrity algorithms to be used for all VPN communications for this community.

Figure 10.8 VPN Properties

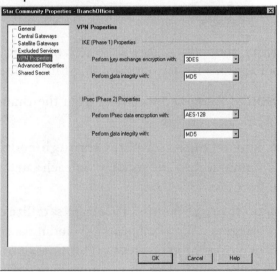

VPN Properties includes the configuration settings most administrators are concerned with. However, more goes on behind the scenes. Check Point's open and configurable nature shows the administrator the default settings and allows them to be changed easily and quickly for all VPNs between gateways partici-pating in the community. This process is shown in Figure 10.9.

Figure 10.9 Advanced VPN Properties

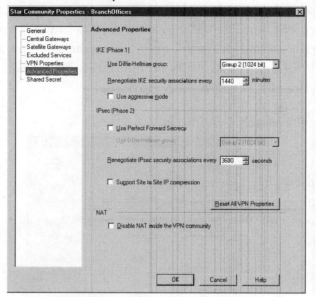

Phase 1 always uses Diffie-Hellman to generate the keys. Selecting which Diffie-Hellman group is used can allow connectivity to other devices that use different levels of security. You can also use Diffie-Hellman to provide added security by selecting the **Use Perfect Forward Secrecy** check box. Here you can also define the length of time between key renegotiations, whether to use IP compression before encrypting the traffic, and whether to use aggressive mode to complete the key exchange in six packets rather than three packets.

The final option in this page is **Disable NAT inside the VPN community**. Because most of the networks behind the VPN gateways will be private (invalid) IP addresses, NAT will likely be applied to allow systems to communicate out to the Internet. By checking this box, any traffic through the VPN will not be subject to NAT rules applied by objects and the NAT Rule Base. It will, however, be subject to IP Pool NAT after the destination gateway has decrypted it, if applicable.

Adding VPN Rules

If you did not check the **Accept all encrypted traffic** check box for the VPN community (refer back to Figure 10.7), you will want to modify your Rule Base so that traffic between LAN and BranchNet is encrypted. Similar to, but not the same as, Traditional mode, this is done by adding two rules to your Rule Base.

You will notice that there is a new column in a Simplified mode policy: the VPN column. You will also notice that the Action column does not have Encrypt or Client Encrypt options. The VPN column defines how rules will be applied to all traffic (encrypted and cleartext), only site-to-site VPN connections, or only traffic encrypted through certain VPN communities. Figure 10.10 shows selection of only the BranchOffices VPN community.

Figure 10.10 VPN Match Conditions

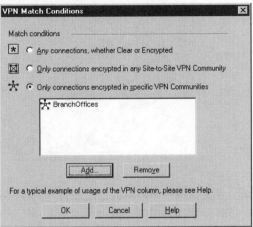

Next you need to define the following rules to allow traffic through the VPN. You could easily create a single rule allowing all traffic through any site-to-site VPN community, but the most advisable technique is to only allow the necessary traffic. To emulate the rules previously shown in the Traditional mode configuration, create the rules as defined next.

One rule specifies the following:

- **Source** LAN
- **Destination** BranchNet
- **Service** Any
- **VPN** BranchOffices
- **Action** Accept
- **Track** Log

The other specifies the following:

- **Source** BranchNet

- **Destination** LAN

- **VPN** Branch Offices

- **Service** Any

- **Action** Accept

- **Track** Log

When the rules have been created, they should resemble Figure 10.11.

Figure 10.11 VPN Community Encryption Rules

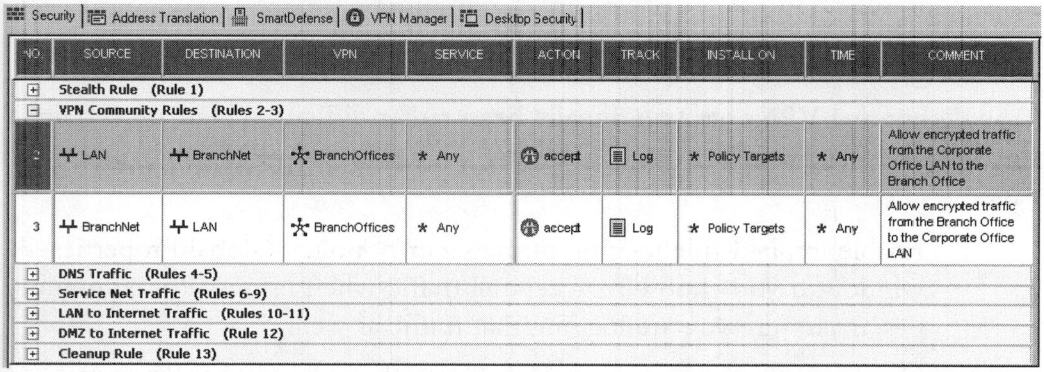

Note that we do not have a rule to allow the IKE traffic to talk from one firewall to the other. As in Traditional mode, this is because it is part of the Global Properties. A rule to allow IKE between the two gateways is only necessary if you have **Accept VPN-1 & FireWall-1 control connections** unchecked in your security policy's Global Properties window. This option is checked by default, so in most cases you won't need a rule to be manually defined.

Now that the rules have been created, let's push the policy and test the VPN.

Testing the VPN

Once the configuration is complete, install the security policy on both gateways. Try to establish a connection from a host in your local VPN domain to a host in the remote gateway's VPN domain. You should see packets with a local source address and a remote destination address being encrypted on the way out the local gateway and corresponding packet decryptions on the remote gateway (see Figure 10.12). If this is not immediately apparent, or if you see errors in the log, refer to the following section for some troubleshooting tips. You should see key install entries in the log, then decrypt and encrypt logs.

Figure 10.12 SmartView Tracker Entries Showing Encrypts, Decrypts, and Key Exchanges

1212	10:34:06	Log	O⤚ Key Ins...		11.12.13.14	15.16.17.18				IKE: Main Mode completion.
1213	10:34:07	Log	O⤚ Key Inc...		11.12.13.14	15.16.17.18				IKE: Quick Mode completion; IKE IDs: host: 11.12.13
1218	10:34:18	Log	O⤚ Key Ins...		15.16.17.18	11.12.13.14				IKE: Quick Mode completion; IKE IDs: subnet: 172.16
1219	10:34:20	Log	O⤚ Key Ins...		11.12.13.14	15.16.17.18				IKE: Quick Mode completion; IKE IDs: host: 11.12.13
1315	10:37:28	Log	Encrypt		172.16.3.2	10.0.0.2	ICMP icmp	2		icmp-type: 8; icmp-code: 0
1318	10:37:37	Log	Encrypt		172.16.3.108	10.0.0.2	ICMP icmp	2		icmp-type: 8; icmp-code: 0
1321	10:37:55	Log	Decrypt		10.0.0.2	172.16.3.2	ICMP icmp	3		icmp-type: 8; icmp-code: 0
1325	10:38:12	Log	Encrypt	H323	172.16.3.2	10.0.0.2	TCP tcp	2		
1326	10:38:13	Log	Encrypt	H323	172.16.3.2	10.0.0.2	TCP tcp	2		
1327	10:38:13	Log	Encrypt	H323	172.16.3.2	10.0.0.2	TCP tcp	2		
1328	10:38:13	Log	Encrypt	T.120	172.16.3.2	10.0.0.2	TCP tcp	2		
1329	10:38:14	Log	Encrypt	T.120	172.16.3.2	10.0.0.2	TCP tcp	2		
1330	10:38:14	Log	Encrypt	T.120	172.16.3.2	10.0.0.2	TCP tcp	2		

Debugging VPNs

Troubleshooting VPNs has traditionally been rather difficult. There are certain steps you can take to make troubleshooting and testing of VPN deployments easier:

1. Enable implied rule logging in the security policy Global Properties window. If you choose to accept all traffic when using VPN communities, make sure you are logging that traffic as well.

2. On the security policy **Log and Alert** tab in the Global Properties window, enable all three encryption-specific log events:

   - VPN successful key exchange

   - VPN packet handling errors

   - VPN configuration and key exchange errors

3. Disable NAT by adding one or more manual rules to the NAT Rule Base that force traffic between opposing VPN domains to be "Original," as in Figure 10.13, or un-NATed. NAT can be used with VPNs; however, disabling it when possible allows for cleaner testing and simpler debugging.

4. Be aware that the gateways participating in the VPN and perhaps the management stations need to communicate prior to the VPN tunnel being established (key exchange, protocol negotiation, and so forth). You may need a rule in your Rule Base explicitly allowing this communication (refer back to the preceding IKE encryption Rule Base examples).

Be aware of where in your Rule Base your stealth rule is and how this might impact such communication. Implied rule and VPN logging, again discussed previously, will show you such communication in a default installation.

5. Remember to test traffic from VPN domain to VPN domain, not from gateway to gateway. Normally, gateways are *not* included in VPN domains, so they cannot provide a platform for reliable tests.

6. Be aware that using just ICMP (Ping) tests may not tell whether or not a VPN is working correctly. This especially applies if you don't have control over the other VPN endpoint. Administrators are often leery of allowing ICMP through their firewall and/or border routers and may be dropping it with implicit or explicit rules before any encryption can take place. A better test, and one that works on any platform with a Telnet binary, is to Telnet to a port other than the traditional port 23, using one that you know is open. So, for example, if your VPN peer has a DNS server in its VPN domain, "telnet *<IP of DNS server>* 53" would show you that you could establish a TCP connection through your VPN tunnel.

7. Your gateway may attempt to encrypt packets, even if key exchange is not complete, causing you to wonder why a VPN is failing to work if encryption is taking place. If you filter your Log Viewer for Key Install under the Action column, you will see key exchange as it occurs. The Info field of each log entry in this case may contain useful error messages relevant to key exchange errors.

8. For every encrypt action on your gateway, your partner's firewall should show a corresponding decrypt action. You may or may not have access to those logs, so the preceding tips can help you test in that case.

9. Look for configuration examples when choosing to interoperate with other non-Check Point devices. Many IKE devices, though certified in many ways to be interoperable, do not choose configurations or negotiate when presented with options during the key exchange. Notorious for this are Cisco devices. In addition, look for the exact device, model, and version in use on the other end. The built-in options and settings will vary between different VPN products from the same manufacturer (for example, Cisco PIX, Cisco VPN Concentrator, Cisco VPN-enabled router) and between versions.

10.   Check to see how the other end is expecting your gateway to present its networks (network address and subnet mask). It may be necessary to change the *ike_use_largest_possible_subnets* option in object_5_0.C to False (True is the default).

Figure 10.13 Address Translation Disabled Between VPN Domains with Manual Rules

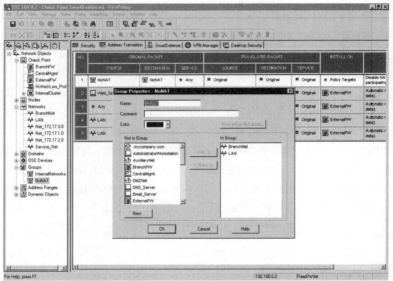

Considerations for External Networks

It is important that all encryption rules have the same exact parameters defined in their respective encryption properties dialog box. Your VPN will likely fail if they do not. This is easy to check when you manage both the local and remote gateways, but it can be harder to verify when the remote gateway is managed by another management station or even another company. Typically this coordination is done via telephone, agreed on ahead of time, as in "We will use IKE with 3DES encryption, SHA-1 data integrity, key exchange for subnets, and no perfect forward secrecy." Most VPN failures are a result of someone changing his or her respective VPN parameters, causing key exchange, key renegotiations, encryption, or decryption to fail.

Configuring a SecuRemote VPN

In this section you will see how to configure your gateway for client encryption with SecuRemote, Check Point's client-to-site VPN tool. First, you will configure your gateway to act as a SecuRemote "server," and then you'll define the SecuRemote users, including their authentication methods. Finally, you will add the appropriate rules to your Rule Base to allow the encrypted communication.

Local Gateway Object

From the Check Point Gateway Properties window on your local gateway (the gateway through which SecuRemote connections will pass), in this case ExternalFW, ensure that VPN-1 Pro is checked in the Check Point Products section. This will enable the VPN functionality on the gateway so that SecuRemote clients are able to access nonroutable networks behind the SecuRemote server (gateway) once they are authenticated and a VPN tunnel is established.

Next, you must define your VPN domain, which in this case defines the networks your SecuRemote clients will have access to once they have been authenticated. Set this as usual in the **Topology** tab of the Check Point Gateway Properties window on your local gateway. For SecuRemote, when using Traditional-mode VPN policies, you need to check **Exportable for SecuRemote** in the **Traditional Mode IKE properties** window (refer back to Figure 10.2). This choice enables clients to download the networks to which they will have access after being authenticated. When Simplified-mode VPN policies are used, you need only add the gateway to the RemoteAccess VPN community. Within the **Global Properties | Remote Access** section are many options that can be used to fine-tune your configuration, as shown in Figure 10.14.

Figure 10.14 Remote Access Window from Policy | Global Properties

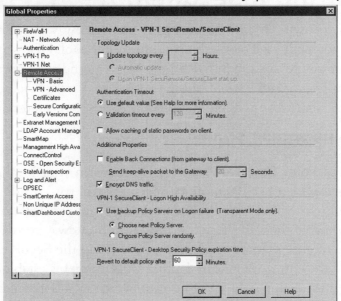

Two configurations should be enabled to ensure that users have the highest likelihood of connecting:

- The first is in the **Global Properties | Remote Access | VPN – Basic** page. The setting **Gateways support IKE over TCP** enables IKE negotiations to be conducted over TCP when necessary. This is important due to the fact that some NAT devices do not correctly translate IKE packets (which are conducted over UDP).

- The second, which is enabled by default, is on the **Remote Access** page of the gateway's Properties. The setting **Support NAT traversal mechanism (UDP Encapsulation)** is enabled by default and provides the ability for clients to function behind NAT devices that do not NAT IPSec traffic correctly. This is mainly because IPSec functions over its own IP protocol (IP Protocol 50), which many devices do not NAT correctly because it is less common than TCP, UDP, and ICMP.

Finally, you must choose the authentication methods your gateway will support. For these exercises, choose **VPN-1 & FireWall-1 Password** on the **Authentication** tab of the **Check Point Gateway** Properties window on your local gateway. If you neglect to check off the appropriate authentication scheme here, your users will all get "Authentication scheme not supported" errors when they attempt to log in.

User Encryption Properties

Assume for this section that you have a preexisting set of users that you want to configure for client encryption. If you have no users defined, refer to Chapter 6 to create a few users before continuing.

Start by opening the Users window by choosing **Users** from the **Manage** menu in the SmartDashboard GUI. Select an existing user and click **Edit**. The User Properties window appears. Select the **Encryption** tab; you are presented with only one option, **IKE**. (Previously, FWZ was also an option here, but it has been decommissioned.) Select **IKE** and click **Edit**. Using IKE, the user's authentication parameters are defined in the Authentication tab and Encryption properties are defined in the Encryption tab. If you use Simplified-mode policies, the Encryption properties are defined globally in the Remote Access page rather than the Encryption tab.

IKE Authentication

Within the IPSec specification, there are only two methods to authenticate an IPSec tunnel: Pre-Shared Secret and Public Key. These options are shown in Figure 10.15.

Because these two options do not provide the flexibility that most companies require, Check Point developed a method to utilize the Public Key option to authenticate users for other authentication methods. This method is called Hybrid Mode Authentication. Hybrid Mode Authentication is enabled by default and is in the **Remote Access | VPN – Basic** page in **Policy | Global Properties**. Using Hybrid mode, users can be authenticated using any of the other available mechanisms within the **Authentication** tab of **User Properties** in addition to the built-in digital certificates, external CAs, and LDAP.

Figure 10.15 IKE Phase 2 Properties

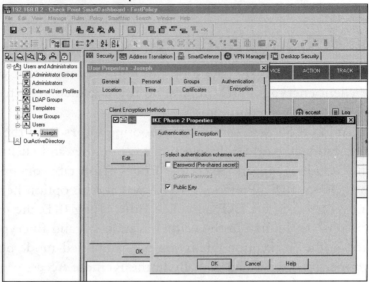

Client Encryption Rules

Your client encryption rule in Traditional mode will look as follows (see Figure 10.16):

- **Source** AllUsers@Any
- **Destination** LAN
- **Service** Any
- **Action** Client Encrypt
- **Track** Log

Figure 10.16 SecuRemote Client Encrypt Rule

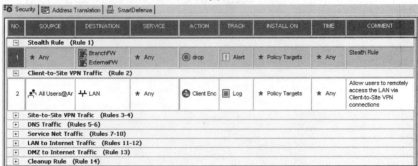

In both Simplified and Traditional modes, the Source column must specify a group of users and a location; the location can be Any, or it can be a specific allowable source network. Destination should be the VPN domain defined for those users on the local gateway object or at least a host inside the VPN domain to which users can connect.

Your client encryption rule in Simplified mode will look as follows (see Figure 10.17):

- **Source** AllUsers@Any

- **Destination** LAN

- **VPN** RemoteAccess

- **Service** Any

- **Action** Accept

- **Track** Log

Figure 10.17 SecuRemote Client Encrypt Rule

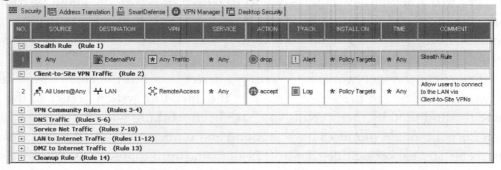

Once the rule is in place in Traditional mode, you can edit the Client Encrypt properties by double-clicking the **Client Encrypt** icon (see Figure 10.18). If the source column of your Rule Base conflicts with allowed sources in the User Properties setup, the Client Encrypt properties will specify how to resolve the conflict. You can specify that the intersection of the allowed user sources and the Rule Base determine when to allow access or to ignore the user database altogether.

Figure 10.18 Client Encrypt Properties

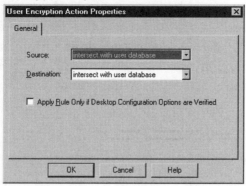

Installing SecuRemote Client Software

The SecuRemote client software must be installed on all the users' workstations or laptops to which you as an administrator would like to give mobile access to your VPN domain. SecuRemote currently supports Windows 2000, NT, 98 SE, XP, and ME and typically requires 32MB to 64MB of RAM and about 6MB of disk space to install. It cannot be installed alongside FireWall-1. There is also a Linux version as well as a Macintosh version that supports OS 8 and OS 9 and a version for Windows PocketPC PDAs.

The client software works by inserting a driver between the client's physical network interface and the TCP/IP stack in the operating system kernel, in the same method used by the firewalls you have been working with to this point. This kernel module monitors both inbound and outbound TCP/IP traffic and intercepts any packet destined for a VPN domain (from topology downloaded during site creation or update). The packet is then handed off to a user-space daemon, which handles user authentication and key exchange with the SecuRemote server, as well as encryption, should authentication succeed.

Installation is handled by a fairly straightforward graphical setup program; however, there are some points worth noting:

- You need to install Desktop Security Support only if you are using SecureClient (see Figure 10.19 and Chapter 11, "Securing Remote Clients"). This is a piece of software that must be licensed separately from Check Point for a fee. If cost is a concern or you are using another desktop firewall solution, you may opt for SecuRemote.

Figure 10.19 SecuRemote Desktop Security Prompt During Installation

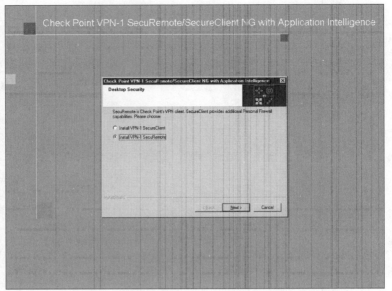

- If you do not install Desktop Security, you will be asked on which adapters to bind the SecuRemote kernel module (see Figure 10.20). You can choose "Install on all network adapters" (which would include Ethernet *and* dialup adapters) or "Install on dialup adapters only." The latter would be appropriate for remote users with a dialup ISP who would never use their Ethernet interface to access the VPN domain from the outside. Mobile salespeople often fall into this category; they use dialup access when on the road and use Ethernet to plug into the LAN when they are in the office. However, for this configuration, other options would work just as well.

Figure 10.20 SecuRemote Adapter Configuration Screen During Installation

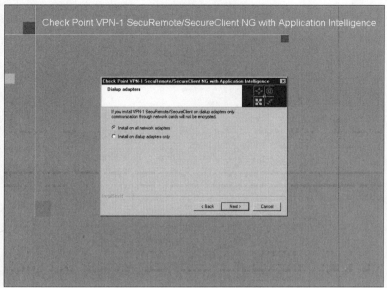

- You can install over an older version of SecuRemote. You will be asked if you want to update the previous version (which saves site and configuration information), or if you would like to overwrite the existing version.

- Although the client software is available for free download, a license is still required on the management station to use SecuRemote with Check Point NG AI.

- The SecureClient Packaging Tool can also be used to create self-extracting, preconfigured packages to distribute to client systems. This requires you to obtain a SecureClient license from Check Point, but it quickly pays for itself in decreased help desk calls.

Using SecuRemote Client Software

Once the client software is installed, you can start the SecuRemote GUI by double-clicking the envelope icon in your taskbar. Before you can use SecuRemote, you must create a new site by choosing **Create New Site** from the **Sites** menu (see Figure 10.21). Enter the IP address or hostname of your SecuRemote server (which is the gateway through which you will be connecting), and click **OK**. The site key information and topology will be downloaded automatically and stored in a file named userc.C on the client, in the SecuRemote installation's database directory.

Figure 10.21 Creating a New Site

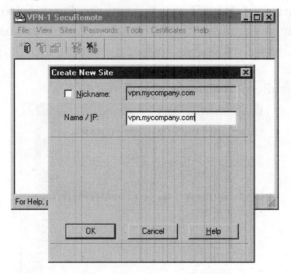

Once a site you have successfully created a site, you can attempt a connection to something in your VPN domain. You should see an authentication dialog box pop up (see Figure 10.22); this is where you enter one of the previously defined usernames and passwords, after which you will be allowed access. This is an example of Transparent mode in action.

Figure 10.22 SecuRemote Authentication Window

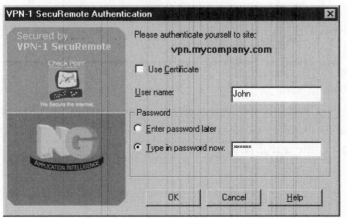

If you want to have a login that functions more like Microsoft's Dial-Up Networking, double-click the envelope in your taskbar and select **Tools | Configure Client Mode**. Select **Connect** and click **OK**. You will be notified that for these changes to take effect, you need to restart SecuRemote. Select **File | Stop VPN-1 SecuRemote** to stop the client, and then select **Check Point VPN-1 SecuRemote | SecuRemote** from the **Start | Programs** menu. Once SecuRemote has initialized and you see it in your taskbar, left-click it, and you will see the connect dialog box shown in Figure 10.23.

Figure 10.23 SecuRemote Connection Window

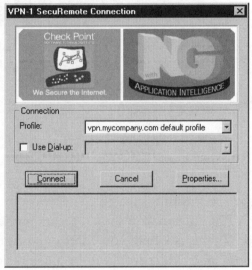

Click **Connect**, and the rest of the login process is completed similarly to Transparent mode. This mode is easier for many users to understand and is probably the most common method of deployment today. To get back to the window shown in Figure 10.21, simply right-click the envelope in the taskbar and select **Configure**.

After a topology change, you need to update the SecuRemote clients so that their topology is in sync with the SecuRemote server. Updating the site can be done manually by right-clicking the site icon and choosing **Update Site**. This works for a small number of clients, but if you have a large number of remote users, you can enable automatic update (in SecuRemote version 4.1 or NG) in one of three ways:

- Prompt the client to update its topology whenever SecuRemote is started by changing *:desktop_update_at_start (false)* to *True* in the *:props* section of the objects_5_0.C file on the management station. This can be refused by the client.

- Prompt for update of *all* defined site topologies whenever SecuRemote is started by changing *:update_topo_at_start (false)* to *True* the *:props* section of the userc.C file on the desktop.

- Force updating of the site topology every *n* seconds by updating *:desktop_update_frequency (n)* to the *:props* section of the objects_5_0.C file on the management station.

Configuring & Implementing…

Making Changes to Objects_5_0.C Stick

Editing the objects_5_0.C file can be tricky—if it's not done correctly; your changes will be lost. You should follow these recommendations when making changes to the objects_5_0.C file on your management server. Note that this file is called objects.C on the firewall module, as it was in past versions of Check Point FireWall-1. Editing this file on the firewall module will have no effect, since it gets overwritten by the objects_5_0.C from the management station during policy installs. In addition, see Chapter 8, "Managing Policies and Logs," for a discussion of the dbedit tool, which can be used to make changes to objects defined in objects_5_0.C. Of course, dbedit should be used to make all changes to the file, but in the event you must edit the file directly, follow these steps:

1. Close all GUI clients.
2. Perform *cpstop* on the management console.
3. Delete or rename the files objects_5_0.C.sav and objects_5_0.C.bak.
4. Back up the original objects_5_0.C.
5. Make the necessary changes to the objects_5_0.C file and save them.
6. Perform *cpstart* on the management console.
7. Install the security policy to all modules.

Secure Domain Login

Secure Domain Login (SDL) enables users to encrypt traffic to a Windows NT domain controller behind a FireWall-1 firewall. Normally, SecuRemote is activated *after* domain login, meaning that domain login is not encrypted. To enable SDL after installation, choose **Enable Secure Domain Logon** from the **Passwords** menu. This will take effect only after a reboot. Note that SDL over a dialup connection is only supported when using the Windows 2000 or NT clients—the 98 or ME clients only support SDL over an Ethernet adapter when configured as part of a domain.

In order to successfully log in to an NT domain, you need to make sure you have the following client settings:

- Your "Client for Microsoft Networks" has "Log on to Windows NT Domain" checked.

- Your dialup profile is configured with your internal WINS server address.

- *Or* you need an LMHOSTS entry that points to your primary or backup domain controllers.

Designing & Planning…

VPN Management

Easy VPN management is directly related to network topology choices. In general, one VPN endpoint with multiple small VPN domains behind it will be easier to manage than multiple distinct gateways, each with one VPN domain. The need for backend security can be best met by using gateways as needed behind the sole VPN endpoint. Each smaller gateway must then be configured to pass through encrypted traffic and key exchange traffic untouched. You can use Table 10.2 to assist in this effort.

Table 10.2 VPN Ports and Protocols

Encryption Scheme	Ports/Protocols Used
IKE	IKE (UDP port 500), ESP (IP protocol 50), AH (IP protocol 51), IKE over TCP (TCP port 500)*, UDP encapsulation (UDP port 2476)*,FW1_topo (TCP port 254), tunnel_test (UDP port 18234)*

* Not always necessary

Summary

Virtual private networks (VPNs) can be used to provide authenticity, privacy, and data integrity. There are two types of VPNs: site-to-site and client-to-site. Both utilize IKE for key management and several encryption algorithms to do the actual encrypting of traffic. The process of establishing a site-to-site VPN can be broken down into three steps: configuring the firewall and/or management stations, configuring the VPN domain, and adding encryption rules to the security policy Rule Base. Establishing a client-to-site VPN is similar, except that users are configured with the proper authentication method, and then the Rule Base is updated with a Client Encrypt rule. Remote users must install the SecuRemote software and download SecuRemote server topology before they can use a client-to-site VPN. Several methods exist for automatically updating site topology. Self-extracting packages can be created to ease the installation and configuration of software onto client systems. (Self-extracting packages are covered in more depth in Chapter 11.)

Solutions Fast Track

Encryption Schemes

- ☑ VPNs can provide privacy, authenticity, and data integrity.
- ☑ Key exchange is public (asymmetric); encryption is symmetric for performance.
- ☑ Beware of the security of proprietary encryption schemes.

Configuring an IKE VPN

- ☑ Double-check encryption rule properties to make sure they are identical.
- ☑ Make sure key exchange rules (if any) are above your stealth rule.
- ☑ Simplified mode can make it easy and quick to bring up even many site-to-site tunnels.
- ☑ It is a good idea to disable NAT for any encrypted traffic between VPN domains.

Configuring a SecuRemote VPN

- ☑ SecuRemote can be used with dialup or Ethernet adapters.
- ☑ Secure Domain Login, or SDL, is possible with SecuRemote.
- ☑ Several methods exist for automatically updating site topology.

Installing SecuRemote Client Software

- ☑ Your main choices when installing the SecuRemote client are whether to bind SecuRemote to all adapters or just your dialup adapter and whether to enable desktop security (see Chapter 11, "Securing Remote Clients").

Using SecuRemote Client Software

- ☑ The IP address or hostname used in creating your "site" is the IP address or hostname of the firewall gateway through which you will be connecting, or, in the case of a distributed installation, the IP address or hostname of that gateway's management console.
- ☑ Topology downloads are saved on the client locally in the file userc.C in the SecuRemote installation directory.

Frequently Asked Questions

The following Frequently Asked Questions, answered by the authors of this book, are designed to both measure your understanding of the concepts presented in this chapter and to assist you with real-life implementation of these concepts. To have your questions about this chapter answered by the author, browse to **www.syngress.com/solutions** and click on the **"Ask the Author"** form. You will also gain access to thousands of other FAQs at ITFAQnet.com.

Q: Why can't I ping such-and-such host in my peer's VPN domain?

A: This may not be allowed by policy. Check your policy's Global Properties, and make sure that ICMP is not being accepted first, before any encryption rules. Try a different protocol if you have no control over the peer policy (for example, Telnet to port 25 on a mail server in the peer's VPN domain).

Q: What does "No response from peer: Scheme IKE" mean when it appears in logs during VPN testing?

A: Confirm that fwd and isakmpd are running on your peer gateway. Isakmpd listens on UDP port 500; you can use the *netstat* command to double-check this (on UNIX platforms and Windows platforms). This message is also seen when the remote VPN peer does not respond to the firewall's request to establish a secure tunnel.

Q: What does the error message "No proposal chosen" mean?

A: The two-encryption rule properties differ in some way, or one gateway supports an encryption method that another doesn't.

Q: I want my salespeople to be able to log on and browse my NT/domain from the field. How can I do this?

A: See the section on "Secure Domain Logon" in this chapter.

Q: I have a really large network, with a lot of VPN traffic to and from multiple VPN domains, and I notice frequent connection interruptions. Why is this?

A: Check to make sure that **Key Exchange for Subnets** is enabled. Check the size of the connection table. Check gateway memory usage and processor load (*fw tab −t connections −s* and *fw ctl pstat*).

Q: What does "gateway connected to both endpoints" mean?

A: This message usually appears due to broadcast traffic that is generated on your internal network. If your encryption rule has your local network in both the source and destination, and the local network object has **Broadcast address included** checked in the network properties **General** tab, you may receive these messages. They are harmless and are merely stating that the source and destination of this traffic match the encryption rule, but both endpoints are connected locally—therefore no encryption will take place.

## Chapter 11

Securing Remote Clients

Solutions in this Chapter:

- Installing and Configuring a Policy Server
- Desktop Security Options
- Installing SecureClient Software
- Logging into the Policy Server

Introduction

If your organization wants to use a virtual private network (VPN) client, but you are concerned about allowing clients' personal computers into your network, do not worry. Check Point solves this problem by giving you control of the remote users' desktop security. You can configure specific properties for your mobile users' desktops, including prohibiting connections to their PC's when they have remote software running. That way, if they are running a Web server on their PC, you do not have to worry about their server being compromised while they have a connection into your private network.

SecureClient software is simply the SecuRemote software package discussed in the previous chapter with additional features. These features include a personal firewall on your mobile users' PCs that you control via SmartDashboard, as well as Secure Configuration Verification (SCV), which allows an administrator to define the attributes of a system secure enough to access the VPN. Within SmartDashboard, you can define detailed policies that SecureClient downloads when a user logs in to your firewall's policy server.

This chapter shows you how to install and configure a policy server, and how to configure different desktop policies for your users. A policy server can reside on one of your firewall modules, or it can be set up as a separate server to strictly enforce clients' security policies.

After describing the policy server in full detail, this chapter shows you how to install the SecureClient software, and how to use the SecureClient Packaging Tool on the Next Generation with Application Intelligence (NG AI) CD.

Installing and Configuring a Policy Server

The first step toward ensuring that your remote users' desktops adhere to your security policies, is to install and configure a policy server. Once the policy server is installed and configured, it will be able to transmit the appropriate security settings to the SecureClient process running on the remote desktops.

Installing from CD-ROM

The policy server can be found on the Check Point NG AI CD-ROM. To install the policy server onto your firewall module, insert the CD-ROM, and from the

Add Products option, choose **Install additional Check Point products**. Then select **SecureClient Policy Server**, as shown in Figure 11.1.

Figure 11.1 Check Point Policy Server Installation

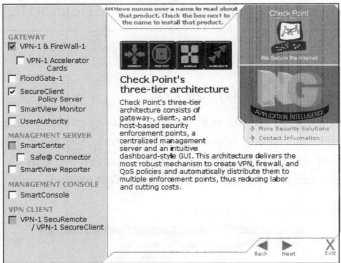

This will load the Check Point installation wizard, which will first check that the VPN-1/FireWall-1 module is installed. If not, you will be required to install the VPN-1/FireWall-1 module prior to continuing with the policy server installation.

The policy server installation will proceed, and will not require any further input. Once it is complete, ensure that you have the appropriate license installed on your firewall and management station. The license on the management station must contain sufficient users for the number of actual users connecting to your environment. The license on the firewall must contain a license for the policy server, which is available with any VPN-1 Pro module. If your firewall license does not have a policy server SKU, you can regenerate it in UserCenter. If you do not know whether your license contains policy server functionality, consult your reseller, local Check Point office, or call Check Point Support and speak to Customer Advocacy.

Now that the policy server component of Check Point NG AI is installed, you can configure your security policy.

Starting with NG FP1, a Software Distribution Server (SDS) is included in the policy server package. NG FP1 and later SecureClient packages also include a Software Distribution Agent, which checks the SDS for updated software revisions using Transmission Control Protocol (TCP) port 18332.

Configuring a Policy Server

The first step in configuring the policy server is to open the policy editor, go to **Manage**, and edit the firewall object. In this example, the firewall object is called *ExternalFW*. From the **General Properties** tab, under the **Check Point Products** section, check **SecureClient Policy Server**, as shown in Figure 11.2.

Figure 11.2 General Firewall Properties

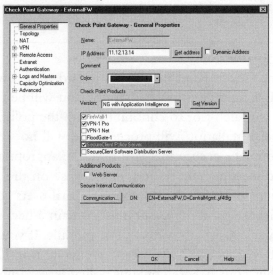

By selecting this option, you are telling the firewall that the SecureClient policy server is installed. You may now continue to configure its remaining options.

Next, go to the **Authentication** tab of your firewall object. Here, you will see a new option that allows you to define a group of users, as shown in Figure 11.3.

Figure 11.3 Authentication Firewall Properties

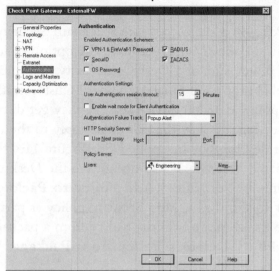

Select the user group that the policy server is going to manage. This user group should contain all of the SecureClient users who will log on to the policy server. If you are not restricting certain users from utilizing the VPN, you may select **All Users**, which allows any defined user to log on to the policy server. In this example, only Engineering users are able to log on to this policy server. Later, you will add all applicable users to this group. Once you install the policy, the policy server will start running.

Desktop Security Options

There are two main areas of the policy editor that are important to desktop security:

- The Desktop Security policy
- The Remote Access global properties.

Both of these enable you to control various aspects of what is transmitted to the SecureClient users by the policy server.

Desktop Security Policy

Located on the main screen of the policy editor, the Desktop Security tab enables you to specify what access your users have. The Desktop Security

Rulebase is similar to the standard Security Policy Rulebase, with some important distinctions.

The Desktop Policy is installed just like a standard Security Policy. When you select **Install** from the Policy Menu, you have the option of installing an Advanced Security policy and/or a Desktop Security policy. Both are selected by default (per the global properties SmartDashboard Customization), and once you install the desktop policy onto the policy servers, they get distributed to the SecureClients as they log in. Only the rules that apply to the user who belongs to the SecureClient desktop will be applied. See Figure 11.4 for an example of a basic Desktop Security Rulebase. If you do not see the Desktop Security tab in SmartDashboard, simply select **File | Add Policy to Package** and check **Desktop Security** to show a Desktop Security policy as part of this policy package. To remove the Desktop Security policy from a package, open the package and select **File | Delete | Policy from Package**.

Figure 11.4 Desktop Security Rulebase

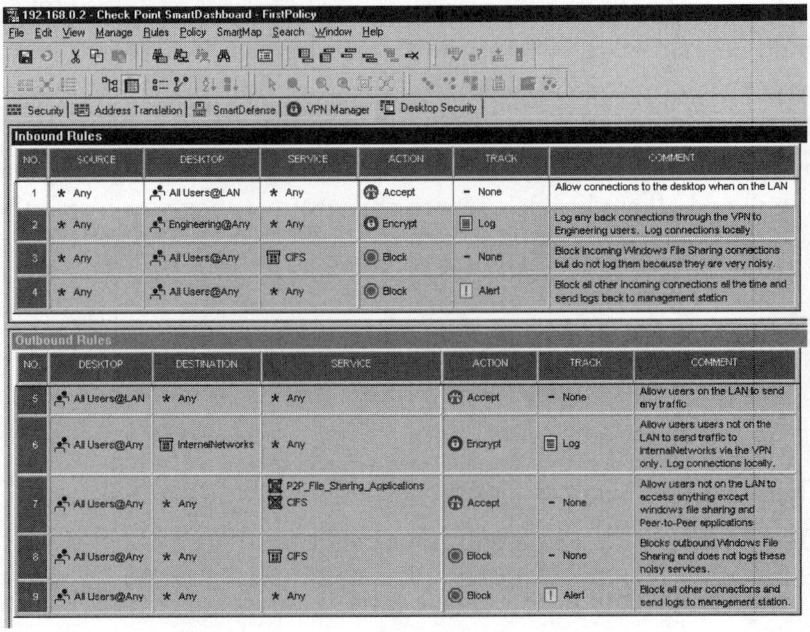

Configuring & Implementing...

SecureClient Logging

Unlike other firewall logs, when you set **Track** to **Log** in the Desktop Security policy, logs are kept on the local SecureClient workstation. These logs can be viewed with the SecureClient Diagnostics Log page, which is included as part of SecureClient installation.

If you set **Track** to **Alert**, the SecureClient workstation will send these log entries back to the policy server, which are then consolidated with the normal FireWall-1 log and viewable via SmartView Tracker.

Notice that unlike the normal security policy, there are Inbound Rules and Outbound Rules. These are inbound and outbound in relation to the desktop system, which will be doing the policy enforcement, not the policy server you are pushing your policy to. In the initial release of Check Point NG, this was one single rulebase, but due to the confusion of many administrators, in NG FP1 and later it has been separated into two sections. Also, even though there are inbound and outbound sections, you do not need to enter each piece of a connection (one in the outbound and a returning packet in the inbound) because all of this functions on connections, not packets. This is because the desktop firewall also utilizes stateful inspection, which keeps track of each session and only permits packets that are known to be part of that session. As a result, you only need to explicitly permit packets in the direction that the connection is initiated.

In Figure 11.4, Rule 1 allows traffic from anywhere to the users' workstations for any service, but only while they are on the local area network (LAN). Rule 2 allows connections to a desktop when a user in the Engineering group is logged into the VPN and authenticated by the policy server. These connections will be logged locally, but not sent consolidated with the logs seen in SmartView Tracker. Note that because Encrypt is selected as the action, only connections via the VPN are allowed by this rule; cleartext connections from across the Internet are not allowed. Rule 3 then drops any incoming Windows file sharing connections and broadcasts, and does not log them. The final Inbound rule, Rule 4, is similar in functionality to the Stealth Rule found in a typical security policy—if not explicitly allowed, block the connection, log it, and the next time that user logs into the policy server, send the logs to be consolidated with the rest of the logs to be viewed via SmartView Tracker or reported on by SmartView Reporter.

The Outbound Rules section contains rules to be applied for connections originating from the desktop system itself. As you can see from the rule numberings, this is a continuation of the same policy. Rule 5 allows users on the LAN to communicate with anything. The assumption here is that the security on the LAN will take care of providing access controls. Rule 6 is for users that are not on the LAN allowing access to anything on the internal network as long as it is over the VPN (due to the Encrypt action). While users are not on the LAN, they still require access to systems on the Internet for Web browsing and other functions. Rule 7 allows them to establish connections to anything on the Internet unless it is a Windows file sharing or peer-to-peer application. Rule 8 blocks connection attempts using Windows file sharing, and does not log them, and Rule 9 blocks all other outbound connections similar to a Cleanup rule in a typical security policy. Because of what is defined before this rule, it will likely only block access to peer-to-peer applications and log them. This will, however, show which users are attempting to use peer-to-peer applications in SmartView Tracker as well as create reports in SmartView Reporter of which users are attempting to use peer-to-peer applications.

The Desktop Security Rulebase adds an implicit rule to the bottom of the rulebase that denies all inbound communication. This means that anything not explicitly allowed in the Desktop Security Rulebase is blocked. Note that packets that are dropped due to the implicit drop rule are not logged; if you want to log drop packets, you can add your own explicit drop rule at the bottom of this rulebase. The Desktop Security Rulebase also has an implicit rule, which allows all outgoing traffic and does not log it. If you plan on restricting what a user is able to access outbound, it is imperative to add a rule similar to Rule 9.

Remote Access Global Properties

The Remote Access Global Properties screen enables you to configure various additional aspects of the SecuRemote and SecureClient desktop environment. Keep in mind that SecureClient uses the same Client Encryption software as SecuRemote, and therefore some of the settings shown in Figure 11.5 apply to both sets of users and some only apply to users of SecureClient.

Figure 11.5 Remote Access Global Properties

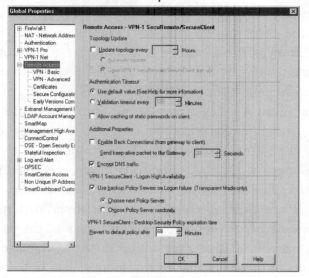

The Topology Update section defines how topology updates will be handled. By default, the client will update its site once a week, but this can be changed to a specific number of hours by checking the **Update topology every** *n* **Hours** checkbox and setting the number of hours. There are also two options:

- **Automatic Update** This tells the client to do the updates automatically when the user connects to the VPN. This is the default.

- **Upon VPN-1 SecuRemote/SecureClient start up** This selection tells the client to automatically prompt the user to connect to the VPN every time the client is started, which is typically whenever they boot the system logs into the operating system (OS) to use it.

Next are the Authentication Timeout settings. You may choose **Use default values**, which allows an Internet Key Exchange (IKE) Phase 1 authentication to be valid for one day. You can choose to lower this value by selecting **Validation timeout every** *n* **Minutes** and selecting the number of minutes. If you select **Allow Caching of static passwords on client**, users with authentication methods of OS or VPN-1/FireWall-1 password will only have to authenticate when SecureClient connects initially.

The Additional Properties section allows an administrator to define whether to allow back connections (connections originating from the LAN directed to the desktop) and if so, how often to send a keep-alive packet to the gateway. This is necessary because connections may time out or fail incoming to the VPN client due to firewall or Network Address Translation (NAT) limitations on devices between the client and the gateway. This ensures that the VPN tunnel is always available. **Encrypt DNS traffic** determines whether Domain Name System (DNS) queries sent by the desktop to a DNS server located on the corporate LAN are to be sent through the VPN tunnel or in the clear.

When logging on to a policy server using SecureClient, one may not always be available. This setting defines what action to take if a policy server is unreachable from the client and the client is using Transparent Mode to connect. (If the client is using Connect Mode, the action to be taken is defined in the Connection Profile.) The two options are fairly self explanatory. **Choose next Policy Server** tells the client to connect in a predefined pattern. **Choose Policy Server randomly** attempts to connect to any of the policy servers in a random method, whereby allowing the administrator to disperse the load on other policy servers in the event that one is down.

The final option on this page (VPN-1 SecureClient – Desktop Security Policy expiration time) deals with how long a policy downloaded from a policy server is valid before the client seeks to update itself and receive a new Desktop Security policy. When half of the time defined here has elapsed, the client will connect to the policy server to retrieve an updated version (if necessary) and start the timer over again. If this renewal fails, after half of the remaining time, a connection will be attempted again. If the client reaches the amount of time set in **Revert to default policy after n minutes**, it will revert back to its default policy. The number of minutes a policy will be valid for can be set by changing the value from 60 (default) to the length of time desired. This means that after 30 minutes it will attempt to renew the policy, then if that fails, after 15 minutes (of the remaining 30 minutes) it will attempt to renew again and so on.

VPN – Basic

Figure 11.6 presents options that deal with the basics of the VPN connection, how users are allowed to authenticate, what connectivity enhancements are enabled, and if they are required to integrate with legacy Nokia VPN clients.

Figure 11.6 Remote Access – VPN Basic Global Properties

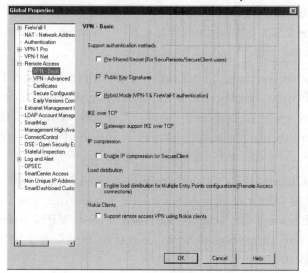

The setting fields are as follows:

- **Support Authentication Methods** IKE itself has two methods for authenticating VPN connections; **Pre-Shared Secret** and **Public Key Signatures** The final option, **Hybrid Mode (VPN-1 & FireWall-1 Authentication)**, is used to authenticate users using other methods (such as SecurID, Radius, and internally managed passwords) as defined on the user's Authentication tab.

- **IKE over TCP** Eventually, one of your users will end up connecting from behind a device that does not support fragmented User Datagram Protocol (UDP) packets correctly, and you will be required to check the **Gateways support IKE over TCP** option. Gateways will always support the standard IKE implementation, which happens over UDP. This allows clients to connect using TCP if it detects a problem using UDP. It should be noted that this option only allows the gateways to use IKE over TCP, this does not tell the clients to use IKE over TCP. The client's setting must be done from the client for Transparent Mode (**Tools | Global IKE Settings**) or using Connection Profiles if using Connect Mode.

- **IP Compression** By selecting **Enable IP compression for SecureClient**, you allow the client to negotiate Internet Protocol (IP) compression parameters during key exchange, which allows the effective throughput to be higher than the actual bandwidth. By setting this, all clients running SecureClient (not available with SecuRemote) will negotiate IPCOMP along with the encryption parameters, which will be reflected in the logs in SmartView Tracker.

- **Load Distribution** The **Enable load distribution for Multiple Entry Points configurations (Remote Access Connections)** selection allows administrators to spread the load (bandwidth and CPU) of client connections across gateways in different locations. Multiple entry points will be discussed further in the Chapter 12.

- **Nokia Clients** For a brief period of time, Nokia was distributing its own VPN solution. It was eventually phased out, but for legacy purposes, checking the **Supply remote access VPN using Nokia clients** will allow Nokia VPN clients to establish a VPN tunnel to a Check Point gateway.

VPN – Advanced

The VPN – Advanced page (as seen in Figure 11.7) presents more options that are typically only changed if you are configuring your VPN in a more specific or advanced fashion.

Figure 11.7 Remote Access – VPN Basic Global Properties

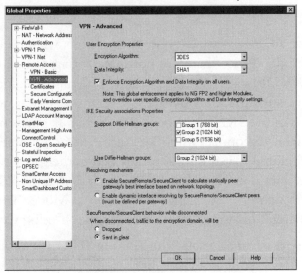

The settings fields are as follows:

User Encryption Properties By default, **Enforce Encryption Algorithm and Data Integrity on all users** is enabled. This allows you to define the Phase 2 encryption properties for all users using SecuRemote or SecureClient.

NOTE

The **Enforce Encryption Algorithm and Data Integrity on all users** option is only available for NG FP2 modules or later. Disable this option if using earlier versions on your gateway(s). If disabled, it can be set on a per-user basis in the Encryption tab of each user's object. For performance reasons, you may wish to select AES-128 instead of 3DES, as it is a less CPU-intensive algorithm for both the gateway and client and has a slightly higher effective key length (AES' 128 bits vs. 3DES's 112 bits). AES-256 is also an option for enforcing the highest levels of security and DES is available for operating in countries where high encryption is not allowed.

- **IKE Security associations Properties** The Diffie-Hellman (DH) group determines the level of encryption used in IKE Phase 1 to exchange keys during IKE Phase 2. This information is downloaded by the client as part of the topology. By default, a new client (no topology yet defined) will use Group 2, so keeping Group 2 enabled is necessary to support the addition of new clients. If using Traditional Mode policies, ensure that the gateway will support the DH groups you specify here.

- **Resolving Mechanism** SecuRemote and SecureClient have the ability to find the interface on the gateway best to communicate with. This is important if you have more than one interface which you want the client to establish a VPN to. For example, if you have one interface for the wireless network and another interface for connections across the Internet, you would want to allow the VPN client to find which one to speak directly with. **Enable SecuRemote/SecureClient to calculate statically peer gateway's best interface based on network topology** will use the primary (external) address of the gateway (on the object's General Properties page) to VPN to only. By selecting

Enable dynamic interface resolving by SecuRemote/
SecureClient peers, you are not enabling the client to try to connect
to each interface, you are only allowing a new option in each VPN
Gateway object's VPN Advanced page called Dynamic Interface
resolving configuration. There you can define whether you wish for an
individual gateway to be resolved statically or dynamically.

■ **SecuRemote/SecureClient behavior while disconnected** In the
beginning, Check Point's VPN clients would simply drop all traffic destined for addresses contained in VPN domains unless it was connected
to the VPN or it recognized that it was on the LAN. This was not
always the ideal option for companies, so Check Point added the option
to simply send traffic in the clear when not connected to the VPN.

NOTE

This option is only valid when the client is in Connect Mode.

Certificates

When users are authenticating themselves to the VPN gateway using Certificates,
there are two options (as seen in Figure 11.8) that become relevant; how to
handle whether the client will check the gateway's certificate and how to handle
the expiration of certificates:

Figure 11.8 Remote Access – Certificates Global Properties

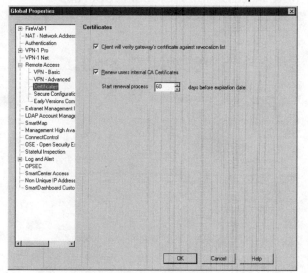

The settings fields are as follows:

- **Client will verify gateway's certificate against revocation list**
  This option tells the VPN client to verify the digital certificate the
  gateway is presenting against the Certificate Authority's Certificate
  Revocation List, to ensure that the gateway's certificate is still valid. This
  is part of any good PKI infrastructure in that digital certificates are continually being compared against published lists of revoked certificates.

- **Renew users internal CA Certificates** This option allows an individual user's certificate to be renewed starting at a specific period of
  time (60 days by default) before it expires, to ensure that the user will
  continue to have access to the VPN without interruption. Certificates
  are valid for two years from the date they are issued by default.

SCV

SCV enables you to control other important aspects of the SecureClient desktop.

Figure 11.9 Remote Access – SCV Global Properties

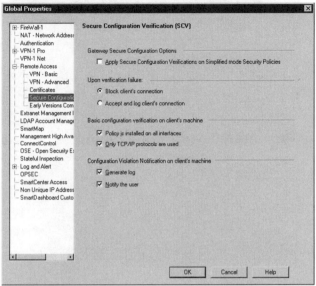

The settings fields are as follows:

- **Gateway Secure Configuration Options** Check the box next to
  Apply Secure Configuration Verification on Simplified mode
  Security Policies to enable the SCV desktop security mechanisms for
  all VPN connections to gateways using Simplified Mode VPN policies.
  Note that SCV is a SecureClient option only. By enforcing desktop
  policies, you may be blocking SecuRemote sessions.

Configuring & Implementing…

SCV and the $FWDIR/conf/local.scv file

SCV options are much more extensive than what is shown in this pane.
The *local.scv* file in the *$FWDIR/conf/* directory is used to define very
granularly how to define a system to be "secure" enough to access the
VPN and pass SCV verification. The options inside the file include IE
Browser configuration, Registry Checks, executing custom scripts,
checking Anti-Virus DAT file versions, checking OS Patch levels and hot
fixes, checking for the existence (or non-existence) of particular pro-

Continued

cesses, checking the local windows user's group, checking the CPU type, and more. The *local.scv* file that is distributed with NG AI has many examples, but is typically not exactly what an organization wants to deploy. You should customize the *local.scv* file before enforcing SCV across your enterprise. A detailed discussion of the SCV policy syntax is available in the *VPN-1 Users Guide for NG AI*.

There is also a graphical user interface (GUI) SCV editor available at www.opsec.com to ease the configuration of SCV options. In addition, multiple vendors such as Trend Micro and Pest Patrol have developed their own additions to SCV to more extensively check their applications. OPSWAT has also developed a number of SCV checks to integrate with Shavlik's HFNetChk/HFNetChkPro, Norton, McAfee, and Internet Explorer as well as validating the hardware identity of client systems. Information on OPSWAT's products can be found at www.opswat.com

- **Upon Verification failure** When a desktop does not pass the SCV checks as defined in this pane and in the local.scv file, you may choose to block connections from that system by selecting **Block client's connection** or simply notify the user (the final option on this page), log that it failed, and allow connections by selecting **Accept and log client's connection**. It is best to simply block the connection; however, when you are beginning to enforce SCV on your user community you may wish to allow the connections, inform the users directly on how to fix their systems (install anti-virus, install Windows patches, and so on), and then after the users have had ample time to update their systems, start blocking connections.

- **Basic configuration verification on client's machine** These basic options have been available since the beginning of SecureClient. During the installation of SecureClient, the user has the option to only install the client on dial-up interfaces, in which case **Policy is installed on all interfaces** becomes relevant. If all interfaces are not protected, the machine may be at risk via the unprotected interface and it will fail SCV. **Only TCP/IP Protocols are used** is also a basic method of checking if non-TCP/IP are in use (such as Internetwork Packet Exchange/Sequenced Packet Exchange [IPX/SPX] or NETBIOS Extended User Interface [NetBEUI]). SecureClient cannot protect these protocols and again, the system is at risk and will fail SCV.

- **Configuration Violation Notification on client's machine** If the desktop fails SCV, you can elect to generate a log locally (**Generate log**) and also **Notify the user** about the failure. If you are going to be blocking connections when verification fails, it is a good idea to notify the user that they are not configured securely and also teach the user how to correct the problem. The error message to display to the user is defined in the *local.scv* file in the **:mismatchmessage** section.

Early Versions Compatibility

This section of the Global Properties window, as shown in Figure 11.10, enables you to configure policies for versions of SecureClient prior to NG.

Figure 11.10 Remote Access – Early Versions Compatibility Global Properties

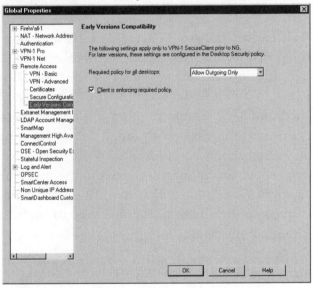

Following are the four policy options in the **Required Policy for all desktops** pull-down window:

- No Policy
- Allow Outgoing & Encrypted
- Allow Outgoing Only
- Allow Encrypted Only

You can see from this list how much more granular the new Desktop Security rulebase is. You can only select one of these policies for all pre-NG SecureClient users, which will work in conjunction with the other Security Configuration Verification options set in the global properties.

- If **No Policy** is selected, there will be no policy loaded on the SecureClient when users log in to their policy server, hence no protection.

- If **Allow Outgoing Only** is selected, only non-encrypted traffic originating from the SecureClient PC will be allowed, and all inbound connection attempts to the SecureClient will be dropped.

- If **Allow Encrypted Only** is selected, only connections to and from the VPN domain will be permitted. For example, with the encrypted policy, mobile users cannot browse Internet sites, but they can download their e-mail from the office while the SecureClient software is running.

- If **Allow Outgoing & Encrypted** is selected, the users can initiate any connections to either the Internet or to the VPN domain, and only encrypted traffic is allowed inbound to the SecureClient.

The **Client is enforcing required policy** option defines whether or not to allow users not configured securely to be able to connect to the VPN and access the LAN.

Traditional Mode (Client Encrypt) Rules

The final step to allowing remote users to use SecureClient when using a Traditional Mode policy securely to a VPN is to set up a client encrypt rule in the standard Security rulebase. This is where the firewall administrator defines the policies that will be installed on the firewall module that will be enforcing the policy and allowing SecuRemote and/or SecureClient users into the VPN domain. (See Figure 11.11.) To do this, open the Policy Editor and add a new rule to the rulebase, similar to the rule used in Chapter 10 for SecuRemote.

Figure 11.11 Client Encrypt Rule

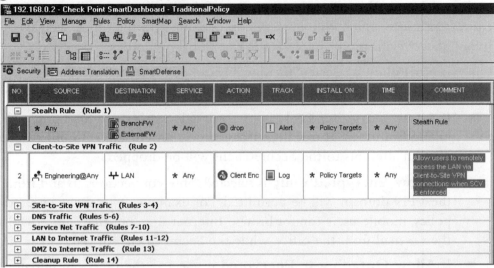

For this example, choose **Engineering** and set **Location** to **No restriction**. The Destination field specifies what objects these users will have access to via the encrypted connection, and Service enables you to further restrict the connection to particular services. Set Action to **Client Encrypt**, Track to **Log**, and ensure that Install On includes the appropriate firewalls.

Now that the rule is configured, there are some additional action properties to consider for SecureClient. To access them, right-click on **Client Encrypt**, and choose **Edit properties**, as shown in Figure 11.12.

Figure 11.12 User Encryption Action Properties

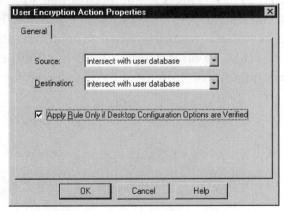

The Source and Destination options discussed in Chapter 10 have not changed. The selection you need to be concerned with is the **Apply Rule only if desktop configuration options are verified**, which relates to the desktop configuration verification options you configured earlier in the global properties and the *local.scv* file. If any of the desktop verifications fail for a particular user, the firewall will not allow the encrypted connection via this rule. This is an effective way to ensure that only properly secured SecureClient desktop users are authenticating and connecting to particular parts of your network. If a user does not have the appropriate desktop policy loaded on their client, they will not have access via this rule. In Traditional Mode, you can have rules that allow SecuRemote users and users that do not pass SCV to connect by not checking the **Apply Rule only if desktop options are verified** option on a per-rule basis. Traditional Mode is necessary to allow connections through the VPN to an anti-virus update server in order to get clients that are failing SCV (because of an out-of-date anti-virus version) up-to-date so that they can be verified by SCV and allowed access to other parts of the network.

Client Authentication supports SecureClient connections as well. To enable this, select **Client Auth** in the action field on a rule, and then edit the **Client Auth Action Properties** and select **Verify secure configuration on Desktop**. This is generally used for cleartext (not encrypted) communication from an internal SecureClient PC.

Simplified Mode Rules

In Simplified Mode, adding rules for SecureClient VPN connections is exactly the same as setting up a rule for SecuRemote connections in Simplified Mode. To not allow SecuRemote connections and only allow SecureClient connections with SCV verified, check the box next to **Apply Secure Configuration Verification on Simplified mode Security Policies** in the Global Properties. Simplified Mode is, as its name suggests, easier to configure but not nearly as flexible as Traditional Mode.

Installing SecureClient Software

Each remote user that will be connecting to your firewall via VPN needs to install the SecureClient software. This software is available on your Check Point NG AI CD-ROM, and the latest version is also downloadable from the Check Point Web site at www.checkpoint.com/techsupport/downloads_sr.html. It is highly recommended that you read the release notes prior to installing or upgrading the SecuRemote/SecureClient software. You will notice that there are two versions on the Web site to download; a self-extracting *.exe* file for end users to run and a compressed *.tgz* version, which is similar to what is provided on the NG AI CD-ROM. The *.tgz* version contains all of the individual files needed by an administrator to create a customized installation, which is discussed later in the "SecureClient Packaging Tool" section.

You may notice that the software package is called SecuRemote/SecureClient. The installation is for both VPN clients, with the important distinction being that SecuRemote does not contain the desktop security components that SecureClient does. This means that with SecuRemote, the user's desktop will not be protected from external attacks, nor will they receive policy updates from your policy server. To install the SecureClient software, perform the following steps:

1. Run the SecuRemote/SecureClient installation program. If you have a previous version of SecuRemote or SecureClient on your workstation, you will be asked if you would like to upgrade or overwrite the old version, as shown in Figure 11.13. Upgrading your previous version of SecuRemote/SecureClient preserves your configuration data, so you would be wise to take this option. Overwriting may be necessary if there is something wrong with the previous version, and you want to start with a clean installation. Also, if you want to switch from SecuRemote to SecureClient or vice versa, choose overwrite, since upgrading will only upgrade the type of client you already have installed. Whichever option you choose, click **Next** to continue.

Figure 11.13 Previous Version Screen

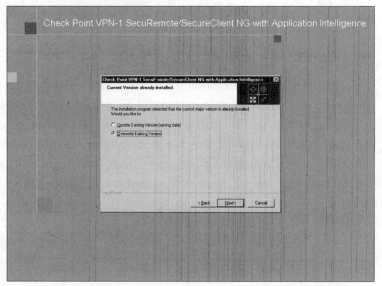

2. Next, you will be asked if you want to install SecureClient or
    SecuRemote, as shown in Figure 11.14. Unless you have a particular
    reason not to provide personal firewall functionality for this client, it
    would be best to take advantage of these additional security features by
    installing SecureClient. Select the checkbox for Install VPN-1
    SecureClient and click **Next**.

Figure 11.14 SecureClient

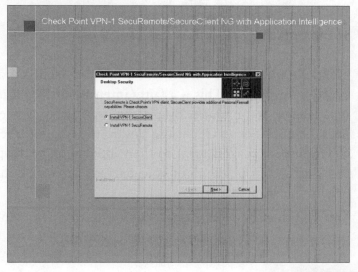

3. Next, you will be asked what network adapters you would like to bind SecuRemote/SecureClient to, as shown in Figure 11.15. The most secure method of running SecuRemote/SecureClient is to bind it to all adapters. Binding to all adapters means that traffic passing through any physical interface on the desktop will be secured and encrypted. Otherwise, it is increasingly possible for unauthorized access attempts via one of the desktop's other network interfaces. This option also relates to the Desktop Configuration Verification where you specified whether or not the policy must be installed on all interfaces. If you selected this option and you do not choose to install on all adapters here, this client will be denied access. Select **Install on all network adapters** and click **Next**.

Figure 11.15 Network Adapters

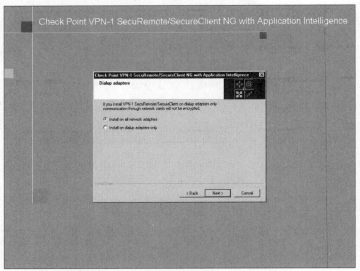

4. Next, the installation wizard will install the SecuRemote/SecureClient kernel into the OS. This is a fairly intensive and delicate process that may take several minutes. By placing itself at the OS level, SecuRemote/SecureClient can ensure the highest level of security, since it will inspect packets prior to their interaction with applications. Note that during this phase, all of your current network connections will be briefly interrupted.

5. You will then be prompted to restart your system, which is required prior to using SecuRemote/SecureClient.

SecureClient Packaging Tool

To reduce the amount of configuration and customization each remote user must perform to their VPN client, Check Point provides the SecureClient Packaging Tool. This tool enables you to create a customized SecureClient package that you can distribute to your remote users. The end result is an easy-to-install, self-extracting SecureClient executable file that is designed to your specifications. The SecureClient Packaging Tool is installed from your Check Point NG AI CD-ROM. The installation of the SecureClient Packaging Tool is part of the Management Clients installation covered in Chapter 2.

1. Once installed, the SC Packaging Tool is run from the **Start | Check Point Management Clients** section. Upon loading the tool, you will see the log-in screen as shown in Figure 11.16. You will log in to the SC Packaging Tool with the same credentials you used to log into SmartDashboard. Click **OK** to log in.

    Figure 11.16 Packaging Tool Login

2. The first time you log in, you will see a blank window. Figure 11.17 shows this window with a list of profiles. You will want to create a new profile. To do this, go to the **Profile** menu, and choose **New**. Click **Next** on the welcome screen.

Figure 11.17 List of Profiles

3. You will now see the General configuration screen, as shown in Figure 11.18. For **Profile name**, enter a descriptive name for this profile. Note that this name can only contain up to 256 alphanumeric characters and cannot contain any spaces. In this case, you will use StandardProfile. The **Comment** section can include a more detailed comment about this profile. Once you have entered these, click **Next**.

Figure 11.18 General Properties

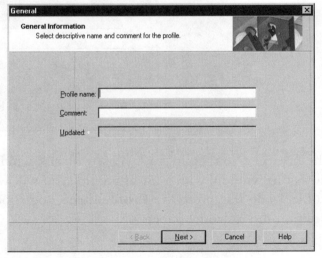

4. Next, you will be presented with your first configuration options, as shown in Figure 11.19. These configurations affect how the end–user will interact with the application. **Transparent mode** watches for packets leaving the desktop directed towards the VPN domain of any of the gateways and prompts for authentication only when it sees traffic destined for one. This can be annoying when a desktop system is continually polling a printer or print server and the client insists on connecting. **Connect mode** is similar to dial-up networking, and therefore end users seem to understand it better. Click on the envelope in the taskbar and it presents a screen that has a button named **Connect**. Connect mode is probably the most widely deployed now.

   The other selection on this page is whether or not to allow the user to change between modes in the SecureClient GUI. For simplicity, most organizations elect to select one mode and not enable mode transition so that helpdesk employees have a single configuration to troubleshoot.

Figure 11.19 Client Mode Configuration

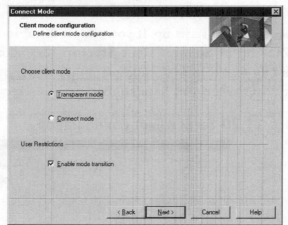

5. You will next see the SecureClient configuration window, as shown in Figure 11.20. The options on this screen are defined below.

   ■ **Allow clear connections for Encrypt action when inside the encryption domain** When selected, this option allows unencrypted connections whenever both the source and destination of the connection are within the VPN domain (for example, when a laptop returns to the corporate campus and attempts to connect to an internal server). When this is the case, clear connections are allowed even if "Encrypt" is specified in the Desktop Security rulebase.

- **Accept DHCP response without explicit inbound rule** By default, SecureClient will accept dynamic host control protocol (DHCP) responses regardless of whether or not they are defined in the Desktop Security rulebase. If you do not select this option, these DHCP connections will only be allowed if they are defined explicitly in the rulebase.
- **Restrict SecureClient user intervention** As described in the window, selecting this object will hide the **Disable Policy** item from the SecureClient menus. This removes the remote user's ability to disable the policy their SecureClient receives from the policy server.
- **Policy Server** When selected, the **Logon to Policy Server at SecureClient Startup** option will result in the remote user being prompted to log on to the policy server defined as soon as SecureClient starts up. If you choose **Enable Policy Server Load Sharing at SecureClient Startup**, the logon request will be randomly sent to one of multiple policy servers.

Click **Next** when you have configured this screen.

Figure 11.20 SecureClient Configuration

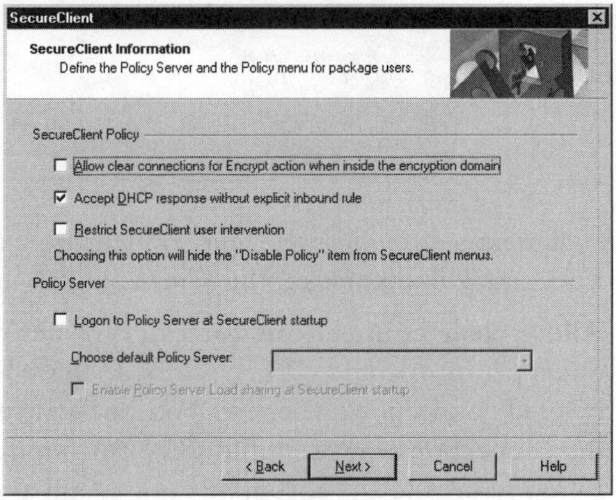

6. You will now see the **Additional Information** options, as shown in Figure 11.21. Here, you can select the options you want to enable for connectivity enhancements. **IKE over TCP** enables the IKE negotiation to happen over TCP port 500 instead of UDP port 500 as necessary, since some devices do not correctly know how to translate fragmented UDP packets. **Force UDP encapsulation for IPSec Connections** is useful in cases when the SecureClient is connected behind a NAT gateway; as some NAT gateways are unable to route ESP/AH packets properly for an Secure Internet Protocol (IPSec) VPN. Some NAT devices do not allow you to set up NAT for these protocols. Basically, it can only handle TCP, UDP, and Internet Control Message Protocol (ICMP). ESP and AH use protocols 50 and 51; these are needed along with the IKE service on UDP 500 for IPSec communication. Table 11.1 shows you which TCP, UDP, and IP protocols each encryption scheme uses. If you have a policy server behind a firewall, these are the ports that you need to open.

Here you are also allowed to define whether or not to give the user the option to stop SecuRemote/SecureClient. Note that even if the user stops SecureClient, the desktop will still be protected because it only stops the service, it does not remove the driver that is doing the enforcement. This screen tells you to decide how to handle connections if the user selects to erase the passwords. You can choose to allow or block (the default) already established connections.

The last option on this page is **to "Use third party authentication DLL**. This is used if you want to use a mechanism outside of what Check Point has provided for authenticating users. Examples of this include biometrics and token-based authentication systems. If you are using a system that has been OPSEC-certified to use Secure Authentication API (SAA), configure this as appropriate per the vendor's documentation.

Click **Next** to continue.

Figure 11.21 Additional Information

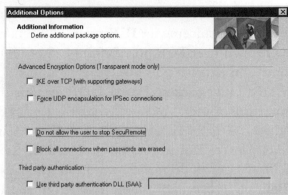

Table 11.1 Encryption Protocols

Encryption Scheme	Ports/Protocols Used
IKE	IKE (UDP port 500) ESP (IP protocol 50) AH (IP protocol 51) IKE over TCP (TCP port 500) * UDP encapsulation (UDP port 2476)* FW1_topo (TCP port 264) FW1_pslogon_NG (TCP port 18231) FW1_sds_logon (TCP port 18232) FW1_scv_keep_alive (UDP port 18233)

* Not always necessary

7. You will now be brought to the **Topology Information** screen, as shown in Figure 11.22. The options in the Topology Information screen include the following:

   ■ **Change default topology port** Topology information is transmitted by default on port 264. For port conflicts or security reasons, you can change this to an alternative port.

   ■ **Obscure Topology on disk** The topology information that FireWall-1 stores in the *userc.C* file can be stored in an obscured (non–human readable) format. If so, you must specify this option. For testing and debugging purposes, it is useful to be able to see the contents of the *userc.C* file. In production, however, there is little need for users to be able to see it.

■ **Accept unsigned topology** If selected, the firewall will accept topology requests even if there is no security signing in place. This is not recommended, since it introduces a possible security hole.

■ **Perform automatic topology update only in "Silent" mode** If enabled, this option causes SecureClient to obtain an updated topology after every key exchange. This is a very useful option.

If you choose to utilize the Partial Topology option, the only information stored in the package about your site will be the system users will have to connect to in order to receive the topology. This is nice in the fact that after the end-user has rebooted, they are prompted to authenticate to download the latest topology information. In addition, if this package falls into the hands of someone outside the organization, the only information compromised is the address of your VPN gateway.

Click **Next** when you have made your selections.

Figure 11.22 Topology Information

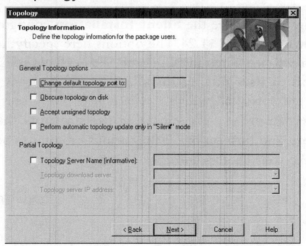

8. This brings up the **Certificates Information configuration** screen, as shown in Figure 11.23. Here, you can select a **Certificate Authority IP Address** and **Port**, which are used to specify the location and port

of your Entrust Certificate Authority server. You can also specify your **LDAP server IP address** and **Port**, which you should use if you are using an Lightweight Directory Access Protocol (LDAP) server as part of your configuration. **Use Entrust Entelligence** specifies whether SecureClient should use this proprietary feature of Entrust. When you have made your selections, click **Next**.

Figure 11.23 Certificate Information

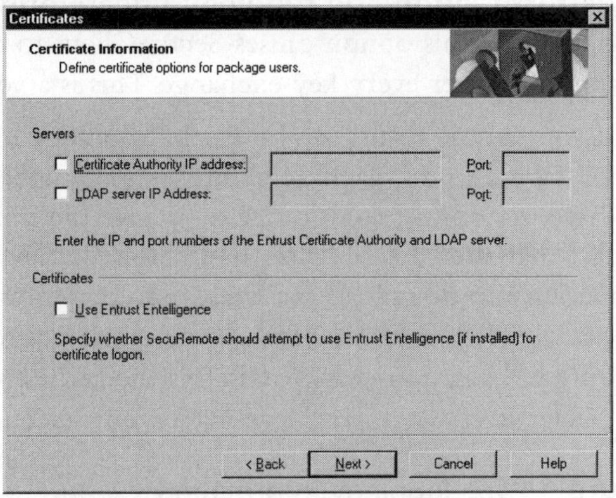

9. Now you will see the **Silent Installation** configuration screen, as shown in Figure 11.24. The options here specify how many prompts the user will see when installing the SecureClient package. The **Don't prompt user during installation** option means that the user will see no prompts at all, which is what Check Point calls a *silent installation*. Alternatively, you can select **Choose prompts that will be shown to users**, and turn on or off the various prompts as per your requirements. Make your choices and click **Next**.

Figure 11.24 Silent Installation

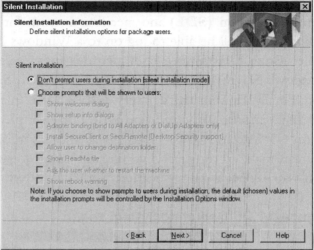

10. You will now see the **Installation Options Information** screen, as shown in Figure 11.25. Here, you can specify the destination installation folder to use, what adapters you want SecureClient to bind to (see above for details), and whether you want the package to install SecureClient by default, as opposed to SecuRemote. You can also choose whether you want the user's system to be restarted by default after installation. Make your selections and click **Next**.

Figure 11.25 Installation Options

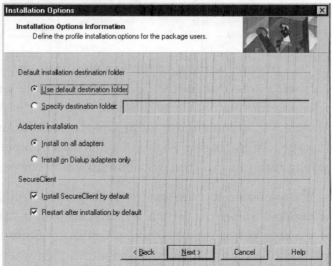

11. Next, you will see the **Operating System Logon Information** screen, as shown in Figure 11.26. Here, you can choose **Enable Secure Domain Logon (SDL)** and specify a timeout for SDL. This means that remote users will be able to log on to a Windows NT domain controller. **Enable Roaming user profiles** means users can use the Windows NT roaming profiles feature over their SecureClient connection. Finally, **Enable third party GINA DLL** enables you to use an external vendor's authentication DLL (for example, Novell's Client32 logon GINA). The *VPN-1 User Guide* also has information on changes you can make to the *product.ini* file and others to streamline the installation process. Make your selections and click **Next**.

Figure 11.26 Operating System Logon

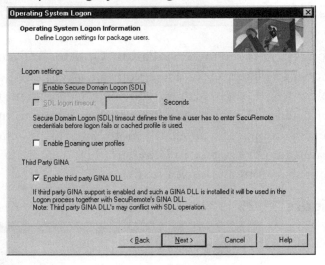

12. You will now be brought to the **Finish** screen, as shown in Figure 11.27. Here, you can choose **NO, Create profile only** to have the packaging tool simply create a profile based on the parameters you have specified. Or, if you choose **YES, Create profile and generate package**, the Packaging Tool will generate a complete SecureClient package that you can then distribute to your remote clients.

   If you choose to generate the package, you will see the SecureClient Packaging Tool wizard, which will first ask you if you want to upload the package you are creating to an Automatic Software Distribution (ASD) S Automatic Software Distribution (ASD) server. If you have one defined, check the box and click **Next** to continue. You will be shown a screen with a prompt for a **Package Source Folder**, which is the location of the SecureClient package on your system. You can either use the package directory on the NG AI CD or you can place it (unzipped) in a directory on your PC. You will also be prompted for a destination folder, which is where the final package executable file will be placed. You will be required to create a package for each platform type (Windows 2000/XP, 98/ME, and NT). It is also useful to number the packages you created (similar to build numbers) so you can tell if someone is using the latest version of the installer and configuration you have defined. Click **Finish** once you have made your selection.

NOTE

If you have a working version of *userc.C* and wish to have all the site information defined (as well as all the other options) as part of the package, do not select partial topology, place your pre-configured *userc.C* into the source directory replacing the stock *userc.C*, and generate the package.

Figure 11.27 Finish

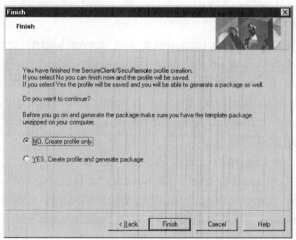

Logging into the Policy Server

Once you create and distribute a SecureClient package to your remote users, they are on their way to securely connecting to your network. After installing the SecureClient package, the policy server needs to communicate with the remote client. This occurs when the user logs in to the policy server, either explicitly or automatically.

When the remote user first loads SecureClient, it automatically tries to log in to the policy server, provided that one is installed on the firewall. The user will be prompted for their log-in credentials and then logged on.

> **NOTE**
>
> If a remote user has IP forwarding enabled on their desktop, SecureClient will detect this, will display a warning to the user, and may disable some functionality as per the security policy. This is an important feature, because having IP forwarding can result in packets entering one insecure interface being transmitted out another interface, which is a security risk.

After successfully logging on, SecureClient will periodically re-log on to the policy server in order to transmit any logs and ensure that it receives any updates to the security policy.

In addition to these automated policy server logins, the remote user may also decide to explicitly log on to the policy server when in Transparent mode. This is useful in cases where the user knows the policy has been updated, such as when they are in contact with the firewall administrator and they want to update their desktop's policy immediately. In Connect mode, the user simply can disconnect and reconnect.

To explicitly log on to the policy server in Transparent mode (since there is no disconnect option for the VPN session in Transparent mode, only Invalidate Passwords), the remote user should go to the **Policy** menu and choose **Log on to Policy Server**. They will see a list of available policy servers to choose from.

Summary

Any security policy is only as strong as its weakest link. A common mistake by firewall administrators is not considering remote users as a possible source of security breaches. This is changing, however, as worms and viruses are propagated by them. Once a remote user is connected to your network, any compromise of that user's workstation could easily result in a compromise of your network.

Check Point's SecureClient and policy server coupled with SCV enable you to reduce the risk of a remote user's desktop being susceptible to a security compromise as well as ensure its level of security. Because remote users are not necessarily knowledgeable about what their local security policy should be or how to implement it, the combination of SCV, policy server, and SecureClient enables the firewall administrator to set the security policy appropriate for remote users, and then push that policy out in a way that is simple and unobtrusive to the user.

The Check Point SecureClient Packaging Tool is an additional component that enables you to distribute preconfigured versions of SecureClient to your users. This eliminates the need for remote users to correctly set up and configure SecureClient, thereby further simplifying the process for remote users to securely connect to the network.

Solutions Fast Track

Installing and Configuring a Policy Server

☑ Install the Policy Server from the Check Point NG AI CD-ROM or from a package off of the Check Point Web site.

☑ Enable the Policy Server as an installed product in your firewall object.

☑ Set the user group to use with the Policy Server in the Authentication tab of your firewall object.

Desktop Security Options

☑ Set up your desktop security rulebase and configure the global policy properties for desktop security.

☑ If desired, configure desktop configuration verification to specify what should happen if the security policy is broken.

☑ Add a client encrypt rule to the standard rulebase and edit the client encryption action properties.

Installing SecureClient Software

☑ Remote users can install SecuRemote/SecureClient directly from their Check Point NG AI CD-ROM.

☑ The latest version of SecuRemote/SecureClient software can be obtained from Check Point at www.checkpoint.com/techsupport/downloads_sr.html.

☑ You can use the SecureClient packaging tool to preconfigure SecureClient, and bundle it into a package that remote users can easily install.

Logging into the Policy Server

☑ When a remote user loads SecureClient, it automatically logs into the policy server and receives the most recent security policy.

☑ SecureClient periodically logs into the policy server (approximately every 30 minutes) to check for any security policy updates, and send logs back to the policy server.

☑ Users can also explicitly log in to the policy server through SecureClient.

Frequently Asked Questions

The following Frequently Asked Questions, answered by the authors of this book, are designed to both measure your understanding of the concepts presented in this chapter and to assist you with real-life implementation of these concepts. To have your questions about this chapter answered by the author, browse to **www.syngress.com/solutions** and click on the **"Ask the Author"** form. You will also gain access to thousands of other FAQs at ITFAQnet.com.

Q: Can I install the policy server on two firewalls for redundancy?

A: You can configure the policy server for high availability, but it is more complicated than simply installing the policy server on two separate firewalls. Consult the Check Point NG AI documentation for details.

Q: What licensing issues should I take into account when installing a policy server?

A: In addition to your existing FireWall-1 licenses, the policy server requires a separate license on each firewall module on which it is installed. You also need to ensure that you have sufficient user licenses for the number of remote users that will be connecting. The user licenses are installed on the Management Module.

Q: I want my salespeople to be able to log on and browse my NT/domain from the field. I also want them to be able to be notified that their NT passwords will be expiring at the same time.

A: See the Secure Domain Logon section in Chapter 10.

Q: I have a really large network with a lot of VPN traffic to and from multiple VPN domains, and notice frequent connection interruptions.

A: Check to make sure that **Key exchange for subnets** is enabled under the firewall workstation object under the **Advanced IKE Properties** tab. Check the size of the connection table. Check gateway memory usage and processor load (*fw tab –t connections –s* and *fw ctl pstat*).

Q: I have a number of employees who connect from the site of another company. The other company's firewall does not let IPSec traffic through. Is there any way I can let them make a VPN connection?

A: Yes, Visitor mode (also called TCP Tunneling) was designed specifically for this purpose. It takes the IPSec traffic, wraps it with Hypertext Transfer Protocol (http), then Secure Sockets Layer (SSL) encrypts the entire thing and sends it over port 443. It will even function through proxy servers. It works amazingly well but at a cost; all of the additional overhead of HTTP and SSL in addition to IPSec means that the bandwidth through the tunnel will be lower and latency may be higher. In case you are wondering, Check Point's firewall can be configured to block Visitor Mode (TCP Tunneling) connections.

Q: I have a single firewall but I want to create a number of ways for users to connect in Connect mode. (i.e., one with IKE over TCP and Force UDP Encapsulation enabled, another with Visitor mode, and a third with Route All Traffic enabled) When I download the topology, I am only allowed to select these options on a per-site basis. How can I provide this functionality to my users?

A: Look at **Manage | Remote Access | Connection Profiles** in SmartDashboard. You can create multiple profiles for a single site. These connection profiles will be downloaded with the topology the next time the client updates itself. Note that once you do this, the downloaded connection profiles are the only ones the user will be able to use and all the connection profiles will be read-only. This read-only attribute removes the ability for the end user to mess it up and eases helpdesk burden tremendously.

Q: I want to use Visitor mode, but SecurePlatform is using port 443, how can I turn off the Web interface on Secure Platform to allow Visitor mode to function on port 443?

A: From the command line, execute *webui disable* to disable the Web interface completely or *webui enable <new port to run web server on>* to move it to another port. Currently, there is no way to bind the Web server to specific IP addresses on the firewall.

## Chapter 12

Advanced VPN Configurations

Solutions in this Chapter:

- **Check Point High Availability and Check Point Load Sharing**

- **Single Entry Point VPN Configurations**

- **Multiple Entry Point VPN Configurations**

- **Other High Availability Methods**

☑ **Summary**

☑ **Solutions Fast Track**

☑ **Frequently Asked Questions**

Introduction

The Internet and Internet services have become increasingly important to businesses over time, and many organizations are choosing to implement measures to keep these services highly available to their staff or to their customers. The first task is identifying which services are business-critical, and then determining the best solution to keep that service available 99.9 percent of the time. The reason that keeping a service available is an issue at all is because the Internet and networking technology is not fail-proof. Your ISP (Internet Service Provider) connection could be down or slow, your internal router could lose its routing table and stop passing packets, or you could have a hardware failure or power failure at any point in the network infrastructure, which could cause any number of service interruptions.

So, what can you do to prevent these outages from happening? Well, you probably can't control them 100 percent of the time, regardless of how much time, money, and effort you put into the project, but you can make a considerable dent in downtime by setting up some redundant systems and configuring them to fail over in the event of a failure.

For example, suppose your company prints a well-known newspaper on the East Coast, and having the Internet available to your reporters is business-critical, since they use this source of information for many of their articles. Therefore, it's your job to have a redundant Internet connection with failover abilities. You could contract two ISPs, have two routers set up at each end of each ISP connection, have two or four firewalls set up to fail over, and have two routers inside each firewall, all plugged into various uninterruptible power supplies (UPSs). This is a complicated configuration, but it can be an operational means to have a high availability connection to the Internet.

This chapter will briefly discuss the Check Point High Availability (CPHA) and Check Point Load Sharing (CPLS) modules, as well as a few network configuration models in which Check Point will allow VPNs (virtual private networks) to fail over. This is only a brief overview; high availability and load sharing using both Check Point's internal and Nokia's IPSO mechanisms are covered in-depth in the sister book to this one, *Check Point NG VPN-1/FireWall-1: Advanced Configuration and Troubleshooting* (Syngress Publishing, ISBN: 1-931836-97-3).

Check Point High Availability and Check Point Load Sharing

High availability can be your best friend, both from a network performance and from a security perspective. Many enterprises are concerned about the firewall being their single point of failure, and some organizations even have a contingency plan allowing for the redirection of traffic around a firewall, should it fail…which is a poor solution, because an attacker could purposely attempt to cause this to happen. With a highly available solution, this won't be necessary.

The first question you have to ask yourself when implementing high availability is: What makes a system available? Is it that the operating system is…for lack of a better term…operating? Is it defined by a daemon on the system, or, like a server group discussed earlier in the book, does it require some sort of agent installed to monitor "upness"? To answer these questions, we'll delve into the mechanics of Check Point High Availability.

Load sharing is simply an extension of high availability that allows all systems in the cluster to process traffic and be active at the same time.

Enabling High Availability (Legacy Mode)

Before you can begin using high availability, or define and join clusters, you have to do some preparatory work. Primarily, you need to make sure that you have the proper licensing in place in order to run the High Availability module, and that high availability is enabled. Then you must begin by defining the configuration and the Internet Protocol (IP) addresses on the future cluster members. The cluster members must have three interfaces, with four interfaces being preferred if you opt to use synchronization on a network separate from the management network. All of the internally facing IP addresses must be the same, as must all of the externally facing addresses. The Check Point High Availability module will make sure that the media access control (MAC) addresses are identical, so there's no need to play around with Address Resolution Protocol (ARP) entries. Figure 12.1 illustrates what a sample network layout for high availability might look like. Note that all of the external facing IP addresses are the same in the diagram (noted as .5 to indicate the final octet) as are the internal IP addresses. The interfaces on the management segment and synchronization network must each use a unique IP address.

Figure 12.1 Highly Available Cluster using Legacy Mode

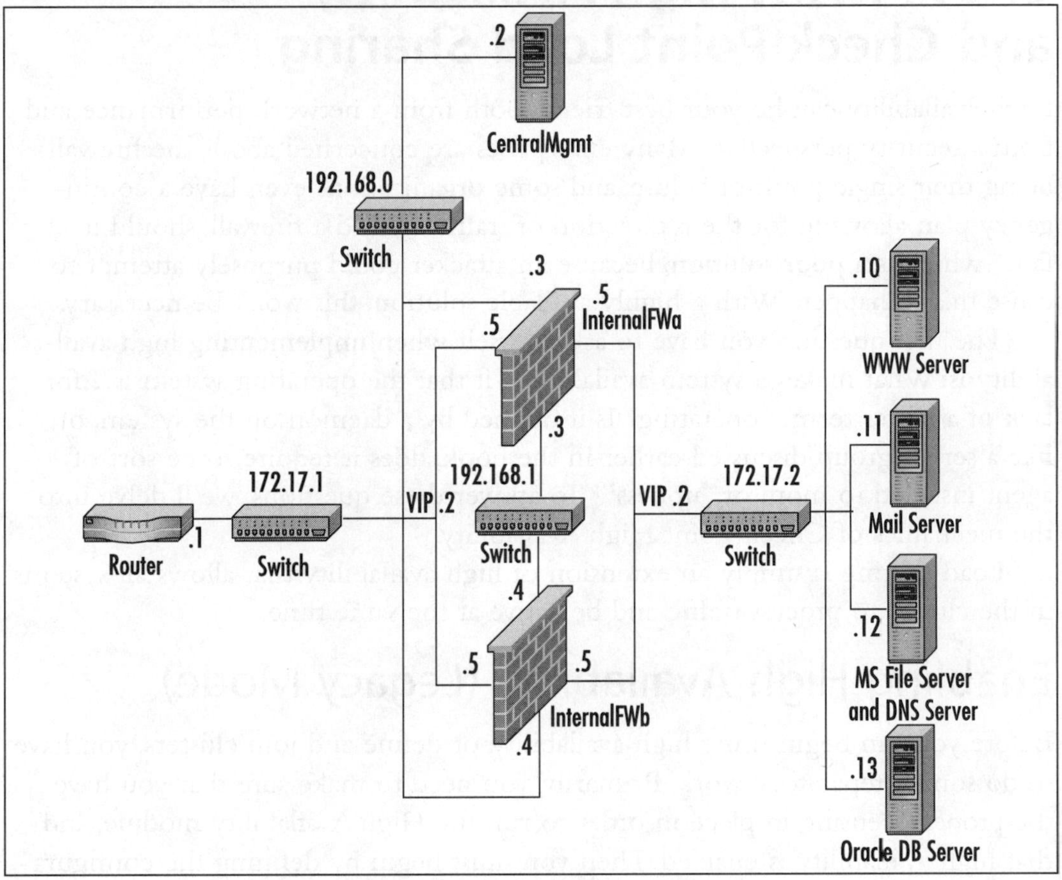

The next step toward gaining the benefits of Check Point High Availability is to enable it on the enforcement module. This is a really easy step, and only involves running the cpconfig command. On UNIX installations, simply run cpconfig, select "Enable Check Point High Availability/State Synchronization" and answer y for yes. Access the High Availability tab in Windows by selecting **Start | Programs | Check Point Management Clients | Check Point Configuration NG | High Availability**. Place a checkmark in the checkbox, indicating that you are enabling High Availability.

Configuring & Implementing...

How does the High Availability Module Select the MAC Address?

There are two distinct types of bootups for a High Availability (HA) member. Initially, at the first boot, there are no real elements of the cluster associated with that machine. The policy has not yet been installed, no priority is associated with the machine, and no gateway priority has been defined. In this case, the gateway begins to look for information by listening on User Datagram Protocol (UDP) port 8116, from an already configured cluster member. If it can't determine information from a configured cluster member, then it looks for information from other machines with its shared IP address. Once it sees that traffic, it will select the MAC address from the machine with the lowest Random ID and use it for its own.

After that initial boot, and after the remaining cluster information has been assigned, the CPHA module looks for packets coming from the primary cluster machine, compares that machine's MAC to its own, and changes its own, if necessary.

Because each system maintains the same IP addresses and MAC addresses on shared interfaces, when a failover condition occurs the standby system simply begins responding to ARP requests and starts processing the traffic. Because the same MAC addresses is used, no information must be updated on routers or other connected servers.

There are some restrictions when implementing a high availability solution. The gateways must be running the same version of Check Point VPN-1/FireWall-1 (VPN-1/FW-1), and they must be on the same platform (for example, you cannot synchronize a Solaris firewall with a Windows NT firewall). Also, you must have a separate management server; the management module cannot reside on a cluster member.

Another wise bit of advice is to configure each cluster member offline; that is, off of the network. While it is good security practice to build machines while they are disconnected from the network anyway, there is a different reason here. Since each machine will be sharing IP addresses, it's nice to avoid address conflicts that might be present if the machines were active on the network segment. Finally, if you are configuring a single entry point (SEP) VPN high availability solution, the VPN domain for the cluster should be a group object containing the cluster member gateways and their respective VPN domains. We'll discuss SEP later in this chapter.

Enabling High Availability (New Mode)

New mode HA is very dissimilar to legacy mode. With legacy mode, there are many limitations, one of which is the fact that all systems utilize the same address on interfaces which are marked for high availability. This has been overcome in new mode. new mode functions in a way that is similar to other HA protocols such as Virtual Router Redundancy Protocol (VRRP) and Hot Standby Routing Protocol (HSRP) in that each system has its own IP address and utilizes a secondary, virtual IP (VIP) address for communicating with other devices on the network. Figure 12.2 shows the differences in IP addressing between legacy mode and new mode. In this configuration, the management station does not have to be on its own network since it can communicate directly with each of the cluster members in this mode.

Another difference in this mode is how traffic is migrated from one system to another. At any one point in time, the VIP will resolve to the MAC address of the active cluster member. The standby system(s) will respond to ARP requests for its native IP address, but not the VIP. In the event that the cluster needs to failover traffic to the standby member, the standby begins responding to ARP requests for the VIP. To speed up the failover, it also sends a gratuitous number of ARP replies/updates to other systems on the network to notify them of the MAC sddress change for the VIP address. This shortens the failover time significantly.

Figure 12.2 Other HA and Load Sharing Cluster Configurations

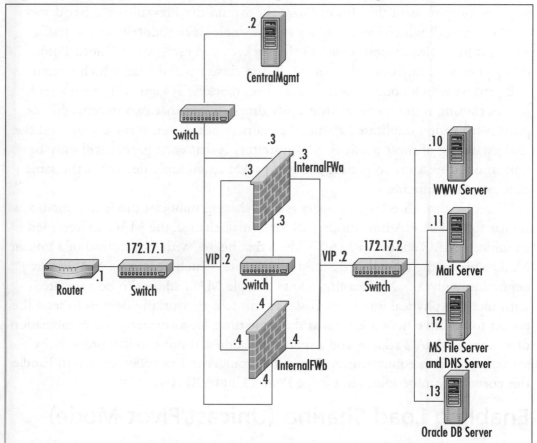

Enabling Load Sharing (Multicast Mode)

Some organizations don't like to hear that they are paying for systems that sit idle. Others may have the need to spread load across multiple systems because of the load a lot of VPN or security servers may generate. This is where load sharing comes into the picture. Load sharing is an extension of the HA modes discussed previously; it will still allow traffic to be dynamically rerouted around a failed gateway to an active one without losing session state, but it also allows all systems in a cluster to be active instead of designating one or more as standby.

Load sharing configuration is a tricky process with a few caveats. You should definitely set it up in a lab before attempting to implement it. One of the biggest caveats is that there are numerous devices out there that it will not interoperate with. The reason for this is that Check Point's load sharing design using multicast requires all systems in the cluster (how else would the firewalls, or other devices on the network which treat the cluster as a single device, distribute the traffic amongst multiple devices) to see all the packets, and using what Check Point calls a "decision function" the devices in the cluster will decide which system will process which connections. This ensures that one system will process each packet causing it not to be inadvertently dropped, but that two systems do not process it causing duplicated traffic. Typical network design is for unicast and the understanding of most network administrators is that each packet will only be sent in one direction, so getting a single packet to multiple devices at the same time is rather difficult.

To solve this, Check Point operates load sharing multicast mode in a method similar to CPHA HA new mode with one small change: the MAC address used is a multicast MAC address (a MAC address that begins with 01:) instead of a unicast MAC address (the type your desktop system uses, which contains a MAC address beginning with 00:). Multicasting allows a single MAC address to be associated with multiple physical interfaces. Basically, this tells networking devices to send the packet to multiple network cards at the same time. Unfortunately, the combination of a multicast MAC address and a unicast IP address is not handled properly by some networking equipment. A short list of routers and switches known to handle this correctly can be found in Check Point's ClusterXL User Guide.

Enabling Load Sharing (Unicast/Pivot Mode)

In the event that you do not have equipment or the inclination to support load sharing in multicast mode, NG with Application Intelligence (AI) adds the option to do load sharing using Unicast MAC addresses instead of multicast ones.

Unicast mode, also called pivot mode, provides a solution to the limitations you may run into in your environment with multicast mode. In unicast mode, the handling of MAC addresses is similar to CPHA new mode in that only one device responds to ARP requests for the VIP address and traffic is sent to only one device. This device, referred to as the *pivot*, handles all the traffic and is the only device to make a decision function. This decision the pivot device makes is which cluster member will process the packet with regards to routing and fire-walling. The pivot device can send the traffic to any of the other devices in the cluster to be inspected or inspect the traffic itself, hence their classification as being active, not standby. Because of the additional overhead of making the decision functions, it will typically handle less traffic than other devices in the cluster.

Other cluster members will not have to make a decision function due to the fact that they will only see traffic they have to process and inspect, so each will process all packets it sees.

In the event that a failure in the pivot mode system occurs, the next highest priority gateway will take over the pivot mode functions reassigning the amount of load the other devices will be responsible for. All traffic, including connections which were processed by the now failed pivot device, will continue to function. When the failed pivot device comes back online, it will reassume the pivot functionalities by telling the current pivot device to fail back to the new pivot device.

Failing Over

Now that we've seen how to enable Check Point's high availability and load sharing functions, your next question most likely harkens back to our earlier wonderings about what classifies a system as "up." When dealing with VPN-1/FW-1, the answer to this question is up to you.

When using the CPHA or CPLS modules, you gain access to the functionality of the **cphaprob** command. This command allows you to define services that are considered critical to the operation of the VPN-1/FW-1 system. There are also some default conditions that must be met for the system to be considered available:

- The fwd process (and other critical pieces on the device) must be running, and must not report any problems.

- The network connection must be active (interface up and link OK).

- The machine must be running.

- A security policy must be installed.

These are, of course, the most basic of conditions. As you've come to expect (and, hopefully, appreciate) Check Point allows you to enhance the granularity of the checking. This is done using the aforementioned **cphaprob** command. This command is used to register additional devices within the firewall machine as critical, so that their failure will cause the preemption of cluster control. The options to this command are displayed in Table 12.1.

Table 12.1 cphaprob Command Options

Command Option	Command Explanation
-d <device name>	Specify a device to be monitored.
-s <status>	The state of the device. Status can be either "ok," "init," or "problem." If the value is anything besides "ok", the device is not considered active.
-t <timeout>	Define a timeout value. If the device doesn't report its status before the timeout expires, the device is considered as failed.
-f <filename> register	Allow the specification of a file containing multiple device definitions.
[-l[a]][-e] list	Display the current state of CPHA devices.
Register	Register the device as a critical process.
Unregister	Remove the registration of this device as a critical process.
Report	Display the status of the HA modules.
If	Display the status of interfaces.
Init	Instruct the firewall to reacquire the shared MAC address.

You can also use the **cphaprob** command with the **state** argument to see the status of the HA cluster. Example output for a two-member cluster might resemble this:

```
$ cphaprob state

Number     Unique Address    State

1 (local)  172.16.1.3        active
2          172.16.1.4        standby
```

You can also check your log files for information about both synchronization and failover.

Firewall Synchronization

State synchronization allows the firewall or VPN module to be really highly available, in the truest sense. Without synchronization, when a failover occurs, the connections that are currently active will be dropped. This may not be that important when dealing with a firewall, for example, when the majority of the traffic through your firewall is destined for the web, but can be disastrous in a VPN context. You probably never want to be without synchronization when dealing with a VPN.

What synchronization does is maintain an identical state table on all of the machines involved in the gateway cluster. This, obviously, uses resources. The synchronization process consumes memory, CPU, and network resources, and depending on the size of the state table, this could be significant.

How does it work? The first thing to understand is that the entire state table is not copied from machine to machine all the time. Obviously, the first synchronization involves the entire state table (called a *full sync*), but subsequent updates only involve the changes since the last update (referred to as a *delta sync*). The updates occur by default every 100 milliseconds, and while this can be changed, the process isn't easy and you'll probably never want to try. Another thing to consider is that processing the updates takes a minimum of 55 milliseconds. If you are maintaining a particularly busy site, one with a lot of Hypertext Transfer Protocol (HTTP) traffic, for example, your state table may have a larger number of changes, and processing may require more time than the minimum.

Also, synchronization is not available when using a multiple entry point (MEP) VPN solution. This is because, as discussed later in this chapter, MEP is designed for use with a physically disperse VPN solution. Synchronization is most often used with a SEP VPN solution. You can see a screen shot of the Synchronization window in the section on SEP. In a truly user-friendly manner, enabling synchronization is as easy as placing a checkmark in the box labeled **Use State Synchronization** on the **Synchronization** tab of the cluster object. Next, you'll need to define the synchronization network by clicking **Add** on the **Synchronization** window. Clicking **Add** will show you a window such as the one shown in Figure 12.3.

Figure 12.3 Add Synchronization Network

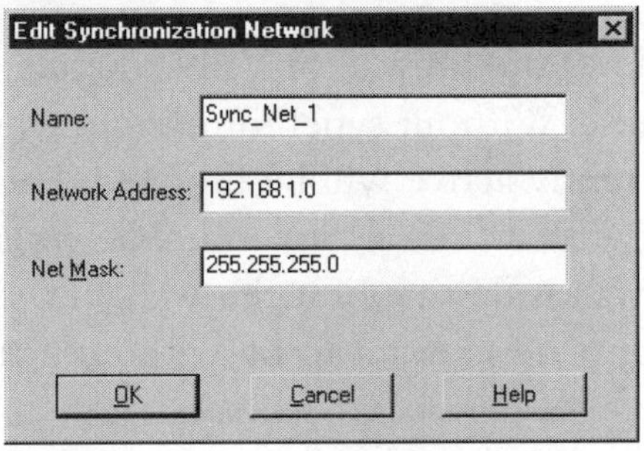

There is a caveat here: Make sure that the synchronization network is trusted. The way to do this is to segment the synchronization traffic from any general-use traffic. In the case of a two-node cluster, you may use a crossover cable, for example. Next, you need to make sure that VPN-1/FW-1 control connections are allowed to pass between the cluster members. Simply make a rule that allows the VPN-1/FW-1 service from member to member.

After you have activated synchronization, you'll want to test it to make sure that it is working. There are a couple of different techniques. The quickest way is to check the size of the state tables on each machine. The command to do this is as follows:

```
fw tab -t connections -s
```

While this is quick, it is the least accurate. Remember, the state table is updated frequently, so there is a chance that the table on one machine could change before you can type the command.

The most accurate method is the use of the **fw ctl** command. Using the **pstat** option will give you the information on the synchronization process (and other processes as well). A sample bit of the output is shown below.

```
sync new ver working
sync out: on   sync in: on
sync packets sent:
total: 2145 retransmitted: 0 retrans reqs:0 acks: 0
sync packets received:
total 2473 of which 1 queued and 31 dropped by net
also received 0 retrans reqs and 2 acks to 0 cb requests
```

Another way to check is to see that two or more firewalls are connected to one another via the **netstat –an** command. We usually run **netstat –an | grep 256**. On Windows machines you can substitute the **findstr** command for **grep**.

The second line is the key to determining the operation of state synchronization. If synchronization is on, then both of these should be on.

Yet another manner is to simply use the SmartView status to view the status of the cluster. The ClusterXL section under each cluster member will revel if there are any problems with the state synchronization.

What if you are working on a particularly busy boundary firewall cluster, where the vast majority of traffic consists of HTTP and Simple Mail Transfer Protocol (SMTP) connections? Each of these connections is relatively short-lived, and might not be the best candidate for synchronization. HTTP, for example, is totally stateless from connection to connection by design, so a failover probably wouldn't be noticed. Does the burden of synchronization outweigh the benefits? If so, you are in luck. You don't have to synchronize every protocol. You can selectively weed out those protocols that are hogging too many resources when compared to the necessity of their HA conditions. This is done by editing the service object, clicking **Advanced** and unchecking **Synchronize connections on Cluster**. Here you also have the option to only synchronize a protocol after it has been open for a certain period of time. This is done using the **Start Synchronizing** *n* **seconds after connection initiation** option.

You can also selectively synchronize certain connections instead of protocols as a whole. Simply create another service object, with the same properties as the original, only with the option to synchronize disabled. Wherever this object is used, the connection will not be synchronized. Note: only one service can have **Match for 'Any'** selected. The one with the Match for 'Any' option checked will be the service with whose properties are used when *Any* is defined for the service in a rule. This can be very useful if you wish to synchronize connections to the e-commerce website, but connections on the same network running through the same cluster for the server only handling advertisement images does not have to be synchronized.

A new feature in Check Point NG with Application Intelligence R55 removes the software version dependence of state synchronization. This allows administrators to remove a system from the cluster, upgrade a single system in the cluster, say from NG AI R54 to NG AI R55, bring it back into the cluster, synchronize with other members, and then take the other systems down—all without anyone losing a connection. This is absolutely necessary in environments where downtime windows are not available or cost money at any time. Check Point calls this a "Zero-Downtime Upgrade".

Single Entry Point VPN Configurations

Single Entry Point VPNs enable your enterprise to deploy a solution that protects what many consider an increasingly critical element of the network. VPNs allow you to extend your enterprise to the remote user, and as more companies look toward telecommuting, remote sales forces, and partner networks, making their availability becomes increasingly important. Gone are the days when a VPN was a novelty or a convenience; today it's a necessity. Also, synchronized connections are a must. You wouldn't want users to notice that their VPN connection was just transferred to another gateway and have to reestablish all their connections.

Another nice feature is the support for SEP (and MEP) VPNs when dealing with both remote clients and with gateway-to-gateway VPNs.

Gateway Configuration

In Chapter 3, you began looking at the means of configuring a high availability solution. In this section, you'll look at this topic in greater depth. Figure 12.4 is presented here as a memory refresher. It shows you the General window used for cluster configuration. As covered in Chapter 3, this window is used to initially identify the information about the cluster, such as the cluster name and IP address and also to specify the Check Point applications installed. Note that the IP address configured here is the cluster IP address. This will be the common IP (or Virtual IP) of the cluster.

Figure 12.4 Gateway Cluster: General Window

You can use the Topology window (Figure 12.5) to specify which addresses reside behind this cluster. This is similar to the features on a single gateway object's interface properties topology window. One of the most common uses of a manually defined VPN domain is to define an overlapping encryption domain for the gateway cluster for MEP (discussed later).

If defining the topology manually, you'll first need to define a network object or objects symbolizing the protected network. Then you'll want to define a group object containing each gateway cluster member, as well as the newly created network object. In Figure 12.5, this group is called InternalVPNDomain. Specifying this object on the Topology window is all you need to do to institute a full VPN domain overlap.

In this window you will also be required to define any clustered addresses (VIPs) that will be used in this configuration. If you are using CPHA in legacy mode, these options will not be available since the interfaces with the same IP addresses will automatically be known as shared interfaces. When the interface names on all the cluster members are similar, it makes sense to name the interface name here (which is arbitrary) similar to what the interface name is on each device.

Figure 12.5 Gateway Cluster: Topology Window

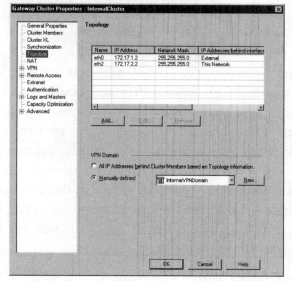

The next window enables you to specify cluster members. Cluster members are the gateways previously defined for inclusion within the cluster. This configuration window is illustrated in Figure 12.6. Note that order is important, as the order that the gateways are listed defines their priority. The order can be shuffled without much effort by the use of the familiar **Increase Priority** and **Decrease Priority** sort buttons. Also, new gateways can be added and old ones simply removed, as well. In this case, the **Edit** button will open the Properties window for the selected gateway, allowing very handy alteration of its settings information.

Figure 12.6 Gateway Cluster: Cluster Members

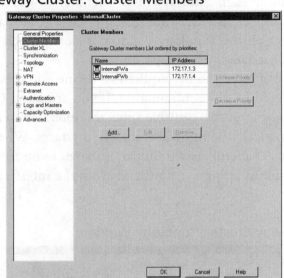

Figure 12.7 shows you how the High Availability or Load Sharing settings are defined. The first options, **High Availability** and **Load Sharing**, define whether the cluster will be operating in an active/standby or active/active configuration. Below the High Availability section, there are two options to define the operating mode: **New Mode** and **Legacy Mode**, defined previously in this chapter. Under the Load Sharing section, there are also two options: **Multicast Mode** and **Unicast Mode**, also described earlier in this chapter.

When using High Availability, there are two options in the **Upon Gateway Recovery** section to define how to handle a gateway that has failed but has now returned to the cluster. These are explained below.

- **Maintain current active Gateway** In this mode, when a primary gateway has failed and subsequently returned to service, it will not regain control of the cluster. Instead, it will assume the role of secondary and remain in standby. This is useful if you opt not to use state synchronization, as it causes the least interference in these cases.

- **Switch to higher priority Gateway** When the primary gateway in the cluster fails and subsequently returns to service, it will retake control of the cluster, assuming that it has been assigned a higher priority (as sorted in the cluster members window).

Also defined on this window is the action to take when a failover situation occurs under **Fail-Over Tracking**, as well as how to share traffic when using load sharing by clicking the **Advanced** button.

Figure 12.7 Gateway Cluster: ClusterXL Window

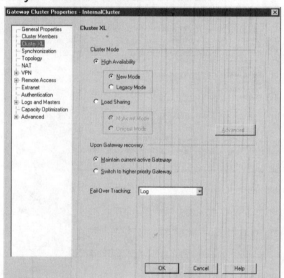

Figure 12.8 shows you the Synchronization window. Synchronization is not required for an HA cluster to function, but it is highly recommended. Synchronization assures that no connections are lost when a failure occurs and connections are migrated to another gateway. It does this by maintaining the state table across all cluster members. This table maintenance has an associated resource cost, which, depending on the size of the state table, can be large. The decision to use this feature is up to you. If you opt for its benefits, you'll need to define a secured network to operate the synchronization over. Note that the network listed in this window will be treated as trusted. The ClusterXL module will trust all messages coming from this network, and, as such, it should be segmented from

normal user traffic. If you opt not to use synchronization, simply uncheck the **Use State Synchronization** field.

Recall from the earlier discussion about state synchronization what the purpose of this mechanism is. Imagine if a user behind your firewall is getting a very large file via File Transfer Protocol (FTP); downloading the newest service pack from Microsoft, for example. If the primary firewall failed and synchronization was enabled, the secondary firewall would take over the connections and the user wouldn't notice the slightest difference. Without synchronization, the transfer would need to be restarted, perhaps with the loss of the already downloaded data.

Figure 12.8 Gateway Cluster: Synchronization

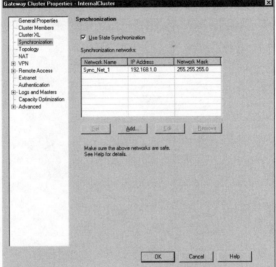

The remaining tabs of the Gateway Cluster are identical to their cousins in the workstation properties. (Refer back to Chapter 3 for a refresher on the Gateway object.) These allow the setting of the same information as for the individual member workstations, except that here the information is defined per cluster. This also means that the information will no longer be configurable on the individual cluster members.

Policy Configuration

When you have finished configuring the cluster and assigning all the proper members, you still need to allow the VPN-1/FW-1 service to pass between the cluster members (unless you still have implied rules enabled). As mentioned earlier, it's best to make sure that the synchronization network is trusted completely. This is easily accomplished by simply not connecting that network to any other machines. You certainly wouldn't want others synching up with your firewalls—that could lead to very bad things.

Not only are these cluster and VPN configurations useful for perimeter gateways, but also for internal networks when internal networks must be secured and users must secure communications to certain servers. With the proliferation of worms and other fast-propagating attacks, the deployment of internal security measures has become more important and more widely deployed.

Multiple Entry Point VPN Configurations

Multiple Entry Point VPN deployments make use of the VPN-1/FW-1 Backup Gateway feature. With this sort of implementation, gateways for logically separated networks can be used to connect to the same destination network, assuming that a link exists between those networks. A diagram of a MEP configuration is shown in Figure 12.9.

Figure 12.9 Simple MEP Illustration

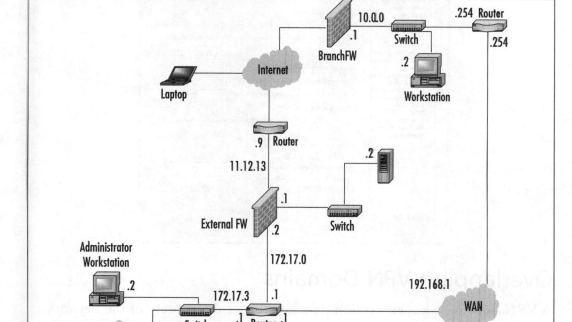

MEP configurations are actually more of a redundancy solution than a true high availability solution. Since the networks are logically (and often geographically) separated, firewall synchronization is not possible (though some support has been added in NG AI R55 when the cluster members are connected to the same layer 2 network). With this being the case, connections cannot be maintained as they can be with a SEP configuration. Instead, when the SecuRemote client's (or SecureClient's) gateway fails, there is a brief pause before the backup gateway is connected. This will cause an interruption in the connection from a user's perspective. Usually this isn't a big deal and users don't notice much. A user browsing the internal website, for example, will simply click the refresh button to continue as normal.

The first step toward setting up a MEP solution is to enable backup gateways on the management server. This is done by accessing **Global Properties | Advanced** and placing a checkmark in the box labeled **Enable load distribution for Multiple Entry Points configurations**, as shown in Figure 12.10.

Figure 12.10 Enabling MEP

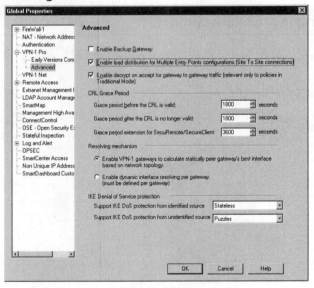

Overlapping VPN Domains

A VPN domain (a.k.a. encryption domain) defines the entirety of the network residing behind the VPN-1/FW-1 device, and also includes the VPN-1/FW-1 gateway(s). Recent versions of VPN-1/FW-1 support the use of overlapping

VPN domains. This inclusion is the key element that allows the implementation of high availability for VPN connections. There are three methods of creating an overlapping VPN domain:

- Partial Overlap
- Full Overlap
- Proper Subset

Figure 12.11 shows you a graphical representation of these VPN domain types in the following order: partial overlap, full overlap, and proper subset. These will be discussed in more detail later in the chapter.

Figure 12.11 VPN Domain Types

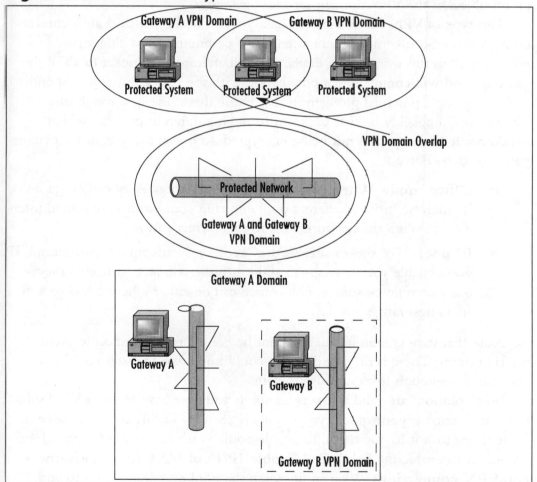

Check Point has included support for all three types of VPN domains with NG AI. Previously, only full overlap and proper subset were supported. This section will look at the particulars of the VPN domains in the next couple of paragraphs.

As mentioned in the first paragraph of this section, a VPN domain consists of the network residing behind the gateway, including that gateway. What this means for you, as a firewall administrator, is that you define a network object consisting of the protected network and then point to that network object within the configuration of the workstation object that is the VPN gateway.

Implementing a fully overlapping VPN domain isn't much more difficult than defining a normal VPN domain. All you need to do is properly define the network object. Simply define a group of network objects containing all of the involved gateways and all of their protected networks, and then point to this new group object as the VPN domain for those gateways.

This type of VPN domain is very handy when dealing with critical connections. When a SecuRemote client attempts to communicate with a server residing within this overlapping domain, it will attempt to connect to all of the gateways, and will complete that connection with the first gateway to respond. This brings up a potential problem in that traffic that came in through one gateway could possibly be sent back out through a different gateway, which would result in that packet not being encrypted. To prevent this from happening, you have two choices.

- **Office mode** When using SecureClient, each gateway can assign users IP addresses from a different pool ensuring connections are routed internally through the network back to the correct gateway.

- **IP pools** For site-to-site, SecureClient, or SecuRemote connections, IP ooools enable you to assign an address to the connection from a previously configured source. This source can be either a network object or an address range.

Note that state synchronization cannot be considered a solution to asymmetric routing. There is no way that you could hope two firewalls could synchronize fast enough to avoid this problem.

Both solutions are valid and very useful. If you ever have to use a VPN solution that doesn't support pools, you'll quickly see why having them available is far superior to not having them. To enable pools, you need to modify the global properties to enable the field called **Enable IP Pool NAT for SecuRemote and VPN connections**. What to do when the pool evaporates is up to you. Figure 12.12 illustrates this window.

Figure 12.12 Enabling IP Pool NAT

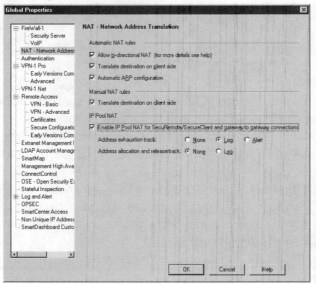

Address exhaustion, which has the familiar three options of None, Log, and Alert, defines what to do when the addresses allocated to your pool are all used. It's not recommended that you select None. Address allocation and release information is a must for debugging purposes. Equate this with DHCP lease information as far as function, and consider the gap in your security policy if you didn't have accountability here.

Backup Gateway Configuration

The backup gateway configuration is much simpler than the SEP configuration. The **Backup Gateway Configuration** option allows you to define a gateway that is the primary endpoint for certain networks with a backup also being able to be an endpoint, but only if necessary. This is essentially because, as mentioned before, this is more of a failover solution than a high availability solution. The gateways aren't clustered and there's no way to synchronize. SecuRemote clients will connect to their primary gateway as normal. If that gateway fails, then the connections are reestablished with the backup gateway. This takes a few seconds, so there will be a momentary interruption in the user's connection. But a momentary interruption is definitely a lot better than one for an extended period of time. If, however, you don't want even a moment's interruption, SEP is the only real way to go (possibly using multiple ISPs).

Designing & Planning…

Why Not Go All Out?

So, you aren't sure if either SEP or MEP is the solution for you. Say, for example, that you have a really mission-critical connection, one that just cannot be down. But you also have a requirement for redundant connections. These redundant connections have to be available even if an entire site goes down.

You have options. There's nothing that says you can't use both SEP and MEP in tandem. You could define an SEP cluster to handle the requirement for the highly available connection and then use MEP to define a redundant backup link!

Once you've enabled backup gateways in the Global Properties, you are able to define them within the gateway's object. On the **NAT** tab of the **Gateway Properties**, you'll see a new checkbox called **Use Backup Gateways:** and an associated pull-down menu. Place a checkmark in this box and select the desired backup gateway from the list, and you're off to the races. The results will resemble the window shown in Figure 12.13.

Figure 12.13 Configuring a Backup Gateway

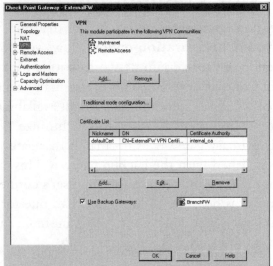

The next thing you will need to do is define how you will be translating incoming connections so that they will get routed back to the appropriate gateway from anywhere on your internal network. You can use office mode for SecureClient connections, which has already been covered, but for all other VPN connections, you will need to use IP pool NAT. First define a network object or address range object for the pool of addresses then go the **NAT** tab of the firewall's object. As shown in Figure 12.14, you will be able to define if you wish to use IP pools for remote access VPN connections (**Use IP Pool NAT for VPN clients connections**) and/or site-to-site connections (**Use IP Pool NAT for gateway to gateway connections**). Select the appropriate boxes and define the IP pool you wish to use next to **Allocate IP Addresses from** section. You can also define how long to reserve each address (because the translations are per-host, not per connection). This is similar to the way a Dynamic Host Control Protocol (DHCP) lease operates.

Figure 12.14 Configuring IP Pool NAT

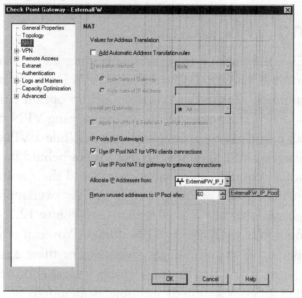

The next step is to define the VPN domain for this gateway. There are really no special tricks involved here. All you need to do is define the proper VPN domain for this gateway, just as you would if you were using a single gateway solution. Figure 12.15 illustrates this window. The gateway will be the primary destination for the network in its VPN Domain, but will also be able to handle decrypting traffic for the encryption domain it is backing up.

Figure 12.15 Selecting the VPN Domain

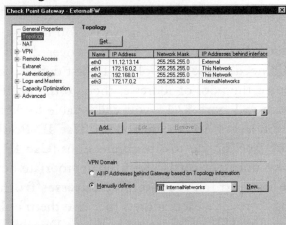

Overlapping VPN Domains

Establishing a MEP configuration using an overlapping VPN domain makes things about as easy as possible. Using the Overlapping VPN Domains option gives equal weight to both endpoints, unlike the Primary/Backup option employed in the Backup Gateways section. In simple terms, an overlapping VPN domain makes the VPN domain of all participating gateways identical. While a VPN domain usually contains a single gateway and the network that resides behind it, when establishing an overlap, the domain contains all of the gateways and their respective protected networks. Configuring a MEP configuration for a fully overlapping encryption setup isn't all that hard. Let's take a look at the steps. Figure 12.16 shows a MEP configuration using a fully overlapping VPN domain. You can refer back to Figure 12.9 for a more specific description of IP addresses. For these examples, you will need to create some network objects and a group with the following networks (netmask of 255.255.255.0 is assumed) and objects included:

- 172.17.2.0

- 172.17.3.0 (previously defined at LAN)

- 192.168.0.0

- 192.168.1.0

- 10.0.0.0 (previously defined as BranchNet)
- ExternalFW object
- BranchFW object

Figure 12.16 Fully Overlapping VPN Domain

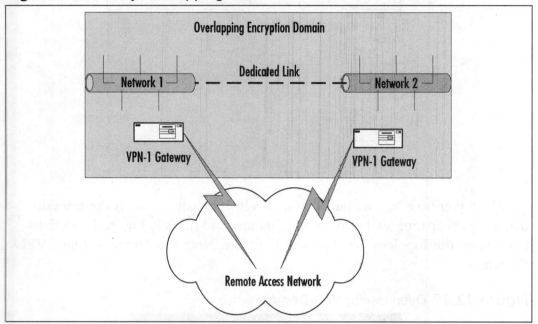

The first step is to define these networks for use within your rulebase. By selecting **Manage | Network Objects | New | Network** from the Policy Editor, you'll be able to create the networks representing your VPN domain. After you have done that, you need to place them all into a group. Select **Manage | Network Objects | New | Group | Simple Group** from the Policy Manager menu, and create a group like the one in Figure 12.17.

Figure 12.17 Overlapping VPN Domain Group

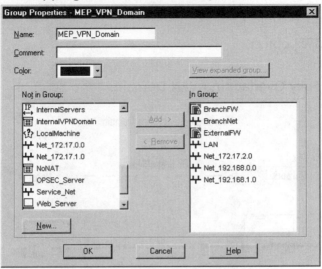

Next, you have to configure this new VPN domain on all of the firewalls that are participating within the configuration, and that's it. Figure 12.18 illustrates what the Topology window will look like. Note the *Manually defined* VPN domain.

Figure 12.18 Overlapping VPN Domain

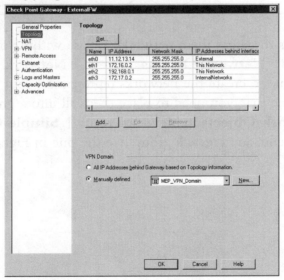

You also must use some means of avoiding the problem of asymmetric routing. Again, IP pools to the rescue unless you're only using SecureClient, in which case you can use office mode. You'll also need to make sure that the routing within your network is properly configured to handle passing the traffic back to the network associated with the IP pool network. To associate an IP pool with the gateway, you first must define an address range or network object that will be used as the pool. After you do that, access the **Check Point Gateway properties** and access the **NAT** window. Place a checkmark in the box marked **Use IP Pool NAT for VPN clients connections** for client-to-site connections or **Use IP Pool NAT for gateway to gateway connections** to site-to-site connections, select the previously defined address range object, and you're ready to go. Figure 12.19 shows you this final configuration window.

Figure 12.19 Using IP Pools

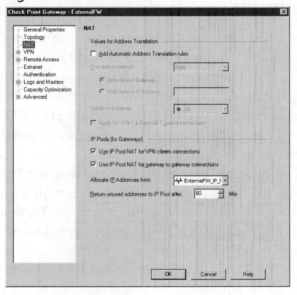

When your SecuRemote clients attempt to initiate a connection, the first gateway to respond will be selected. This is a pretty simple method and is one of the reasons that this configuration is so straightforward.

Other High Availability Methods

So far, this chapter has discussed some generic high availability configurations, and has only mentioned using the Check Point HA and Load Sharing modules.

There are, however, other ways to create high availability. Many vendors have developed HA solutions for Check Point VPN-1/FW-1, and some of them are very good. A popular choice is RainWall from Rainfinity (www.rainfinity.com).

Hardware products can also be employed to provide the load sharing and high availability between firewalls. One notable hardware solution is the Foundry ServerIron XL content switch. This product was the first to be OPSEC-certified to provide full failover support, including the failover of active VPN sessions. ServerIron also supports clustering and synchronization of its load balancers, so that they are not a single point of failure. Also, the configuration commands for this switch are nearly identical to those of the Cisco IOS, which makes the learning curve simpler. You can see a full listing of Check Point OPSEC-certified products at www.opsec.com. Discussion of the configuration for each of these products is beyond the scope of this book and is best obtained directly from the vendor.

Routing Failover

Another failover method is to use a routing protocol to handle moving traffic around a downed firewall. The most popular method of implementing this is by using the Virtual Router Redundancy Protocol. Numerous platforms currently support VRRP, including the Nokia appliance. For those readers with a networking background, think of VRRP as a takeoff on HSRP.. The firewall software will have to take over the duties of synchronization, but that's not unusual to the HA solutions we've looked at.

Configuration of VRRP is outside the scope of this text, but we can discuss some of the more general points that you'll be dealing with. First, you need to decide which version of VRRP you want to implement. There are two versions in common use: VRRP v2 and VRRP Monitored Circuit. Unless you have a pressing need to use VRRP v2 (address-space exhaustion, backward compatibility, etc.), you should opt for Monitored Circuit. In either of these configurations, you may experience problems with asymmetric routing. One of the main differences in v2 and Monitored Circuit is the convergence time, that is, the time it takes for a failure to be detected and corrected. In earlier versions of IPSO, convergence time could be over eight seconds. Using Monitored Circuit, the convergence time is less than one second. Like HSRP, VRRP uses HELO messages, sent at a default interval of one second, to a multicast destination (which must be allowed in the rulebase) to announce their status. This HELO message includes a priority, which is used to determine which gateway should be the active member of the cluster. If the primary machine detects a failed interface, for example, it would decrement its priority, thus notifying the backup gateway to take over the cluster. Remember to include all of the firewall interfaces in the tracking list. It wouldn't do much good if the outside interface was down, but not tracked, and the inside interface was still taking traffic.

A more complete discussion of VRRP is available in the *Check Point NG VPN-1/FireWall-1: Advanced Configuration and Troubleshooting* book published by Syngress as well as the *Nokia Network Security* book.

For other routing-based configurations, in NG with Application Intelligence, Route Injection into your internal routing infrastructure based on VPN Tunnel availability was added (referred to as the Route Injection Module or RIM). And in NG with Application Intelligence R55, ISP redundancy was also introduced for SecurePlatform and Nokia IPSO.

Summary

While you might not be using, or even considering, implementing a Highly Available solution within your network, it is a good idea to be aware of the capabilities that Check Point VPN-1/FW-1 offers you.

If you are currently using a highly available solution, this coverage may have given you food for thought and perhaps some new configuration techniques. While most of the focus of this chapter was on the VPN aspects of HA solutions, keep in mind that HA is also a valuable solution for any mission-critical network boundary with cleartext traffic as well.

Finally, this chapter also gave some attention to third-party solutions for HA, such as VRRP and hardware options for high availability. While this book can not go into much detail on the vast amount of HA solutions out there (Windows 2000 clustering and IBM HACMP as two examples), hopefully you have something new to chew on and research.

Solutions Fast Track

Check Point High Availability and Check Point Load Sharing

☑ Remember that the Check Point High Availability and Load Sharing modules are separately purchased products. With the pricing at the time of this writing it is included in new Enterprise and Express gateway licenses. However, if you have old licenses, you may need to upgrade your license to use the features. Contact your Check Point authorized reseller for the most up-to-date pricing information. Basically, make sure that you have the proper license before using it.

☑ If using state synchronization, don't be afraid to tailor the synchronized protocols.

☑ Be sure that you have properly defined the necessary components using the **cphaprob** command.

Single Entry Point VPN Configurations (SEP)

☑ Synchronization is a must with a SEP VPN.

☑ Before enabling a SEP gateway configuration, make sure that clusters are enabled in the Global Properties and that HA has been turned on each enforcement module.

Multiple Entry Point VPN Configurations (MEP)

☑ Remember that a MEP solution is the most simple of failover solutions; synchronization of connections isn't available.

☑ Use office mode (for SecureClient only), IP pools, or NAT to circumvent problems associated with asymmetric routing.

Other High Availability Methods

☑ VRRP is available with a number of solutions including Nokia's appliances.

☑ It is wise to select an OPSEC certified hardware solution.

Frequently Asked Questions

The following Frequently Asked Questions, answered by the authors of this book, are designed to both measure your understanding of the concepts presented in this chapter and to assist you with real-life implementation of these concepts. To have your questions about this chapter answered by the author, browse to **www.syngress.com/solutions** and click on the **"Ask the Author"** form. You will also gain access to thousands of other FAQs at ITFAQnet.com.

Q: I've been told that state synchronization uses authentication between cluster members. My machines are connected via crossover cable. Is there a way to disable authentication?

A: Indeed there is. You simply need to edit the $FWDIR/lib/control.map file and add the sync directive to the line that currently reads: "★ : getkey,get-topo,gettopossl,certreq/none." Contact Check Point Technical Support or at a minimum view SecureKnowledge Solution ID: 55.0.5956173.2652048 before making changes to the control.map file as it can cause you endless headaches and expose you to security risks if you make incorrect changes.

Q: In prior methods, I had to edit the sync.conf file and run the **putkeys** command in order to establish synchronization peers; is this no longer the case?

A: You are referring to what is called the Old Sync Method. VPN-1/FW-1 NG AI uses what is known as the New Sync Method, and this configuration is all GUI-based. No need to meddle with the sync.conf file anymore (note that you still *can* use the old method, but then you *must* use the **putkeys** command).

Q: I have a Nokia appliance but I am confused about the capabilities of ClusterXL on IPSO and the need for VRRP. How is this configuration special?

A: ClusterXL when referring to IPSO-based appliances simply means state synchronization. VRRP and Nokia's clustering technology handles sending traffic to one gateway or another. In this case, VPN-1/FW-1 simply processes any and all packets it sees and then updates other members via state synchronization. Make sure you do NOT check ClusterXL in the "Products Installed" part of the Cluster object's configuration. The 3rd Party Configuration page will allow you to specify if you are using Nokia VRRP or clustering and set the appropriate parameters.

Q: I can't seem to find the configuration information I'm looking for in SecureKnowledge or on Check Point's website. Is there somewhere else I should be looking?

A: Yes, Check Point's online help is pretty good in NG AI. When you're looking at a screen just click the **Help** button to find configuration examples as well as discussions of what each option does. Check Point has examples of how to migrate from a legacy HA installation to new mode HA or *Load Sharing with Minimal Effort or Minimal Downtime*, as well as many others common configurations. There are other resources on the Internet as well, but check out the online Help; it may save you a lot of time.

## Chapter 13

SmartDefense

Solutions in this Chapter:

- **Understanding the Theory of SmartDefense**
- **Using SmartDefense**
- **Understanding Network Security**
- **Understanding Application Defense**
- **Updating Smart Defense**

☑ **Summary**

☑ **Solutions Fast Track**

☑ **Frequently Asked Questions**

Introduction

The basic principle of any firewall is to allow access to legitimate services while denying all other network access. Although in the past this level of security may have been sufficient, in today's world of increasingly sophisticated network-based applications comes the threat that malicious users may be able to exploit vulnerabilities in these applications. As a result, the simplistic "permit or deny" firewall model is no longer effective on its own as a successful network security defense mechanism.

SmartDefense, a key component of Check Point's VPN-1/FireWall-1 NG with Application Intelligence, is the solution to the problem permitting legitimate access to a network resource while protecting that resource from malicious attacks.

SmartDefense's underlying methodology is to monitor network traffic flowing through the firewall, comparing characteristics of the traffic to patterns known to be indicative of malicious activity. Suspicious activity is logged, and notifications may be sent so that the network administrator can choose to take action against the threat. SmartDefense supports the detection of five categories of attack: Denial of Service (DoS) attacks, Transmission Control Protocol/Internet Protocol (TCP/IP) attacks, application attacks, port and IP scanning, and worms.

With new attacks constantly being designed, it is not sufficient protection to have a static list of algorithms for SmartDefense to use to compare to network traffic. As a result, Check Point offers a subscription service, whereby SmartDefense can be kept constantly up to date on newly released attack algorithms. Updating SmartDefense is a simple, one-step procedure, with the intention that updates may be performed frequently, without tying up significant time or resources.

Understanding the Theory of SmartDefense

SmartDefense takes a different approach than a standard intrusion detection system (IDS). It does not attempt to counter each new attack that is discovered; instead, it protects your network against entire classes of attacks. SmartDefense performs strict sanity checks on packet headers and protocol data to prevent any malformed information getting into your network.

For example, instead of watching for an extensive list of attacks that can be used against DNS servers, SmartDefense will check DNS packets for compliance with the RFC standard for DNS packets. This behavior can protect against a large number of current and future exploits, without the need for continual signature updates. This method, of course, will not protect against every available attack, because many attacks are difficult to distinguish from valid traffic flows. Some of these checks may also be too strict and will subsequently drop valid traffic that is required for your applications to function properly, which is why you have the ability to change the sensitivity levels or even turn off the protection entirely.

Using SmartDefense

In earlier versions of VPN-1/FireWall-1, configuring the features now available in SmartDefense was a complicated process, involving manual editing of text configuration files and in-depth knowledge of how each protective measured worked. Thankfully, Check Point has now put all these features into an easy-to-understand component of the SmartDashboard that is much easier to configure.

All SmartDefense options are accessible under the **SmartDefense** tab in SmartDashboard, as shown in Figure 13.1.

Figure 13.1 The SmartDefense Tab

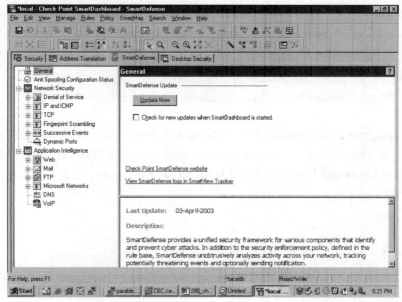

The initial SmartDefense screen includes links to update SmartDefense, which will be discussed later on, and allows you to enable the option of having SmartDefense automatically check for updates on startup. There are also links to the SmartDefense logs in SmartView Tracker, which tracks all traffic flowing through the firewall.

Choose **Anti Spoofing Configuration Status** to see a report of any interfaces on the firewall for which you have not enabled antispoofing, as shown in Figure 13.2. It is important to enable antispoofing for all interfaces; otherwise, your hosts are susceptible to spoofing attacks, in which the attacker is able to trick the firewall into perceiving the attacker's IP address as one that is allowed to inside hosts.

Figure 13.2 The Anti-Spoofing Configuration Status Window

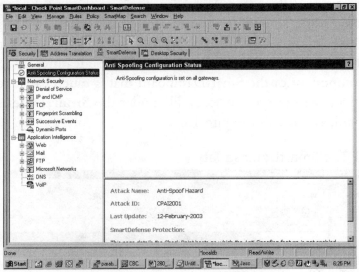

You configure antispoofing by opening the properties of your firewall object, choosing the **Topology** tab, and ensuring that each interface is either set to **External** or **Internal** but *not* **Not Defined**, as in Figure 13.3.

Figure 13.3 Topology Configuration

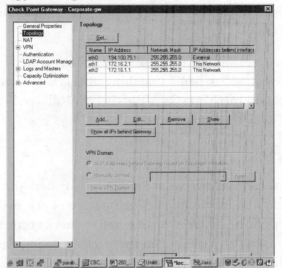

Let's now examine in further detail the additional components of SmartDefense that are geared toward protecting your network from specific types of threats.

Understanding Network Security

The Network Security section of SmartDefense provides protection against many of the standard network-based attacks that can affect systems on your network. In contrast to the Application Intelligence section, which is geared toward protection that involves inspection of application content, these defense mechanisms rely on the detection of properties of IP packets and traffic flows.

Denial of Service

SmartDefense offers protection against three types of DoS attack. The motive of any DoS attack is to take advantage of a vulnerability in an application or operating system to cause a system to become unresponsive to legitimate users. By detecting activity that could be indicative of such an attack, you have the ability to deny access to the offending user, leaving the system available for general use.

The three types of DoS attack that can be detected are:

- **TearDrop** Detects overlapping IP fragments.

- **Ping of Death** Detects fragmented, oversized ICMP requests.
- **LAND** Detects packets that are modified to match unusual specifications.

The only option available for each of these attacks is to adjust the action that VPN-1/FireWall-1 will take when a matching attack is detected. Note that even if you choose not to log these attacks, VPN-1/FireWall-1 will still block traffic that is suspected to be a DoS attack.

IP and ICMP

The IP and ICMP section allows you to protect your network from various common Layer 3 and 4 vulnerabilities. A mandatory check is the Packet Sanity verification, which performs a number of routine checks on each packet to ensure that nothing unusual is present in the packet header, size, and flags. The Max Ping Size option allows you to specify the maximum size, in bytes, of ICMP packets, alleviating the risk of having your network congested by oversized and excessive ping floods.

Next, choose the **IP Fragments** option, as shown in Figure 13.4.

Figure 13.4 IP Fragments

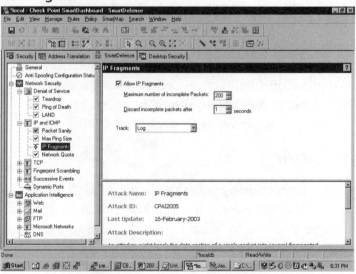

Enabling **Allow IP Fragments** is a good idea because legitimate packets may need to be fragmented if they exceed the maximum transmission size. The risk is that malicious users may try to hide what they are doing by fragmenting their packets so that SmartDefense does not recognize their attack. A good compromise is to set a limit on the maximum number of incomplete packets and to set SmartDefense to disregard incomplete packets after a certain amount of time (one second is a good default).

The **Network Quota** section, shown in Figure 13.5, allows you to protect your network from DoS attacks that are based on sending an excessive amount of traffic through your firewall.

Figure 13.5 Network Quota

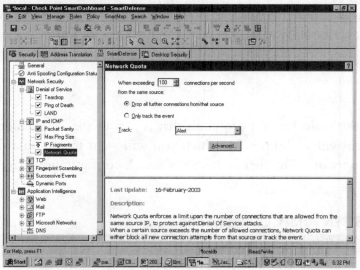

This feature will either drop or track any connections from the same host that exceed the specified number of connections per second. The default is 100, a good starting point; most legitimate network use will not result in more concurrent connections than that.

Developing & Deploying…

Unusual Applications

The concurrent connection setting in SmartDefense is one example of a setting that needs to be tuned according to the applications running on your network. You may have an unusual application that legitimately opens a high number of concurrent connections, which would be blocked by SmartDefense's default setting. This is why SmartDefense cannot be expected to work "out of the box"—you need to spend the time tuning its settings to your specific network requirements.

TCP

TCP, one of the main Layer 4 protocols that is part of the IP protocol suite, has several inherent vulnerabilities for which you will want to use SmartDefense to protect your network. The first is the SYN attack configuration screen, shown in Figure 13.6.

Figure 13.6 SYN Attack Configuration

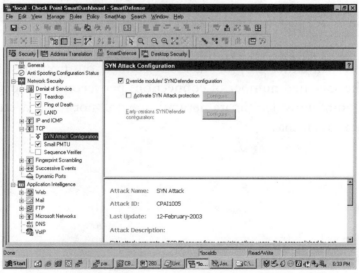

By selecting **Override modules' SYNdefender Configuration**, you ensure that the policy you set on the management console will be pushed and enforced by all the enforcement modules. Select **Activate SYN Attack Protection**, and choose **Configure**, as shown in Figure 13.7.

Figure 13.7 SYN Attack Configuration

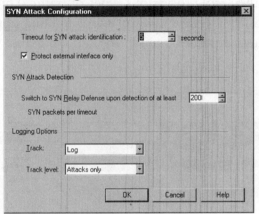

The **Timeout for SYN attack identification** is how long SmartDefense will wait before it considers a packet that has not received an acknowledgment to be part of an attack. The **Switch to SYN Relay Defense upon detection of at least...** option specifies how many SYN packets per timeout should be received before switching to SYN relay defense mode. This mode puts the firewall between the external host and the inside host so that unacknowledged packets do not reach the server; the firewall performs the handshake on behalf of the server, thereby shielding it from this type of attack. The default of 200 packets per timeout is a good starting point.

The next option (shown in Figure 3.6 underneath the SYN Attack Configuration option), is to protect against small PMTU attacks. This attack involves the offending host sending a large number of very small packets. The targeted host's resources are tied up in responding to all these packets, so it can no longer serve legitimate requests. To prevent this type of attack, set a minimum packet transmission size (MTU). At least 350 bytes, which is the default, is recommended.

Finally, the sequence verifier (also shown in Figure 13.6), when enabled, allows SmartDefense to keep track of the sequence numbers of packets to ensure each packet's validity. This ensures that packets that are out of sequence, but not meant for legitimate reassembly in the case of packet fragmentation, are not able to enter your network.

Fingerprint Scrambling

A remote host may attempt to collect information about hosts within your network based on how they reply to various types of traffic. This process is known as *fingerprinting*. The SmartDefense fingerprint-scrambling options aim to eliminate the threat of fingerprinting by rendering unidentifiable the information that hosts send in reply.

Damage & Defense...

Keeping OS Information Hidden

It is good practice to keep all information about operating system type and version private. A malicious user with knowledge of what operating system your hosts are running is much further along in terms of developing an attack than one who is yet to determine this information. Attacks are often geared toward a specific operating system type or version, so fingerprint scrambling helps keep this information private, lessening the risk of a successful exploit.

Three types of fingerprint-scrambling are available: ISN spoofing, TTL, and IP ID. *ISN spoofing* involves modifying sequence numbers of the three-way handshake to make operating system detection impossible. TTL, or *time to live*, removes an external user's ability to determine the number of hops between themselves and an internal host. *IP ID* instructs the firewall to assign its own identification number to each IP packet, thereby masking the type of operating system an internal host is running, since an external user may be able to determine the type of operating system by the identification number that is assigned.

Successive Events

The successive events section allows you to track repeated events that could be a sign of malicious activity. These events include:

- **Address spoofing** Occurs when an external user attempts to represent himself or herself as coming from an IP address with authorized access to your network.

- **Local interface spoofing** Occurs when an external user attempts to attack the firewall by representing him or herself as coming from an authorized IP address.

- **Port scanning** Occurs when an external user scans through multiple TCP or UDP ports on an internal host.

- **Successive alerts** Occurs when VPN-1/FireWall-1 generates a certain number of alerts in a certain amount of time.

- **Successive multiple connections** Occurs when a certain number of concurrent connections are opened from one external host to one internal host.

Dynamic Ports

The Dynamic Ports section, shown in Figure 13.8, allows you to specify how the firewall should treat applications that attempt to open ports dynamically. An example of such a service is File Transfer Protocol (FTP), which normally attempts to use ports above 1024 for data transfers.

Figure 13.8 Dynamic Ports

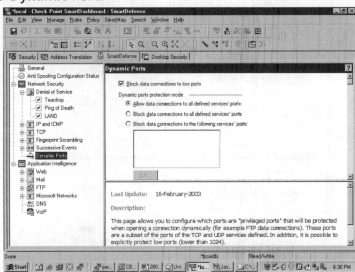

The first option, **Block data connection to low ports**, should be enabled unless you have a specific reason to do otherwise. Low ports (below 1024) should normally be used only by standard services, and so should not be used dynamically. Next, you have the option to either allow or block connections to defined services. A defined service is one that you have explicitly allowed access to in the Rule Base, so here you can choose whether or not these services' dynamic port requests will be permitted or denied. Alternatively, you can choose to block dynamic port requests to a list of specified services.

Understanding Application Intelligence

The second section of SmartDefense, Application Intelligence, focuses on attack detection that is application specific. This includes applications such as HTTP, Mail, FTP, Microsoft Networks, DNS, and VoIP. SmartDefense is able to examine properties and data within the packets that travel to and from these applications and detect suspicious signs.

General HTTP Worm Catcher

The first type of HTTP protection offered is the HTTP Worm Catcher, shown in Figure 13.9.

Figure 13.9 General HTTP Worm Catcher

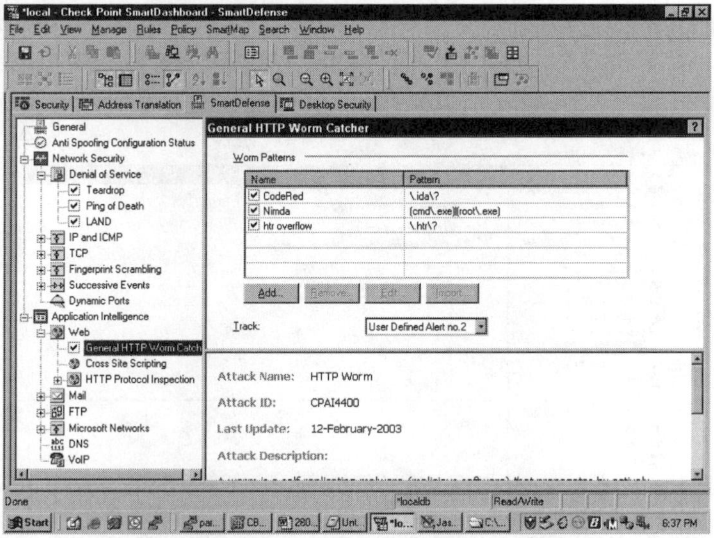

Recently a number of HTTP worms have been released on the Internet that have had a significant impact on the availability of many corporations' network resources. These worms typically exploit vulnerabilities in HTTP clients and servers, using these vulnerabilities to both infect the affected server or client and spread itself to other potential hosts.

The HTTP Worm Catcher, operating within the kernel of the server running VPN-1/FireWall-1, is configured to watch for specific strings. If one of these strings is detected in HTTP traffic flowing through the firewall, SmartDefense will take the action specified in the Track setting. Patterns can be added, removed, and edited manually, imported from a file, or updated automatically through the SmartDefense update mechanism.

HTTP Protocol Inspection

A second layer of HTTP protection is available via HTTP protocol inspection, accessible under the **HTTP Protocol Inspection** tab, shown in Figure 13.10.

Figure 13.10 HTTP Protocol Inspection

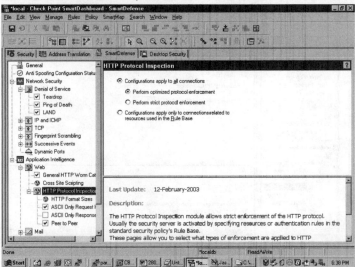

When enabled, the two ASCII header options, for requests and responses, prevent other types of data from being used in header transmission. Since all header requests and responses should be standard ASCII text, there is no valid reason to allow non-ASCII data. This type of data could be used in an attempt to overload the HTTP server's buffer, as a DoS attack.

The **HTTP Format Sizes** tab, shown in Figure 13.11, allows you to configure other aspects of what constitutes acceptable HTTP parameters. Setting the maximum URL length, which defaults to 2048 bytes, eliminates the threat of a malicious user entering an extremely long and invalid URL in an attempt to cause the HTTP sever to malfunction. Although all HTTP servers should have this vulnerability patched by now, it still cannot hurt to leave this option enabled.

Header restrictions, for length and number, defaulting to 1000 bytes and 500 respectively, are used to prevent malicious users from transmitting an excessive number of HTTP headers to your HTTP server or from sending unreasonably large HTTP headers. Both of these attacks would be launched in an attempt to cause a malfunction of your HTTP server—either to gain unauthorized access to it or simply to deny legitimate users access.

Note that in the case that any of these limits are exceeded, VPN-1/FireWall-1 drops the connection so that the suspicious traffic does not even reach the HTTP server.

Figure 13.11 HTTP Format Sizes

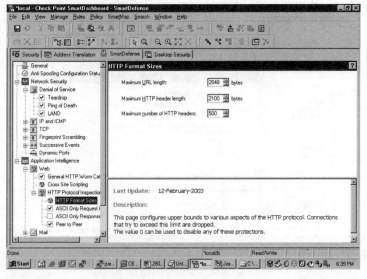

Cross-Site Scripting

The **Cross Site Scripting** tab, shown in Figure 13.12, allows you to configure the firewall to protect against attacks that are designed to steal users' confidential information. Malicious users employ two methods to do this: obtaining information stored in cookies on Web servers and causing Web servers to run scripts that end in users sending their information directly to a third party.

Figure 13.12 Cross-Site Scripting

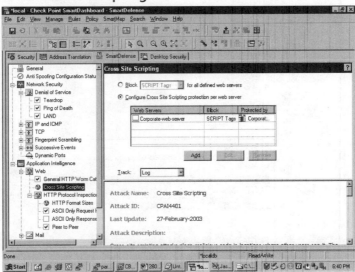

Both of these methods involve uploading a script to a Web server that instructs it to pass saved cookies to a third-party site or to send a form to users that will direct entered information to a third party. Although it is important to ensure that your Web server is patched from vulnerability to this attack, SmartDefense adds extra protection by denying HTTP POST requests and URLs that include scripts.

Configuration options for cross-site scripting include a setting to block script, HTML, or all tags for all defined Web servers, or, for additional granularity, you have the option of blocking scripts by individual Web server.

Peer-to-Peer Blocking

The **Peer to Peer** tab, shown in Figure 13.13, allows you to control users' access to the various peer-to-peer networks such as Kazaa, Gnutella, ICQ, and AIM. SmartDefense comes with the most common of these controls already configured, so all you need to do is enable or disable them based on your corporate policy concerning access to these services. You may also add more peer-to-peer networks, as long as you know the header name and value that SmartDefense should use to identify traffic bound for the service.

Figure 13.13 Peer-to-Peer Blocking

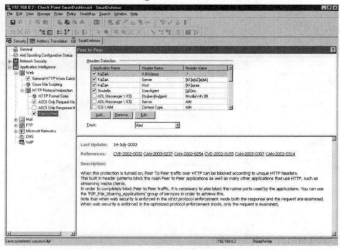

File and Print Sharing Worm Catcher

The File and Print Sharing Worm Catcher, located on the **Microsoft Networks** tab under **File and Print Sharing** (see Figure 13.14), extends SmartDefense's worm detection capability to Microsoft file shares. Just as with the HTTP Worm Catcher, SmartDefense comes preconfigured with a number of worm patterns that you may enable or disable, and you can add or import new patterns. Enabling this option protects Windows systems within your network from NetBIOS worms and from the Windows 2000 CIFS vulnerability.

Figure 13.14 File and Print Sharing

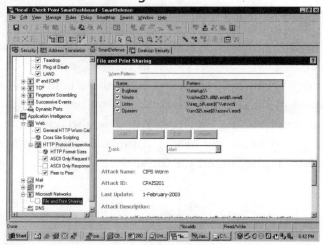

Updating SmartDefense

Keeping SmartDefense up to date is key to maintaining its ability to protect your network. From the general SmartDefense menu, shown in Figure 13.15, you will notice that in addition to the **Update Now** button used to update SmartDefense, you have the option of having SmartDefense check for updates whenever SmartDashboard is started. Given the importance of frequent updates, it is a good idea to enable this feature.

Figure 13.15 SmartDefense Update

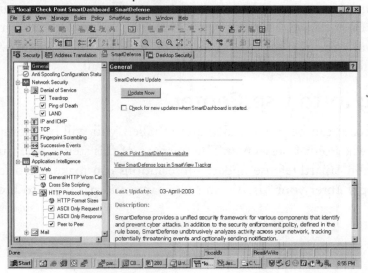

An important thing to keep in mind regarding SmartDefense updates is that you need to have a current subscription license in order to receive updates. This license also entitles you to receive SmartDefense advisories, which include useful information that will assist in developing your security practices and defense strategies.

A number of types of updates are supported by VPN-1/FireWall-1 NG with AI's SmartDefense:

- **Dynamic attack protection** These updates are for the core aspects of SmartDefense, allowing it to protect your network from newly discovered types of attacks.

- **INSPECT updates** These updates augment the INSPECT scripts based on new vulnerability information.

- **HTTP worm signature** Used to keep SmartDefense up to date for protection against newly released HTTP worms.

- **CIFS worm signature** Similar to HTTP worm signatures but for protection against CIFS worms.

- **New services** SmartUpdate will add protection for new services not originally part of its knowledge base.

- **P2P application signatures** Protection for point-to-point applications such as instant messengers.

Once SmartUpdate completes its update, a notification popup window will be displayed to notify you. However, it is important to note that even though at this point your management console has been updated, the updates will not reach the enforcement point until you do a policy install.

Logging In to UserCenter

Before an update can be downloaded and installed, you will be prompted to log in to the Check Point UserCenter. The purpose of this step is to ensure that only users with valid SmartDefense update subscriptions can make use of downloaded updates. Simply enter your UserCenter username and password to proceed.

Summary

SmartDefense is a key component of VPN-1/FireWall-1. Although the fundamental aspect of any firewall is to permit or deny traffic based on a set of rules, today's world of more sophisticated applications brings the need for protection against attacks that cannot be prevented with a standard Rule Base. By combining an easy-to-use interface with powerful attack detection and notification, SmartDefense allows firewall administrators to extend the protection that VPN-1/FireWall-1 provides to the application layer.

SmartDefense offers protection against numerous types of attacks, including HTTP worms, cross-site scripting, and vulnerabilities inherent to point-to-point applications.

Due to the nature of the protection that SmartDefense provides, it would not be effective without frequent updates. New worms and exploits are constantly being developed, and so SmartDefense must adapt to offer continued protection. The SmartUpdate feature, along with a current subscription license, provides a painless and efficient way to keep SmartDefense current.

Solutions Fast Track

Using SmartDefense

☑ Configure SmartDefense from the SmartDefense tab in SmartDashboard.

☑ Ensure antispoofing is enabled for all interfaces.

Understanding Network Security

☑ Configure DoS attack detection for TearDrop, Ping of Death, and LAND attacks.

☑ Enable IP and ICMP protection to defend your hosts from Layer 3 and 4 attacks as well as TCP protection for other Layer 4 vulnerabilities.

☑ Enable fingerprint scrambling to block outside users from collecting information about hosts on your network.

☑ Configure detection of successive events and restrictions on dynamic ports to further secure your network.

Understanding Application Intelligence

☑ Configure the general HTTP Worm Catcher and HTTP protocol inspection to detect exploits of Web server vulnerabilities.

☑ Enable cross-site scripting protection to detect attempts to steal users' information.

☑ Configure peer-to-peer blocking to place restrictions on peer-to-peer traffic to services such as Kazaa.

☑ Enable the File and Print Sharing Worm Catcher to detect worms transmitted through Microsoft file shares.

Updating SmartDefense

☑ Use the **Update Now** feature to begin the update process.

☑ Log in to your UserCenter account to install an update.

☑ Install the policy on all your enforcement points once an update has completed to ensure they all receive the update.

Frequently Asked Questions

The following Frequently Asked Questions, answered by the authors of this book, are designed to both measure your understanding of the concepts presented in this chapter and to assist you with real-life implementation of these concepts. To have your questions about this chapter answered by the author, browse to **www.syngress.com/solutions** and click on the **"Ask the Author"** form. You will also gain access to thousands of other FAQs at ITFAQnet.com.

Q: Will SmartDefense inspect traffic that is permitted by the standard Rule Base?

A: Yes, SmartDefense inspects all traffic flowing through the firewall, whether it is permitted or denied by a rule.

Q: Instead of configuring SmartDefense to detect ICMP attacks, wouldn't it be a better idea to deny all ICMP to my network?

A: ICMP is a useful tool for determining connectivity to and from hosts, but because it is susceptible to attacks, disabling it will provide the best level of defense. If you do leave it enabled, SmartDefense will provide a good level of security.

Q: If I have SmartDefense inspecting HTTP traffic to prevent exploits of my Web server, do I still need to spend time keeping the Web server updated?

A: Even though SmartDefense will detect all known exploits, it is always good practice to keep all software on any server up to date. Besides the fact that two levels of defense are better than one, there may be vulnerabilities that are patched through software updates that SmartDefense has not yet been updated to detect.

Q: Instead of using SmartDefense to block access to peer-to-peer networks, can't I just deny this traffic via a rule in the Rule Base?

A: The problem with attempting to block access to these services with a deny rule is that many of them use a wide variety of ports, some of which may be used for other applications. If you block access to these ports, those other applications would stop functioning. The SmartDefense solution is to identify peer-to-peer traffic by inspecting the content of packets.

Q: How often should I update SmartDefense?

A: The best thing to do is to check the Check Point Web site frequently to see if any new exploits have been detected and added to SmartDefense. If a newly discovered vulnerability affects an application on your network, it is especially important to update SmartDefense immediately. Signing up for the SmartDefense mailing list is a good way to be notified of newly discovered vulnerabilities.

Class C Subnet Mask Cheat Sheet

This cheat sheet can come in handy when working with network addresses and subnet masks. A standard netmask is written 255.255.255.0 which is equivalent to the aggregate /24. Using aggregates has become popular because computer people tend to be lazy and it only requires three keystrokes.

Table A.1 Netmasks and Aggregates

Netmasks and Aggregates			
Subnet Mask	255.255.255.0	**Hex Mask**	0xffffff00
Subnet Bits/Aggregate	24	**Host Bits**	8
Number of Subnets	1	**Hosts per Subnet**	254
Network Address	**Host IP Range**	**Broadcast Addresses**	
.0	.1 - .254	.255	
Subnet Mask	255.255.255.128	**Hex Mask**	0xffffff80
Subnet Bits/Aggregate	25	**Host Bits**	7
Number of Subnets	2	**Hosts per Subnet**	126
Network Address	**Host IP Range**	**Broadcast Addresses**	
.0	.1 - .126	.127	
.128	.129 - .254	.255	
Subnet Mask	255.255.255.192	**Hex Mask**	0xffffffc0
Subnet Bits/Aggregate	26	**Host Bits**	6
Number of Subnets	4	**Hosts per Subnet**	62
Network Address	**Host IP Range**	**Broadcast Addresses**	
.0	.1 - .62	.63	
.64	.65 - .126	.127	
.128	.129 - .190	.191	
.192	.193 - .254	.255	
Subnet Mask	255.255.255.224	**Hex Mask**	0xffffffe0
Subnet Bits/Aggregate	27	**Host Bits**	5
Number of Subnets	8	**Hosts per Subnet**	30
Network Address	**Host IP Range**	**Broadcast Addresses**	
.0	.1 - .30	.31	
.32	.33 - .62	.63	
.64	.65 - .94	.95	
.96	.97 - .126	.127	

Continued

Table A.1 Continued

Network Address	Host IP Range	Broadcast Addresses	
.128	.129 - .158	.159	
.160	.161 - .190	.191	
.192	.193 - .222	.223	
.224	.225 - .254	.255	
Subnet Mask	255.255.255.240	**Hex Mask**	0xfffffff0
Subnet Bits/Aggregate	28	**Host Bits**	4
Number of Subnets	16	**Hosts per Subnet**	14
Network Address	**Host IP Range**	**Broadcast Addresses**	
.0	.1 – .14	.15	
.16	.17 - .30	.31	
.32	.33 - .46	.47	
.48	.49 - .62	.63	
.64	.65 - .94	.79	
.80	.81 - .94	.95	
.96	.97 - .110	.111	
.112	.113 - .126	.127	
.128	.129 - .142	.143	
.144	.145 - .158	.159	
.160	.161 - .174	.175	
.176	.177 - .190	.191	
.192	.193 - .206	.207	
.208	.209 - .222	.223	
.224	.225 - .238	.239	
.240	.241 - .254	.255	
Subnet Mask	255.255.255.248	**Hex Mask**	0xfffffff8
Subnet Bits/Aggregate	29	**Host Bits**	3
Number of Subnets	32	**Hosts per Subnet**	6
Network Address	**Host IP Range**	**Broadcast Addresses**	
.0	.1 – .6	.7	
.8	.9 - .14	.15	
.16	.17 - .22	.23	

Continued

www.syngress.com

Table A.1 Continued

Network Address	Host IP Range	Broadcast Addresses
.24	.25 - .30	.31
.32	.33 - .38	.39
.40	.41 - .46	.47
.48	.49 - .54	.55
.56	.57 - .62	.63
.64	.65 - .70	.71
.72	.73 - .78	.79
.80	.81 - .86	.87
.88	.89 - .94	.95
.96	.97 - .102	.103
.104	.105 - .110	.111
.112	.113 - .118	.119
.120	.121 - .126	.127
.128	.129 - .134	.135
.136	.137 - .142	.143
.144	.145 - .150	.151
.152	.153 - .158	.159
.160	.161 - .166	.167
.168	.169 - .174	.175
.176	.177 - .182	.183
.184	.185 - .190	.191
.192	.193 - .198	.199
.200	.201 - .206	.207
.208	.209 - .214	.215
.216	.217 - .222	.223
.224	.225 - .230	.231
.232	.233 - .238	.239
.240	.241 - .246	.247
.248	.249 - .254	.255

Continued

Table A.1 Continued

Subnet Mask	255.255.255.252	Hex Mask	0xfffffffc
Subnet Bits/Aggregate	30	Host Bits	2
Number of Subnets	64	Hosts per Subnet	2
Network Address	Host IP Range	Broadcast Addresses	
.0	.1 – .2	.3	
.4	.5 - .6	.7	
.8	.9 - .10	.11	
.12	.13 - .14	.15	
.16	.17 - .18	.19	
.20	.21 - .22	.23	
.24	.25 - .26	.27	
.28	.29 - .30	.31	
.32	.33 - .34	.35	
.36	.37 - .38	.39	
.40	.41 - .42	.43	
.44	.45 - .46	.47	
.48	.49 - .50	.51	
.52	.53 - .54	.55	
.56	.57 - .58	.59	
.60	.61 - .62	.63	
.64	.65 - .66	.67	
.68	.69 - .70	.71	
.72	.73 - .74	.75	
.76	.77 - .78	.79	
.80	.81 - .82	.83	
.84	.85 - .86	.87	
.88	.89 - .90	.91	
.92	.93 - .94	.95	
.96	.97 - .98	.99	
.100	.101 - .102	.103	
.104	.105 - .106	.107	
.108	.109 - .110	.111	
.112	.113 - .114	.115	

Continued

Table A.1 Continued

Network Address .118	Host IP Range .119	Broadcast Addresses.116 .117 -
.120	.121 - .122	.123
.124	.125 - .126	.127
.128	.129 - .130	.131
.132	.133 - .134	.135
.136	.137 - .138	.139
.140	.141 - .142	.143
.144	.145 - .146	.147
.148	.149 - .150	.151
.152	.153 - .154	.155
.156	.157 - .158	.159
.160	.161 - .162	.163
.164	.165 - .166	.167
.168	.169 - .170	.171
.172	.173 - .174	.175
.176	.177 - .178	.179
.180	.181 - .182	.183
.184	.185 - .186	.187
.188	.189 - .190	.191
.192	.193 - .192	.195
.196	.197 - .198	.199
.200	.201 - .202	.203
.204	.205 - .206	.207
.208	.209 - .210	.211
.212	.213 - .214	.215
.216	.217 - .218	.219
.220	.221 - .222	.223
.224	.225 - .226	.227
.228	.229 - .230	.231
.232	.233 - .234	.235
.236	.237 - .238	.239

Continued

Table A.1 Continued

Network Address	Host IP Range	Broadcast Addresses
.240	.241 - .242	.243
.244	.245 - .246	.247
.248	.249 - .250	.251
.252	.253 - .254	.255

Subnet Mask	255.255.255.255	Hex Mask	0xffffffff
Subnet Bits/Aggregate	32	Host Bits	0
Number of Subnets	255	Hosts per Subnet	1

Index

Syngress: *The Definition of a Serious Security Library*™

Syn·gress (sin–gres): *noun, sing.* Freedom from risk or danger; safety. See *security.*

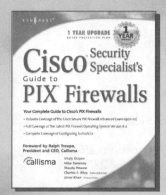

Cisco Security Specialist's Guide to PIX Firewall

Demystifying the task of implementing, configuring, and administering Cisco's PIX firewall appliances, this book delivers a total solution both for managing these widely used devices and for passing the challenging Cisco Secure PIX Firewall Advanced Exam (9E0-571), a prerequisite for gaining prestigious Cisco Security Specialist 1 certification. Packed with insider tips and techniques on protocols, hardware and software components, troubleshooting and more, this powerful advisor illustrates attack concepts, explains must-know networking principles for optimizing and integrating PIX firewalls, sets forth real-world configuration and administration examples, and helps users master Cisco's infamous command line interface.

ISBN: 1-931836-63-9

Price: $59.95 USA $92.95 CAN

Managing Cisco Network Security, Second Edition

Offers updated and revised information covering many of Cisco's security products that provide protection from threats, detection of network security incidents, measurement of vulnerability and policy compliance, and management of security policy across an extended organization. These are the tools that you have to mount defenses against threats. Chapters also cover the improved functionality and ease of the Cisco Secure Policy Manger software used by thousands of small-to-midsized businesses, and a special section on Cisco wireless solutions.

ISBN: 1-931836-56-6

Price: $69.95 USA $108.95 CAN

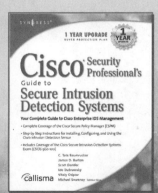

The Cisco Security Specialist's Guide to Secure Intrusion Detection Systems

Cisco Security Professional's Guide to Secure Intrusion Detection Systems does more than show network engineers how to set up and manage this line of best selling products ... it walks them step by step through all the objectives of the Cisco Secure Intrusion Detection System course (and corresponding exam) that network engineers must pass on their way to achieving sought-after CCSP certification.

ISBN: 1-932266-69-0

Price: $59.95 US $79.95 CAN

solutions@syngress.com